QUESTIONS & ANSWERS:
BUSINESS ASSOCIATIONS

QUESTIONS & ANSWERS:
BUSINESS ASSOCIATIONS

Multiple-Choice and Short-Answer Questions and Answers

Second Edition

DOUGLAS M. BRANSON
W. Edward Sell Chair in Business Law
University of Pittsburgh School of Law

ISBN: 9781422490853

> NOTE TO USERS
> To ensure that you are using the latest materials available in this area, please be sure to periodically check the LexisNexis Law School web site for downloadable updates and supplements at www.lexisnexis.com/lawschool.

Editorial Offices
121 Chanlon Rd., New Providence, NJ 07974 (908) 464-6800
201 Mission St., San Francisco, CA 94105-1831 (415) 908-3200
www.lexisnexis.com

MATTHEW◆BENDER

DEDICATION

For Clare, Annie, and Elizabeth

ABOUT THE AUTHOR

Douglas M. Branson has occupied the W. Edward Sell Chair in Business Law at the University of Pittsburgh since 1996. Prior to 1996, he was a Professor of Law at the Seattle University (1973 to 1996). He also regularly visits the University of Alabama School of Law, where he has twice held the Charles Tweedy Professorship. He also holds the rank of Permanent Fellow at the University of Melbourne (Australia) where each year he has taught (with Professor J. Farrar) the corporate governance class to Master of Law students. He has been a visiting professor at Arizona State University, Cornell University, the University of Oregon, Washington University (St. Louis), and the University of Washington (where he was the Condon-Falknor Distinguished Professor), among others. He has taught the basic course in business organization law for over 30 years.

Professor Branson has also taught in New Zealand, South Africa, Malaysia, Hong Kong, Indonesia, Ireland, Spain, France, and England. He has been a Fulbright-sponsored lecturer at University of Ghent (Belgium) and a U.S. State Department-sponsored lecturer at several universities in the Ukraine. He has been a USAID-sponsored consultant to the Republic of Indonesia on matters of corporate law, corporate governance, and capital markets law. He has worked on similar projects for Macedonia and Afghanistan, endeavoring to aid those countries in modernizing their economic laws.

He is the author of over 70 law review articles and more than a dozen books. His books include the leading treatise *Corporate Governance* (1993) (with annual supplements); *Problems in Corporate Governance* (1997); *Understanding Corporate Law* (1999; 2d ed. 2004; 3d ed. 2009) (with Arthur Pinto); *No Seat at the Table: How Law and Governance Keep Women Out of the Board Room* (2007); *Business Enterprises: Legal Structures, Governance and Policy* (with Joan Heminway et al., 2009); *The Last Male Bastion: Gender and the CEO Suite at America's Public Corporations* (2010); *The Russell Sage Handbook of Corporate Governance* (Thomas Clarke & Douglas Branson eds., 2011); and *Tastes of Nuoc Mam: Service in the Brown Water Navy and Visits to Vietnam* (2011).

PREFACE

Today the obligatory law school "elective" is "Business Enterprises," or "Business Organizations," rather than "Corporations." Not too many years ago, the principal business law course was "Corporations." Most law students regarded the Corporations course as obligatory, even though their law school offered the course as "elective."

By contrast, a course in partnership law was a true elective, often combined with agency in "Agency and Partnership." Often, together, the two courses, Corporations and Agency and Partnership, constituted the entire array of business organization electives offered.

The modern Business Enterprises course includes materials on the law of partnership, limited partnership, and professional service corporations, as well as traditional corporations. The course also includes materials relating to two new kids on the business enterprises block, namely, limited liability partnerships (LLPs) and limited liability companies (LLCs). Many law schools offer a second elective entitled "The Law of Unincorporated Business Entities" which is much broader than the old Agency and Partnership course. Some law school casebooks include materials on contractual alternatives to firms (business enterprises) such as relational contracts of one sort or another (franchises, strategic alliances, distributorships, employment contracts).

Thus, the basic course is far less monolithic than it used to be. In fact, the course may be bewildering at times. This book is an attempt to (1) allay some fears by putting organizational and legal issues in context across the range of forms of business entities you may encounter in a basic course, and (2) use factual settings to aid you in developing your capacity for "issue recognition" — that, at times, elusive quality both law professors and bar examiners look for in the examination process.

One other stress-relieving piece of advice I offer to you is born of my 30 years' teaching experience. Don't look for overarching themes here. One way to view corporations (or business enterprises) is as a composite of six or eight stand-alone topics, including formation of the entity, issues relating to legal personality (liability on preincorporation contracts, piercing the corporate veil, etc.), finance, rudimentary managerial accounting, governance (Political Science 101), fiduciary duty, shareholder litigation, and mergers and acquisitions. To an extent, partnerships and other subjects are similar. As you utilize these Questions, remember also that often there is not a single correct answer. Rather, there usually is a "best answer." Part of learning and practicing law is learning to make informed judgments, informed in part by your knowledge of the law, your knowledge of human nature, and plain old common sense. This book attempts to help you gain those as well as issue recognition skills.

Since the first edition a number of changes have taken place and developments have occurred, many of which I have incorporated in this new edition. They include the following:

1. Model Business Corporation Act (MBCA) Changes. Although the MBCA is not the law, it is the basic pattern for the corporate law of 39 states and highly influential in all jurisdictions. The ABA Committee on Corporate Laws promulgated complete new editions of the statute in 1969 and in 1984 (sometimes referred to as Model Act Third). The original statute dates from 1950. The Committee, however, also continually attempts to update the statute between complete restatements. Since 2004, the Committee has been especially busy tinkering with various aspects of the model law.

2. Delaware General Business Corporation Act. Similarly, the Delaware Bar Corporate Law Revision Committee has authored a number of changes to the Delaware corporate statute, although not as many as the ABA Committee. The legislature and governor of Delaware have adopted and signed these suggested changes into law.

3. "Wall Street Reform and Consumer Protection Act" ("Dodd-Frank") was signed into law by the president in July 2010. The Act runs to over 700 pages. Buried within it are a number of provisions affecting corporate governance and corporate finance. The most publicized developments allow certain shareholders to nominate directors for office, to be listed in the corporation's own annual proxy statement, rather than independently in an insurgent's own (very expensive) proxy materials. The Act also requires large public corporations to hold advisory votes on executive compensation ("say on pay"). Together with the Sarbanes-Oxley Act of 2002, Dodd-Frank represents a trend of federal government incursions in what historically has been governed by state law.

4. As usual, the United States Supreme Court has been busy in this area. The Court has decided cases on the proper standard for judging the level of advisors' fees for investment companies (mutual funds); the statue of limitations for securities law actions; the liability of secondary actors in securities transactions, an issue it has visited twice before; and the extraterritorial application of U.S. securities laws. All of these cases have impacts on business enterprise and corporate law.

5. State court decisions. As usual, state courts have gone about their business, deciding a number of business law disputes.

PREFACE

I have tried to include some of those recent developments in this revision although the focus remains on inculcating in students the fundamentals.

I would like to thank Dean Mary Crossley at the University of Pittsburgh for a summer research grant which enabled me to complete this revision. My principal contact at LexisNexis was (and is) Jennifer Beszley.

Professor Douglas M. Branson
Pittsburgh, Pennsylvania

July 2011

TABLE OF CONTENTS

TABLE OF CONTENTS

QUESTIONS

Dahl, Olson, and Erickson have a successful (very successful) business equipping and guiding fishermen who come to Northern Minnesota to catch fish. Under the DBA (Doing Business As) statute, they have registered the name "Pike Patrol." When Dahl and Olson found they had more business than they could serve properly, they contacted Mike Dooley and Virgil Flowers. "You guys purchase the necessary equipment (cushions for their boats, spare rods and reels, life jackets, etc.)," which they did to the tune of $1,813.97 and $1,943.63, and "we will assign to you any client overage, that is, over 6 but only up to 10."

During that summer and the following, Pike Patrol had six to eight clients every day. Moreover, high-roller clients from Chicago and the "cities" (Minneapolis-St. Paul) came to Northern Minnesota to fish and paid high fees. But Pike Patrol ceases doing business, leaving a substantial bank balance. Dooley and Flowers' lawyer contends that the arrangement constituted a partnership and that Dooley and Flowers are entitled to 2/5ths of the bank balance.

1. You are Dahl, Olson, and Erickson's lawyer. What response do you make?

    (A) Dahl et al. never intended to form a partnership.

    (B) The dollar amounts Dooley and Flowers received may have varied greatly but those amounts were wages, not partnership shares.

    (C) The equipment Dooley and Flowers purchased remained their separate property.

    (D) Dooley and Flowers received wages; provided their own equipment as would an independent contractor; never made a contribution to partnership property; and never voted or otherwise participated in upper-level decision making. Further, there was no partnership agreement, oral or otherwise; no partnership tax return ever was filed.

Sam is a coach and former track star at Home State University ("HSU"), located downstate. Charlene coaches at a different school upstate, but was a basketball star at HSU. Dave is a wealthy industrialist who lives in the center of Home State. Through his support for HSU athletics, Dave has become friends with Sam and Charlene.

Sam and Charlene have obtained the rights to distribute Zeus running shoes in Home State. Dave has agreed that the inventory of Zeus products may be maintained in Dave's warehouse in Central City. Dave's company will supply a part-time shipping clerk. Dave has put up $225,000 necessary to finance the inventory from Zeus. For his contribution, Dave is to receive 7 percent interest plus 6 percent of the profits. Sam is to sell Zeus products to retailers downstate. Charlene is to sell Zeus products to retailers upstate. Sam and Charlene are to receive 10 percent commission. Sam, Charlene, and Dave are to share equally anything left over after payment of expenses, including commissions.

Sam, Charlene, and Dave visit you in your office. Their discussion raises a number of questions.

2. What is the nature of the legal relationship among the parties? Are there alternative ways in which

their relationship might be characterized?

ANSWER:

Partnership.

3.   What type of agreement would you draft for them if they requested you to draft an agreement? What would be three salient features of the agreement?

ANSWER:

4.   What might happen if they did not go to the expense of having you, as their attorney, draft an agreement? What is their probable relationship, and what are the consequences of that relationship?

ANSWER:

Liam and Clare each own an Irish pub in Kansas City. To cash in on the microbrew craze, Liam and Clare wish to go together to establish a small microbrewery that will supply two or three locally brewed beers to each pub. The brewery will be located off-site, in the industrial section of Kansas City. The premises will be leased.

5.   If Liam and Clare do nothing more than jointly sign the lease, hire the brewmeister, and purchase supplies and equipment, their new enterprise will be:

    (A)   A partnership.

    (B)   A joint venture.

    (C)   A limited liability company.

    (D)   Both (A) and (B).

Return to the facts of Question 2. Eighteen months later, Home State experienced the rainiest winter in its history. Sam and Charlene receive reports from retailers that much of the merchandise shipped to them is water damaged. Sam and Charlene visit Central City and the warehouse. They find the roof leaking badly. The shipping clerk's duties have been delegated to an after school part-time high school student who has given free shoes to all of his friends, and who never inspected the inner portions of the warehouse where the bulk of the inventory has been stored and the leaks occurred. Dave has become obsessed with competing in Northern Pike fishing tournaments all around Home State, leaving the student unsupervised. An estimated $150,000 of inventory is worthless. Sam and Charlene are furious with Dave. They want to end the business relationship.

6.   What actions should Sam and Charlene take in order to end the relationship?

ANSWER: *Can Be ended @ anytime*

7.   Do Sam and Charlene have any legal rights against Dave? If they file a court complaint, what theory or theories should they pursue in their case?

ANSWER: *yes DoL*

In 1970, Jennifer, a real estate developer, and Veronica, a wealthy investor, undertook the purchase and rehabilitation of a small shopping center. Their agreement provided that Veronica was to receive 40 percent of the net cash flow for the first five years and 50 percent thereafter, until year 20. At that time, the venture was terminable upon the will of either.

In 1988, the original owner, Eldridge, approached Jennifer with news that the lessee had vacated the adjoining parcel, which Eldridge also owns. Extracting a pledge of confidentiality from Eldridge, Jennifer enters into a lease for parcel two. At year 20, she terminates the relationship with Veronica, enters into her own lease for parcel one, and develops the two parcels into a regional mall, with three flagship department stores and other major retailers. Not until year 26 does Veronica discover what has happened. She then sues Jennifer for violation of her duty of loyalty.

8.   Which of the following approximates Jennifer's exposure in Veronica's suit?

   (A)   She owes no duty of loyalty because "greed is good" and social policy dictates that she be able to maximize her own economic welfare.

   (B)   She has diverted a partnership opportunity, must "account" to the original partnership for all her illicit gain, and likely will have a constructive trust placed upon her entire new venture, with the original partnership as the beneficiary of the Trust.

(C) Same as Answer (B), but she is only liable for the gain that is causally related to the diversion of the opportunity, as opposed to that portion of the gain attributable to her skills as a real estate developer.

(D) She owed a duty of loyalty to Veronica and the venture, but she did not violate it because the new opportunity was not within the scope of the original venture and was not, therefore, a partnership opportunity.

The Moss family owns your client, Happy Volvo and Jaguar. Sterling Moss, the fleet sales manager, telephones you, his attorney and counselor. He has received a telephone order from the managing partner of Wycoff and Van Duzer ("WV"), a law firm with 30 partners. The managing partner has placed an order for 40 luxury automobiles. The purchase is to be financed though Happy Volvo and Jaguar's in-house finance department. Sterling wants to know what, if any, partnership paperwork he needs before he accepts and places the order with the factories for the new cars.

9.   You tell him:

   (A)   The managing partner, or any partner, has the authority to do such a deal. Go ahead and place the order.

   (B)   Ask around to determine if the managing partner has done transactions like this in the past. If he has, there exists "implied actual" authority. Go ahead and place the order.

   (C)   The managing partner, by being given the title, an office, letterhead stationery, and so on, has the "apparent authority" to do the deal. Go ahead and place the order.

   (D)   Do not place the order. Require that WV produce a certified copy of a valid resolution adopted by the partners at a partnership meeting.

Turner and Kelley are law partners. Turner's practice is primarily divorce while Kelley does general civil litigation. Without Kelley's knowledge, Turner has been promising divorce clients high rates of return (12–14%) if they leave the proceeds of divorce settlements with Turner. Your client, Norma, left $400,000 with Turner, who paid her high interest for five years.

Turner has now filed personal bankruptcy and is judgment proof. He stopped paying interest last year. The entire affair turns out to have been a "Ponzi scheme." You represent Norma in a suit against Kelley and the law firm. The defense proposes to put on the stand the state bar association president and partners from two other local law firms who all will testify that investing client funds is not "carrying on in the usual way the business" of a law partnership under Uniform Partnership Act ("UPA") § 9(1) or Revised Uniform Partnership Act ("RUPA") § 301.

10.   Is there a good argument for excluding the testimony?

   (A)   Yes, the proper test is the reasonable expectations of third parties and the public regarding what law firms do.

   (B)   No, Norma was contributorily negligent in leaving the settlement proceeds with Turner.

   (C)   No, the testimony is relevant as expert testimony about the scope of the ordinary practice of law.

(D)   It is a toss-up. The judge could rule either way without abusing her discretion.

Joseph and Larry have practiced law together since law school graduation two years ago. Joseph discovers that Larry is a techno-geek, who orders computers, printers, servers, and other computer accessories on a weekly basis. Their law office is filled with black and white plastic cows from Gateway. Larry's excesses vastly inflate the firm's accounts payable. Joseph has asked Larry to stop, to no avail. Joseph has also sent a registered letter to Gateway to cease shipments, but Gateway keeps shipping product anyway.

11.   What is Joseph's next step in solving this Question?

    (A)   Notify Gateway that, as partner, Larry has no authority to bind the partnership in these matters.

    (B)   Invoke a partner's veto powers under the emergency doctrine and declare that Larry no longer has power to bind the partnership, notifying creditors.

    (C)   Associate a new partner and then vote 2-1 to restrict Larry's authority.

    (D)   Dissolve the partnership "by the express will of any partner."

Summers and Dooley had a refuse collection business. For the summer season, Summers wanted to take on (hire) a third person. Dooley said "no." Summers hired a helper anyway, to whom he paid $12,000. Summers now sues Dooley for reimbursement of half ($6,000).

12.   You are the municipal court judge, presiding at a bench trial of Summers's claim. What result?

ANSWER:

TOPIC 5:	QUESTIONS
PARTNERSHIP DISSOLUTION	

Ken does home remodeling for a larger San Francisco area contractor. Ken would like to strike out on his own, but needs a certain amount of capital to purchase tools, a truck, and for working capital. He approaches Barbie, who is an old friend of his. Barbie agrees to contribute $25,000 to the enterprise. Ken will solicit clients, bid the remodeling jobs, and do the work. They will split the profits 50-50. They shake hands on the deal.

Fast forward one year later. Due to the dotcom bust, far fewer homeowners are remodeling. Ken has "burned through" the $25,000 investment. He and Barbie agree that the venture is to end. Ken will go back to working for large contractor. Barbie asks Ken to contribute $12,500 to her so that they will "come out even."

13. What should Ken and Barbie do to dissolve their partnership?

(A) Ken should pay the $12,500 to her because, unless otherwise agreed, partners share the losses in the same proportions as they share the profits.

(B) Ken owes nothing to Barbie because while she contributed capital he contributed his labor. A California court would regard the contributions as offsetting.

(C) Actually, Barbie owes Ken $12,500 because his labor, at his usual rates, has a reasonable value far in excess of her $25,000, to wit, $50,000.

(D) Barbie owes Ken $25,000 on the same grounds explained in Answer (C).

Roberta, a prominent dentist, and her son, Robert, a high school teacher, several years ago purchased a beach house. Roberta contributed $140,000 and Robert $10,000 as down payment on the $350,000 purchase price. Robert has used his carpentry skills to fix up the house, adding a new family room and master bedroom. Roberta and Robert have now sold the house for $800,000. Robert paid bills at the local lumberyard to the extent of $20,000. The partnership owes $30,000 for property taxes, the plumber's bill, and the electrician's bill.

14. Make up a worksheet distributing the proceeds.

ANSWER:

Dowe, Cheatum, and How have a successful contracting and earth moving business which owns a great quantity of heavy equipment (bulldozers) and such. How wishes to withdraw from the partnership (he is moving to Santa Fe). Their agreement, which you checked, says nothing about dissolution.

15. What are the default rules they would have to work around?

(A)   They have to sell everything off, reducing it to cash because a withdrawal by a partner dissolves the partnership. They then pay How his share.

(B)   How has disassociated from the partnership, an act which does not dissolve the firm. So Dowe and Cheatum can sell some equipment (not all of it), or obtain a bank loan, etc., pay How his share and go about the business as a continuation of the same firm.

(C)   How's withdrawal is a wrongful dissolution. How is entitled to nothing. Moreover, Dowe and Cheatum can sue How for any damages to the partnership his dissolution has caused.

(D)   The agreement must work around the default rule, providing that upon withdrawal a new partnership automatically comes into being and the business carries onward. Check again.

Pat and Mike have a partnership that owns two Irish taverns, one on the North Side, where Pat lives, and one on the South Side, where Mike lives. The taverns are pretty much identical, in decor, revenues, expenses, and so on. There are a few other assets (a pickup truck, extra chairs and tables, etc.). Pat and Mike have decided, quite amicably, to go their separate ways. They have asked you as mediator to *apply the partnership rules*, effectuating a split-up between them.

16.   You should "decree" as follows:

(A)   Pat gets the North Side and Mike gets the South Side with the other assets being split equitably among them.

(B)   Both taverns and the miscellaneous assets are to be sold with the cash proceeds split 50-50 if either Pat or Mike insists.

(C)   Each gets an election to take a tavern or cash.

(D)   Pat gets the North Side and Mike gets the South Side with the other assets being sold at auction, the proceeds of which are to be divided equally between them.

Ken and Barbie now have another business. They are theatrical agents. So far, in five years, they have paid off the debts they incurred when they formed the business, except for a $50,000 note payable to Barbie. Barbie has developed an impressive client list, which includes Meg Ryan, Sean Penn, and Melanie Griffith. Ken has only a few clients, mostly bit-part character actors. Ken does manage the office and has installed the computer system. He also performs numerous tasks for Barbie's clients.

Ken and Barbie start bickering. Ken complains about Barbie's extravagant lunches and her club memberships. Over a weekend Barbie moves her files across the hall to a new office she has rented. She sets up shop without Ken. She begins to make money hand over fist. Ken is angry.

17.   Does Ken have a claim?

(A)   No, not without a partnership agreement. The withdrawal of a partner dissolves the partnership. Such a dissolution is wrongful only if it contravenes some provision of the partners' agreement.

(B)   Yes, the partnership had an implied term, which was to pay off the debts incurred in its formation. Barbie's dissolution of the partnership prior to that time is wrongful.

(C)   Yes, a partner at will is not bound to remain in the partnership, but she must exercise her right to withdraw in good faith and consistent with the fiduciary duties partners owe one to another.

(D)   No. This is a free country. Barbie did not take anything that belonged to Ken.

Dave, Nick, and Shane have a partnership, Kingston Boats, which for many years has built wooden sailboats. The last few years, however, Shane has misappropriated tools from the shop, failed to work a 40-hour week (or even a 20-hour one), demanded that his son be made a partner, demanded that a certain employee be discharged (even though no cause existed), and refused to return partnership books and records (which he took home with him).

Dave and Nick have had it. They confer with their attorney, who examines their written partnership agreement. The agreement confers upon the partners the right to expel a partner. Dave and Nick tell Shane that he is expelled.

18.   What are the consequences?

(A)   The partnership is dissolved and they must sell the assets, pay off the debts, and make distributions to the partners. If they do not do so, a court may order a judicial sale of the partnership assets.

(B)   Dave and Nick could be sued for wrongful expulsion.

(C)   Because they have not caused dissolution wrongfully, Dave and Nick may carry on the business, provided they pay Shane his fair share.

(D)   Dave and Nick should sell the assets, move locations, and open a new shop under a new name.

Flog, Browbeat, and Harass is a 30-lawyer firm. Heather is a young partner in the firm. She has worked extensively on the XYZ account. Over the past few years, she has noted that the supervising partner, Johnson, has inflated the hours billed to XYZ, sometimes by a factor of 40 or 50 percent. Finally, Heather could take it no longer. In June, she reported the over-billing to the managing partner.

In August, two of the management committee partners requested an interview with Heather. They reported to her that their investigation had uncovered no intentional over-billing of XYZ. They also stated that she should begin to look for work elsewhere. Her partnership draw would continue only until December 31.

19.   Can they get away with such an injustice?

(A)   Yes, partnerships are consensual. The partners may expel her if the partnership agreement so provides.

(B)   They may expel her, but only for cause.

(C)   No, they violated the fiduciary duties partners owe one to another.

(D)   No, the rules of professional responsibility are implied terms of the partnership agreement and Heather had a duty to take reasonable remedial action to avoid the consequences of known violations by another lawyer in the firm.

You are at your 10-year law school reunion picnic. It is August. Megan Mulcahy, a former classmate, takes you aside. Megan is a very successful personal injury practitioner in the mid-size law firm of Rose & Rose. In confidence, she tells you that she is going to form her own firm on January 1. She plans on taking two junior partners and one associate attorney with her.

20.   What should she do between August and the date of departure?

ANSWER:

Same facts as in Question 20, but now you are counsel to the firm of Rose & Rose and it is a year earlier. The partners ask you to draft provisions in the partnership agreement that will regulate, if not prevent, opportunistic withdrawal by partners of the firm.

21.   What sorts of provisions would you recommend?

ANSWER:

The six members of the "Brady Bunch" all went to undergraduate school together. They have all now obtained professional degrees in law, medicine, dentistry, and so on, returning to Home Town to practice. They are all married, for the most part to fellow professionals. As two-wage-earner families, they have been taking a beating on federal income taxes.

Jack Brady has located a 60-unit townhouse apartment complex in State College, home to the large state university in the state of Wigmore. The complex needs some repairs and cosmetic improvement, but it is available at a very reasonable price of six times the gross rentals. The Bunch has decided to make a near full-price offer on the property. They seek your advice on the form of business they should set up before making their bid or, in the alternative, once their bid is accepted.

22.   You recommend that they:

    (A)   Form a general partnership (either at will or for a term of years). That way they can all participate in the management of the complex, choosing the color of paint for the units, and so on.

    (B)   Form a corporation. The tenants will be undergraduates, who from time to time injure themselves doing "wild and crazy things." You have to have liability insurance, but the limited liability a corporation would afford would give added protection and peace of mind to the investors.

    (C)   Form a limited partnership, combining attributes of a general partnership and a corporation well suited to this type of venture.

    (D)   Form a limited liability company.

The Brady Bunch has purchased the apartment complex. Jack Brady has agreed to serve, and is serving, as the general partner. June and Jill Brady are interior decorators. They will leave the interior decoration (new curtains, color of paint, new cabinets and countertops in some units) to a decorator in State College, but June and Jill wish to have the power to review the decorator's choices, reversing any decision with which they do not agree.

Also, as a financial control, the Bradys want to require that Jim Brady's signature be required on checks, in addition to general partner Jack Brady's signature.

23.   Can they set it up this way? The State of Wigmore has the original Uniform Limited Partnership Act (1916).

    (A)   Both arrangements are permissible.

    (B)   Jim can countersign the checks, but Jill and June should refrain from interfering in choice of interior decoration schemes.

(C) Jill and June may supervise the decorator, but Jim should not countersign the checks.

(D) Neither arrangement is permissible.

Jack Brady has decided that, after all, he does not wish to serve as general partner. He has substantial personal assets, as do all the other partners. He does not want his assets subject to the risk of suit by a college student who injures himself on the premises, or on the note given to the appliance dealer for purchase of new home appliances for the apartments.

Jim Brady responds with the idea that they form a corporation, Brady Management, Inc., which will act as the general partner of Brady Bunch Limited Partnership No. I (limited partnership repeat syndicators are fond of Roman numerals). That way no one will have general liability. They also can use the corporation to be the general partner for Brady Bunch Limited Partnerships Nos. II, III, IV, and V, if they eventuate. The Bradys themselves will serve as the directors and officers of the corporation.

24. Jim Brady asks you, "Did I come up with a good idea?"

    (A) No. The service by limited partners as directors and officers of the incorporated general partner is participation in the control of the business of the partnership that will result in general liability.

    (B) No. A court will hold the limited partners liable by piercing the corporate veil of the general partner, reaching their pockets in their shareholder capacity if, for example, they do not carry adequate liability insurance and otherwise capitalize the corporation. Creditors and tort claimants are thus adequately protected.

    (C) No. It is a tossup whether a court in the State of Wigmore would adopt Answer (A) or Answer (B), so why chance it?

    (D) The Bradys should campaign for Wigmore to adopt the RULPA, which clearly permits a corporation to serve on a limited partnership's board as a general partner.

Your friend Evelyn is a law librarian who, over the years, has been a persistent real estate investor. She does not own real estate directly. Rather she has purchased units of participation in limited partnerships that, in turn, purchased a number of commercial and multi-family real estate developments.

Evelyn has decided to take early retirement. She intends to move to Sun Valley, Idaho, and become a professional snowboarder. She wishes to cash in her units of participation to raise cash to purchase a Hummer and a condominium at Elkhorn, near Sun Valley.

25. She seeks your advice. What do you tell her?

ANSWER:

Myron has had a vineyard and winery in the Eola Hills region of Oregon's Willamette Valley for 20 years. He has built up the business from near nothing to a probable market value of $7 to $10 million (an exact valuation is difficult to pin down). He produces Pinot Noir wines that have won many gold and silver medals and are served in fine restaurants up and down the West Coast. Myron has four children, all grown. None is too far away, but none works in the winery, at present.

At age 59, Myron has begun to think about his mortality. The value of his winery is spiraling upward, he is thinking of expansion which will increase the value even more, and he wishes the winery to be preserved intact because one or two of his sons or daughters very well might take it over upon Myron's death or retirement. He worries about federal estate taxes, the payment of which might force the sale of the winery.

26.   In what form of entity should he put the winery?

   (A)   General partnership.

   (B)   Limited partnership.

   (C)   Corporation.

   (D)   Limited Liability Company.

Note: LLC statutes and jurisprudence draw both on partnership law and on corporation law. By this point, you should have a feel for partnership law, but not for corporation law doctrine, such as veil piercing, upon which LLC law draws. It may, then, be a good idea to re-read the next several Questions after you have studied the corporate law Questions, infra, which lay out the corporate law version of the doctrine.

Recall that the Brady Bunch chose a limited partnership as the form of entity they would use to acquire a 60-unit apartment complex. The limited partnership hybrid, roughly half partnership, half corporation, would have given them two of three attributes they would like to have. They would have limited liability and "flow through" tax treatment. The downside was that someone (possibly a corporation) had to be the general partner and that the limited partners could not participate in control of the business, at least without risking their limited liability status. For example, Jill and June could not oversee the interior decoration of the units.

27.   Is there any form of entity that will give them all, or most all, of what they want?

    (A)   A corporation.

    (B)   A "subchapter S" corporation.

    (C)   A limited liability company.

    (D)   A family limited partnership.

Clare, Erika, and Rachel are top-flight women professional golfers who have played on the LPGA Tour. They have acquired, as tenants in common, an option on 285-acre parcel 10 miles outside of Taos, New Mexico, where they live in the off-season. They plan to develop the parcel into a destination resort golf course, with a name designer such as Jack Nicklaus or Robert Trent Jones, Jr.

The business plan for "Clare's Glen" is for the three promoters to contribute the option, and $1.5 million, for a 51 percent interest. They will sell 100 proprietary membership interests for $35,000 each, using the $3.5 million to finish paying for the land and for construction of the golf course. Once the course is up and running, they will sell further non-proprietary memberships at a price to be determined.

28.   What would be a good choice of entity for this venture?

    (A)   A Sub S corporation. The flow through of losses in early years may be taken as deductions on members' personal tax returns, but members will have limited liability if some one gets it in the head by an errant golf ball.

    (B)   This is perfect for a manager-managed LLC: limited liability, flow through tax treatment, some participation by the members in design of the facility, and centralized management.

(C)   A limited partnership, which would result in limited liability, flow through tax treatment, and would keep the members out of the promoters' hair, would be a good choice.

(D)   Eventually, Clare, Erika, and Rachel will need a corporation, so why not start out that way.

Joe, Jim, and Warren have an earth moving business. Joe and Warren are brothers. Jim is their cousin. The company, Parrot Head Contractors, LLC ("PHC"), bought some of the heavy equipment (bulldozers, dump trucks, excavators) on installment contracts, with very little down, but leased most of it. PHC carries only $100,000 liability insurance, far above the state law minimum of $20,000, but still rather low.

The owners are absentee owners. Joe drops by the "shop" every few weeks to check on things. They have few, if any meetings, but do keep in touch by telephone. Their records are in disarray. Basically, Warren and Jim let Joe "do it." Joe does it, but in a lackadaisical fashion.

The owners used an LLC so that Warren, who is rather well-to-do, could have the depreciation on the purchased new equipment "flow through" for deduction on his personal tax return.

One day a speeding PHC dump truck failed to make "dead man's curve." The out-of-control truck rammed through a chain link fence into the premises of "Deadman's Curve Pet Kennels." A number of prize show dogs were injured, disfigured, or killed. The damages easily exceed $1 million. The assets of PHC are no more than $150,000 plus the $100,000 in auto insurance.

29.   Can the kennel owners hold Warren and Jim personally liable for the $750,000 shortfall?

(A)   Piercing the corporate veil is just that, a corporate law doctrine that has no application to LLCs.

(B)   The doctrine has application when the LLC form has been abused, but must be modified to accommodate the greater informality contemplated by the LLC form of entity.

(C)   The veil of limited liability of an LLC, which shields its owners from liability for LLC torts or contract breaches, should be pierced when the owners have inadequately capitalized the LLC or intermingled their affairs with those of the LLC, to the detriment of third parties.

(D)   The LLC statute's provision of limited liability to "partners" is unconstitutional under state constitutions' remedies clauses, which guarantee to citizens of the state the civil law remedies they would have had as the common law existed at the time of statehood.

PHC is a Nebraska LLC. An accident involving a PHC-owned truck occurred outside of Council Bluffs, Iowa. Assume that the Iowa court held PHC and its three members (Joe, Jim, and Warren) personally liable. Warren and Jim now seek indemnity, or, in the alternative, contribution, from Joe.

30.   What law governs? What result?

ANSWER:

Players on the Chicago Cubs Baseball Club form an LLC to manufacture and market hats, shirts, baseball bats, and other items with players' likenesses or personal logos on them. Some items include groups of players. The reason for the effort is that, in the hypothetical year, the Cubs seem destined to win the National League championship (something they last did in 1945, and barely missed doing again in 2003) and the World Series (something they have not done since 1908). Fifteen players are participating, ranging from some of the stars (Sammy Sosa, Kerry Woods) to a utility infielder and a couple of seldom-used relief pitchers.

The group also is negotiating with Citizens Bank for a revolving line of credit so that funds will be available to gear up quickly for the large production increases and increased marketing anticipated if, indeed, the Cubs are World Series bound. Citizens wants additional security for the loan, but the players are not willing to give unlimited guarantees of the LLC's bank indebtedness.

31. How would you set up the financial provisions of the operating agreement?

(A) Rely on the LLC statute default rule, which probably provides for members' capital accounts akin to those for partners in a partnership.

(B) Assign negotiated percentages to players, with the stars having greater percentages than the relievers, and provide for an LLC "limited by guarantee" to satisfy the bank.

(C) Just negotiate the percentages. Maybe some of the players will give the bank second mortgages on their homes.

(D) Issue stock certificates to the players, who will then "pledge" some of their shares to Citizens Bank.

32. In the facts of the Question 31, how do the Cubs players make decisions and conduct day-to-day business?

(A) Have a member-managed LLC. In dealings with third parties, any member may bind the company.

(B) Have a manager-managed LLC. Provide in the articles or certificate that only the manager(s) may bind the LLC.

(C) Provide for officers (CEO, COO, CFO, or President, Secretary, and Treasurer) and provide further for annual election of officers by the members.

(D) Hire an outside firm of consultants to run the operation for the players.

Assume that the players elect relief pitcher Art Fowler as the manager. Art is an older player, at the end of his career, who almost never plays, but has significant business experience. Art predicts that little-used utility infielder Roy McMillan will star in the stretch run at the end of the season. Art had 10,000 McMillan t-shirts printed. McMillan never plays. Only two t-shirts are sold (for McMillan's two children).

Also, at the end of the season, the LLC has a considerable amount of Sammy Sosa paraphernalia in inventory. Art proposes to buy the inventory at 60 percent of cost.

33. Is Art potentially liable for losses due to his miscalculation in the t-shirts?
ANSWER:

34. May Art purchase the inventory and sell it for his own account during the off season?
ANSWER:

Now assume that the Cubs are successful down the stretch. The LLC is selling hats, shirts, and other sportswear items as fast as they can be put on the shelves. Hal Jeffcoat is one of the Cubs' relief pitchers. Hal resides with an aged uncle, George Jeffcoat, who used to be in the sportswear business.

Just before the trading deadline, the Cubs trade Hal to the San Diego Padres. Hal wants to provide for his uncle by giving him his 4 percent share in the LLC.

35.   Can Hal do so?

(A)   Yes, this is a free country. Common law prohibits restraints on alienation.

(B)   Hal can transfer his right to receive distributions, but Uncle George may not participate in the management or conduct of the LLC's business unless the operating agreement so provides or all of the members consent.

(C)   Hal may transfer nothing without the consent of his fellow members.

(D)   Hal can place his LLC interest in trust for the benefit of Uncle George.

Sammy Sosa has turned his season around. In late June and throughout July, he went on a home run spree that has him on pace to set yet another major league home run record. Through his agent, Sammy has informed Art Fowler, the LLC manager that "Sammy wants out." Supposition is that, with his turnaround, Sammy thinks he can do better marketing hats, t-shirts, and other items on his own.

36.   LLC manager Fowler consults you. Can Sammy do that, he asks?

(A)   Yes. LLC statutes commonly provide for member dissociation.

(B)   Yes, but he may be liable in damages for a "wrongful" dissociation.

(C)   LLC statutes are silent on the subject. Unless the LLC operating agreement provides for disassociation, we are in legal limbo here.

(D)   No. An implied provision of the agreement is that the LLC is formed for the major league baseball season, including the World Series. Any attempt to withdraw before that time would be null and void.

37.   Assume that Sammy does withdraw, effective July 31. What happens thereafter?

ANSWER:

The law firm of Bacon, Lettuce & Tomato ("BLT") has 100 partners. For many years, the firm was organized as a partnership. Twenty years ago the firm reorganized as a professional corporation ("PC"). The PC form allowed the partners to enjoy limited liability as to some passive real estate investments. The firm also has a stock portfolio in which it owns substantial amounts of stock in several high-tech corporate clients. Limited liability gives some comfort as to those investments. The PC Act enacted by the State of Huey exempts from limited liability the professional activities of the firm and its employees, as many such statutes do.

Three years ago, however, the firm's offshore banking group, comprised of partners 99 and 100, was accused of aiding and abetting a money-laundering scheme by one of the group's clients. The suit arose because an associate attorney working with the group failed to do the required due diligence on the transaction and, arguably, partners 99 and 100 failed to supervise the associate properly. The court held BLT liable for $13 million. Because the firm only had $10 million in malpractice insurance, the partners each had to contribute $30,000 to make good payment on the judgment.

Partners 7 and 8, members of the very conservative, pinstripe-wearing onshore banking group, consult you. They wish to reorganize again.

38. What is the best choice of business entity?

    (A) Corporation.

    (B) Limited Liability Company.

    (C) Partnership.

    (D) Limited Liability Partnership.

Roy Bean and his sister Gail, both well-to-do dentists, own Roy Bean's Exotic Food of All Nations. Gail has also become hostess of a popular cooking show on local television. Roy and Gail have an existing store that, after three years, has become profitable, at least in the busy months of the year. In the coming year, they plan to lease premises and open three new stores in the Birmingham, Alabama metro area. The leases will have seven- to eight-year terms. The business plan, which they prepared for the bank, shows the stores breaking even in the fourth year. As they embark upon this expansion, they consult you, their attorney, for advice.

39. Your advice to them is:

    (A) Do nothing and operate as a general partnership.

    (B) Form a corporation and elect subchapter "S" status under the Internal Revenue Code.

    (C) Hire counsel in Wilmington and form a Delaware corporation.

    (D) Hire you to draft a detailed partnership agreement.

Reed Bailey practices law with six partners in a boutique litigation firm. Last year Reed got hit with a malpractice claim in which the settlement exceeded the group's malpractice policy limits. Each partner had to chip in $40,000. They do not wish to see that happen again.

40. What alternatives do they have?

    (A) Remain a partnership because the bar association rules require it.

    (B) Form a corporation and elect subchapter S, as above.

    (C) Form a professional service corporation.

    (D) Form a limited partnership with Reed as the general partner.

Buddy Bonds wishes to incorporate his luxury car business and, as his lawyer, you concur. Buddy, his business, and you all are located in the State of Nirvana, which has the latest Model Business Corporation Act.

41. Buddy should form his corporation by filing articles of incorporation with the Secretary of State (or similar official) in:

    (A) Nirvana.

    (B) Nevada.

(C) Delaware.

(D) Offshore (Cayman Islands, Bermuda, the Bahamas, or the Netherlands Antilles).

Buddy's luxury car business, Bay Area Luxury Car Operation (BALCO) has been very successful. Buddy is thinking big time. He wishes first to re-incorporate in Nevada (the Delaware of the West).

42.   Advise Buddy on the mechanics of how it should be done.

    (A) He should form a shell corporation in Nevada, naming it BALCO Nevada. He would then merge his Nirvana BALCO into BALCO Nevada, then amending the name to delete "Nevada."

    (B) His corporation should adopt a plan of domestication, as now provided for in the MBCA.

    (C) You should tell him to hire a high-priced big city lawyer who knows how to do these things.

    (D) It cannot be done. Once in Nirvana, always in Nirvana.

You are a partner in a law firm. Associate Rosa comes to you. "Mr. Kelly has asked me to incorporate Ms. Stewart's business. I never took business organizations in law school. Help! What do I do? And, please don't tell Mr. Kelly that I came to you."

43.   What will you tell Rosa to do?

ANSWER:

44.   Rosa returns with the stamped ("Filed") articles in hand. She says, "I have looked through some old files. Here are some of the things I obviously should do. What comes next?"

    (A) Draft bylaws for conduct of the corporation's internal governance.

    (B) Order a corporate minute book with stock certificates, blank stock records, and a corporate seal.

    (C) Call the clients in and hold an organizational meeting.

    (D) All of the above.

Brittany and Posh form a company to produce music. Posh suspects that Brittany, if given the chance, would use corporate resources to open a splashy new nightclub as a venue for her performances. In their preliminary meeting with their attorney, Posh voices her concerns and Brittany agrees to any reasonable measure that would rein in or check her expansionary desires.

45.   The simplest way for the attorney to implement Brittany and Posh's meeting of the minds would be:

   (A)   Drafting a hold harmless agreement making Brittany responsible for any losses occasioned by unauthorized expansion of the corporation's business.

   (B)   Doing the same in an employment agreement that outlines Brittany's responsibilities.

   (C)   Drafting a narrow purpose article in the articles of incorporation.

   (D)   Having Brittany post a bond, with a commercial surety thereon.

Silver Wings is a discount airline licensed to fly from Seattle, Washington, to several California cities. Wiley Post, a senior pilot (and no relation to Wiley E. Coyote), decides that on the return trip from San Diego, he will divert to Las Vegas to see his lady friend, who lives there. While on the ground in Las Vegas, Wiley tells the cabin crew to take on any additional passengers, at least if they pay cash.

46.   Wiley's acts constitute:

   (A)   An *ultra vires* act.

   (B)   A "frolic and detour" by an agent.

   (C)   An illegal act.

   (D)   A breach of contract.

Ashbury Corp. builds railway carriages. Its articles' purpose clause states that the purpose of the corporation shall be to "build and sell railway equipment." Ashbury Corp. has signed a contract to build a railway line and railway bridges in Guatemala. While the contract has remained wholly executory, the price of steel has risen dramatically. If Ashbury performs, it will lose great amounts of money. The Ashbury CEO consults you.

47.   Are any of the following possible means to escape performance under the contract?

   (A)   Have a friendly shareholder bring suit to enjoin performance of the contract on grounds that is *ultra vires*.

(B)   Allege mutual mistake of fact and seek reformation of the contract.

(C)   Negotiate a new due date for performance and hope that the price of steel declines.

(D)   Defend any later suit bought by the Guatemalan railway authorities on grounds of fraud.

48.   What are five reasons the *ultra vires* doctrine has less viability today?

ANSWER:

For years, Gyro Gearloose has had his heart set on owning a Dunkin Donuts franchise in his hometown of Altoona. When retail space became available across from the Altoona police station, a prime location for a donut shop, Gyro signed a five-year lease, as follows: "Altoona Dunkin Donuts, Inc., Gyro Gearloose." Alas, Gyro does not get the Dunkin Donuts franchise.

49. He visits you to ascertain who is liable on the lease:

    (A) Neither corporation nor promoter Gyro is liable because a non-existent corporation may not act.

    (B) The corporation is liable, but only if it comes into existence.

    (C) Only Gyro is liable as the corporation did not exist and he failed to disclose that fact.

    (D) Both the corporation, when and if formed, and Gyro are liable.

Now assume the opposite. Dunkin Donuts and its area representative approve Gyro for the franchise. As in the previous Question, the prime space has become available, but Gyro has not yet signed a lease. Gyro has surveyed the market. He wants to quickly place an order for a precise Swiss donut-making machine (those people are very good at holes). He is in a hurry and wants the machine to arrive before he opens the shop. Gyro visits your office. In very unsophisticated fashion, he asks "what paper work do I need from you as my lawyer before I can get going on this thing."

50. You should reply:

    (A) Merely hold on to the written offers and have the corporation accept them when it comes into being.

    (B) Sign binding contracts, but make certain that you sign indicating the non-existence of your principal and your representative capacity, and look to the corporation for indemnity.

    (C) Sign, as in Answer (B) above, plus provide in the contract for a future novation when the corporation does come into existence.

    (D) Sign binding contracts, but look to the corporation for indemnification if and when it is formed.

Now reconsider the Gyro Gearloose hypothetical one additional time, but from yet another perspective, that of the corporation after it has been formed. Assume that there are three other participants, each of whom (and Gyro as well) owns 25 percent. Gyro has correctly signed and provided for novations in each of the three principal contracts and a number of other contracts.

51. At the organizational meeting, the participants should:

(A) Review and affirmatively repudiate any contracts not suitable for the new enterprise.

(B) Merely instruct the active manager to accept no benefits from certain of the contracts found to be inappropriate.

(C) Purchase a newspaper advertisement stating that "Dunkin Donuts, Inc." will no longer consider itself liable on the following contracts.

(D) Do nothing, at least with promoter's contracts, at the organizational meeting.

Soupy Sales is forming a corporation with Smokey Robinson and Brenda Lee. The business of the corporation is to rent a hanger at local airfield in Eugene, Oregon, and operate a small (two airplane) charter service. Soupy visits lawyer Lash Larue who tells Soupy that the articles were filed in Salem (the state capital) days earlier.

Acting for the corporation, Soupy then buys a computer on credit from IBM, buys two airplanes from Cessna (again on credit), and signs the lease for the hanger. Lash then telephones Soupy to say "Whoa. It seems my secretary put the articles on top of the filing cabinet, from whence they fell between the cabinet and the wall. They were never filed in Salem. I am sorry to say you don't have a corporation after all." IBM, Cessna, and Landlord sue Soupy, Smokey, and Brenda personally.

52.   The best defense is:

    (A)   De jure corporate status.

    (B)   De facto corporate existence.

    (C)   None, because Oregon has the MBCA, which the Oregon Supreme Court has held abolished the de facto corporation defense.

    (D)   Lack of knowledge because the MBCA has been revised to supersede in part holdings such as that by the Oregon Supreme Court.

The Fratelli brothers form a corporation, Mystic Pizza, Inc. The articles list their lawyer as their registered agent and registered office to which the Secretary of State sends the annual report form. The Fratellis, however, lose contact with their lawyer, who eventually moves away. Annual reports aren't filed. Franchise taxes aren't paid for three years. From a telephone call to the Secretary of State, "Chunk," the largest and nicest of the Fratelli brothers, discovers that the corporation had been dissolved. He is worried that they might be personally liable on corporate obligations. He is worried that the IRS might seek back taxes from the Fratellis, treating corporate earnings as partnership earnings. Chunk wants Mystic Pizza, Inc. brought back to life.

53.   Can you do it?

ANSWER:

Melba and Marvin form a corporation, Collateral Estoppel, Inc. ("CEI"). They capitalize it for $10,000 in return for common stock. They then have the corporation acquire the assets of the Arrow Bar for $50,000, payable as follows: $7,500 cash down payment and a promissory note for $42,500 to sellers. Later, Melba and Marvin cause the corporation to borrow $42,500 from local bank, paying off the seller of the Arrow Bar. Local bank, though, requires Melba and Marvin personally to guarantee CEI's note to the bank.

Late on Super Bowl Sunday, a customer left the Arrow Bar in an inebriated condition. Driving away, a few blocks later the customer hits Jay Harrow, who is out riding his Harley Davidson. Jay suffers serious injury. His damages are well over $500,000. The State of Concussion has a commercial Dram Shop Act. Customer has only minimal insurance ($10,000) and few other assets. Melba and Marvin have caused CEI to purchase liability insurance, but the policy limit is $100,000.

Jay Harrow brings suit under the Dram Shop Act and for negligence, naming CEI, Melba, and Marvin as defendants. He adds a third claim of "corporate disregard," asking the court to disregard the corporation's existence, thereby "piercing the veil" of limited liability that ordinarily exists. You are the judge's law clerk. She asks your opinion on whether to pierce.

54.   Select from the following.

   (A)   Yes. The capital is $7,500 and it "is trifling or illusory compared with the business to be done [size or volume] or the risks of loss," which are significant in the bar business.

   (B)   Yes. The capital is $50,000 and is trifling, given the risks of loss.

   (C)   No, the capital is $150,000 and is adequate and, besides, few courts pierce the veil based upon thin or inadequate capitalization alone.

   (D)   No. Melba and Marvin cannot be personally liable.

Ken Kenyon owns a California warehouse and a manufacturing facility, which he has leased for 20 years to AgriPac, Inc. AgriPac enters bankruptcy. Back East, Inc. ("BEI"), a billion dollar company, has an interest in expanding to the West Coast. It forms a subsidiary corporation AgriEast, Inc. to acquire the assets and assume some of the contracts of AgriPac out of bankruptcy.

BEI puts in its own officers as directors and officers of subsidiary AgriEast. Within a year, all of the managers of AgriEast have been dismissed, their functions assumed by BEI under a "services agreement" under which AgriEast pays its parent corporation $1 million plus 40 percent of earning before taxes, interest, depreciation, and amortization. Soon AgriEast's top customers are being billed by BEI. Correspondence with AgriEast's top customers and bankers often is on BEI stationery, signed by BEI managers in upstate New York, where BEI is headquartered.

After two years, BEI fires everyone at AgriEast and closes shop. Discovery shows that all the top AgriEast customers are now BEI customers. BEI capitalized AgriEast with only $1,000 of its own money, causing AgriEast to borrow $70 million to operate.

Kenyon now has an empty warehouse and manufacturing facility, with 15 years left on the lease. He has been unable to rent the facility. He calculates that he is losing over $1.5 million per year. Kenyon has filed a complaint alleging breach of contract against AgriEast (which has no money).

55.   Kenyon should amend his complaint to:

   (A)   Allege personal liability of BEI's officers and directors.

   (B)   Pierce the corporate veil to reach the assets of BEI.

   (C)   Add allegations of a conspiracy to defraud, naming BEI's officers, BEI, and AgriEast as co-conspirators.

   (D)   Seek the intervention of the activist New York Attorney General because BEI abused the corporate form when it formed AgriEast as a New York corporation and capitalized it for only $1,000.

On a brisk spring night, Captain Jennifer Bright exited the Pipeline Club in Valdez, Alaska, fortified against the night with a number of vodka tonics. Once aboard her ship, an oil supertanker, Captain Bright prepared to go to sea. Casting off all lines, the supertanker ventured out into pristine Prince William Sound. Although still in confined waters, Captain Bright went below to her cabin. Unaware of shoal water, the first mate drove the giant ship aground, ripping open its hull, spilling millions of gallons of crude oil. Eventually, the damages to the environment and to the Alaskan fishing community totaled $15–20 billion.

Injured parties sued BigGasCo for negligence in hiring and negligent entrustment, among other things. BigGasCo had ample evidence of Captain Bright's propensity to "drink and drive." Discovery reveals, though, that the *supertanker*, and every other tanker in the BigGasCo fleet, is each owned by an individual corporation. In turn, BigGasCo Transportation owns each of those brother-sister (sibling) corporations. BigGasCo Transportation, in turn, is owned by BigGasCo. The assets available to satisfy any judgment plaintiffs may obtain include one large tanker with a hole in the bottom and liability insurance of several million dollars.

56.   The judge hearing the case should rule as follows:

   (A)   This is an "outrage" and BigGasCo and BigGasCo Transportation should be liable.

   (B)   Each and every subsidiary was the "alter ego" and "mere instrumentality" of the parent and should have its "corporateness" disregarded.

   (C)   It is permissible to compartmentalize a business in this way (through use of multiple corporations).

   (D)   BigGasCo and BigGasCo Transportation should be indicted, but that is for the state or federal prosecutors to decide.

Coach Walker is concerned that his football players have neither sufficient summer employment opportunities nor sufficient summer income. Along with boosters of State U's football program, Walker organizes a light hauling and moving enterprise.

In each city around the state, he forms a corporation, organizing 12 in all, including Peoria Movers, Inc. Walker is the sole shareholder of each of the 12 corporations. Each corporation buys two trucks from local Chevrolet dealers, all of whom are big State U boosters. The corporations purchase the trucks with little down payment ($5,000), giving a promissory note for the remainder of the purchase price of each truck ($16,000). Each corporation obtains liability insurance, but only the minimum $20,000 required by the financial responsibility law in the State of Butkus. Each corporation hires five or six football players, paying each of them $20 per hour.

One hot July day, linebacker Dizzy Doubtful is exceeding the speed limit in a Peoria Movers truck, loaded with 100 cases of canned Spam. He turns left suddenly, across oncoming traffic. Grammar school teacher Millie Mild is unable to stop her Chevrolet Geo Metro. She collides with Dizzy. Spam is everywhere. Instead of the usual case with a Geo Metro (Spam in a can), Ms. Mild is in a can in Spam. Dizzy is uninjured, but clearly was at fault.

Millie Mild is seriously injured. She is off work for months, has to go through painful rehabilitation, and is left with considerable pain.

57.   Who should Millie Mild sue and why?

(A)   State U, as vicariously liable (*respondeat superior*) for Walker's activities.

(B)   Walker, as the owner of Peoria Movers, Inc.

(C)   All 12 corporations.

(D)   Both Answers (B) and Answer (C).

58.   In theory, in which sort of case should it be easiest to pierce the corporate veil?

(A)   Contract claims by financial institutions such as banks.

(B)   Tort claims (like Millie Mild's in Question 57).

(C)   Contract claims.

(D)   Corporate group claims involving title to real property.

Returning to the facts of Question 55, Ken Kenyon brought suit in California against AgriEast, Inc. and its parent company, Back East, Inc. ("BEI"). BEI has moved to dismiss on grounds of lack of territorial jurisdiction. It has no presence in California other than through its subsidiary, which leased the warehouse. BEI not only has no "minimum contacts" under *International Shoe*, it claims to have no contacts at all.

You are the judge's law clerk. She has promised BEI's lawyers an answer by this afternoon so that they may be able to catch an airplane back to the East Coast.

59.   What is your advice?

ANSWER:

Now switch hats. You are an attorney working on Ken Kenyon's case. The case is now in discovery. You are back in New York going through boxes of documents. You find an email from the Chief Executive Officer ("CEO") of Back East, Inc. to Kenyon. The date of the email is shortly before Kenyon signed the ancillary documents relating to assumption of the lease by AgriEast, Inc. the subsidiary BEI formed to acquire the assets of California-based AgriPac.

The closing of the email reads as follows: "And you know, Ken, Back East has been in business for over 100 years. Don't be nervous about this lease. Back East stands by its commitments and will be good for it."

60.   What have you found?

(A) A smoking gun.

(B) Good evidence for the piercing the veil aspect of the case.

(C) Circumstantial evidence of direct liability.

(D) Nothing of significance.

Some years ago Hans, Franz, and Volker started a microbrewery, making beer in Franz's garage and marketing it under the "Homburg" name (with a hat on the label). Up until two years ago, they operated as a partnership at will. During the partnership years, it was a labor of love. Each of the partners put varying amounts of money into the business, but they always operated as equal one-third partners. Their partnership capital accounts were as follows: Hans $120,000, Franz $70,000, and Volker $20,000

The brewery did well until a few years ago. New microbreweries began springing up everywhere. Sales fell off. Homburg suffered its first ever losses.

Hans, Franz, and Volker consulted a lawyer who advised them to incorporate, in part to avoid personal liability should the business continue to slip. Lawyer set up the "capitalization" of Homburg, Inc. as follows: Promissory Note due Hans $100,000, Promissory Note due Franz $50,000, Common Stock (100 shares each), Hans $20,000, Franz $20,000, Volker $20,000.

Sales continued to dwindle. Homburg, Inc. entered bankruptcy, listing $500,000 in liabilities and $300,000 in assets. Hans has filed proof of claim for $100,000 and Franz for $50,000.

61.   You represent Grosse Bank, which Homburg owes $200,000. Your strategy should be:

(A) Attempt to pierce the corporate veil, holding the "partners" personally liable.

(B) Seek out any affiliated corporations or other entities, attempting a "sideways" piercing of the veil.

(C) Undertake extensive discovery to ascertain if Hans, Franz, or Volker somehow held themselves as responsible for corporate obligations.

(D) File a motion in the bankruptcy court asking that the corporate debts purportedly owing to Hans and Franz be subordinated (pushed down or to the end of the line).

Now assume that, instead of failing, the Homburg microbrewery (Question 61) operates successfully for a number of years. The "partners" (Hans, Franz, and Volker) have expanded the operation from one state to three. Since then, a number of competing microbreweries have started up, and price competition has become fierce. Unable to withstand the competition, Homburg, Inc. starts its downward slide, ending eventually in bankruptcy.

62.   Can Grosse Bank make a claim that Hans, Franz, and Volker should have put in more capital as the "business to be done" expanded? Can they pierce the corporate veil or subordinate

shareholder-owned debt based upon the thinly capitalized nature of the expanded business?

ANSWER:

Beau, Luke, and Uncle Jesse are forming a stock car racing company. Needless to say, limited liability, and probably incorporation, are good ideas, although some attorneys might form a limited liability company ("LLC"). Regardless of the form of entity, corporation or LLC, a capital structure has to be set up for accounting and legal purposes.

Beau and Luke are each going to put in $15,000. Uncle Jesse will contribute the racecar and the lowboy trailer they use to haul around the car. The parties agree that the racecar and trailer have a value of $15,000.

63. The best capital structure for Duke Racing, Inc. would be:

   (A) Common stock for the boys and preferred stock for Uncle Jesse.

   (B) Common stock for the boys and a loan by Uncle Jesse.

   (C) All common stock.

   (D) Common stock for each and a loan by each.

The articles of incorporation of Duke Racing, Inc. authorize issuance of up to 400 shares. At the corporation's organizational meeting, 300 shares are issued. Two years later, Uncle Jesse wishes to retire. The corporation buys back Uncle Jesse's 100 shares. Later on Beau and Luke have a falling out. With the director who replaced Uncle Jesse, Roscoe P. Coletrain, Luke attempts to have the corporation issue 200 shares to Boss Hog, a disreputable local mogul.

64. Does Beau have an argument for injunctive relief on pure technical grounds?

   (A) Yes, the issuance of 200 additional shares is clearly an "over issue," that is, an issuance that exceeds the 100 remaining authorized shares. In order to issue 200 shares, the directors must seek shareholder amendment of the articles to increase the number of authorized shares.

   (B) No, under the Model Business Corporation Act, shares that are repurchased by the corporation revert to the status of authorized, but unissued, shares. Therefore Duke Racing had authorized 200 additional shares which could be sold to Boss Hog.

   (C) Yes, the shares that were repurchased from the corporation became "treasury shares."

   (D) No, even if treasury shares existed, the directors have power to re-issue them.

Assume the same facts as in Question 64, but Beau and Luke have no cash. Instead, Luke offers a contract to serve part-time as the racing team's mechanic in return for his stock. Beau, who has no mechanical skills, offers his personal $15,000 promissory note for his stock. Uncle Jesse's racecar, the "General Beauregard," has a market value of no more than $5,000. You are their business lawyer. You practice in a jurisdiction that has never updated its corporate laws.

65.   You should:

(A)   Advise the boys that they may not contribute promissory notes or future services for stock.

(B)   Advise Uncle Jesse that what he receives will be "watered stock" and that, upon any insolvency, the creditors of the corporation may seek to hold him liable for the "water."

(C)   Call Roscoe P. Coletrain and report these guys to the attorney general.

(D)   Set par value low, say $1.00 per share, and have each pay in only that amount with respect to their stock.

Again, assume the same facts as in Question 64, except that you are in a jurisdiction that has the latest, fully upgraded Model Business Corporation Act ("MBCA"). Luke contributes his contract, Beau his promissory note, and Uncle Jesse his racecar.

66.   What would an accurate balance sheet look like?

ANSWER:

Clare, Erika, and Rachel were on the college golf team together. Clare and Rachel play on the Lady Professional Golf Association ("LPGA") tour. The three women have developed a line of clothing and golf accessories. They are going to form a company that Erika, who was a business major in college, will manage. The company will manufacture the clothing in the Republic of Indonesia. The three have decided that a minimum startup capital would be $2.5 million, $1.5 million of which they will raise from wealthy investors, asking 15 each to contribute $100,000, for a 49 percent common stock interest. The three principals will contribute $1 million and the designs and logo for a 51 percent stock interest.

67.   Questions of securities law aside (they must register the stock with the SEC, or have an exemption from registration, and almost always will rely on an exemption), what paperwork should Clare, Erika, and Rachel have ready when they solicit the wealthy investors?

(A)   None, as they know most of these people very well.

(B)   Stock certificates that they can "fork over" in return for $100,000 checks.

(C)   Sample clothing and accessories with certificates of authenticity.

(D)   Short agreements called "subscription agreements" which the "subscribers" will sign.

You are a hot shot Silicon Valley business lawyer who represents venture capital firms. Your client, Kleiner Perkins, has reached a decision to invest $30 million in "mid-stage" venture capital in an e-commerce company known as Webvan, Inc. Webvan has been gearing up to take grocery orders over the Internet. The company will then use a fleet of vans to deliver groceries to customers' front doors.

68.   The Kleiner Perkins partner has asked your advice on what form the investment should take and what necessary steps have to be taken by the attorneys who represent Webvan. What should you advise?

(A) Make a loan and take only a small stock interest so that if the company fails, Kleiner Perkins will be a creditor.

(B) Take all common stock. If the company is wildly successful, Kleiner Perkins will own a chunk of it.

(C) Do something in-between, such as take a preferred stock that can convert into common stock if the company is wildly successful.

(D) Talk them out of the investment, as groceries-by-Internet is an idea whose time has not yet come.

In the beautiful Shenandoah Valley of Virginia lies the heart of the East Coast's apple industry. Many years ago two orchard owners — Golden Delicious and Granny Smith — joined fortunes to form the Winchester Apple Co., which they subsequently incorporated. Today, the Delicious family and the Smith family still own the company's common stock 50-50. The Delicious family consists of two children, Gomer Golden Delicious, who is now CEO, and his sister, Gretchen, who lives "down the Valley" in Woodstock, Virginia.

By contrast, the Smith family consists of eight children who, by and large, are spread all over the U.S., in Seattle, Portland, San Francisco, Albuquerque, New Orleans, Tupelo, and Tuscaloosa. Only one sibling, Sarah, remains in Virginia.

Sarah reports to her siblings that Gomer has offered her a lucrative position as a "marketing consultant." The position carries with it a new leased Mercedes automobile.

69. What should the old, trusted family lawyer have anticipated and done 10 years ago when the first generation was alive and still held the stock?

(A) Anticipated a "divide and conquer" strategy by the Delicious family, which could be foiled by creation of class, or "group," voting for directors.

(B) Created a "put" in either family that would give each a right to force the sale of all the stock to a third party.

(C) Purchased directors' and officers' ("D & O") liability insurance that would pay damages in event of a breach by Gomer of his fiduciary duties.

(D) Nothing. A certain amount of politics and maneuvering is to be expected in any corporation.

Fabulous Foods, Inc. is a confectionery company. The company's common stock is traded on the New York Stock Exchange. An inner circle of shareholders, which holds about 15 percent of the common stock, consists of the third generation of the company's founders and the company's long time top managers. The inner circle and Fabulous's management are worried about a hostile takeover. Fabulous has no debt, ranks number two or three in every market in which it has products, and has $100 million in cash or cash equivalents. There has also been much recent consolidation in the food industry, not only through friendly mergers, but also by hostile takeovers.

The Fabulous board of directors is conducting its annual "fly away" board retreat at a resort in Vermont. The board has asked the founding family members to join the board for an afternoon. The board has also asked you, a New York takeover lawyer, to address them on a takeover defense they could quickly implement.

70. You should prepare to advise them on:

(A) A defensive acquisition that would result in an antitrust obstacle to any merger that the likely hostile bidders could pursue.

(B) A "scorched earth" defense plan in which the corporation would make pre-arranged plans to sell off its best assets to various competitors.

(C) Issuance of "super stock" or "super voting stock" to the inner circle.

(D) Arrange in advance a defensive merger with a "white knight."

Beau, Luke, and Uncle Jesse (see Questions 63–66) have had some racing success. In the last year, they have garnered $200,000 in prizes against $30,000 in expenses. They have put much of their winnings into spare parts (extra engines, tires, etc.), a backup racecar, and a used Winnebago motor home. They also wish to each take $10,000 out of the corporation.

71. Can they do so legally?

ANSWER:

Buddy Boy Broadcasting ("BBB"), Inc. is located in the State of Bond. BBB has radio stations in three middle-sized markets and has been quite successful. The founding shareholder, Bill ("Buddy Boy") Bradford, age 63, owns 40 percent of the company. Bill's son, Bobby, and their partner Bart, both younger men, own 30 percent each. Bill plays golf to a 7 handicap and wishes to retire to Prescott, Arizona. Bobby and Bart are willing to aid Bill in doing so by having the corporation buy out Bill's interest. The price is $4,500,000, to be paid over 15 years.

You are the corporate lawyer. The commercial lawyer down the hallway in your firm has drafted the promissory note that Bobby and Bart will sign on behalf of BBB, Inc. The note provides for quarterly payments of $75,000 each year with simple interest at 8 percent per annum, payable on the outstanding balance with each quarterly payment. Your partner has also drafted the repurchase agreement by and between BBB, Inc. and Buddy Boy.

72. Are there any corporate law issues with which you have to deal?

(A) No, the parties' agreement should pretty well take care of it. At closing Buddy Boy will hand over his share certificate and the corporation will deliver the promissory note and a check for the first installment to Buddy Boy.

(B) Yes, the repurchase of shares at such a high price is bound to be a violation of the fiduciary duties Bobby and Bart owe to the corporation.

(C) No, a long-term repurchase of shares is an unregulated transaction in which the parties are free to engage.

(D) Yes, the transaction is a distribution and therefore must be tested for legality using the statutory tests discussed in Question 68.

In Question 72, the attorney for the corporation will have to pass on the condition of the corporation, after giving effect to the distribution. In other words, is the corporation financially strong enough to undertake a $4.5 million commitment? Assume, though, that subtracting the total liabilities from the total assets produces a balance sheet net worth of only $1 million.

73. Does that end the inquiry, foreclosing the transaction?

ANSWER:

It is 2020. The United States is in the midst of another hi-tech and dotcom boom. Your client is Bob Bates, IV (a.k.a. "Quad") — or, rather, his company, MacroSoft, Inc. Quad has formed a company that has successfully developed new products, including "Doors 4.0." Quad and six software "buddies" from Lakeside High School own 51 percent. Seven older investors ("the angels") own the remaining 49 percent, having chosen to take common stock rather than preferred or convertible preferred stock other angels or venture capitalists often prefer (see Question 65). The company was formed under a recently updated version of the MBCA, but the articles of incorporation provide for preemptive rights. The MacroSoft business plan is to "go public" six months from now if favorable stock market conditions hold.

You and Quad are in a coffee shop drinking a quad latte. Quad relates to you: "You know, the underwriters I have talked to say we have to get rid of preemptive rights before any public offering. What are preemptive rights? But first, can we get rid of them?"

74. What is your answer?

    (A) "Maybe not," because the preemptive right is an important and valuable ("vested") property right. If any shareholder objects, you cannot amend the articles to eliminate them.

    (B) "Yes," a public offering under the Securities Act of 1933 automatically eliminates preemptive rights.

    (C) "Yes," by amendment of the articles of incorporation via a majority shareholder vote, which we know we can obtain as we know 10 of 14 shareholders are clearly in favor.

    (D) "Yes," because the latest version of the MBCA does not recognize preemptive rights.

Quad resists governmental regulation. Quad has come up with a plan to sell MacroSoft shares at a series of seminars he and his founding shareholder friends intend to put on in motel and hotel conference rooms in Washington, Oregon, and California.

75. What do you think of Quad's plan?

    (A) It is a free country. He ought to be able to raise capital any way he wishes.

    (B) Under the federal Securities Act of 1933, the corporation must register the shares with the Securities and Exchange Commission (SEC) or have an exemption from registration. Generally speaking, open-ended "general solicitations" of the kind Quad has planned never are exempt.

    (C) He would be violating state law because under state securities laws ("blue sky" laws), the corporation must register or have an exemption from registration in each state in which the securities will be offered for sale (here Washington, Oregon, and California).

(D) He and MacroSoft would be violating both federal and state securities acts and Quad might very well end up in jail if he keeps up his defiant attitude.

On January 30, Arctic Aloha, Inc. ("AA"), an Anchorage, Alaska travel company owned by 20 equal shareholders, receives a merger proposal from Happy Hawaii Holidays ("HHH"). The proposal, which appears to be attractive, states that it is good for 30 days. Many of AA's shareholders, however, have escaped the brutal winter to vacation in sunnier climes, including Costa Rica, Fiji, and Belize. They are unavailable until late February. AA's bylaws state that the annual meeting of shareholders is to be held on the first Monday of March each year. AA's board chair, Tony Knowles, consults you regarding what to do.

76. What is your advice to Tony Knowles?

(A) Call a special meeting of the shareholders for mid-February and take action, no matter what.

(B) Wait until the annual meeting in March — HHH won't care about the deadline.

(C) Agree to the merger, seeking shareholder approval in April.

(D) Call a special meeting, but only after a feasibility study of whether and on what date a quorum might be obtained.

Whistling "Belize Navidad," Barbara mails a letter from the former British Honduras to Anchorage and Tony Knowles stating that "I hereby appoint you my agent to vote my 100 shares in favor of proposed merger and to act on such other matters as may properly come before the meeting." By contrast, from the Cook Islands, Betsy mails a letter to Tony stating "I vote my 100 shares in favor of the merger with HHH." Eleven shareholders voted for the merger and nine voted against. You are the election judge.

77. Did the merger pass?

ANSWER:

The Whaler Corp. (owned by the descendants of Bob Marley) proposes to acquire the Jonah Corporation in a friendly merger. The Jonah boys are hesitating, however. After the merger they will own only 25 percent of the bigger company. They fear that in this merger "they will be swallowed up." Whaler's attorney replies that he will cap the board size at 10, insure that the Jonah boys have 3 of 10 directors, and have an 80 percent quorum and voting requirement both for shareholders' and directors' meetings.

78. How should the Jonah boys react to the offer on the table?

(A) Snicker. This is America and majority always rules.

(B) Snicker because courts are openly hostile to such arrangements on the grounds that the resulting veto power, or "negative control," often results in "the tyranny of the minority."

(C) Seriously consider it as statutes now make clear the authority for greater than majority quorum and voting requirements.

(D) Walk. From their point of view, mergers of small companies into larger entities are problematic at best.

Return to the facts of Question 76. While on the beach in the Cook Islands, Betsy meets an attorney who tells her that her absentee ballot is no good. Also, Betsy begins to change her mind about the AA-HHH merger. She now opposes it. So she hops an Air New Zealand flight from Raratonga to Los Angeles. She transfers from Terminal "A" to Terminal "G," just in time to catch an Alaska Airlines flight to Anchorage. She arrives just an hour before the meeting. Breathless, she telephones her friend Bobby Joe, who tells her that only 10 shareholders will be present in person or by proxy.

79.   What should she do?

   (A) Stay away to prevent a quorum ever from assembling.

   (B) Don't stay away because she could be held liable for breach of her fiduciary duty.

   (C) Attend, see which way the wind is blowing, and leave if the wind seems against her, thus "breaking" the quorum.

   (D) Make a "special appearance" and protest the lack of a quorum.

Recall that on January 30, Tony Knowles, the board chair, discussed calling a special shareholders' meeting to discuss the HHH merger proposal. Assume that, on February 1, the AA board of directors called a special shareholders meeting for February 28.

Casey acquired his shares in AA at a very late date, February 20. Casey has some definite thoughts on the AA merger.

80.   Is there any chance that Casey will be able to vote at the February 28 meeting, even though he acquired his shares only eight days earlier, or has Casey "struck out"?

   (A) He cannot vote because he acquired his shares after the date on which the board of directors called the meeting.

   (B) He cannot vote because he acquired the shares after any "record date" the board of directors may have set in order to determine which shares are eligible to vote at the meeting.

   (C) He cannot vote because only shareholders of record on the corporation's books may vote, and corporations close the transfer books after the meeting has been called, but before the corporation sends out notice of the meeting.

   (D) He has a good chance of being able to vote. He should call up his seller, asking her to give him a proxy to vote the shares at the meeting.

Clintmarts, Inc. is a leading retailer based in Arkansas with a five person board of directors, elected annually. The corporation is privately held by two factions: the Clintons, who own 730 of 1,000 shares, and the Gores, who own the other 270 shares. Clintmarts, Inc. has cumulative voting for the election of directors. Some years, Great Aunt Mary, who lives in New York, and owns 200 percent of the Clintons' 730 shares, does not show up for the meeting.

At tomorrow's annual shareholders' meeting the two families will convene to elect five directors. You are huddled with the Gores at the Best Western, plotting strategy for tomorrow.

81. How many directors will the Gore family be able to elect at the meeting?

(A) One.

(B) Two.

(C) Three.

(D) None.

Suppose that the Clintmarts, Inc. articles of incorporation provide for a "staggered" or "classified" board of five directors. The board is divided into three classes of two, two, and one director each, each class to be elected for three-year terms.

82. Now how many directors can the Gores elect?

(A) One.

(B) None.

(C) Two.

(D) Three.

Uncle Jimmy Watson is the scion of the family that owns Sherlock Holmes, Inc. The company produces hound's-tooth hats, capes, and meerschaum pipes. Jimmy has given away much of the stock to the second and third generations of the Watson family. He now owns only 40 percent. But he continues to rule with an iron fist. Jimmy signs everything on behalf of the company without consulting anyone. He has not accepted advice or held a meeting in 10 years.

83. Younger Watsons want a forum in which they can discuss company affairs and, if necessary, reproach Uncle Jimmy. Can you get them one?

ANSWER:

Shareholders of the Winchester Apple Co. (Question 69) are widely scattered. They do not wish to travel back to Winchester from all around the country merely to attend and vote at routine shareholders' meetings. Winchester Apple Co. is incorporated in a jurisdiction with the Model Business Corporation Act.

84. May the company's attorney just send them a resolution and have each of them sign it?

(A) Such informal action is only permitted when an emergency exists and the emergency doctrine is invoked.

(B) Action by informal consents is permitted in lieu of a meeting if the shareholders' consents are unanimous.

(C) Shareholders' unanimous written consents may only be utilized for special and not for annual shareholders' meetings.

(D) The annual meeting must be held.

Hunter Boat Works, Inc. is a publicly-held company, incorporated and having its principal place of business in Connecticut. Its bylaws state that the annual shareholders' meeting will be held on the first Monday in March, unless the board of directors otherwise decides. Traditionally, the corporation holds the meeting at its headquarters in New London, but another bylaw gives the board the right to designate the place of the annual meeting.

Hunter has learned that a large East Coast company, Bangor Junta, has acquired from institutional investors a large block of stock and is in the process of negotiating two more "block" purchases which will give Bangor Junta numerical control or nearly so.

Hunter's board holds a special meeting early in December. The directors take two steps: first, they advance the annual meeting date to the last week of December; and, second, they designate the place of the meeting to be North Pole, Maine, where Hunter has a fiberglass resin storage facility. Due to exceptional snowfall, North Pole is under 10 feet of white stuff. Ingress and egress is only by snowmobile from the next town.

Bangor files suit in Litchfield, Connecticut (home of the U.S.'s first law school) to enjoin the shareholders' meeting. You are the law clerk to the state trial judge. She asks you to snowshoe over to the county law library and come back with some advice for her and the legal research to back it up.

85. What is your advice?

(A) Advancing the meeting date is permissible, but the relocation to North Pole is not. Order the meeting to be held in Connecticut.

(B) The meeting can stay in North Pole, but the annual meeting must be held after the year has ended (and not before).

(C) Both actions are permissible under the language of duly adopted bylaws.

(D) Both actions are permissible in themselves, but "inequitable action does not become permissible simply because it is legally possible."

Indiana Jones has been presented with the opportunity to do a three-year archaeological dig in the jungles of Myanmar (Burma). The difficulty is that Indiana and his sister, Jennifer, each inherited 35 percent of Bullwhip, Inc. Through their combined ownership, they control the board of directors.

Indiana wishes to go off on his dig without being bothered about Bullwhip affairs. Jennifer is quite willing to vote Indiana's shares for him because she realizes the Jones siblings must stick together, lest they lose control of the Bullwhip board. She also, however, does not want Indiana to be able to show up at the last minute, second guess her decisions, and try to vote his shares.

86. What voting device will get the job done for them?

(A) A proxy, with Indiana as the proxy giver and Jennifer as the proxy holder.

(B) A proxy styled as "irrevocable."

(C) A shareholder's voting agreement (a.k.a. a "pooling agreement").

(D)   A voting trust with the trusted family lawyer as the trustee.

Recall from Question 69 that the eight Smith children, who collectively own 50 percent of the common stock of Winchester Apple Co. in equal shares, are spread out geographically. To maintain their share of control on the board of directors, the Smith children have to "stick together." Otherwise, Gomer and Gretchen Delicious, who both remain in or nearby Winchester, may pursue a "divide and conquer" strategy.

87.   Question 69 raised the possibility that class voting (Smith common and Delicious common) could effectuate a power sharing arrangement between the two groups. If the Delicious children refuse the articles of incorporation could not be amended to provide for class voting. How else could you allay the Smiths' concerns?

(A)   Have the seven younger Smith siblings give an irrevocable proxy to the eldest of the eight brothers and sisters.

(B)   Have the eight siblings sign an agreement to vote their shares as they all may agree and, if they fail to agree, to designate their trusted family lawyer to vote their shares by proxy.

(C)   Start negotiations to sell to the Delicious family.

(D)   Have the eight Smith siblings sign an agreement to vote all their shares as the majority of them agree.

Suppose the Smith siblings try a pooling agreement, but it does not work. Many of them are young and are prone to argue over the most minor points. For two years now, it has been extremely difficult even to marshal a majority on any given point.

88.   What might be a solution now?

(A)   Now have the seven younger siblings give an irrevocable proxy to the eldest of the eight brothers and sisters.

(B)   Sell. The situation is impossible.

(C)   Convey the shares to a trusted family adviser who will convey back all but the voting rights, which she will retain for 10 years.

(D)   Modify the existing pooling agreement to provide for plurality rather than majority control of the pool.

Now assume that one sibling protests about Environmental Protection Agency wastewater permit requirements at Winchester Apple's plants. He says "give me proxies," or "make me a voting trustee," or "all of you who think environmental laws are a crock join me in a pooling agreement" and "we'll put directors in office who, as much as possible, will direct the company's managers to skirt and evade the environmental laws of the U.S. and the Commonwealth of Virginia."

89.   Will the scheme work?

ANSWER:

R. D. Hoe Co. is a publicly-held garden implement manufacturer, with approximately 400 shareholders, many of whom live in the community in which Hoe is located. Hoe has done well, but the last several quarters failed to meet analysts' projections by a few pennies per share. The board of directors therefore fired the CEO, Jimmy Stewart, whose life is no longer wonderful. Mr. Stewart has been extremely popular, both at Hoe and in the community. He has served as a youth coach, as a scout leader, and on the boards of several community organizations. He personally knows and is friends with a number of Hoe's rank-and-file shareholders.

At the annual shareholders' meeting, the hotel ballroom is packed to the rafters. A shareholder steps to the microphone, propounding two resolutions:

1. That by resolution the shareholders hereby resoundingly voice their praise and affection for CEO Jimmy Stewart for all the great work he has done at the Hoe Co. and in the community.

2. The shareholders move that Jimmy Stewart be re-hired as the CEO of the R.D. Hoe Co.

Both motions are seconded, multiple times.

90.   You are corporate counsel, seated on the dais next to the board chair, who is presiding over the meeting. The chair leans over, whispering to you "What should I do?"

   (A)   Personnel matters and appointment of corporate officers are part of the corporation's business and affairs. By law, the directors, and not the shareholders, manage the business and affairs of the corporation.

   (B)   Allow discussion of both resolutions, but allow a vote only on resolution one, which is purely advisory, and rule resolution two "out of order" for the reasons stated in Answer (A).

   (C)   Allow discussion of and voting on both resolutions which, even if passed, are purely advisory, but are not "out of order."

   (D)   Same as Answer (C), but only if resolution two is re-phrased in advisory or precatory language (*i.e.*, "The shareholders *recommend* that the board of directors rehire Jimmy Stewart as the CEO of R. D. Hoe Co.").

91.   But as a shareholder how do you know, or how can you get started in finding out, about the performance of R.D. Hoe Co. during the years Jimmy Stewart was the CEO?

ANSWER:

Bert Lahr, a shareholder in R.D. Hoe, has to be away at his daughter's wedding in Indiana, Pennsylvania (actually the real Jimmy Stewart's hometown). He wants to hear the meeting and to vote for Jimmy when the time comes. The folks at Hoe, although opposed to Jimmy, will do whatever it takes to enable Bert to do this.

92.   How would you set it up for him?

ANSWER:

Five shareholders of Allegheny Forest Products, Inc. ("AFP"), a publicly-held corporation, are in your office. Together they own 7 percent of the outstanding common shares. One is a professor at Carnegie-Mellon University, another is a professor at the University of Pittsburgh, one is an Episcopal minister, another owns a French bakery, and the last is the lead oboist with the Pittsburgh Symphony. They are aghast at the way in which AFP is laying waste to the Laurel Highlands in the Allegheny Mountains of Pennsylvania by clear-cutting forests. They want it stopped.

The questions come tumbling forth from the mouths of all five. They are prepared to sally forth now in Saabs and Volvos to enlist other AFP shareholders for their campaign.

93. Which of the following options is their best course of action?

    (A) Wage a proxy fight, electing their own slate of directors.

    (B) File a lawsuit, alleging, *inter alia*, breach by the AFP directors of their fiduciary duties.

    (C) Engage in vigorous advocacy, designed to sway both public and AFP shareholder opinion.

    (D) File a shareholder SEC Rule 14a-8 proposal, with supporting statement, which management will have to include in its (and the company's) annual proxy statement.

Francophile, Inc. is a diversified food products and import-export company, with $150 million in annual sales and $10 million in annual profits. One line of products it imports is pâté de foie gras, produced through forced feeding geese and harvesting their oversized livers. Francophile sells about $80,000 in pâté de foie gras each year.

Audubon, a Francophile shareholder, has presented management the following proposal: "Resolved, the shareholders recommend that the board of directors form a committee to study the methods whereby the company's French supplier produces its pâté de foie gras and report to the shareholders its findings." Audubon has already been rebuffed. Francophile management told him in no uncertain words: "It's our pâté and we'll import it if we want to."

94. Audubon consults you. What is his next step?

    (A) Proceed to federal court, filing a complaint and motion for preliminary injunction.

    (B) Enlist the aid of seven or eight other shareholders to put pressure on the company.

    (C) File a complaint with the SEC.

    (D) Await the outcome of the company's request from the SEC of a "no-action letter."

Fritz, Maria, Kristen, Hans, and Volker each own 20 percent of Barvarian Pretzel Co (BP), a very successful prepared foods manufacturer (of pretzels and bratwurst) incorporated in South Dakota. Fritz, Maria, and Hans usually have coffee together in the town café each morning, where they discuss and usually agree on corporate business. Often, then, one or the other of them sees Kristen or Volker, or both, around town (at the bank, having lunch). Hans et al. tell Kristen et al. what has been agreed-upon, and they usually agree as well. They seldom have formal sit-around-the-table meetings.

The coffee klatch group though now has agreed to a plan to merge with a mid-size manufacturer of German condiments (hot mustards, pickle relish, etc.). Hans and Kristen oppose this.

95.   What should Hans and Kristen do?

(A)   They can do nothing because majority rules, even if acting informally rather than at a meeting.

(B)   Withhold their consent because to be effective informal action must be unanimous.

(C)   Sue the coffee klatch group for breach of fiduciary duty, requesting a temporary restraining order or preliminary injunction against any further steps toward merger.

(D)   File complaints with the South Dakota Secretary of State and the Attorney General.

At the annual shareholder's meeting of Foster's Supply (Supply), a publicly-held company, Tom, Dick, and Harry run for the board of directors. There are 1000 of 1500 shares outstanding present (in person or by proxy) at the meeting. Tom receives 600 votes, with a further 200 votes marked "withhold authority" (SEC proxy regulations do not permit "no" votes in the election of directors unless the corporation's articles or bylaw provide for them). Dick receives 475 votes with 300 marked "withhold authority." Harry receives 375 votes while proxies representing 400 shares are marked "withhold authority."

96.   Who is elected and who is not? Under a majority voting scheme? Under a plurality voting scheme? Under a Pfizer, or "plurality plus" voting scheme?

(A)   Under a majority scheme, Tom is elected but Harry and Dick are not.

(B)   Under a plurality voting scheme, all are elected because the number of votes (even though not a majority in Dick's and Harry's cases) cast in favor exceeds the number cast against, given the presence of a quorum at the meeting.

(C)   Under a Pfizer scheme, all are elected but Harry must tender a letter of resignation which the board may then accept or reject because the number of withheld authority votes exceeds the number of yes votes.

(D)   All of the above.

Under the Dodd-Frank enactment of 2010, and the SEC's Rule 14a-11 (effectiveness temporarily suspended), the officers and directors of Goggle, Inc. must include in their own proxy statement nominees for director positions whom certain shareholders put forth. Not any shareholder may do so. To be eligible, the shareholders must own 3 percent or more of the company's shares and have held shares for two years. Sergei and Brin, the guys who run Goggle, want to know if they can put other requirements in place, such as a requirement that at least half the directors have backgrounds in information technology, or that they drive Toyota Priuses (or similar hybrids).

97.   Can Goggle put additional roadblocks in the way of shareholder proxy access? How would they go about it?

(A)   No, the restrictions would be in conflict with the federal shareholder proxy access statute and regulation and, therefore, would be invalid under the Supremacy Clause.

(B)   "Reasonable" restrictions on the nomination of director candidates, usually implemented by a bylaw, have always been permitted by state corporate law and presumably would be undisturbed by the new federal requirements.

(C) The drafters of the MBCA have also added a statutory provision attempting to make even clearer the powers described in (B).

(D) The Dodd-Frank provisions and SEC regulations for shareholder access to the corporation's proxy machinery constitute an illegal taking under the Fifth Amendment and are therefore unconstitutional.

A current feature of the activist shareholder (labor union pension funds and public employee pension funds) landscape is propounding proposed amendments to bylaws. Although shareholders have limited powers, and still more delimited powers of initiative (removal, nomination, and election of directors), they do have shared powers over the bylaws (shared with the board of directors). One fertile area for activism: proposals in the form a bylaw amendment requiring that the corporation reimburse expenses shareholders may have incurred in making nominations to the board. So assume that a shareholder at Goggle has nominated Larry Ellison and Zach Zuckerman for the board. Both Larry and Zach lost in the election but the shareholder has presented to Sergie and Brin a request for reimbursement of $350,000 in expenses.

98. Advice for the Goggle guys?

(A) Both the MBCA and the DGCL contain amendments enabling corporations to adopt such bylaws (which we assume a previous shareholder proposed and Goggle has by bylaw implemented).

(B) A corporation's business and affairs are managed by, or under the supervision of, a board of directors. A proposal for reimbursement to shareholders would violate this central precept of corporate law and is therefore void.

(C) It's okay to reimburse the shareholder if Goggle is incorporated in an MBCA state which has adopted all the recent amendments; it is not enabled in Delaware.

(D) Ellison and Zuckerman are directors and founding shareholders of competitors of Goggle. They are not eligible for service on the Goggle board.

The directors of Old Sooner Bank, Inc. are unhappy with the performance of the CEO, Barry Nelson, who is also a director. There are five directors, but two are elderly and, by and large, inactive. The remaining two directors, Watts and Nichols, go to the bank's offices. As Watts and Nichols materialize in his office, Nelson jumps up from his desk and disappears. Watts yells after Nelson, "You're a lousy CEO and we are bouncing you out of office."

The following day Nelson is driving by the Old Sooner offices. Through the plate glass window, he sees Watts and Nichols in the lobby. Nelson parks his SUV. He strides into the lobby. He begins to tell Watts and Nichols what a dirty trick they pulled the previous day. Nichols, however, shouts Nelson down. "One, two, three," he yells, "Now you are removed as CEO." Watts yells, "I concur" and the two directors walk out of the bank.

99.   Nelson asks, "Am I really out as CEO?" What is your answer?

    (A)   Yes, by arguing, Nelson waived any objections to lack of notice, constituted a quorum (3 of 5 directors), and was validly removed by a majority vote at a special meeting (2 of 3).

    (B)   No, there must be formal notice and a formally convened meeting to remove a corporate official.

    (C)   Yes, actually he was removed on the previous day by the unanimous vote of the active directors.

    (D)   No, there must at a minimum be notice to the two absent directors.

Your client, Sammy Sosa, comes to you, saying, "Boy, do I have a great new endorsement. Maury Holland, who is a director of Nike, gave me a signed offer sheet for an endorsement deal on a new line of softball and baseball outfits."

100. Does Sammy have a deal?

ANSWER:

Fred Stewart is a director of a large corporation that owns a string of car dealerships. Fred is part of a contingent on the board that is against expansion, especially into lower priced new automobiles. He believes it best to stick to top-of-the-line dealerships such as Mercedes, Range Rover, and BMW. Fred's two allies in this regard are absent from the meeting.

There are seven directors in all, with four present at this meeting. Fred does not like the way the discussion is going. A director he thought was neutral is nodding his head, seemingly in agreement. A motion to enter into an agreement for a Mini-Cooper franchise seems to be imminent.

101. Can Fred suspend effective or valid action by absenting himself from the meeting?

ANSWER:

Sydney Delong, CEO of a newly-public dotcom, Runners.com, seeks your advice about the governance of his company. The board of directors now consists of Syd, his twin brothers (who own substantial blocks of shares), and two "outsiders," one of whom is the track coach of the local university and the other of whom is the company's lawyer.

102. How large should the board be? Who should, and who should not, be on the board?

    (A) Everything is fine. Don't worry. Be Happy.

    (B) Get rid of the brothers and the lawyer. Expand the board to seven members.

    (C) Get rid of the "cronies" and expand the board to 13 or 15.

    (D) Have a board of 24, but run most things through an executive committee of three or so members.

You and Syd are on a long run together. Midway through the run Syd asks, "As a public company, what board committees should we have? Who should be on them? Are there any legal requirements, or is this all just recommended?"

103. Somewhat breathless (Syd is a killer to run with), you reply:

    (A) Nothing is required. It is all just "good practice," aspirational "stuff."

    (B) If you ever list Runners.com's shares on the New York Stock Exchange (NYSE), you will then have to have an audit committee at that time.

    (C) You must have, at a minimum, audit, nomination, and compensation committees comprised of independent directors.

    (D) The Sarbanes-Oxley Act of 2002 ("SOXA") (the post-Enron federal legislation) now requires all public companies to have an audit committee, with mandatory responsibilities. Other committees are highly recommended, but not required.

Stoneham owns a plurality (35%) of the outstanding shares of a minor league baseball team, the Reading Retrievers. The field manager, "Tug" McGraw, owns 8 percent. A local judge, Stan Wettick, has recently purchased another 8 percent. The three of them, representing 51 percent, sign a contract. The contract provides that each will use his best efforts to keep the other in office as a director of the Retrievers' organization, which has a five-person board. The contract provides further that, as directors, the signatories will use their efforts to keep Stoneham in as president, McGraw as vice-president, and Wettick as secretary-treasurer.

Wettick repeatedly catches Stoneham with his "fingers in the till." He instructs employees that, under no circumstances, are they to permit Stoneham access to any cash. In retaliation, Stoneham rallies McGraw and one other director. The three directors vote to fire Wettick and remove him as a director.

Stan ("Stan the Man" when he played college baseball) loves the Retrievers. He is crestfallen. He wants his jobs back.

104. What can you do for Stan?

    (A) Get him back on the board but, as a corporate officer, he serves at the board's pleasure. Despite the contract, he cannot get his job as treasurer back. He may, however, be able to obtain damages.

    (B) Get an injunction. He can get back on the board and in his office as treasurer.

    (C) Nothing. He is out of both offices.

    (D) Nothing and he may be liable to Stoneham for defamation of character.

Rob, Bill, and Sally form a company (Tree Top) that sells and services various manufacturers' products in the Pacific Northwest. They "rep" products used in the orchard industry. They sign a contract providing that Rob will devote half of his time as CEO and interface with the various manufacturers, Bill will work half time as VP Administration and Secretary Treasurer, and Sally will work full time as VP Sales, traveling 30–35 weeks per year, selling equipment to orchardists throughout the Northwest. Rob and Bill are each to receive $50,000 in annual compensation plus 2 percent of sales. Sally is to receive $70,000, plus 4 percent of sales up to $300,000, 6 percent of sales over $300,000, and 8 percent of sales over $750,000.

The company succeeds, mostly because Sally excels at her job, but Bill has a falling out with Sally. At a board meeting, Rob and Bill vote to dismiss her as VP Sales. Sally is in a panic. As with many small companies, her primary livelihood will come not from her investment as a shareholder, but from her employment as a corporate officer/employee.

105. Can Sally get her job back?

    (A) No, the case upon which the previous Question is based (*McQuade v. Stoneham*) disposes of the issue.

    (B) Maybe. The contract is not valid and she is an employee at will. But, her dismissal constitutes breach of the implied covenant of good faith and fair dealing which courts regard as an implied term of the employment at will relationship.

    (C) Yes. The law has changed. Courts enforce such agreements where all owners (shareholders) are signatories.

    (D) Yes. Same as Answer (C), but in addition courts have come to recognize the importance of the employment relationship for shareholders in small companies.

Same hypothetical except that there exist two other shareholders who hold 7½ percent each. Rob, Bill, and Sally, the only ones to sign the agreement, own 85 percent. There is no fraud or sharp dealing involved. It is simply that one minority shareholder of Tree Top has retired to Florida and the other is just impossible to reach, either in person or on the telephone.

106. Can Sally get her job back?

ANSWER:

Now Bill and Rob have a change of heart. They realize how great and valuable Sally is to Tree Top, Inc. As directors, they convene a meeting and award her a lifetime contract as VP Sales.

107. Is that money in the bank, or is the contract subject to doubt?, Sally asks.

    (A) Lifetime contracts for anything are never valid.

    (B) It may be an impermissible abdication by the board of its power and future boards' power.

    (C) Same as Answer (B), but it may be able to be fixed.

    (D) Rob and Bill are wishy-washy and treacherous. Sally should start her own company.

Tree Top becomes successful beyond Rob, Bill, and Sally's wildest dreams. Through private placements of securities, Tree Top now has 570 shareholders. The corporation sells products worldwide — in New Zealand, Australia, the People's Republic of China, throughout Europe, and in the Eastern United States. PriceWaterhouseCoopers ("PWC"), one of the "Big Four" (didn't there used to be eight?) accounting firms, audits the corporation's annual financial statements.

Rob and Bill, though, have tired of the business. Rob wishes to resume his career in Irish literature, in which he has developed an international reputation. Bill wishes to play more golf and spend time with his children. PWC comes to their rescue. PWC offers to provide human resources, bookkeeping, accounting, information systems, legal, marketing, employee benefits, actuarial, valuation, and general management services to the corporation under a 10-year contract, with renewals by mutual agreement for five-year terms thereafter.

108. Is this a good idea?

    (A) Yes, no worries, mate. Be happy!

    (B) No, PWC is not the right firm. Find another accounting firm.

    (C) No, it very well could be invalid as an overly broad delegation and, hence, an impermissible abdication by the board of directors of their duty to manage, or to oversee management of, the corporation's business and affairs.

    (D) No, it could be invalid as in Answer (C), and also illegal under the Sarbanes-Oxley Act ("SOXA"), at least insofar as PWC tries to provide both audit and "consulting" or management services.

A large, publicly-held movie production company, Two Fisted, Inc., has three directors (John Wayne, Dean Martin, and Dorothy Lamour) who dominate its board. The "magnificent three" convince the rest of the board to create an executive committee, staff it with the magnificent three, and delegate to it all powers of the full board of directors, except declaring dividends and recommending mergers to shareholders. A dissident director, Don Knotts (a.k.a. Deputy Barney Fife), consults you about challenging this arrangement.

109. What advice do you give?

    (A) You can't challenge it because the decision to delegate is protected by the business judgment rule.

    (B) It is not wise to challenge it because it is an efficient arrangement.

(C) It is an overly broad delegation that constitutes an abdication by the full board of its responsibilities.

(D) You should challenge it as an overly broad delegation, which violates the statutory provision on the permissible scope of delegations to board committees.

There has been a wave of consolidation in the movie industry, which has involved several hostile takeover bids. Two Fisted, Inc. has been reviewing its shark repellent provisions (a.k.a. "porcupine provisions"). These are structural defenses put in place by likely takeover targets, such as staggering (classifying) the board of directors and resurrecting a requirement that directors may be removed only "for cause."

Dean Martin wishes to discuss "poison pill" defenses, also known more euphemistically as "shareholder rights plans." These are rights, usually to purchase additional securities on favorable terms, given to existing shareholders, or owners of shares for more than five years, and so on. There are hundreds of variants, but one broad division is rights to purchase shares in the existing target company ("flip in" poison pills) versus right to purchase shares in any entity into which the target may later be merged ("flip over" poison pills).

Pills become "activated" by a hostile bidder reaching a "trigger" or "triggering" level of ownership, often 15 or 20 percent of the voting shares. If a pill is activated, and enough target shareholders exercise their rights, the bidder is diluted back down to a lower percentage of ownership (say, 3% or 5%).

Dean wants to insure that a bidder doesn't acquire Two Fisted shares right up to the triggering level (say, 19.9%), thereafter waging a proxy fight to gain control of the Two Fisted board. The new board then could "de-activate" or "defuse" the poison pill.

110. How could Two Fisted respond to such a series of tactical moves by a bidder?

   (A) Make the pill a "dead hand" poison pill which may only be de-activated by directors who were in office at the time the pill was adopted.

   (B) Make it a "no hand" poison pill which simply cannot be de-activated by anyone (old or new directors) until six months have passed.

   (C) Combine the poison pill with a staggered board and a removal for cause requirement.

   (D) They can't do anything. There is no way to "bullet proof" a poison pill.

Dorothy Lamour and Dean Martin are angry with dissident director Don Knotts. They wish to remove him from the Two Fisted board. The difficulty is that Knotts is "squeaky clean." He attends every board meeting. He has served long and well on the Two Fisted audit committee. He is clean as a whistle.

111. Can they remove Knotts?

   (A) No, removal of a director requires proof of cause and a vote of a majority of the shares in favor of removal.

   (B) Under modern statutes, removal is by shareholder vote "with or without cause." They can remove him if they can get the votes.

   (C) Same as Answer (B), but they must give Knotts notice of the charges being made about his performance and an opportunity to defend himself.

(D) Dean, Dorothy, and the other directors may vote to remove him.

Now assume that Two Fisted is a California corporation with cumulative voting for directors.

112. Are there any further wrinkles to Knotts's removal?

ANSWER:

Now assume the opposite. Don Knotts is not "squeaky clean." He has sexually harassed female workers at Two Fisted, Inc. He has his "buddies" from his acting days, including Otis, who often is inebriated, hanging around corporate offices and using corporate facilities. Don has "gone bad" and there is no doubt about it.

But every time Two Fisted's board and shareholders seek to remove him, Don and his friends (Otis, Andy, Opie — but not Aunt Bea — she fell out with Don several years ago) all vote against his removal. Through cumulative voting, they then keep re-electing him.

113. What can the other Two Fisted directors and shareholders do? Do they have to put up with this behavior for the foreseeable future?

(A) No, they may go to state court and seek his removal on ground that "the director engaged in fraudulent conduct with respect to the corporation or its shareholders, grossly abused the position of director, or intentionally inflicted harm on the corporation."

(B) No, under the Sarbanes-Oxley Act of 2002 ("SOXA") they may obtain a "lifetime ban" forbidding his service as a director or officer of a publicly-held company.

(C) Yes, they have to put up with Don, but perhaps they can get a protective order against Otis hanging around the corporate offices.

(D) No, they should cause the corporation to sue Don for breach of fiduciary duty and Otis, Andy, Opie, et al. for "aiding and abetting" breaches of fiduciary duty.

Doug Day Trader had an account with a small brokerage firm, Edward D. Moans, Inc, that had three principals, each of whom acted as broker, shareholder, and director. Doug lost $100,000 before he swore off day trading. Moans is now defunct. Doug telephones Director One at her office, asking if Moans, which is in the process of winding up, will compromise Doug's debt for $30,000. Director One agrees.

Later, Doug sees Director Two at their health club, working out in the weight room. Doug tells Director Two about the conversation with Director One. Director Two shrugs his shoulders and walks away. Doug paid the $30,000 and considered the score settled.

There is no evidence of the whereabouts of Director Three or even if the position remains open. Rumors are that Director Three took his Lonely Planet Guide and headed to Myanmar long before Moans ceased business.

Creditors then threw Moans into an involuntary bankruptcy. The trustee in bankruptcy has sued Doug for $70,000.

114. You are law clerk to Bankruptcy Judge Phil Brandt. What result?

(A) Doug is forgiven. Director One's acts as agent bind the corporation.

(B) Doug owes $70,000. Only valid, formal action by the full board of directors may compromise a debt.

(C) Doug is forgiven. Informal action by some directors with acquiescence or ratification by the others will suffice.

(D) Doug is forgiven. The corporation (and the trustee) is estopped from pursuing him.

Same facts as in Question 114, except that Doug Day Trader has been to see Director One. She has agreed to compromise the debt. Doug then comes to see you. Instead of being a law clerk to a bankruptcy judge, you are now in private practice.

115. As Doug's personal lawyer, what do you tell him to do?

ANSWER:

Runners.com, *supra*, has entered into a merger agreement with Triathlon, Inc. The Runners board has approved the merger. The agreement requires that the Runners board of directors use "best efforts" to obtain shareholder approval of the merger. Runners' board, though, has found that Triathlon's raw materials and inventory are obsolete and probably unsalable, greatly reducing its value as a merger partner. The directors, who no longer favor the merger, fell between a rock and hard place.

116. What can they do?

ANSWER:

Clowns by Bozo, Inc. is a small corporation of fun-loving shareholders, directors, and employees. They wish to have the highest ranking officer denominated "Chief Bozo." The second ranking would be "Clarabelle." The treasurer would be "The Rich Bozo," and so on.

117. Can they change the officers' titles as they wish to?

   (A) No. There must be a minimum of a president and a secretary and the same person may not hold both offices.

   (B) No. There must be a president, one or more vice presidents, a secretary, and a treasurer.

   (C) No. Under modern statutes, there must be a Chief Executive Officer ("CEO"), a Chief Operating Officer ("COO"), a Chief Financial Officer ("CFO"), and so on.

   (D) Yes. They can have "such offices as are designated by the bylaws or by the board of directors," with whatever titles they wish, or no officers at all, so long as the board designates someone "to prepare minutes of directors' and shareholders' meetings and [to] maintain and authenticate records of the corporation."

Your client is a contractor. She has just signed a contract with a major Fortune 1000 company to build a new 700,000-square-foot manufacturing facility in Sweet Home, Oregon. It is a fixed-price $19.4 million contract. Her attorney asks her what kind of documentation she got from the other side. Haughtily, she replies: "I don't need any documentation. I have the CEO's signature on the contract." The attorney replies, "Well, I'm not so sure. You better let me do some checking."

118. Who is right?

ANSWER:

One fine October day, as you gaze out the window of your Chicago office, you receive a telephone call from a client, Glenn Grant, Inc. Glenn Grant is a mid-size Chevrolet dealer. On the other end of the line is the Fleet Sales Manager at Glenn Grant. Excitedly he reports, "I just received an order from Air Wisconsin (a large Midwest commuter airline) to purchase 100 trucks. This is great because business has been so slow the last several months. I am dealing with their purchasing agent. What kind of paperwork do I need from a legal standpoint, counselor?"

119. Your reply?

   (A) None. The purchasing agent has inherent authority to enter into transactions of this kind.

    (B) Just obtain a personal guarantee from the purchasing agent and one or more other corporate officers.

    (C) Obtain a "third-party legal opinion" from Air Wisconsin's outside law firm that the purchasing agent has authority.

    (D) Request that the corporate secretary provide you with a certified board resolution either authorizing the purchasing agent to enter into the transaction or delegating to the purchasing agent authority to enter into transaction below a certain dollar amount.

Same facts as in Question 119, except the order is for 25 medium-size pickup trucks and it is a credit rather than cash transaction.

120. What are the other questions the attorney might ask?

    (A) What color are the trucks being painted, what are the logos, and so on?

    (B) Have you ever dealt with this guy (the purchasing agent) before?

    (C) Can you find out when the next Air Wisconsin board of directors meeting takes place?

    (D) Does Air Wisconsin have divisions or subsidiaries engaged in business other than air transport?

Same facts again as in Question 119. This time, however, the order is five trucks. Also, Glenn Grant's Fleet Sales Manager tells you, "This is the first order we have ever had from Air Wisconsin, but we certainly would like to get their business."

121. Do you advise him to do the deal?

ANSWER:

One more question before we leave Air Wisconsin behind. Now, your client is Chicago-based Citizens' Bank. The bank is pondering a construction loan for a facility in Phoenix, Arizona. Based in Denver, the borrowing company, Rub-A-Dub, manufactures hot tubs and home spas. It wishes to expand to the Southwest. The loan amount is $1.8 million. The company has sales of $12 million in Denver, but it also has $6 million in other debt.

The Citizens' Bank loan officer tells you that the transaction would be "kind of iffy" for the bank but, coincidentally, Rub-A-Dub has proposed a form of guarantee of its indebtedness to Citizens' by Air Wisconsin. The commitment for the guarantee is on personalized Air Wisconsin stationery, signed by Air Wisconsin's treasurer. The loan officer has verified that, indeed, the person signing is Air Wisconsin's treasurer.

122. What should the bank do?

    (A) Make the loan because express actual authority exists.

    (B) Treasurers have inherent authority to do this sort of thing.

(C) The last item on the checklist, apparent authority, furnishes the basis for the bank making the loan.

(D) Do not make the loan because it has neither rhyme nor reason. It simply lacks common sense.

Alan Associate is second chairing a trial. Alan's law firm represents plaintiff shareholders suing over the failure of Old Line Insurance, a regional medical malpractice carrier. The defendants are the directors of Old Line. At their meetings, the directors never discussed or otherwise inquired into the adequacy of Old Line's reserves. When malpractice claims increased, and the payout per claim also increased, Old Line had insufficient reserves to carry it through the tough times. When Old Line began to fail, the state insurance commissioner put the company into receivership. The shareholders lost the entire value of their investment.

The defense is about to put on the stand directors from three or four other insurance carriers. The tenor of their testimony is that, in companies of this size, insurance company directors do not concern themselves with the adequacy of reserves, relying entirely upon management and the company's actuary.

123. Alan rises to object to the testimony. His best objection is:

    (A) Irrelevant. What other insurance carriers do is of no moment because they are not defendants in this case.

    (B) Irrelevant. The custom in the trade or profession is irrelevant, or of limited relevance, because the whole trade or profession may have been laggard in the adoption of acts and practices that could have prevented the harm.

    (C) Hearsay. The testimony is offered to prove what a collegial group does in board meetings and other board members are not present and therefore cannot be cross-examined.

    (D) None. The testimony is relevant.

The directors of Old Line include an actuary who practices her profession through her own actuarial firm and a corporate lawyer from a large multi-service metropolitan law firm. The board also includes the son and daughter of the controlling shareholder, who is the CEO. The daughter is a senior in college, majoring in Irish poetry. The son is a third-year law student. Neither the son nor the daughter attended board or committee meetings regularly. Neither did anything to familiarize themselves with the insurance industry or with Old Line or current issues it faced.

124. If you had to assess the prospects of liability, which of the following would be your best estimate:

    (A) The actuary and the attorney may well be liable, but the son and daughter are not.

    (B) The son and daughter are liable, but the lawyer and actuary are not.

    (C) All four have valid defenses.

    (D) All four would appear to be liable.

Two other Old Line directors defend on other grounds. John Bares Fortippton was the former CEO of Big Time Insurance. He now lives most of the year at his farmhouse in Vermont. What meetings he participates in, he participates by conference telephone call. In his deposition, he testified that he allowed his name to be added to the Old Line board to enhance Old Line's prestige.

John Pont, a retired university administrator and coach in Bloomington, Indiana, attends meetings, but only when they concern the company's business in Indiana. He testifies that he was added to the board to help it drum up and service business in the Hoosier State.

125. Does either have a shot at a valid defense?

    (A) No. Each and every director must bring their abilities to bear on the full range of issues the board confronts, or should confront.

    (B) Yes. In its judgment the board may add members to the board of directors based upon their prestige value.

    (C) Yes. Companies that do business over a broad geographical area need to allocate directors' seats geographically.

    (D) No. Directors who fail to attend all, or most all, of the board's meetings will be liable for violation of their duty of care.

Cambridge Bank is an old-fashioned bank. It has one office, three tellers, a cashier, a president, and a seven-person board of directors, which meets quarterly, but after the bank has closed for the day. Cambridge Bank also has no computers. All recordkeeping is done by hand. The cashier takes slips from the tellers, makes entries in the journal and ledgers by hand, and counts the cash at the end of each day.

The cashier is a young fellow. The last two years he has arrived at work in a new Saab convertible. He has taken to wearing Armani and Versace suits. No one has taken particular notice of these events.

While in the last three years the bank has seemed very busy, deposits have continued to drop. Finally, the outside auditors call in all of the depositors' passbooks. The passbooks show deposits exceeding those recorded in the ledger by over $250,000 annually. Deposits actually have increased, but the cash is gone.

The cashier breaks down and confesses. Alas, he has spent all the money on wild Club Med "sophisticated singles" vacations and first class air tickets. The bank is defunct.

Disgruntled shareholders sue the cashier, the president, and the directors.

126. Who would you rather defend?

    (A) The cashier. Sounds like a fun guy.

    (B) The directors. Nothing put them on notice that wrongdoing may have taken place.

    (C) The president. He had severe insomnia the last several years so he has not been too watchful during the day.

    (D) The state banking commission, which should have caught on to the scheme and nipped it in the bud.

Aged director Bill Veeck has been on the board of Ruckers, Inc. for 15 years. The Ruckers board meets monthly. Mr. Veeck has been troubled by a persistent lung infection. In September, he decides that he would rather not face the cold Ohio winter. He leases a home on Siesta Key, below Sarasota, Florida. After the October board meeting, Mr. Veeck journeys down to Sarasota. He misses the November meeting. He participates by conference telephone call in December. In addition, each month the Ruckers corporate secretary federal expresses a "board packet" (trial financial statements, minutes of previous meeting, reports, etc.) to Mr. Veeck, which he takes great care to review. He also misses the January meeting.

Still not well, Mr. Veeck decides to stay in Florida until April or May. He seeks your advice about what he should do with regard to his Ruckers board commitment.

127. What is your advice?

(A) He should charter planes and attend meetings in Ohio. Directors have an affirmative duty to attend board meetings.

(B) He should resign. He has missed too many meetings already.

(C) He absolutely cannot miss any more meetings.

(D) A director's duty is to keep informed, and a good way to do that is to attend meetings. But, directors are entitled to be ill, and to take time to recover from their illness. He should try as best he can to participate by telephone conference call and continue to review carefully his board packets. Reassess the situation in May.

Same facts as in Question 126, except assume that the directors do meet during the workday; moreover, they meet at the bank. They can easily observe the youthful cashier rising toward opulence in terms of his wardrobe, automobile, and general lifestyle.

128. Did their observations trigger a duty to conduct an investigation or cause one to be conducted?
ANSWER:

CB Foods, Inc. is a large, publicly-held company in the fruit, frozen vegetable, and canned meat business. CB's annual sales exceed $1 billion. The company has 6,000 employees, many of whom operate 42 plants located in various parts of the United States. In its business, the company generates large amounts of waste products (vegetable and animal matter), solvents (de-greasing agents used on its machinery), and waste water (especially in processing fruits and vegetables).

You are the newest lawyer in the CB law department, which has four lawyers. The Chief Legal Officer ("CLO") calls you into her office. She says, "Our outside law firm thinks we need a legal and environmental audit of all our operations. You are newly out of law school. Is this necessary (it will cost a lot of money) or is it just a ruse to get more legal fees out of us?"

129. Your reply?

(A) Absent notice (red flags), management and the board of directors have no duty to make inquiry. Let sleeping dogs lie.

(B)   In *Graham v. Allis-Chalmers Manufacturing Co.*, 188 A.2d 125 (Del. 1963), the Delaware Supreme Court specifically held that, absent "knowledge or suspicion of wrongdoing," directors have no duty to "put into effect a system of watchfulness" which might bring possible violations of law to their attention.

(C)   Our company has "huge" potential exposure under the environmental laws (Clean Water Act, etc.). It just makes economic sense to put in place some monitoring and compliance system.

(D)   In a corporation of any size or complexity, the directors' duty of care requires them to put in place adequate monitoring and compliance programs.

The Airplane Factory, Inc. manufactures windshield, double- and triple-pane skylights, and other products of Plexiglas. It got its start, and its name, manufacturing canopies for aircraft. Today it has 100 shareholders and sales of $50 million.

Two years ago the company founder, Walter Hoy, insisted that the Airplane Factory acquire a shower door fabricating facility in Florida. Very little, if any, due diligence was done about the Florida facility. At the meetings that discussed the acquisition, Walter shouted down any opposition. Two of the other directors are his sons, Doug and Phil, who vote with their Dad.

The outside directors, Dan and Valerie, were put on the board by the public shareholders. They opposed the acquisition, suspecting that Walter pushed it so hard because the shower door facility was near his favorite golf course in Florida, but they did not voice their opposition. They simply remained silent when the matter came up for a vote.

The acquisition proved to be a disaster. There were undisclosed environmental problems that forced the closure of the facility nine months after the acquisition. Losses exceed 15 million. The environmental exposure has yet to be assessed. Shareholders have sued Dan and Val.

130.   Defend them (if you can).

(A)   They did not agree to the acquisition so they have no responsibility.

(B)   They were helpless and could do nothing.

(C)   By remaining silent, they are presumed to have assented to the action taken (the acquisition) but, even had they voted "no," Walter would have taken the action. Hence there is no causation.

(D)   They have no defense. A fair inference is that a protest of some sort would have caused Walter and his sons to stop, or at least re-think, the acquisition.

Ted MacDonald was managing director of Country Joe's Hardware, which had two outlets in Missoula, Montana. Ted is a somewhat erratic, sometimes diligent manager. Most days he pursues his hobby, competing in fly fishing tournaments throughout the West. He manages at night. His management style consists of writing hundreds of little notes to himself, which he stores in a bulging shirt pocket. He always overstocked the fishing department, but the stores never had enough lumber to satisfy demand.

Country Joe's has now gone "belly up." Ted and his board of directors have been sued by shareholders. Discovery in the lawsuit reveals that the corporation's decline in profitability tracks chronologically with the arrival of Home Base, Home Depot, and Wal-Mart in Missoula.

131. You are the high-priced litigator flown in from Billings to get Ted and his directors out of this mess. Can you?

ANSWER:

Rosten Stamps, Inc. is a large, wholesale dealer of stamps for collectors. Rosty, the CEO and a director, causes the corporation to sell quite a number of commemorative stamps to the U.S. Postal Service for face value. He did so all in one morning, based upon his astrological chart for the day. A year later stamps surge in value, tripling over a few weeks' time. Shareholders have now sued.

132. Defend Rosten.

    (A) He in fact exercised that amount of care that a reasonable director would exercise in a like position in similar circumstances. Stamp dealers are quirky.

    (B) His decision is protected from judicial review by the business judgment rule.

    (C) All the shareholders can prove is a possible profit forgone and not any loss or damage to the corporation, so no duty of care violation.

    (D) His conduct is indefensible.

Sam and Dave's, Inc. manufactured beach wear and bright Caribbean-style clothing. Sam and Dave then caused the corporation to diversify into winter sports clothing. Because of their South Florida location, however, Sam and Dave are unable to judge fashion trends in ski wear. In addition, their product reaches Northern and Western markets well after the season has commenced. In the expansion, Sam and Dave's, Inc. loses its Aloha shirt.

After two years' large losses, Sam and Dave close the ski wear business. At the annual shareholders' meeting, Sam and Dave have a pre-meeting reception at which hors d'oeuvres and wine are served. At the meeting, Sam and Dave describe to the shareholders why "they, too, are victims." The shareholders then vote 68-32, ratifying the actions of the past two years, including the ill-fated expansion. A disgruntled shareholder consults you.

133. Can you challenge the action taken at the meeting (with a good chance of success)?

    (A) Yes. Blanket ratifications ("all acts in the past year") are worthless.

    (B) Yes. This is not a blanket ratification, but it does constitute a "waste" of corporate assets beyond shareholders' power to ratify.

    (C) No. Majority rules. Shareholders may ratify anything except illegality or self-dealing.

    (D) Yes. The shareholders could ratify, but ratification must be based on full disclosure, which does not appear to have taken place.

Jerome Von Gherkin is the CEO of a large, publicly-held company. He is approaching retirement and holds 4,000,000 shares of the company. The company, Trans Wheel, has a share price that has languished in the high $30s for several years, even though the book value of the company is $45 per share. A few months ago, Von Gherkin had the CFO, Noble Roman, "run the numbers" on a purchase of the company using its cash flow to service (pay interest on) the debt that would be incurred if Von Gherkin and the other senior managers bought up all the shares currently held by the public (a "leveraged buyout ("LBO")" or "management buyout ("MBO")"). Roman reported back that a buyout would be feasible at prices up to and slightly beyond $60 per share.

There were no third-party buyers at $61–62 per share, so Von Gherkin went to see a well-known financier, Jay Ghoul. Ghoul offered to buy the company at $55 per share, but also insisted upon an option to purchase 1,000,000 Trans Wheel shares from Trans Wheel at $38 per share and a "no shop" clause. Under the latter arrangement, the Trans Wheel senior management would not be able to test the market to see if a better price could be obtained.

All of the foregoing occurred on a Friday and the following Monday. On Tuesday, Von Gherkin then called a special meeting of the Trans Wheel board of directors for Friday morning. You are personal counsel to two outside directors of Trans Wheel.

Using cell phones, they telephone you during a break in the meeting. Von Gherkin has asked for approval by the board of the buyout by Jay Ghoul after only an hours' meeting. He has not even presented them with the documents for the proposed transaction. He has started pounding the conference room table.

134. What should you tell them to do?

   (A) Go ahead and vote for the deal. $55 is a good price and the business judgment rule will protect you.

   (B) $55 may be a good price, but you do not know that for certain. Insist upon seeing:

   (1) the deal documents,

   (2) Roman's report,

   (3) an independent valuation expert's report ("fairness opinion" — usually done by an investment banker in larger transactions), and

   (4) an adjournment until next week at a minimum.

   (C) Von Gherkin and perhaps other insiders are pushing too hard. Do (1)–(4) above also exclude Von Gherkin and any other insiders from the decision-making process.

   (D) Do (1)–(4) from Answer (B), meet in executive session as in Answer (C), hire an independent investment banker and independent law firm to represent the ad hoc committee of directors, meet over several sessions before calling the question, and leave an "out" for the directors should a clearly superior bid surface.

You work for an older lawyer who does very little corporate work. He asks you to draft articles of incorporation for a new corporation. The venture, a software firm, is to have five close friends, all software engineers, and six passive investors as the initial shareholder group. They already have three pieces of "hot" software ready for the market. The business plan is to go public in 18 to 30 months.

135. What optional charter or articles provision should you think about including?

   (A) Preemptive rights.

   (B) Par value for shares.

(C) Opt-out provisions, capping or eliminating money damage liability for duty of care violations.

(D) None.

Sir Arthur Anderson is a director of Energy Corp. He is aware that Andrew Fields, the CFO of Energy, has procured a waiver of the Energy Corp. code of ethics, allowing Fields to serve as the general partner of limited partnerships which will do large amounts of business with Energy Corp. The Audit Committee, which granted the waiver, has provided that the Finance Committee will exercise oversight over this conflict of interest and waiver. But the Audit Committee failed to notify the Finance Committee. With no supervision whatsoever, Fields is making extra money hand over fist ($43 million in the last two years). Sir Arthur knows all of these facts (told to him by friends on the two committees and others at Energy Corp).

136. What should Sir Arthur do?

(A) Let a sleeping dog lie. A director may have state law duties of disclosure to shareholders (the duty of candor) but not to the board of directors or fellow members of it.

(B) Meet with Fields and urge him to "come clean" with the committees.

(C) Disclose to the Finance Committee that they have responsibilities here, ones of which they may not be aware.

(D) Telephone business reporters at the Houston Chronicle, alerting them to a "hot story" in Houston community.

The board of Borgen Stanley had noted that the corporation had on hand excess cash of $500 million. Desiring to lie low for a year, after a quick canvas of the markets, the board directed the CFO to invest the cash in tax-free municipal bonds earning 5 percent interest. Uncertainty in the markets, occasioned by the impending invasion of a Middle Eastern country by an allied force, soon thereafter pushed interest rates to 16 percent in the short term bond market. With all of that excess cash, Borgen Stanley could have earned considerably more in the high-yield bond market.

A shareholder has sued the board, seeking to hold liable its members for the hurried decision they made. The judge asks you, his law clerk, what decision he should make and why on the board members' motion for summary judgment.

137. You recommend that the judge:

    (A)   Grant the motion. The law charges boards of directors, not judges, with management of the corporation's business.

    (B)   Grant the motion. Courts will not second guess business decisions made in good faith by duly elected corporate officials.

    (C)   Grant the motion. The board of directors complied with the "business judgment rule."

    (D)   Deny the motion. The board of directors failed to comply with the business judgment rule.

The Birmingham Barons are a class AAA (one level below the major leagues) minor league baseball team. They play their home games at beautiful Black Warrior Stadium, which sits on the banks of the Black Warrior River. The Barons' majority shareholder, Wimp Sanders, a successful local car dealer, fervently believes that "God intended baseball games to be played outdoors in the afternoon." Black Warrior Stadium thus has no lights; it cannot accommodate nighttime baseball.

Recently, a celebrated athlete (some say the most celebrated of all time) has decided to try his hand at baseball, with the Barons no less. His presence on the team would triple attendance, that is, if the Barons played night baseball.

Instead, the Barons continue to lose money each year. Year after year the Barons' board summarily votes to continue to have the team play day baseball only.   .

Shlensky, a rabid baseball fan, is a minority shareholder in the Barons, who has given up on the major league team he formerly supported and moved to Birmingham. He has sued Sanders and the other board members for breach of the duty of care.

Shlensky says that if the directors only conducted the most perfunctory market study they would see that the team could make considerably more money playing nighttime baseball, especially given the presence of the aforesaid celebrated athlete.

138. Does Shlensky's suit have a chance of a "cup of coffee" in the "bigs" of litigation?

    (A)   Yes, it does. The directors have not made an "independent" decision or judgment. They have merely rubber stamped the controlling shareholder's decision.

    (B)   No, it does not. Absent fraud or *ultra vires* acts, directors' decisions are protected from judicial scrutiny by the business judgment rule.

    (C)   No, it does not. The directors have no personal financial stake in the outcome and therefore they and their decision are protected by the business judgment rule.

    (D)   Yes, it does. The directors failed to comply with the business judgment rule.

Assume that, in Question 138, the seven directors of the Birmingham Barons are: the outside lawyer whose firm does $300,000 in legal work for the Barons each year; Wimp Sanders's long-time Saturday morning golf partner; the owner of the radio station that broadcasts the Baron's games; a senior vice-president of the Barons in charge of marketing; an accounting professor who, in addition to his director's fees, receives a $25,000 consulting contract each year and who chairs the audit committee; Wimp Sanders's nephew, Sandy Sanders; and, of course, Wimp, himself.

Assume further that the directors did discuss and deliberate the question of night baseball over three successive meetings, culminating in a formal 6-0 vote, Wimp abstaining.

139. Can you nonetheless challenge the defense of the business judgment rule?

ANSWER:

Change the hypothetical once again. The directors are not as described in Question 139. Instead, they are all pillars of the Birmingham business community. None has financial ties to the Barons or its controlling shareholder. They are CEOs and business leaders. Only one or two have social ties to Wimp Sanders.

When confronted by the shareholder demand to consider playing night baseball, the directors hire a consultant, Reggie Doby. Reggie quickly renders onto the board a written report. The report purports to find a trend back to daytime baseball, at least by minor league teams operating in cities with more than 400,000 inhabitants. Reggie also openly discloses that he is the president of a not-for-profit organization named "Daytime Baseball Boosters, Inc."

Following receipt and review of the report, the Barons' directors now vote 6-0, Wimp abstaining, to continue playing daytime baseball only.

140. Would you as a plaintiff's attorney still take the case of the complaining Barons' shareholder?

    (A)   Yes, the directors have a duty of care. Receipt of one report by a biased consultant, quickly produced, does not measure up to the directors' duty.

    (B)   No, how much information is enough information is itself a matter of business judgment. Along with its other elements, the business judgment rule requires some care and not necessarily due care.

(C) Yes, directors making such a decision have a duty not just of due care, but of the utmost care.

(D) No, decisions of independent directors, as here, are unassailable.

Now assume that the relatively disinterested Barons' board receives the consultant's report and decides to do it one better. The board votes 6-0, Wimp abstaining, to have their baseball club play only early morning baseball. Among other things, in order to avoid the afternoon heat, the Barons will commence games at 7:00 AM. Doubleheaders (successive games played back-to-back) will commence at 5:45 AM. The twilight doubleheader of old will be replaced by the "dawn doubleheader." Reporting on these developments, sports writer Lash Larue writes of the Barons board of directors, "Where are they coming from?"

141. Can a shareholder's attorney argue for non-application of the business judgment rule?

ANSWER:

Leaving baseball for politics, the local state telephone company in the state of Mercury (Mercury Bell) equips the State Democratic Committee ("SDC") with banks of telephones for phone-a-thons and provides a myriad of other telecommunications services. After the elections, SDC has a huge $4 million telephone bill which it cannot pay.

SDC seeks forgiveness of the debt. Mercury Bell's board of directors deliberates. Forgiveness of the debt might well serve the company's best interests as both the new governor of Mercury and the house and senate leaders are newly elected Democrats. The company has several important measures on its legislative agenda.

None of the directors serves on the SDC or otherwise has an interest in the subject matter of the decision. The board receives reports from the CFO and the company's attorneys. The CFO opines that forgiveness of the debt will not put the company in any financial strait. Only the attorney has a caveat. She reports that the forgiveness of the debt may be construed as an indirect gift to partisan campaigns for political office and, hence, illegal. She indicates that she will do further research on the question. The board, however, is impatient. They decide to vote. They forgive the debt.

142. An irate Mercury Bell shareholder consults you. Is the Mercury Bell board's decision shielded from judicial scrutiny by the business judgment rule?

(A) Yes. The directors made a decision or judgment, they reasonably informed themselves, and they rationally believed the decision made was in the best interests of the corporation.

(B) Yes. The directors exercised not only some care, as the rule requires, but due care.

(C) Yes. A fundamental principle of life is that she who gets along goes along. That principle applies to corporations as well as human beings.

(D) No. Although arguably the technical elements giving rise to business judgment rule application are present, the judgment does not pass the smell test. The directors have not made the decision in good faith.

Senior management at PCS 2000, a publicly-held telecommunications company, is concerned over a sudden spike in the trading volume of PCS 2000 stock. They have reason to believe that the active takeover players, the Pike brothers, are the ones acquiring the stock. The PCS 2000 board of directors has convened in special meeting to consider adoption of shark repellent measures that would enable them to ward off any hostile takeover bid. They have asked you, as counsel, to address the board and then guide them through the process of adopting takeover defenses.

143. Which of the following should you advise them *not* to do?

(A) Insure that any defense measure "is reasonable in relation to the threat posed."

(B) Convene the independent directors in executive session (*i.e.*, without the senior managers present) for the final discussion and actual adoption of the defenses.

(C) Stagger the board of directors into three classes and resurrect a requirement of removal for cause only.

(D) Adopt a scorched earth policy of sorts, giving a crown jewel option to purchase their prized subsidiary at a favorable price to a friendly competitor in a neighboring state.

Now assume that the Pike brothers file a Schedule 13D with the SEC. Anyone, acting either alone or as a group, acquiring 5 percent or more of a public company must within 10 days file a form with the SEC revealing their identity and other information. The Pike brothers announce 15 percent ownership and an intention to make a cash offer for a majority of the PCS 2000 shares at 30 percent over the market price of $20, or $26 per share. PCS 2000 convinces a friendly competitor, Firstwave Communications, to make a rival bid at $28 per share.

The Pike brothers rise to the occasion, bumping their offer to $30. Firstwave matches that bid. The Pikes then raise their offer to $33.

The PCS 2000 board meets, with the senior managers excluded from the meeting. Afterward, the board recommends that shareholders accept the $30 Firstwave bid. The directors themselves will tender to Firstwave. They also have caused PCS to issue an option to Firstwave to acquire authorized, but unissued, PCS 2000 shares equivalent to 25 percent of the PCS 2000 outstanding shares (a so-called "leg up" or "lock option" designed to encourage a favored bidder).

One of the reasons the PCS 2000 board states for favoring the Firstwave offer is that Firstwave has promised to keep all, or most all, the incumbent PCS managers in place.

Peter Lynch's mutual fund owns two million shares of PCS 2000. He is hopping mad. Success of the inferior bid will cause him to leave $6 million "on the table."

144. Does the business judgment rule forestall any meaningful challenge to the action by the PCS 2000 board?

(A) Yes, the directors carefully examined the competing offers and made a decision or judgment.

(B) Yes, the directors took action that was "reasonable in relation to the threat posed" by the Pike brothers' ownership.

(C) No, because once it becomes certain that the target company will be sold or broken up, directors cease to be "defenders of the corporate bastion" and must conduct an auction for the benefit of the owners.

(D) No, because the directors had a conflict of interest and were more interested in taking care of the incumbent management at PCS 2000 than in serving shareholders' best interests.

The Special Litigation Committee ("SLC") of the board of Orson's Beans, Inc., a specialty coffee importer and retailer, has found that, as a complaining shareholder had alleged, two insider directors (the CEO and CFO) have abused their positions by padding expense accounts, maintaining a vacation home at corporate expense, and purchasing a nine-meter sailboat with corporate funds. The SLC has found that in the derivative action the company could recover approximately $75,000 from one director and $65,000 from the other. The two directors have resisted paying anything.

As to the lawsuit, based upon the drain on executive time and the negative effects on Orson's Beans employee morale, the SLC proposes to recommend that the court dismiss the derivative suit as "not in the corporation's best interests." You are special counsel to the SLC. You were away on a short vacation and they met without you.

145. Should their report go forward in its present form? Can they do this?

(A) No. Courts have taken a dim view of the use of "makeweight" factors such as the drain on executive's time in SLC recommendations that lawsuits filed on behalf of the corporation not continue.

(B) Yes. The board manages the business and affairs of the corporation, including litigation filed in its behalf. Under the business judgment rule, courts may not review the board's determination that litigation should cease.

(C) No. The directors on the special litigation committee have not exercised sufficient care in informing themselves about the subject matter of their decision.

(D) No. The Orson's Beans board of directors had its opportunity to pursue the wrongdoers when it learned of their actions. It should not be given a "second bite at the apple" through the use of a litigation committee or otherwise.

Full Sail, Inc. is a successful microbrewery that has two product lines: Golden Ale and Amber Lager. The board proposes to sell off a brewery and product line (Golden Ale). Director Augie Birch is interested, but believes that, if he bids on the proposed Golden Ale "spin-off," he will be "held hostage." Augie is the wealthiest of the directors. Augie, therefore, has his cousin, Portia Porter, form a new corporation. That entity purchases Golden Ale.

Five years later Golden Ale has proven to be wildly successful. A Full Sail director, however, learns that Augie has been the one behind the new venture all along. Full Sail has demanded that Augie turn over his stock in the new business, "lock, stock, and barrel."

146. Should Augie defend or should he attempt to settle?

   (A) Defend. The new corporation paid an objectively verifiable "fair" price for the Golden Ale line. Full Sail has not been damaged.

   (B) Defend. Most of the increase in value can be proven to be due to Augie's management effort and expertise. Damages due to Full Sail will be small, if any.

   (C) Defend, but have Augie resign from the board and make his resignation retroactive.

   (D) Settle. Augie has breached his duty of loyalty, he is liable not only for any damage to the corporation, but also for an illicit gain, and the likely remedy is constructive trust in favor of Full Sail for all of the stock, despite clear evidence of the factors cited in Answer (B).

El Cid, Inc. is a publicly-held steel producer located in Toledo, Ohio. El Cid has modern plants, but has had losses for four consecutive years, mainly due to foreign competition. El Cid's board of directors has recently been approached by a Scottish consortium that wishes to purchase El Cid's facilities, which consist of five plants employing 4200 individuals. The directors' due diligence reveals that the Scots have broken up and sold off two similarly situated steel producing companies in Europe.

While the El Cid directors deliberate, the El Cid employees propose a purchase ("leveraged buyout") to be financed by a major Toledo bank. The offer is firm and in writing, but is for 15 percent less than the Scots' offer. Revlon to Sth

147. El Cid director Chuck Beston consults you. What do you tell him?

   (A) Reject the employee bid. Once it has become certain that the company is for sale, your duty ceases to be a defender of the corporate bastion and you must conduct an auction (the Delaware *Revlon* standard). Shareholders will sue and you will be held liable if you accept the lower bid. (B) Reject the employee bid. Although many companies have adopted in their mission statements and elsewhere a stakeholder model, which posits duties for directors to employees, local communities, the environment, customers, suppliers, and others, as well as shareholders, El Cid has not done so. Again, sell to the highest bidder.

(C)   Consider the employee bid. In the meanwhile, do legal research to determine if Ohio has a statute such as Indiana's that directs Indiana courts specifically to disregard Delaware precedents such as *Unocal* and *Revlon*.

(D)   Consider the employee bid. And you don't need to do any research because Ohio has a so-called "non-shareholder constituency" statute which provides that directors may consider the "interests of employees, suppliers, creditors, or customers, the economy of the State and the nation, and the long-term as well as the short term interests of the corporation, including the possibility that these interests may best be served by the continued independence of the corporation."

Amelia Earheart sits on the boards of both Otter Aircraft, Ltd. and Owens Corning Composites, Inc. ("OCC"). Otter has been purchasing from OCC composite wing assemblies for its new Tri-Otter commuter airliner. The Otter purchasing department has been purchasing approximately $900,000 of wing assemblies per year. Otter's annual sales are $100 million. Amelia has discovered these facts.

148.   Need Amelia take any action?

(A)   No. She has no conflict of interest because the transactions are not material as a percentage of Otter's sales or profits.

(B)   No. She has no personal interest in the subject matter other than the "interlocking" directorate position.

(C)   Yes. She must disclose to the Otter board of directors her interest in the transaction (namely, the interlock) and have the disinterested directors approve (or reject) the transaction with OCC.

(D)   Maybe. She must disclose and receive board approval if she participated in or influenced negotiation of the transaction.

Bob Sole is a director and CEO of Sunsweet Juice Co. The corporation processes fruit for its own brand of juice and for other labels as well. The corporation has now decided to divest itself of the bottling plant and vehicle fleet utilized for the latter endeavor.

Trent Mott, first cousin and childhood friend of Bob Sole, bids at the appraised market price. Or, more accurately, he bids in the name of a corporation he has formed for the purpose of acquiring the assets.

The jurisdiction has adopted the Model Business Corporation Act ("MBCA") in its entirety.

149.   Does the transaction require any special scrutiny or treatment?

(A)   No. Under the MBCA, doing business with a director's first cousin or with an entity controlled by him is not a defined "conflicting interest" transaction.

(B)   Yes. Under the MBCA, common sense prevails. A transaction with an entity controlled by a director or officer's cousin involves a conflict of interest. The transaction should receive special scrutiny by the disinterested directors.

(C)   Yes. The MBCA leaves conflicts of interest undefined. It is a question of fact whether or not specific dealings involve a conflict.

(D) Yes. Bob Sole has a conflict of interest as a matter of law.

Assume, though, that Bob Sole proposes to sell the private label operation to Trent Lott for a price that, at best, is on the low side of the range of prices that could objectively be called fair. The disinterested directors have voted to approve the transaction.

150. Does that end the inquiry?

ANSWER:

The Klein and Lauren families own a corporation which produces designer jeans. Dissatisfied with a lack of bank financing, the Klein family boycotts meetings, concentrating its resources on real estate ventures. Determined not to permit a listing ship to capsize, the Laurens loan personal funds to the corporation at a high rate of interest that reflects of the speculative nature of the enterprise. They also cause the corporation to enter into and pay a substantial, but justifiable, management fee to themselves.

The ship is soon righted. The enterprise is profitable again. The Kleins, however, sue, alleging that the Laurens have "violated" the interested director statute.

151. Megan Lauren consults you. Is the Kleins' claim a good one?

(A) Yes. The law requires full disclosure and the vote of a disinterested decision maker (directors or shareholders). Otherwise the loan transaction is voidable.

(B) No, but the burden will be on the Laurens to demonstrate why they did not comply with the statute.

(C) No, the statutes are safe harbors, but non-exclusive safe harbors, rather than mandatory commands. The directors alleged to have had a conflict may always prove the fairness of the transaction.

(D) Yes. If directors or shareholders loan funds to the corporation, they must do so at a low interest rate.

Three directors of the Blue Moon Motel Co., Ltd, own a parcel of property which they believe to be a prime motel site, located as it is just off a major interstate highway. They have had the property appraised. They now propose to convey to Blue Moon at the appraised value. At the directors' meeting convened to approve the land transaction, one of the directors looks up and notes, "A quorum of disinterested directors would be three. There are only two of us without any interest in this transaction. Counsel, what do we do?"

152. Your reply?   Directors on Both side

(A) Because you cannot obtain a quorum, the directors must convene a shareholders' meeting, seeking shareholder approval.

(B) Modern interested director statutes provide that, for quorum purposes, interested directors may be counted.

(C) The board is paralyzed. The only recourse is to seek court approval.

  (D) In most states, the attorney general, who has general supervisory power over corporations, has a procedure for seeking approval.

Having surmounted the lack of a quorum question, the two Blue Moon directors not in the ownership group engage in self-examination. One, Barney, says to the other, Otis, "Hey, you know Andy [owner of 40 percent of the stock and one of the land owners] put me on the board about 4 years ago." Otis responds, "Well, do you think you can be impartial on this deal?" Barney thinks and says, "Yes, I live here and members of my church would never let me forget it if I let something slide by."

 153. Can Barney remain on this committee of two?

  (A) No, he is not a disinterested director.

  (B) No, he is not a "qualified director."

  (C) No, realistically his relationship with Andy is a material relationship which would "reasonably be expected to impair the objectivity of [his] the director's judgment."

  (D) Yes, standing alone, having been nominated or elected to the board by a director or ex-director will not disqualify."

Using his corporation, Tenore, Ltd., Luciano Havarotti proposes to purchase, from Three Tenors, Inc., a valuable piece of downtown real estate. He further proposes to construct a building in which will be housed offices, a rehearsal hall, and prop storage for the city's civic opera. Luciano will then donate the refurbished building to the local opera. The Three Tenor board approves the conveyance, with Luciano absenting himself from the final board deliberations and abstaining from the vote.

Luciano neglected to disclose that the conveyance by him to the civic opera will be of a life estate in the realty, with the remainder to Luciano's children.

There has been a change in board membership. The nature of the realty conveyance has also come to light. The new directors, lead by Placido Tomingo, are angry. Placido asks you to sing an aria on "Luciano's treachery" as he calls it.

 154. Can the corporation void the transaction?

ANSWER:

Dunhill Pharmaceuticals is a profitable Arkansas corporation that produces generic drugs. The corporation's shares are traded OTC. The class of shares is also registered with the SEC under the Securities Exchange Act of 1934 § 12(g).

Dunhill, Staha, and Hall increase their collective ownership of Dunhill to 50.5 percent. They then cause the board of directors to be downsized from seven to three directors. As directors, they then vote themselves annual compensation of $10 million each. They also authorize personal lines of credit for themselves from the corporate treasury. They each may borrow from the corporation up to $10 million.

 155. They are capable managers, but can they do this? What prevents them from such a power play?

  (A) Nothing if their approval process met with the elements of the business judgment rule.

(B)   The "reasonable relationship" test which requires that a reasonable relation exist between the services rendered and the compensation paid to a corporate officer.

(C)   The reasonable relationship test plus the Sarbanes-Oxley Act of 2002, which would prohibit the line of credit (loan) transaction.

(D)   The reasonable relationship test, Sarbanes-Oxley, and the fiduciary duty of loyalty.

Bucket of Chicken (BOC) is a publicly-held, mid-size poultry and fried chicken restaurant chain. The shares trade at $40 per share but have languished between $38 and $42 per share. Several officers and directors are quietly campaigning for the board to reset the exercise, or strike price, for the options, to $27, the price 18 months ago, from $37, the price which the option grant contains. Other of the directors, who have a strong feeling that BOC will have a gangbuster year next year, want to persuade the board to authorize an exceptionally generous grant of options this year, with an exceptionally short one-year vesting period (graduated vesting over 2–5 years has been the pattern). Others of the directors desire the full board to do so but only after April, when the market will have adjusted to some press releases containing some bad news (loss of a large Department of Defense contract) and the strike price on the new options will be much lower.

156.   You advise the full board, and not any particular individual within it. What advice would you give at the meeting at which individual directors make various motions to do these things?

(A)   The board of directors sets the compensation of officers and directors. Whatever they choose to do, at least if none of them personally benefit, is protected by the business judgment rule (BJR).

(B)   In theory, the BJR does protect compensation decisions by directors who have no disabling conflicts of interest in the matter but the BJR does not fully protect them if options or benefits' terms violate a written plan disclosed to shareholders or disclosed and voted upon by shareholders.

(C)   Backdating options is permissible but spring-loading (extra or extraordinary grants before the corporation announces positive news) and bullet-dodging (waiting to make option grants until negative news has taken the market price, and therefore the strike price, to a lower level) are verboten.

(D)   The other way around — backdating options is forbidden but spring-loading of options or bullet-dodging with option grants are normal and permissible corporate practices.

Versace, Gucci, and Feragamo are the senior executives (CEO, CFO, and COO, respectively) of Romeo Fashions, a publicly-held fashion house and retailer of designer goods. In the past year, each of the top three executives has received performance bonuses totaling $25 million. Together, the three exercised stock options reaping them profits totaling an additional $120 million.

In late February, after the audit of the previous years' results is nearly complete, the accountants from Heat Barwick request a conference with the top three managers. Heat Barwick reports that, in the fourth quarter of the previous year, Romeo had booked $100 million of revenue for goods that were not sold; rather, they had been shipped to exclusive retailers in Milan, New York, Beverly Hills, and so on, on consignment. Due to a slow holiday season, the retailers were returning most of those goods unsold. Romeo Fashions will have to make an accounting restatement of earnings, writing down fourth quarter earnings by $100 million.

The SEC has also announced that Romeo, Versace, Gucci, and Feragamo are the targets of a formal SEC investigation. It seems as though Romeo has twice in the past three years reported glowing earnings only later to be required to take write-downs.

157.   The three executives wish to know the worst-case scenario.

    (A)   The SEC will give them a slap on the wrist and there will be a flood of "stock drop" civil law suits filed on behalf of shareholders. They will be in court for years to come, but the situation is manageable.

    (B)   There will be civil lawsuits and, under the Sarbanes-Oxley Act of 2002, the three executives will have to forfeit to the company all of their incentive-based (bonus and stock option) compensation for the past year.

    (C)   Civil law suits and, under the Sarbanes-Oxley Act, the SEC may seek to bar the three from service as officers or directors of publicly-held companies, based upon their "unfitness" to serve. Such a "bar order" may be for a period of years or a lifetime ban.

    (D)   Civil suits, forfeiture of incentive-based compensation, and lifetime bar orders may all be the consequences of the earnings restatement.

Bing Weldon is the gravel pit king of central Iowa. He owns a number of pits personally. He also is a director and shareholder of a corporation, Pet Rocks, Inc., which owns the second largest gravel pit in Iowa. Pet Rocks also owns an undivided one-third interest in the mother of all gravel pits, the What Cheer Crescent. It also has made an offer, and received a counteroffer, which it has under consideration, from the owner, for the second third. As to the third "one-third," after protracted negotiations to obtain a long-term leasehold, Pet Rocks has come away empty.

When he receives this news, Bing Weldon drives over to the Elks Club. He importunes the two other Crescent owners to sell him both the second and the third undivided "third." Bing breaks the impasse with one of the owners by promising to give the owner's mother, who lives on the property, a life estate in her lot and flower garden.

Bing ends up nearly cornering the gravel market. He is wildly successful. Pet Rocks' directors are angry. Much of that success could have been theirs.

158.   What result if Pet Rocks' directors sue Bing?

    (A)   He has usurped (diverted to his own use) a corporate opportunity, in breach of his duty of loyalty. They should be able to obtain a constructive trust on the other 2/3rds of What Cheer Crescent.

    (B)   They should succeed as to the middle one-third, but the corporation had no "interest or expectancy" in the last one-third.

    (C)   They should prevail because what Bing did was not "fair."

    (D)   They will not prevail because, on the way over to the Elks Club, Bing mailed his resignation to the corporation.

It is 1931. Loft, Inc. is an ice cream parlor and soda fountain company. The directors and senior executives are seeking ways in which to cut costs. For years, the corporation has bought syrup for its soda fountain soft drinks from Coca-Cola. Coca-Cola, however, will not negotiate a price reduction, despite Loft's volume purchases. The board, therefore, directs the CEO, Charles Guth, to explore alternatives to Coca-Cola.

In his market research, Guth discovers a little company with a cheaper product. Its name is Pepsi Cola. Loft knows a good deal when he sees one. He forms a company in his wife's maiden name. Using that company, he purchases the secret formula and the trade name to develop Pepsi Cola out of bankruptcy. A year into that process Guth quietly resigns his position with Loft.

Five years later the Loft board of directors learns of what Guth has done. They sue him.

159. What result?

    (A) Guth is not liable because the corporation had no "interest or expectancy" in the Pepsi Cola opportunity.

    (B) Guth is liable because the opportunity is in a "line of business" in which the corporation is engaged or might reasonably be expected to be engaged, but he is liable only for the value of the opportunity at the time it was diverted.

    (C) Guth is liable and a court will place a constructive trust on the stock of his new company without inquiry as to whether increments of value resulted from the nature of the opportunity or from Loft's own efforts (the "no inquiry rule").

    (D) Guth is not liable because his wife owns the stock.

Celeste is vice-president (information technology) for Hemlock Forest Products, Inc. While at a fundraiser for the school her children attend, Celeste is approached by John Barbar, whose opening conversational gambit is, "Say, you're with Hemlock Forest Products, aren't you?" Barbar then describes a process he has developed for recycling used lumber into wood chips. The breakthrough is that the process removes nails and other impurities.

Celeste telephones several acquaintances in the industry. They are extremely skeptical that it can be done, but emphasize the potential if it can. Celeste also speaks with a banker and a Small Business Administration (SBA) counselor. She has one additional conversation with Barbar.

Celeste resigns from Hemlock. She and Barbar form a new corporation, obtain an SBA guaranteed loan from the bank, and build a prototype. In no time, they are licensing the technology to all the major forest products and paper producing companies, except Hemlock. Hemlock hauls Celeste into court. You are defending.

160. What is the theory of your defense?

    (A) Recycling used lumber is neither in the line of business of a major forest products company nor in any line of business which such a company is likely to pursue.

    (B) Hemlock had no "interest or expectancy" in the opportunity.

    (C) Hemlock was in financial difficulties and, therefore, would not have had the wherewithal to pursue the technology. Hence, the opportunity was not a corporate opportunity.

    (D) Celeste breached no duty to Hemlock because, upon forming a resolve to develop the technology, she promptly resigned.

Miss Jean Brody has her own company — Brody Prime, Ltd. — which has speculated in Federal Communications Commission ("FCC") cellular telephone licenses. She holds licenses for several service areas in south central Wisconsin. She also sits on the board of the Yelm Telephone Company in southern Minnesota. Yelm is an old-fashioned local service provider with hard wires running from customers' homes and businesses to Yelm's exchanges.

Several cellular licenses along the Minnesota-Wisconsin border come onto the market. Jean asks all of her Yelm director colleagues whether Yelm has an interest, but does so individually, rather than at a board meeting. They each say "no," the CEO adding that Yelm has little cash right now because it has been building out a cable television system. Jean and Brody Prime then sign a contract to purchase the licenses.

Before Brody Prime closes on the deal, Firstwave Communications, a full-service (cellular, internet access, cable television, and traditional telephone service) Illinois telecommunications company announces a merger with Yelm.

Firstwave sues Brody Prime and Jean, asking that a constructive trust be placed on the contract to purchase the cellular licenses.

161. Is there a corporate opportunity?

(A) Yes, because a director may not divert an opportunity that rightfully belongs to the corporation's prospective merger partner.

(B) No, because Answer (A) is incorrect, Yelm's line of business did not include cellular, Jean did not learn of it by virtue of her position, and Yelm has no interest or expectancy (indeed, it turned the deal down).

(C) Yes, because cellular is a line of business in which Yelm might reasonably be expected to engage.

(D) No, because Miss Jean Brody was in this business long before she became a member of the Yelm Telephone board of directors.

Brothers Hector and Ajax operate a successful business that exports scrap metal. Each owns 35 percent. The former manager, Rosen, comes into the office one day. Rosen owns 20 percent. Friends and employees own the remaining 10 percent.

Rosen is moving to Bisbee, Arizona. He inquires if the corporation will buy back his shares. The brothers confer. They respond that the corporation has no interest, but it would give Rosen $5 per share. Rosen departs on friendly terms.

Ajax then excuses himself, saying he has an errand to run. He intercepts Rosen in the parking lot. He offers Rosen $12 per share. Rosen accepts.

Using his newly acquired majority control, Ajax puts his business associates on the board. They promote Ajax to CEO, at a greatly increased salary. Meanwhile, Hector languishes. His salary increases, but only slightly. He moves down the hall, to a distant office.

162. Hector consults you. Weren't the Rosen shares a corporate opportunity? Didn't Ajax usurp it?

ANSWER:

163. In Question 159, *supra*, Guth approaches you shortly after he had learned that the fledgling Pepsi brand has become available. What procedures should you recommend be followed if an opportunity is a "corporate [or partnership, or LLC, etc.] opportunity," or potentially so?

ANSWER:

Fred Waters owns the movie rights to "Teenage Mutants." Michael Sizemore asks Waters to join the Sterling Productions board of directors. Waters thinks it would be divine to do so.

Shortly thereafter, the Sterling board discusses another property, "Nail Polish," but declines the movie rights. Mr. Waters acquires "Nail Polish."

Waters then forms his own production company, Sparkling Waters, Inc, employing his children, Rickey Waters and Victoria Waters. They successfully produce "Mutants" and "Polish." Waters then has a falling out with Sterling and resigns from the Sterling board. Michael Sizemore demands a cut of Sparkling Waters's profits for the Sterling treasury.

164. What result?

    (A) No cut. A director may compete with the corporation and, of the two properties, Sterling had no rights in one and turned down the other.

    (B) Big cut. A director may not compete with the corporation if the jurisdiction follows the "line of business" test.

    (C) Partial cut. Sterling may seek profits of "Polish" but not of "Mutants." Sterling never gave Waters permission to take up the "Polish" opportunity.

    (D) No cut. It is outlandish to think that a director (as opposed to an employee) may not pursue his own business interests.

Sparkling Waters, Inc. receives a very attractive acquisition offer from a larger company, Musical Waters. The original bid was for a cash merger at 52 percent over the current Sparkling share price. Retaining an independent law firm and a financial adviser, an independent committee of the Sparkling board persuades Musical to raise its bid to a 60 percent premium. When the time comes to make a recommendation to Sparkling shareholders, however, a majority of the full Sparkling board recommends against the offer, explaining that they believe that after Sparkling produces several more of its highly popular productions, even higher bids will emerge. In truth, the ex-spouse of the Sparkling board chair is the CEO of Musical; several other Sparkling directors' ex-spouses or ex-partners are executives of Musical; two ex-Sparkling directors serve on the Musical board; and a great deal of enmity flows between persons on one company back toward persons at the other company, and vice versa. The shareholders vote the offer down by a close vote. Sammy shareholder sues the Sparkling board.

165. What result?

    (A) Sammy loses. The directors were diligent and none of them had a conflict of interest (pecuniary interest in the outcome). They acted lawfully as well. No duty of care, duty of loyalty, or duty of lawfulness violation.

(B) Sammy wins. Directors have an overriding duty to be truthful and to make full disclosures to their shareholders in all matters, across the board.

(C) Sammy loses. None of the directors or officers lives in the same household as the officers and directors of Musical and hence no conflict of interest exists.

(D) Sammy wins. As a matter of state law, directors may not have a duty to make full disclosure across the board, although when they do speak they must be truthful. When they seek shareholder approval or consent, however, they do have a duty of full disclosure (the "duty of candor") which may arise even though nothing amounting to a duty of loyalty violation may exist.

Arkansas Aluminum (AA) is a large *Fortune 500* company. Among its far-flung assets are a number of bauxite mines located in Western Australia. For over 20 years, twice a week a large bulk container loaded with bauxite leaves Perth, Australia (the most isolated city in the world), making its way across the Indian Ocean. Once across the Indian Ocean, the AA chartered ships unload at the government-owned aluminum smelter in Bahrain, the largest smelter in the Middle East. The Bahrain government recently filed suit against AA. It turns out that for 17 years, or longer, mid-level AA employees have made gifts and paid bribes to Bahrain government employees, who looked the other way while AA overcharged for the bauxite. The 17 years' overcharges amount to at least $1 billion U.S. or more. AA has a 13-person board of directors. Eight of those directors have each served on the AA board for 12–13 years while three other directors have served even longer — 16 to 18 years. Your law firm represents the Hawaiian Hula Dancers Union Pension fund, which owns AA stock (which has nosedived since news of the Bahrain lawsuit hit the newspapers).

166. You are the corporate lawyer advising the litigation partner in your firm about what theories the lawsuit should pursue.

(A) Duty of care violations by the directors.

(B) Duty of loyalty violations by the directors.

(C) Illegal acts, namely, payment of bribes in violation of the Foreign Corrupt Practice Act of 1977.

(D) Sustained and systematic failure of the duty of oversight (ordinarily care) which constitutes an exercise in bad faith and therefore a duty of care violation.

MidAmerican Bank operates branches in eight Iowa counties. It is a conservative institution that has instilled the loyalty of the local farm populace over the years. Approximately 35 individuals own MidAmerican shares. Old time director W.C. Fields, from the larger city up the river (Bettendorf), contacts the children of the deceased founder of MidAmerican. The children, Barbara and Lynn Menke, are married with young families.

Fields offers the Menke daughters $12 per share for their father's stock, 20 percent of the total outstanding, which they inherited. Later, he bids against himself, raising the price to $15. Each Menke daughter then sells, grossing over $200,000 each.

Two months later, Floatman's Bank, a bigger St. Louis bank, makes a friendly tender offer (or takeover bid — the terms are used interchangeably) for MidAmerican shares at $30 per share. Barbara and Lynn have learned that Fields went around to several of the region's towns (Burlington, West Point, Madison) buying up other shares at $12 and at $15.

Barbara and her sister feel abused. They are in your office in Keokuk, Iowa.

167. What course of action should the sisters pursue?

    (A) A federal claim for insider trading pursuant to SEC Rule 10b-5 and the Securities Exchange Act of 1934.

    (B) A state law claim of breach of fiduciary duty under the "special facts" doctrine.

    (C) Answers (A) and (B) are equally advisable.

    (D) A state law fraud claim.

For the last seven or eight years, employees of Good News Gas Co. have been prospecting for natural gas deposits in north central Wyoming's Powder River basin. They drill a test well on one of their leases. The well comes in "gang busters," sending a strong signal that the Good News may be the largest natural gas field ever discovered in North America. The employees quickly cap the well and remove the drilling rig.

Knowing also that natural gas prices are approaching an all time high, two employees, Cal Twitty and Jack Owens, drive to a nearby roadhouse with a pay telephone (cellular calls can be traced). They telephone several stockbrokers each, placing large (but not overly large and therefore suspicious) orders both for Good News common shares and for call options to purchase such shares.

Cal and Jack then call Good News headquarters in Denver. They report to Vice President for Development, Marty Robbins, who tells Cal and Jack to keep it under their hat for a few days. He then buys up shares and options on shares.

Finally, the "good news" is announced at a press conference. Director Ferlin Husky, who is in attendance, whips out his cell phone. He purchases Good News shares, as does his broker. Within a month the share price has gone from $14 to $40.

168. Who is liable and for what?

   (A) They all are liable for the profit made and, in addition, for a civil penalty for up to three times the profit made (or the loss forgone, in cases of insiders selling on negative news) (Insider Trading Sanctions Act of 1984) and possible criminal penalties.

   (B) Ferlin would not be liable. He did not trade (or "tip" his broker to trade) until after the information was disclosed.

   (C) Only Marty Robbins is liable. He is a corporate officer. Cal and Jack are just petroleum engineers, rank-and-file employees who owe no one fiduciary or similar duties.

   (D) None of them are liable. This kind of trading keeps share markets efficient, moving share prices in the right direction and is also the very type of incentive based compensation we wish to encourage.

Vincent is a financial printer in New York City. He is a savvy and creative blue-collar guy. In the course of his work, he reviews printer's proofs of "offers to purchase" in takeover bids. Drafts of these documents, and their contents, are communicated to Vincent's employer in absolute secrecy. The name of the target corporation is encrypted until the final press run.

The cipher for the target company name, though, has to have the same number of characters as the real name. Also, by reading the narrative, Vincent can uncover much information. For example, he might discover that the target is in the forest products industry, is headquartered in Erie, Pennsylvania, and has 10 characters in its name.

In the evening, on his way home from work, Vincent exits the subway one stop early, in order to visit the World's Greatest Library, the New York Public Library.

He quickly researches the subject and finds Hammerhill Paper (10 characters) is located in Erie. Vincent buys the stock, albeit in the modest amounts his financial circumstances permit.

The medium premium over market price in takeover bids for much of the 1980s was as high as 50 percent. Knowing in advance who a takeover target is, and buying shares in it is the stock market equivalent of "shooting fish in a barrel."

Vincent has done this eight times, amassing $80,000. Then the SEC finds out. They bring a civil suit against Vincent in federal district court. In return for getting off with a consent decree, Vincent agrees to disgorge those profits.

But eight or nine financial printers have done this. To make an example of him, the SEC refers the case to the United States Attorney, who prosecutes Vincent criminally. You are defense counsel.

169. What is a good theory of your defense?

   (A) This is good old American ingenuity and should be permitted.

   (B) Inside information comes from a source within the company whose shares are being traded. This information comes instead from a person (the takeover bidder) purchasing, or about to purchase, target company shares. It is market information, information about the market for the company's shares, rather than classic inside information, information about the company itself (a new discovery, a major new contract, an earnings report, etc.).

(C) The events took place wholly within New York City, in a few-block area. Interstate commerce is not involved, the jurisdictional means are absent, and the federal court has no subject matter jurisdiction.

(D) Vincent occupies no fiduciary or similar position vis-à-vis those with whom he traded. He is a stranger to them and owes them no duties.

State U football coach Knute Olsen is attending a track meet at a local high school because his daughter is running in the 800-meter race. Coach Olsen sits behind Local Public Company CEO and his spouse. CEO is talking to his spouse about leaving the next day, a Sunday, to travel to New York, where he will be meeting with investment banking firm Silverman Sachs. In the same conversation, CEO talks about mergers and about XYZ Co.

Putting two and two together, Coach Olsen calls local auto dealer, who sponsors Coach's television show. On Monday, they purchase 20,000 XYZ shares.

Sure enough, on Wednesday, a cash acquisition of XYZ by Local Company is announced. The cash merger price is at a 48 percent premium over market. Coach Olsen and friendly auto dealer sell on Friday. Their one week profits are a whopping $1.9 million.

The SEC sues Coach Olsen and local auto dealer.

170. What is their best defense?

(A) They have none. Coach Olsen is a tippee and local auto dealer is a remote tippee. Both are liable.

(B) Coach is liable but, as a remote tippee, local auto dealer is not liable.

(C) The information is market information rather than inside information so that the "disclose or abstain" prohibition does not apply.

(D) The coach is only an eavesdropper, not a tippee, and therefore neither he nor local auto dealer is liable.

Horatio worked at a major Chicago bank on a team that analyzed leveraged buyout proposals. (In a leveraged buyout ("LBO"), managers or others borrow heavily to purchase the publicly-held shares of a company, using the assets and cash flow of the company as security for the loan.)

After the bank terminated his employment six months ago, Horatio kept his corporate identification, which he wears suspended from his neck. He has a magnetic key card for the elevator. He also long ago befriended the Saturday morning security guard who watches over the building lobby and elevators. The guard believes that Horatio still works for the bank.

On Saturday mornings, Horatio buys a coffee "to go," passes through the lobby, greeting the security guard, and rides the elevator to the 40th floor, where he rifles the desks of his former co-workers. He identified nine LBO targets. Eight of the transactions went forward. With some uncles, cousins, and college friends, Horatio has an "investment club" that has invested heavily in LBO target company shares. The club has made $2.3 million in profits. Horatio receives 30 percent.

171. Horatio is liable for insider trading, but in what capacity?

(A) Insider.

(B) Temporary insider.

(C) Tippee.

(D) Thief (or misappropriator).

Dan Baty owns 61 percent of the common shares of Northwest Transportation, Inc. and sits on the board of directors. A partnership of which Dan is a member owns three cargo vessels. The partnership proposes selling the three vessels, at a price to be determined by an appraisal, to Northwest. In turn, Northwest needs the additional cargo capacity. The transaction would be a large one for Northwest, doubling its fleet of vessels and having a monetary value in the range of $60 million.

The Northwest board of directors ties 2-2, with Dan abstaining. The transaction is not approved. The board does vote, 4-0, to call a special shareholders' meeting at which the shareholders will vote on the proposed transaction.

172. Under the traditional view of a controlling shareholder's responsibilities, may Dan vote at that meeting?

ANSWER:

Kramer causes his corporation, Cosmo Entertainment ("CE"), to gain majority share control of Coffee Shops, Inc. ("CS"), a major owner of New York corner restaurants. Kramer puts his friends, George, Elaine, and Newman, on the CS board of directors. Over the ensuing months, Kramer causes the board, by 3-2 votes, to declare a number of extraordinary dividends and to pay large sums to CE for "consulting, feasibility studies, and indirect overhead expense." The cash drain leaves CS unable to pursue its expansion plans. CS had planned to replicate its successful formula in Baltimore, Boston, Hartford, and other East Coast cities.

George's father, Frank "Serenity Now" Costanza, is a minority shareholder in CS. He has already decided to sue.

173. Who should Frank sue and why?

(A) No one. Majority rules and Kramer (CE) has a majority.

(B) The majority shareholder (Kramer and CE) because their activity, or some of it, amounts to a waste of corporate assets.

(C) The three directors (George, Elaine, and Newman) because they have been "puppet directors," serving Kramer's rather than the corporation's best interests, and therefore have violated their duty of loyalty to CS.

(D) All of them: CE, Kramer, George, Elaine, and Newman.

Orson's Beans, Inc. has grown tremendously, developing coffee shops throughout the country and coffee plantations throughout the world. Orson's has purchased interests in various countries. It owns 72 percent of its Costa Rican subsidiary, 95 percent of its Javanese (Indonesian) subsidiary, and 100 percent of its Brazilian subsidiary.

Ray Folger, a minority shareholder in the Costa Rican operation, has several complaints. First, whenever Orson's develops new coffee, Orson's commissions the Javanese or the Brazilian subsidiary to produce it. Costa Rica has gotten no new business opportunities. Second, Orson's frequently does not take up all of Costa Rica's beans even though Orson's has an output contract with the subsidiary. Third, for what production it does take up, Orson's consistently pays Costa Rica's invoices late, running as much as nine months behind.

174. Does Ray have a legal basis for any of his complaints?

  (A) Yes. Orson's has breached its fiduciary duty by using its control to breach the contact.

  (B) Yes. Orson's has usurped a corporate opportunity.

  (C) No. The business judgment rule shields from scrutiny decisions by the parent corporation's board of directors, absent waste of corporate assets.

  (D) No. The directors have to do as they see fit in order to compete with Starbucks.

Poor Mrs. O'Brien. Her late husband worked for years as the plant superintendent of Punxsutawney Tool & Die Corp., owned by Bill Murphy and his family. Over the years, Bill issued stock to his best employees. Mr. O'Brien came to own 10 percent of the company shares. Those shares passed to his widow, who now lives on a fixed income in Florida. So does Bill Murphy.

His sons, who together own 52 percent, have caused the company to repurchase their dad's remaining 300 shares (30%) for $1,500 per share. Bill will receive the $450,000 in quarterly installments, with interest at 9 percent, over five years.

Over the preceding years Ms. O'Brien has explored selling her shares. There is no market, other than the two Murphy boys. They have offered to buy her shares, but at a lowball price (once for $200 and another time for $275).

Ms. O'Brien would love the same corporate buyback deal that Bill Murphy got. She could really use the $150,000 plus the interest to pay bills and to buy a condo.

175. Can Ms. O'Brien obtain "me, too" relief if the Murphy boys snub her?

   (A) No. Her only claim is a derivative one against Bill Murphy. Such a claim is on the corporation's behalf. Any payback (recovery) will require Bill to pay the money received back to the corporation.

   (B) Yes. In closely-held corporations, the participants owe fiduciary duties one to another, akin to partners in a partnership. The remedial implication is that, because a duty owed directly to her has been violated, Ms. O'Brien may be able to obtain "me, too" type relief.

   (C) Yes. She should petition a court for involuntary dissolution of the corporation on grounds that she is being oppressed.

   (D) No. This is America and majority rules.

Older brother David used to run the family business, a statewide chain of multiplex movie theaters. David, a bachelor, took many vacations to Club Meds in the Caribbean and elsewhere and played golf twice per week. In the meanwhile, David's smarter (and steadier) young brother, Rick, worked his way up in the business. Eventually, Rick became CEO and David stepped down to be a vice president, thinking it would be a rotation every two or so years (but it turned out to be permanent).

At a Super Bowl party hosted by their elderly father, David brought with him a lady friend whom the father found objectionable. The father then changed his will, leaving Rick 60 percent of the shares and David only 40 percent. Six months later the father died. When the will was read, David was not overly disturbed, as most of the real estate and other physical assets were owned by limited partnerships of which he and Rick were 50 percent owners.

Rick thrived on his now nearly complete command of the business. He put his own business associates in the three non-family directorships. At board meetings, Rick seldom would recognize David. When David did speak, Rick would make sarcastic comments such as "Why aren't you out on the golf course?" or "What do you know? You never even finished college."

The company had several very successful years. Each year the board rewarded Rick with substantial bonuses and raises, to the point at which Rick's salary was double David's. Most years David got no raise at all. The board rewarded Rick with a new company-owned Mercedes Benz and a company airplane which Rick and his family could use up to 100 hours per year for personal use. Meanwhile, David was still driving his nine-year-old company-owned Ford Taurus on which the "Check Engine" light had been on for two years.

David consulted a lawyer. Through the grapevine, Rick found out about it. The following Monday he had David's personal effects moved to the smallest office, at the end of the hall. He had David's company car repossessed. He stopped including David altogether at important meetings. This now has gone on for over a year. Fed up, David consults you.

176. What is your advice?

    (A)   Grin and bear it. You are benefiting through significant increase in the value of your limited partnership interests.

    (B)   Sue. Rick's perks and benefits represent self-dealing and a breach by him and the other directors of their duty of loyalty.

    (C)   Sue. Invoke the closely-held status of the corporation and the *Donahue* principle. Ask for "me, too" type relief.

    (D)   Sue and go "all . . . the . . . way." Ask for involuntary dissolution of the corporation on grounds that you are being oppressed.

Heavenly Acres is a gated, upscale condominium development in Lynwood, Washington. Asian developers acquired the real estate, built the units, and sold them for $750,000 each. The developers also formed a Washington corporation, Heavenly Acres Management (HAM, Inc.) to act as the managing agent.

Well, HAM has not been in evidence for several months. The shrubbery is overgrown, the grass is two-feet high, oil stains blotch the parking area, the gutters are filled with decaying leaves, and so on. A homeowners' committee comes to see you. You find that HAM filed articles of dissolution 14 months ago but neither its directors nor its shareholders have done anything since that time. In fact, they have all returned to their homes on the other side of the Pacific Rim.

177. What advice? What is the group's best action?

    (A)   Because HAM has become a de facto non-entity, the unit owners can form a new corporation and have the owners' association contract with the new company.

    (B)   They should try to track down the absentee HAM people in Asia. Meanwhile, they should cut the grass, bale the clippings, and sell the bales for hay.

    (C)   Under a new ground added in 2008, MBCA corporations can file for "involuntary dissolution" when a corporation has begun but then abandoned dissolution proceedings.

(D) They should find and sue the people in Asia. That's what lawyers are for: suing people.

TOPIC 26:
SHARE TRANSFER RESTRICTIONS (BUY-SELL AGREEMENTS) AND COMPREHENSIVE SHAREHOLDER AGREEMENTS

Seven Springs is a small ski resort, opened in the late 1940s by two families who enjoyed skiing. Over the years, Seven Springs has acquired additional property, added new ski lifts, and opened a hotel and restaurant. Through gifts and bequests, the number of shareholders has increased to 34, but all are members of several extended families: the Steep and Deep families on the one hand, and the Groomed and Gradual families on the other.

Many years ago, the shareholders all signed a "buy-sell" agreement. The agreement provided that, before any shareholder could sell, she had first to offer her shares to the other shareholders, on the same terms as the third party was willing to agree to ("right of first refusal"). The existence of the agreement is conspicuously noted in the margin of each Seven Springs share certificate, in accordance with Uniform Commercial Code § 8-218.

Now the entire Steep and Deep clan proposes to sell. They wish to sell to a larger company, Vermont Ski Corp. The Groomed and Gradual families oppose this. They invoke the buy-sell agreement. The Steeps and the Deeps reply, "This is not a sale, it is a merger, and we have you outvoted (19-15)."

178. What result?

(A) A merger occurs by operation of the law (filing articles of merger after the requisite shareholder vote has been obtained) and is not a sale. The agreement does not apply.

(B) In effect, the shareholders "sell" their shares when they vote on the merger, which will result in their receipt of Vermont Ski Corp. shares. The agreement applies.

(C) Such agreements are invalid as restraints on alienation.

(D) Their refusal to abide by the agreement constitutes fraud.

Ira and Aaron have a very successful nuclear pharmacy business that stocks and delivers radioactive substances to radiologists and oncologists in a three-state area. They own 40 percent each. They are married to two sisters, Eva and Za Za. They have in place a succession plan under which their assistants, Finbar and Declan, each of whom has a PhD in nuclear pharmacology and each of whom owns 10 percent, will succeed them. In part to provide for their spouses, Ira and Aaron have also negotiated a lengthy agreement covering various corporate affairs. The agreement provides that corporate officers' salaries may not increase more than 3 percent over the Consumer Price Index increases in any given year; that after a $1 million dollar surplus has been maintained all corporate profits will be distributed as dividends; that the corporation will at all times keep in place a subchapter S election with the Internal Revenue Service; that Finbar will be president and Declan secretary-treasurer for a period of 10 years, terminable only upon good cause shown and four month's notice, and renewable for seven year terms thereafter; that the agreement will terminate only upon the death of the survivor of Eva and Za Za.

179. Why is this agreement invalid?

(A)   Because the agreement is an attempt to conduct the affairs of a corporation as though it were a partnership.

(B)   Because provisions of the agreement would "handcuff" future boards of directors, limiting their discretion.

(C)   This or that restriction on the board of directors is very much necessary, as in the guarantees of long-term employment, but in toto the agreement goes too far.

(D)   Beyond articles, bylaws, buy-sell, and employment agreements, such comprehensive shareholder agreements are the most frequently seen in smaller and mid-size corporations. Both case law and statutes uphold them.

Sam Malone is a director of Cheers, Ltd., the United States subsidiary of an English pub chain. Sam has been sued under the Massachusetts Dram Shop Act. One of the pubs served an excessive amount of alcohol to Norman Wendt, who thereafter had an accident in which his spouse, Vera, was slightly injured. Sam was in the pub when Norman was served. Count one of Norman's complaint was dismissed for failure to state a claim. Count two was dismissed because the short two-year statute of limitations had run. Norman took a non-suit on count three. The trial court did hold a trial on the Dram Shop Act claim, finding Sam liable, but only for $8,000 in damages. Sam presents to Cheers a $450,000 legal bill.

180. Is Sam entitled to indemnification?

(A) No, because he has not been "wholly successful on the merits."

(B) Yes, because as to three claims he was "wholly successful, on the merits or otherwise."

(C) No, because directors are not agents of the corporation and are not entitled to the indemnification agents may obtain at common law.

(D) No, because the corporation's director and officer ("D & O") policy has lapsed.

Ten years after law school, a law school classmate calls. Her mother, Mary Matriarch, has been asked to join the board of the local Old Noble Savings and Loan. Mary has considerable personal assets she wishes to protect, but she really wishes to join that board. Your classmate retains you to examine the current arrangements and then bargain for a package that will give Mary Matriarch maximum protection.

181. What are the features you would examine?

(A) Provisions implementing permissive indemnification provisions and a contract guaranteeing Mary those rights (two-legged stool).

(B) Same as Answer (A), plus D & O insurance or some other funding source (indemnification may only be as good as the ability to pay) (three-legged stool).

(C) Same as Answer (B), plus a provision in the articles exculpating directors from money damage liability for duty of care violations (four-legged stool).

(D) Same as Answer (C), plus a contractual right for advance of expenses (monies to retain counsel) given the proper affirmation and undertaking (four-legged stool plus).

Victoria has information she no longer wishes to keep secret. She has filed an individual action alleging misleading disclosure in a merger involving Unlimited, Inc., a publicly-held corporation in which she owns shares. She has filed with the court a request to view Unlimited's shareholder list. She states as her purpose a desire to inform other local Unlimited shareholders of the pendency of her lawsuit against Unlimited and its directors.

Unlimited's house counsel thinks that Victoria's attorney seeks the list so that she may solicit other shareholders to join the suit. She therefore favors denial of access to the shareholder list on grounds that, by providing the list, Unlimited would be aiding and abetting an ethics violation.

182. You are associate general counsel. Your boss seeks your opinion. Do you give Victoria access to the list?

   (A) Yes, she has alleged a proper purpose and the mere potential of an ethics violation is not adequate grounds for denial of access.

   (B) No, proper purpose is an issue of fact. We can delay her for at least a year until she gets a trial or other hearing where she can establish her purpose.

   (C) No, this is just the type of "fishing expedition" which courts have condemned.

   (D) Yes, under the Model Business Corporation Act she is entitled to view the shareholder list as of right. She need not even allege a proper purpose.

David Falconer is a disgruntled shareholder of Roadstar, Inc., a manufacturer of truck bodies. Roadstar is a small, publicly-held company with 150 or so shareholders and a five-person board. Falconer is disgruntled because a truck fabricator just breached a contract for delivery of 1,000 truck bodies over two years.

Falconer has learned that the fabricator, Drummond Co., is owned by cousins of Reid Manley, Roadstar's CEO and largest shareholder. Reid's brother, Mark Manley, also sits on the Roadstar board, as does their father, John Manley. Cancellation of the order means that Roadstar will have a loss rather than a healthy projected profit this year and next. The other two directors, a banker named Baker and a law professor at State U named Andreen, seldom attend board meetings.

Falconer is incensed because the Manleys have done nothing regarding the breach, allowing it to happen with nary a protest.

183. What is the nature of his claim, against whom would he file his claims, and what is the nature of the action overall?

ANSWER:

Before Falconer can even file his claim, he obtains more "bad news." At a Roadstar board meeting, the Manleys declare an extraordinary dividend of $30 per share (the stock sells for $15), payable only to those shareholders who have held shares for five years or longer. Falconer has held his shares for four years.

The day after the dividend is paid, the Manleys sell all the company's assets to Drummond Co. There is no shareholders' meeting or other formal action. There is just an announcement to the local press, prepared on stationery with the Manley family coat of arms.

184. Falconer now is triply "frosted." What are his claims now?

   (A) He merely has further derivative claims against the Manleys for breach of fiduciary duty.

   (B) He has a direct claim for the discriminatory dividend because he can allege "separate and distinct injury," an injury not all shares have suffered.

   (C) He has direct claims both as to the discriminatory dividend ("separate and distinct injury") and for the denial of voting rights to all the shareholders, even though suffered in common with all of the shareholders.

   (D) He has no claim. The board "rules."

It is 1955. In your office is Patsy Cline, a professional singer, who owns shares in Mift & Co., a publicly-held meat packing company. Patsy has a number of complaints. Mift's directors approved the acquisition of a Beefalo ranch from the CEO's nephew. Several directors took for themselves an opportunity to expand into emerging post-war European markets. The directors have approved a severance package ("golden parachute") for the CEO that is excessive by any measure. In short, she claims numerous breaches of fiduciary duty that may be vindicated, if at all, through a derivative action.

185. Patsy wishes to proceed if (1) she will not receive adverse publicity, and (2) out-of-pocket costs are not too high. How would you advise her?

ANSWER:

Saul Meinberg has been a customer and shareholder of South Shore Bank. He has also been a thorn in the bank's side. He has filed three lender liability suits against the bank, all of which settled for nuisance value. Saul waged an unsuccessful proxy campaign to gain a seat on the board of directors.

Saul now brings a lawsuit alleging that South Shore's losses over the last two years were the result of gross mismanagement. He is joined by his cousin, Phillip Meinberg, who purchased a large block of South Shore shares last month, which are held in "street name" by his broker, Berrill Mynch. Saul and Phillip are represented by Saul's nephew, Avi Meinberg, a newly-admitted member of the bar who has, so far, specialized in personal injury litigation.

186. You represent South Shore Bank. What arguments do you make in your motion to dismiss?

   (A) Lack of contemporaneous ownership (Phillip).

   (B) Lack of contemporaneous ownership and lack of record ownership (Phillip).

   (C) Lack of contemporaneous ownership, lack of record ownership (Phillip), and unclean hands (Saul).

(D) Lack of contemporaneous ownership, lack of record ownership (Phillip), unclean hands (Saul), inadequate representation (Saul), and inadequate representation (both Saul and Phillip as to their lawyer).

Along with several minority shareholders, Hans and Franz own a fitness salon, Club One, Inc. In order to diversify, they formed a new corporation, Pump You Up, Inc. ("PYU"). They transferred their Club One shares to PYU. They also caused PYU to form a second subsidiary, Free Weights, Ltd., that sells weightlifting equipment.

Hans now brings a lawsuit complaining that Franz has been using Club One facilities for taping Franz's fitness and distance learning television show ("I pump up your body as well as your mind").

187. Can Hans maintain the lawsuit?

    (A) No, he is an owner of PYU shares, not Club One shares, and so he has no contemporaneous ownership.

    (B) Yes, courts recognize as an exception to contemporaneous ownership a double derivative action, in which, for example, an owner of shares in a parent corporation complains of wrongdoing in a subsidiary.

    (C) No, Hans does not have clean hands.

    (D) Yes, Hans is an adequate representative.

First-year law student Clarissa received a telephone conversation from her cousin Vinnie, a lawyer. You are Vinnie's supervising partner in the law firm of Pesci & Tomei. Clarissa owns 100 shares of WCI. Vinnie has prepared a class and derivative action with Clarissa as plaintiff, attempting to block the proposed WCI merger with North Pittsburgh Systems, Inc. ("NPSI"), a publicly-traded regional telecommunications company. Although she never heard of the merger, or of the proposed lawsuit, Clarissa quickly reads the complaint and signs it.

Several months later, at her deposition, Clarissa testifies that she knew she owned the stock, that she received a call from Vinnie, whom she believes to be "brilliant," that she met with him, asking "Are you sure about this?" and, after he assured her he was, she signed the complaint.

The following day the defense firm of Crushem, Bashem & Sanctionem requests that you see that the complaint is withdrawn or they will seek sanctions against you, Vinnie, and Clarissa.

188. Should you fold the tent?

    (A) No. The prevailing standard is to file allegations based "upon information and belief," and signed by an attorney. That is all the defense is entitled to.

    (B) Yes. Derivative actions are an exception, in which the plaintiff herself must sign a "verification," swearing that, unless otherwise stated as being based upon "information and belief" the plaintiff believes the matters alleged to be true.

    (C) No. Courts, including the United States Supreme Court, have interpreted verification as meaning only that someone, not necessarily the signing plaintiff herself, has investigated the allegations and believes them to be true.

(D)   Yes. Crushem, Bashem, and Sanctionem is a large and powerful law firm. Sanctions could ruin your career. It is not worth the chance.

Richie and Potsie have a rapidly growing nine-store Happy Days CD and video chain in Milwaukee, Wisconsin. Richie, who owns 52 percent, has just gone through a divorce. Potsie, who owns 25 percent, relates to you that Richie has used corporate funds to purchase a new home in Whitefish Bay (for cash), a 32-foot sailboat (for cash), and a luxury automobile (for cash). Potsie is concerned that Happy Days will no longer be able to pay suppliers, who demand cash on delivery already because Happy Days has made late payments recently.

Representing Potsie, you have been downtown to see Arthur Fonzarelli, the attorney who represents Happy Days and Richie Cunningham. You had a seemingly productive meeting, with Arthur showing sympathy for Potsie's plight. When you return to your office, a fax from Arthur is waiting. The fax from Fonzarelli states that if you dare file a lawsuit without first making a demand on the Happy Days board of directors (Potsie, Richie, Mr. C, Big Al, and Chachi), Fonzarelli will seek sanctions against you.

189.   Potsie pleads that something must be done quickly. Should you file suit and seek a preliminary injunction against Richie's use of corporate funds?

(A)   No, a plaintiff must first make a demand that the board of directors take action and then wait a reasonable time for them to do so before filing.

(B)   Yes, demand is excused if it would be a futile act. If a reasonable doubt exists as to whether, in acting upon the demand, the board would come under the protection of the business judgment rule, then demand is excused.

(C)   Yes, demand would be excused because of the threat of irreparable harm to the corporation if there is significant delay.

(D)   Yes, demand might be excused on three alternative grounds: futility, threat of irreparable harm, and the closely-held corporation exception.

Potsie then proceeds to file a complaint. The corporation appears by its attorney, Fonzarelli, who moves for dismissal on grounds that no demand has been made and that demand was not excused. Assume that the court rules against him, holding that demand was indeed "excused."

Fonzarelli then requests a lengthy continuance, pending the corporation's formation of a special litigation committee ("SLC") of the board of directors and an investigation by it of the alleged wrongdoing.

190.   Will the court grant the continuance?

(A)   Yes, use of the SLC for the corporation to "find its voice" in derivative litigation has been a recognized procedure for over 25 years.

(B)   No, even if just by its inaction, the board permitted the looting of the corporation by Richie in the first place. Letting the board now resolve the question of a lawsuit against Richie is akin to "letting the foxes guard the chicken coop."

(C)   No, a majority, or at least half, of the directors are disabled. The board has no power to appoint a committee.

(D)   No, the board had its chance. Why give it a "second bite at the apple?"

But Potsie, Richie, and Arthur Fonzarelli are not in New York. They are in Wisconsin. No Wisconsin appellate court has made a choice from among the menu of choices as to the standard of review of SLC determinations.

191. What are the Wisconsin court's options?

ANSWER:

The possible standards of review of SLC determinations are not all judicial in origin. The ALI Corporate Governance Project and the American Bar Association's Model Business Corporation Act have legislative suggestions. Potsie and his counsel should examine the Wisconsin statutes to see if the legislature has enacted one or the other of these suggested or "model" provisions or, perhaps, some set of "home grown" provision.

192. What might they find?

ANSWER:

Assume that Potsie and his attorney decide to proceed directly to court, alleging that demand was excused because most of the directors were related to or dominated by Richie. As Potsie is in his lawyer's office, verifying the complaint, he asks innocently enough, "What about the other shareholders? There are nine of them. Do we have to notify them or something?"

Or, assume further, that Happy Days has become a publicly-held corporation. Instead of nine other shareholders there are 900, or 9000.

193. Is demand upon shareholders required as well?

ANSWER:

The Happy Days case settles several months after it is filed. The settlement involves the board's adoption of a strongly-worded policy statement concerning use of corporate funds or other assets. Richie does not have to return any funds or make any payments to the Happy Days treasury. He does have to sign the corporation's new code of conduct for offices and employees.

Arthur Fonzarelli and Potsie's attorney, Laverne, appear in court. The settlement also provides for payment to Laverne by the corporation of a fee of $340,000, computed as follows: 1000 hours, at her normal billable rate of $200 per hour, or $200,000, times a multiplier of 1.7, or $340,000. The multiplier is based upon the alleged presence in the case of various "enhancement factors," such as difficulty of the case, prestige of opposing counsel, presence of novel legal issues, and so on.

194. Both sides urge the court to approve the settlement. You are the court. Should you?

   (A) No. An attorney's fee may be ordered or approved for payment by the corporation only in cases in which the attorney's efforts have created a common fund of some sort that benefits all shareholders.

(B)   Yes. Either a common fund or a common benefit justifies approval of a fee. The common benefit may be "corporate therapeutics" of the sort that occurred here (a bylaw change, adoption of a code of conduct or policy statement, and so on).

(C)   No. This is the very type of contrived "cosmetic settlement" that benefits only the lawyers and not the shareholders. In effect, Laverne "sold out" the class.

(D)   Yes. Courts have awarded fees to plaintiffs' attorneys even in cases in which the plaintiff recovered no damages, if the litigation produced intra-corporate reforms or some other form of common benefit.

Midwest, Inc. is a publicly-held electric utility based in the heartland. It produces steady, but unspectacular, earnings gains each year. The company has also steadily expanded through acquisitions of companies with adjacent service areas, creating economies of scale that many of its competitors do not have. The CEO and several of the directors see the company's great value, but the stock market does not. The share price drifts sideways despite quarter after quarter of earnings gains. Then, in the "dog days of summer," the company announces that State of Nirvana's public utility commission ("PUC") will hold rate hearings in which the commission may order rate cuts of up to 20 percent. The stock price now drifts — not sideways, but downwards.

The CEO and some of the directors know that the PUC announcement is all political grandstanding by a newly appointed chairperson. But, they take advantage of the lower stock price to team up with Sam Tycoon to make an offer to purchase the company. CEO manipulates the process throughout by influencing selection of the members of a board committee that is to represent shareholder interests, and of advisers to the committee (lawyers and investment bankers) who are not independent, but are beholden to the CEO.

In "cash merger" (see Question 181 *infra*), the CEO's group buys out the company for a very small premium over the temporarily depressed market price. The proxy merger statement, which seeks shareholder votes in favor of the transaction, contains numerous misrepresentations, such as ballyhooing the "independence" of the committee and its advisers and failing to disclose that in July the share price had been slightly higher than the price being offered in October.

195. A group of retired persons who hold Midwest stock thinks the deal "stinks." They want you to represent them. What action should you bring on their behalf?

(A)   A derivative suit alleging breach of the duty of loyalty by the CEO and buyout group and duty of care claims against the other board members.

(B)   A suit alleging material misrepresentations and non-disclosures in the proxy statement.

(C)   Both derivative claims and non-disclosure claims.

(D)   An action under the dissenters' rights provisions of the statute permitting a shareholder to dissent from a merger and seek a judicial appraisal of the value of his shares.

Advent Software, Inc. has been sued in federal district court by a shareholder, P. Cameron Devore, alleging that, in its initial public offering ("IPO"), Advent failed to disclose that a significant line of software inventory had become obsolete and would have to be written off, which subsequently has occurred. Plaintiff Devore also claims failures to disclose that the Advent CFO and comptroller (chief accounting officer) sold Advent shares after the IPO, but before the inventory write-off had been disclosed. The CFO is also a director, but Devore studiously avoids any violation of fiduciary duty claims. The Advent share price dropped 20 percent when the inventory write-off was disclosed.

Devore's interrogatory answers reveal that he owns 10 shares of Advent. Under occupation, he lists "contract attorney — part time." Finally, answering an interrogatory about other investments, Devore lists positions in some 300 high-tech stocks.

You work for the Palo Alto, California firm (Sue, Grabitt & Run) that is defending Advent. Your firm has received an inquiry from the attorney who represents an institutional investor, The Golden Bear High Tech Fund, which owns 10,000 shares of Advent. He, and Golden Bear, have been watching the suit with some interest.

196. Any ideas on the management of this litigation? What should be the first step?

    (A) Have Golden Bear appear and the court will substitute Golden Bear as the "most appropriate plaintiff" because, more than likely, Golden Bear will have the largest financial stake of any shareholder appearing before the court.

    (B) Check the court file for the certificate required to be filed by Devore and his attorney. Move to disqualify Devore if he has been a plaintiff more than three times in the past three years, if he is being paid any kind of "incentive" bonus, or if he failed to file the required certificate.

    (C) Move to dismiss because scienter has not been pled with the requisite particularity.

    (D) Move for sanctions, and an award of all defense attorneys' fees, on grounds that the complaint was not based upon an adequate factual investigation or upon existing law or a good faith argument for an extension of existing law.

As it turns out, Devore and his attorney never filed the certificate required by the Private Securities Litigation Reform Act of 1995 ("PSLRA"). They take a voluntary non-suit (dismissal) of their federal court action. They then re-file the same suit against Advent Software under state securities law, in state court. They add some state corporate law claims of mismanagement.

197. What is your strategy for the defense now?

    (A) Request a continuance. Expand the board of directors and form a special litigation committee to deal with the suit.

    (B) Remove the suit back to federal court, under the Uniform Standards Act. In federal court, the suit once again becomes subject to the PSLRA.

    (C) Move to dismiss for lack of subject matter jurisdiction.

    (D) Remove to federal court as in Answer (B), request a continuance, and then form an SLC, as in Answer (A).

On and off over the years, Alaska Air Group, Inc. and Aloha Airlines have discussed combining forces. They operate the same type of aircraft. Their route systems are contiguous, but yet there is no overlap. Senior managers have even thought of a logo, "Aviation Pioneers in the 49th and 50th States." The CEOs of both companies have conferred. Both agree that the deal should continue to go forward. Alaska's CEO would be CEO of the new venture. The Aloha CEO would serve as Chief Operating Officer ("COO") of the new venture. Informally, the CEOs have both consulted with a majority of their respective directors, all of whom approve of the idea.

198. What form should the "deal" take? What "deal structure" would you recommend?

   (A) A statutory merger.

   (B) Alaska should buy Aloha shares in the open market.

   (C) Alaska should make an offer directly to Aloha shareholders to purchase their shares for cash (cash tender offer).

   (D) Alaska should make an offer directly to Aloha shareholders to exchange their shares for Alaska shares (stock tender offer or, perhaps, mandatory share exchange).

M & N Machinery Co. manufactures large metal stamping presses, in turn used by manufacturers of appliances, motor vehicles, and so on. From time to time, these presses cause serious injuries to persons who operate them. There is no statute of repose. Suits are brought by workers who have been injured by presses M & N manufactured 20 and 25 years ago.

Cincinnati Milling and Machine, Inc. ("CMM") wishes to acquire M & N, which holds a number of valuable patents and some very modern physical facilities that CMM would like to own. One item on CMM's priority list right now, though, is preservation of cash. Another is avoidance, if it can, of succession to M & N's products liability exposure.

199. What deal structure might accomplish CMM's objectives?

   (A) Statutory merger.

   (B) Cash for assets.

   (C) Stock for assets.

   (D) Stock tender offer.

Assume that, after the merger of Alaska and Aloha Airlines, the senior managers decide to attempt synergistic gains by acquisition of radio and television stations in the new airline's primary service areas, Alaska, Hawaii, and the Pacific Northwest. Once the airline owns the broadcast media, it can begin low cost, or no cost, saturation advertising, luring passengers from cold climates (Alaska) to warm ones (Hawaii), and from warm climates (Hawaii) to cooler ones (Alaska and the Pacific Northwest). Don Mo has agreed to do some of the commercials.

A complication that arises though is that the Federal Communications Act provides that broadcast licenses are not transferable. The license must be continuously held by the original licensee. Alaska-Aloha is about to acquire Fisher Broadcasting, which owns radio and television stations in the Pacific Northwest. The respective CEOs have already partially negotiated the deal structure. It is to be a stock-for-stock acquisition. The agreed upon ratio is to be between 1.5 and 1.8 Alaska-Aloha ("AA") shares for each Fisher share (called a "collar"). The exact ratio will be determined by stock market conditions on the date the corporate combination takes place.

200. How do you get around the FCC obstacle?

    (A) A statutory merger, but a reverse one.

    (B) Stock for assets transaction.

    (C) A reverse merger with an Alaska-Aloha subsidiary ("reverse triangular merger").

    (D) It cannot be done. The business plan (airlines and TV stations) is real dumb. Discourage the client in any way you are able.

General Eclectic Corp. ("GE") is a large capitalization public company with 30,000 shareholders, who own 250 million outstanding GE shares. GE proposes to acquire, via statutory merger, a small, publicly-held software firm, say, Advent Software in Questions 196–197 *supra*. In the merger, GE will issue one million new GE shares to the several hundred owners of Advent Software shares.

GE's corporate secretary telephones you. She objects to the deal structure. "Do you realize that it will cost $2.7 million for us [GE, she means] to have a special shareholders' meeting and to solicit proxies to be voted in favor of the merger at the meeting?" She pauses for a moment. "This is a rinky-dink acquisition. There has to be a better way, counselor." She hangs up, banging the telephone handset on to its cradle.

201. With ringing in your left ear, you ponder. Is there a better way?

    (A) Have General Eclectic re-incorporate in a jurisdiction with a small-scale merger statute (Answer to Question 181 *supra*).

    (B) Do the transaction as a triangular merger so as to avoid the necessity of a shareholder vote in the acquiring corporation (GE).

    (C) Do the transaction as a cash merger. GE directors alone (*e.g.*, without any shareholder approval) have the authority to spend the money.

    (D) Structure it as a "double phantom reverse consolidation."

Now assume that General Eclectic has approached Advent's senior management with a merger proposal. GE has been rebuffed. GE's intelligence sources tell GE not even to try because Advent's senior managers and board of directors have pledged not to be taken over "at any cost" (or at *almost* any cost).

GE really wants to make this acquisition as Advent makes the software that runs sophisticated medical device and defense systems of a type that several GE divisions manufacture. The timing is good as well. Both the market and Advent's share price are down, within 10 percent of their three-year low.

202. What should GE's strategy be?

(A) Wage a proxy contest. Obtain enough proxies from enough Advent shares to elect a new board of directors who will agree to propose a plan of merger.

(B) Go directly to the Advent shareholders offering to purchase "any and all shares" for a premium of 45 percent over the market price. In other words, make a hostile takeover bid.

(C) Go directly to the Advent shareholders but, in order to save cash, offer them GE shares (stock tender offer).

(D) It cannot be done. It is always necessary first to obtain an agreement approved by a majority of the target company directors.

Although it once was, Hoyne Industries, Inc. is not an industrial company any longer. The company owns four ski resorts, two in the upper Midwest and two in the Intermountain West. The company began with Hoyne Mountain, a ski resort in upper Michigan. Hoyne has been profitable for 15 successive years. It has utilized its cash flow to purchase the two Western resorts and to modernize all its facilities, which now have new spacious lodges and high-speed quad chair lifts on all ski runs.

Last year there was no snow, other than man made, at three of Hoyne's four resorts. The company was barely profitable. The share price (stock ticker DHIL, for Downhill) retreated from the $19–20 range to the $13–14 range, which is approximately book value. The company has over 3,000 shareholders. It is traded on the NASDAQ.

Worried that the corporation had possibly become vulnerable to a hostile takeover bid, the directors classified the board into three classes, each to serve a three-year term, and installed a requirement that shareholders could remove directors "only for cause." They also caused to be issued to the shareholders rights to acquire preferred shares which become exercisable should anyone acquire more than 20 percent of Hoyne's voting shares. The relative rights and preferences of the preferred shares enable the holder to purchase up to five shares of any corporation into which Hoyne may be merged for every Hoyne share presently owned and to do so at a very advantageous price. The latter takeover defense is a "poison pill plan," euphemistically called a "shareholder rights plan" by corporate America.

203. Can Hoyne's directors do these things or will a reviewing court strike them down?

(A) Probably not. The court will review the defenses and their adoption very closely, applying a duty of loyalty analysis that will strike down a defense if the primary motivation behind adoption was entrenchment of the current board and management.

(B) The court will uphold the board classification scheme, which clearly is permitted by statutes, but will strike down the poison pill plan, which has no statutory authorization.

(C) The court will strike down the board classification scheme, as it clearly is an entrenchment device, but will uphold the poison pill defense plan.

(D)   Using duty of care analysis and the business judgment rule, the court will uphold both of these "shark repellent" or "porcupine" provisions.

Now assume that Hoyne's directors ascertain that, indeed, a bidder is on the scene. Vader Enterprises has filed a Schedule 13D with the SEC. The 13D discloses a 12 percent ownership stake in Hoyne Industries. At an emergency special meeting, Hoyne's directors vote to give an option on the two Western ski resorts, at a favorable price, to Luke Skywalker, Inc., another recreation company.

Hoyne's directors also approve and announce a defensive self tender for up to 40 percent of their stock, at a 35 percent premium over market price ($17 as opposed to $13). The fine print in the self tender excludes any shareholder who owns 10 or more percent from participating.

204.   Assess for Hoyne's management the likelihood that each, or either defense, will withstand judicial scrutiny (Vader has already announced that its attorneys are preparing to seek a preliminary injunction in the courts).

(A)   The self tender is discriminatory, but the crown jewel option is okay. The selective self tender clearly violates the bedrock corporate law rule that a corporation must treat all shares of the same class equally.

(B)   Both defenses are overreactions and will be struck down as "disproportionate to the threat posed."

(C)   Both defenses will pass muster because their adoption by independent directors after duly informing themselves brings the business judgment rule into play, shielding the defenses from judicial examination.

(D)   The selective self tender is okay, but the granting of the crown jewel option, especially at such a preliminary stage, is "disproportionate to the threat posed" and will be struck down.

Now assume that other bidders come forward. Vader Enterprises makes a formal bid at $17.50 per share. Vale Ski Corp. enters the fray with combined stock and cash offer valued at $19.00 per share. Vader increases its bid to $19.50. Aspen Ski Corp. enters with a bid of $21.00 per share. Vader tops that at $21.50. Hoyne's board of directors rescinds the "crown jewel" option granted to Luke Skywalker, Inc., which seems to disappear to a planet far, far away.

Informally, the Aspen management lets Hoyne's managers and directors know that their $21.00 per share bid is a "first and final offer." Hoyne's directors consult with you. They wish to tender their own shares to Aspen. They also wish to recommend the Aspen bid to their rank-and-file shareholders. Last of all, they wish to grant to Aspen a "leg up" option on approximately 20 percent of Hoyne's authorized, but unissued, common stock. Their reasoning is that Aspen is an experienced ski resort operator who will not make any radical changes in operations or management staffing while Vader is an unknown quantity.

205.   What is your call?

(A)   They may do all three things, no questions asked.

(B)   The sale of their own shares is permissible as is the recommendation, but the leg up option is questionable, as there still seem to be three bidders for the company.

(C) The sale is permissible, but as to the other actions at this point "[t]he directors' role has changed from defenders of the corporate bastion to auctioneers charged with getting the best price for the stockholders at a sale of the company."

(D) None of the actions is permissible.

Now assume that Luke Skywalker, Inc. ("LSI") did not disappear to a planet far, far away. Instead, LSI has been on the scene for a number of months. Hoyne and LSI have worked out a merger in which each of the two companies will have six directors on a twelve-director board. The office of CEO will first go to Hoyne's current CEO, but after four years will rotate to the much younger LSI CEO.

The plan of merger the two companies have developed also devotes significant resources to preserving the two companies' cultures. Both companies specialize in operating ski resorts that cater to children and families. Both have a philosophy of "groomed and gradual" for maintenance of their ski runs rather than the "steep and deep" philosophy of Aspen, Vale and Vader, all of whom cater to the jet set and the beautiful people.

The merger agreement also has several "deal protection" measures. It has a "no shop" clause that prohibits Hoyne or its directors from soliciting another bidder. It also has a "no talk" provision that, similarly, prohibits furnishing any non-public information to any potential bidder. There is a termination, or "goodbye fee," provision under which Hoyne must pay to LSI $40 million (approximately 5 percent of the value of the transaction) if, for any reason, the merger is not consummated.

The LSI bid is valued at $19.50 per share and is in stock. Recall that Aspen has offered $21.00 in cash and Vader $21.50.

206. Don't the Hoyne directors have a *Revlon* duty to conduct an auction?

(A) Yes, they do. Revlon contains no qualification of its command to conduct an auction.

(B) No, in a merger of equals ("MOE"), the parties are free to "just say no" to other bidders, especially when other values, such as preservation of a unique corporate culture, are at stake.

(C) Yes, they have to go for a clearly superior bid, as here, even if they might not have to entertain a marginally better one.

(D) Yes, and by locking in the inferior bid the Hoyne directors have violated their fiduciary duties.

LSI is extremely worried about the presence of other bidders. LSI's CEO, Han Solo, is afraid the deal could fall apart. As originally stated, Hoyne had given LSI a crown jewel option on its Western ski resorts. Han Solo insists that the option be re-instated. He also insists that generous payment terms be added. If the option is exercised, LSI need make only token payments for the first five years, followed by ten years of installment payments. Lastly, on behalf of LSI, Solo re-insists on payment of the $40 million termination fee to LSI by Hoyne if, for any reason, the transaction is not consummated.

Vader then comes in with a new $24.50 bid. Recall that the LSI bid is in stock valued at $19.50.

207. What should the Hoyne directors do?

(A) Stay with LSI. A contract is a contract and should be honored, especially in a merger of equals situation.

(B)   Nothing in a contract can override directors' fiduciary duties. If, in order to comply with what duty requires, they have to breach a contract, so be it. They must be prepared to be held liable for breach of contract.

(C)   The state anti-takeover statute permits directors to accept clearly inferior offers if the offer, and bidder, will, in the judgment of directors, better serve the interests of other corporate constituencies, such as consumers and employees.

(D)   The business judgment rule will protect the Hoyne directors' decision from judicial scrutiny, whatever it is.

You represent North Pittsburgh Systems, Inc. ("NPSI"), a publicly-traded regional telecommunications company that has successfully branched out into provision of Internet service and LAN networks. NPSI is a Pennsylvania corporation. Wild and Wireless, Inc. ("WAW"), a larger company, has made a hostile bid for NPSI's shares at a 50 percent premium over market price. WAW's purchase offer states that it will oust the managers of NPSI, installing new, younger managers at greatly increased salaries. WAW may also cause NPSI to sell some of its wireless assets to WAW. WAW reveals that it has already acquired a 21 percent stake in NPSI.

NPSI's directors oppose this potential drastic change in the company's business methods. They wish to pull out all the stops in defending against this unwanted intrusion into the affairs of their company.

208.   You advise them:

(A)   Under Pennsylvania's takeover statute, having due regard to the interests of employees, customers, suppliers, and so on, as well as those of shareholders, the directors may adopt relatively radical takeover defenses, such as adoption of a poison pill plan.

(B)   That, under Pennsylvania's takeover statute, NPSI may declare that the shares held by WAW have already lost their power to vote.

(C)   Seek an injunction because some of the proposed actions by WAW, if entered into, violate the Pennsylvania takeover statute's business combination provisions.

(D)   Do all of the above, as Pennsylvania's anti-takeover statute combines all three forms of "second generation" state takeover regulations in one "belt and suspenders" rust belt enactment.

PRACTICE FINAL EXAM: QUESTIONS

PRACTICE FINAL EXAM

INSTRUCTIONS: This practice examination consists of 28 questions, 21 of which are multiple choice questions and 7 of which are short answer essay questions. Suggested time for the examination is two hours.

Grant and Joseph are law students at Atlas State University. Early in their first year of law school they each contributed $2,500 to their business venture. With the funds, Grant and Joseph purchased computer hardware (peripherals mostly, such as printers, DVD drives, and so on). Grant and Joseph rent the equipment to their fellow law students. Joseph, however, has run up large bills with Dell and Gateway, ordering new equipment left and right.

209. What advice do you give Grant to rein in Joseph and get the business back on the right track?

    (A) Notify Gateway and Dell that Joseph is no longer authorized to place orders.

    (B) Notify Gateway and Dell and return the merchandise.

    (C) Dissolve their "partnership at will."

    (D) Sue Joseph for breach of fiduciary duty.

The Revised Uniform Partnership Act provides that partners owe no fiduciary duty of care to one another. Under case law prior to the Act, it was a matter of debate whether partners owed each other a duty of care.

210. What are the ramifications if, under the local law in your jurisdiction, no duty of care exists? How would you advise new partners to conduct themselves in relation to the partnership's business?

ANSWER:

Percy Partner opposed the United States's initiation of the war in Iraq. With thousands of others, Percy demonstrated in the streets of New York. Many of the partners in Percy's law firm (Sue, Grabbit & Run) were irritated at Percy's public opposition to the war. In a weekend partners' meeting, a majority of the partners voted to expel Percy from the partnership, in gross violation of Percy's First Amendment rights. Percy is bewildered.

211. Can he win a suit for wrongful expulsion?

    (A) No, the partnership agreement probably has a clause providing for exclusion by majority or supermajority of the partners.

    (B) Yes, any such clause would be void as against public policy if exercised in such a way as to deny a partner her fundamental constitutional rights.

    (C)   Yes, the remaining partners violated their fiduciary duty of loyalty toward Percy.

    (D)   No, such "guillotine" clauses have been upheld in a wide variety of circumstances, as in keeping with the consensual nature of the partnership relationship.

Roger and Randy have had a law firm for over five years. Roger is a successful personal injury attorney who recently had two million-dollar-plus settlements, with several more in the pipeline. Randy handles all of the office practice (wills, forming corporations and LLCs, and so on). Randy also handles administration of the firm, supervising clerical personnel, preparing the tax returns (state and federal), ordering supplies and equipment, and the like.

Roger then leaves the firm, setting up as a sole practitioner. Randy and Roger's partnership agreement provides that the minimum duration of the partnership will be until all of the startup borrowing has been repaid to Bank A ($20,000 remains unpaid).

212. What are two or three claims Randy might pursue against Roger?

ANSWER:

Dora Bay LLC operates a long shoring venture in Ketchikan, Alaska, loading logs and other cargo onto ships bound for Asia. The LLC's operating agreement provides that Dora Bay will be a member-managed LLC. The five members of the LLC never have meetings. They rely on word of mouth, one to another. They also have kept very poor records. A tugboat company is suing the LLC and its members personally for unpaid bills.

213. Should the members be held personally liable?

    (A)   Yes, lack of formalities is a ground for "piercing the veil" and denying members limited liability.

    (B)   No, LLC statutes contemplate informality, which alone should not be grounds for piercing the veil.

    (C)   Yes, because maintenance of books and records is a statutory requirement which the Dora Bay LLC members have violated.

    (D)   Yes, because LLC members have no limited liability if they permit the LLC to engage in ultra hazardous activities such as long shoring.

Stuart, Vijay, and Fred are golf professionals. They propose to develop a championship caliber golf course in Virginia's Shenandoah Valley. They propose to sell 100 memberships for $75,000 each.

214. Would a manager-managed LLC be a good vehicle for their golf course development? Why?

ANSWER:

Twenty partners from Bacon, Lettuce & Tomato ("BLT"), a large Chicago law firm, have split off from BLT. They wish to form a new firm that will specialize in real estate development and commercial litigation. They consult you as to what legal form their new law firm should take.

215. What is your advice?

    (A) Limited Liability Partnership ("LLP").

    (B) Corporation.

    (C) Limited Liability Company ("LLC").

    (D) General Partnership.

Gyro Gearloose has obtained approval for a Dunkin' Donuts franchise. The franchise agreement will have a five-year term. Gyro has also located suitable commercial real estate space in which to locate his franchise. The landlord requires a five-year lease. Gyro's two college friends, Bart and Ernie, will each contribute $20,000 for a collective 49 percent interest in Gyro's new company. You have advised Gyro to wait until you have formed a corporation for him, entering into contracts only on behalf of an existing corporation, but Gyro is impatient. He is set to sign the lease and the franchise agreement on behalf of the corporation to be formed. If he can avoid it, though, Gyro does not wish to be personally liable on the five-year lease and the franchise agreement

216. Your advice to Gyro?

    (A) On both the lease and the franchise agreement, indicate clearly that the corporation does not yet exist ("a corporation to be formed").

    (B) Indicate clearly his representative capacity ("By Gyro Gearloose, Promoter").

    (C) Provide for a substitution of the corporation for Gyro when the corporation does come into existence (a future "novation").

    (D) All of the above.

Country Joe is your client. He tells you that he wishes to form a Delaware corporation for his startup taxidermy business. His non-lawyer friends at Big Sky Country Club have told Joe that Delaware corporations are "the best."

217. Why should Joe, other things being equal, stay at home, having you form a Montana, rather than a "runaway" Delaware, corporation?

ANSWER:

Lumber Company, Inc. ("LC") agreed to supply plumbing supplies to your client, Mitchell Plumbing, at very advantageous prices (15–20 percent below what Mitchell had been paying for supplies). Open market prices for plumbing supplies then rose dramatically. LC refused to furnish the supplies or otherwise honor the contract. Mitchell was forced to "cover" in the open market, paying 20 percent more than it had been paying and 40 percent more than the contract with LC had provided. In the meanwhile, relying on its contract with LC, Mitchell had bid on a number of jobs. Mitchell was the low bidder on all of them. Mitchell has completed the work but has suffered significant losses on each job, all due to the inflated price of plumbing supplies.

Mitchell has sued LC. At the mediation (the State of Wigmore has mandatory pretrial mediation), LC's counsel shows the mediator the LC articles of incorporation. Those articles provide that LC's purpose is limited to "sales of lumber and plywood products." Wigmore is a Model Business Corporation Act jurisdiction.

218. What is your response to the mediator?

   (A) LC will be unjustly enriched if Mitchell is stuck with the losses.

   (B) Lumber and plywood are building products as are plumbing supplies. Hence, LC had implied power to agree to furnish plumbing supplies.

   (C) A statute in Wigmore estops the corporation itself (as opposed to a shareholder) from raising lack of power or capacity in dealings with third parties.

   (D) *Ultra vires* cannot be raised in a case in which one side has partly performed.

Dr. X and Dr. Y invest in an antique sports car collection owned by Sterling Moss. The business plan is to rent the automobiles to movie and television production companies for use in period pieces. Sterling's lawyer is supposed to form a corporation, but goes halibut fishing in Alaska without filing the articles of incorporation she prepared. Meanwhile, Sterling contracted to buy five exceedingly rare Aston-Martin (James Bond) automobiles. The seller has now sued Dr. X, Dr. Y, and Sterling personally for the $500,000 due on the contract of purchase for the Aston-Martins.

219. Assuming a Model Business Corporation Act jurisdiction, how would you defend Dr. X and Dr. Y?

   (A) Invoke the de facto corporation doctrine.

   (B) Argue that Sterling may be liable but Dr. X and Dr. Y are not because they had no knowledge of the failure to form the corporation.

   (C) Argue that Dr. X and Dr. Y are not liable because they never purported to act on behalf of a corporation; only Sterling did.

   (D) There is no defense. Either a corporation exists for all purposes ("de jure") or it does not exist. It is an "either or" proposition. Try to settle the case.

Five middle class couples are opening a French café. They plan to serve baked goods, sandwiches, good coffees, and the like in the suburb where they live. If the business goes well, in three to four years they may open a second cafe in an adjoining suburb. They have no plans beyond that. They purchase their products (croissants, pan du chocolat, and so on) from a bakery in downtown New Orleans. Each couple has agreed that it will contribute $10,000 to the corporation, Marche Francais, which will conduct the business. The funds will be used to purchase equipment, furnishings and fixtures and for working capital.

220. What is the best capital structure for Marche Francais, Inc.?

   (A) All common stock, in equal proportions to each couple's capital contribution.

   (B) A small amount of common stock, along with convertible cumulative preferred shares to each participating couple.

(C) Common stock to each and a loan by each, say, $4,000 in stock and a $6,000 promissory note from the corporation to each couple.

(D) Common stock to each couple, and authorize cumulative preferred in the articles of incorporation so as to be able to fund any future expansion.

Bill, Pauline, and Steve are shareholders (1/3, 1/3, 1/3) of a computer software company, Pear, Inc. Pear has been quite successful in selling its products. Pear has $100,000 in cash but $300,000 in accounts payable. Pear also has $1,000,000 in accounts receivable, none of which are "stale." Pear's other assets and liabilities are negligible, at least on the balance sheet. Pauline and Steve have made offers on new houses that have been accepted. They wish to have the corporation declare a dividend of $200,000 each, $600,000 in all, to help them make the down payments on their new homes.

A prospective venture capital investor requests that Bill, Pauline, and Steve obtain a letter of opinion from their counsel (you) that the distribution (dividend) is legal. Pear is incorporated in a Model Business Corporation Act jurisdiction that has a "double insolvency test" for distributions to shareholders.

221. What advice do you give to the Pear shareholders and why?

(A) Do not pay the dividend because doing so will cause an "impairment of capital."

(B) The dividend cannot be paid because, giving effect to the payment, Pear will be insolvent in the equity sense (not able to pay its debts as they become due), but not in the balance sheet sense (assets exceed liabilities).

(C) The dividend cannot be paid because, giving effect to the payment, Pear will be insolvent in the balance sheet sense but not in the equity sense.

(D) Wait. Once Pear has collected $800,000 or more of the accounts receivable the dividend can be paid.

Drs. Ward, Mulligan, Tice, and Eddy (1/4, 1/4, 1/4, 1/4) form a professional service corporation in which each invests $750,000 in order to purchase state-of-the-art diagnostic equipment. It is absolutely essential to them that they have the ability to preserve their proportionate ownership interests. They therefore wish to limit the ability of a majority to issue additional shares, which would have the effect of diluting any shareholder's interest in the corporation.

222. What steps would you take to accomplish this objective for them?

(A) Draft a share transfer restriction (buy-sell) agreement.

(B) Draft a share transfer restriction (buy-sell) agreement and insure that preemptive rights exist to govern issuances by the corporation.

(C) Opt into the preemptive rights provision of the Model Business Corporation Act alone.

(D) Draft a share transfer restriction (buy-sell) agreement, insure that preemptive rights exist to govern issuances by the corporation and in the articles of incorporation negate common law exceptions to preemptive rights.

Activist shareholders in Northern Pines, Inc., a publicly-held corporation with approximately 900 shareholders, wish to force the corporation to cease the practice known as "clear cutting" on Northern Pines lands and further to present to the shareholders for approval a "forestry stewardship plan." One central ingredient of such a plan would be to provide for selective harvest of trees rather than clear cutting.

223. Which of the following represents a cost-effective alternative for the activist shareholders to achieve one or more of their goals?

(A) Filing suit against Northern Pines's directors seeking an injunction to stop the practices.

(B) Enlisting the support of 20 or so institutional investors who own 40 percent of Northern Pines's common shares.

(C) Filing an SEC Rule 14a-8 proposal requesting that the directors propose an amendment to the articles of incorporation prohibiting clear cutting and requiring periodic forestry stewardship plans.

(D) Waging a proxy contest, seeking votes to remove the incumbent directors and replacing them with a slate of activist shareholders and others who oppose clear cutting.

You represent a publicly-held company, Sovereign Semiconductor, Inc., whose senior executives feel that the corporation may be vulnerable to a hostile takeover bid. The corporation's eight directors are elected annually.

224. What "shark repellent" package (three or four elements) comes to mind? What steps need to be taken to implement it?

ANSWER:

Partridge Orchards, Inc. is a very successful food products company, producing fruits, jellies, jams, and juices that it markets to supermarkets up and down the East Coast of the U.S. The six siblings who inherited shares as members of the Partridge family (which controls 50 percent of the corporation) are young and cannot get along regarding determination of corporate policy or who should be on the board. They fight all of the time. When they can agree to have meetings to discuss corporate affairs, which is seldom, they are at each others' throats within five minutes.

225. What is a potential solution to this closely-held corporate governance predicament?

(A) Draft 5- or 10-year irrevocable proxies running to the eldest sibling, Paulette, who is 23 years of age.

(B) Implement a voting trust arrangement with the trusted family business adviser as trustee.

(C) Have the six siblings enter into a shareholders' voting (pooling) agreement under which all six agree to vote as a majority of them (four) may agree.

(D) Have the six siblings enter into a shareholders' voting (pooling) agreement under which, failing to agree unanimously, they appoint the trusted family business adviser to vote their shares.

As a director of XYZ Co., Bruce Lee used his own share ownership (16%) and cumulative voting to elect himself to one of seven director positions on the board of directors. Thereafter, Lee has sexually harassed various female employees of the company and kick boxed two of his fellow directors to oblivion. You are counsel to XYZ. Shareholders, directors, and senior managers have all insisted that "Lee must go."

226. How do you get rid of him?

   (A) Convene a special shareholders' meeting to remove him as a director by majority vote, with or without cause.

   (B) Go to court, alleging that he has grossly abused his position and that his removal would be "in the best interests" of the corporation.

   (C) Democracy is democracy. You have to live with it.

   (D) Allege cause (probably required by articles or bylaws), convene a special shareholders' meeting, and remove him as a director by majority vote.

227. In shortened form, list five elements of the business judgment rule "safe harbor" for directors and senior executives.

ANSWER:

Sam and Dave's, Inc., a clothing manufacturing company whose principal offices and manufacturing facility are in South Florida, lost money by investing significant sums in Sam's cousin's nightclub in Michigan and then failing to monitor the club's (lack of) progress. Two shareholders, Lamont and Grady, who each own 10 percent of the shares, are implacable in their anger over the losses due to the ill-fated nightclub diversification. Sam asks if it can be fixed at the annual shareholders' meeting in two weeks.

228. Can Sam and Dave obtain protection by a favorable shareholder vote?

   (A) No, "waste" or a gift of corporate assets is not ratifiable.

   (B) Yes, just include a standard resolution ratifying all acts of the past year.

   (C) Yes, if specific disclosure is made concerning the investment and the ensuing losses and a majority of the shareholders approve.

   (D) No. Fiduciary duty (the duties of care and loyalty) are duties that are owed to each and every shareholder. A breach of those duties may only be ratified by a unanimous shareholder vote.

Sybil, the wealthy mother of your law school classmate Sylvia, wishes to join the board of Old Squirrel Savings and Loan, an Ohio-based publicly-held regional thrift institution. Old Squirrel has had a history of bad investments (loans). Old Squirrel's directors have been sued for breach of the fiduciary duty of care in the past. Now, however, Old Squirrel seems mostly, but not completely, out of the woods. The derivative suits various shareholders have filed have all been settled or otherwise disposed of.

Sylvia has sought to dissuade her mother from joining the Old Squirrel board of directors. Alternatively, Sylvia has urged her mother to delay so that the picture can clarify even more. Sybil, however, is insistent. She feels this is her window of opportunity. On her mother's behalf, Sylvia seeks your advice on how Sybil may best be able to protect herself and her assets, which are considerable.

229. What advice do you give Sylvia regarding Sybil?

(A) Purchase a significant amount of stock in Old Squirrel so that you have a say in removing (or not slating for re-election) under-performing directors.

(B) Do not join the board unless Old Squirrel has Directors and Officers' ("D & O") liability insurance.

(C) Negotiate a contract with Old Squirrel on Sybil's behalf with multiple protections (*e.g.*, indemnification, insurance, other funding sources for indemnification, exculpatory charter provisions) that will protect Sybil regardless of a change of control, falling out, or subsequent charter amendments.

(D) Review carefully the Ohio corporate law indemnification provisions and determine whether the corporation has implemented them. Insist on implementation if the authority to indemnify granted by the statute has not been fully, or largely, implemented.

The senior executives of PSC, Inc. have noticed that, in recent weeks, the average daily trading volume in PSC shares (traded NASDAQ) has tripled. After learning, by way of an SEC Schedule 13D filing, that Hannibal Lector has acquired over 12 percent of PSC's shares, PSC's senior executives propose to give an option to purchase the new PSC Portland, Oregon new state-of-the-art manufacturing facility to a friendly "white squire" investor, Norm Rice. Rice, a wealthy Seattle investor, already owns 15 percent of PSC's shares.

230. What should the PSC directors do before approving (or not approving) management's proposed "crown jewel option" defense strategy?

(A) Nothing, other than insure that the business judgment rule safe harbor protects them and any decision they may make.

(B) Conduct an investigation to determine if a credible threat exists to PSC's means of doing business.

(C) Conduct an investigation, as in Answer (B), and also insure that the defense is proportionate to the threat posed.

(D) Conduct an investigation and adopt an irreversible poison pill takeover defense.

In the previous Question, PSC's directors panic. Many of them have valuable consulting contracts with PSC that they will lose, along with the perks and pay from their director status, if a change of control occurs. In a tumultuous two-hour meeting, PSC's directors adopt a drastic (although not irreversible) poison pill defense.

In response, Lector publicly disavows the takeover plans he had announced earlier. The price of PSC shares, which had climbed on the prospect of a possible takeover, drops. Lector also silently sells the shares he has already acquired, pushing the PSC share price down further. Shareholder D. Vader files a suit against PSC and its directors, alleging breaches of the duty of care and loyalty. You are the litigator hired to defend the directors.

231. What should be your early responses to the suit?

(A) Recommend expansion of the PSC board of directors and creation of a special litigation committee ("SLC"). Request an adjournment of the court proceeding while the SLC investigates Vader's allegations.

(B) Same as Answer (A) and also hire reputable independent counsel (who has done no work for the corporation or its directors in the past) to represent the SLC.

(C) Let the suit proceed, filing a motion for summary judgment on business judgment rule grounds after the facts have been developed through discovery.

(D) File a motion to dismiss on grounds that demand was required and has not been made.

The Zook brothers, Zach and Jack, own movie theater properties across the state of South Carolina. For tax reasons, the brothers hold the real property 50-50 through a series of limited partnerships. When the father and family patriarch died, he left shares in the operating company, Silver Screens, Inc., 51 percent to the younger and more educated Zach and 49 percent to the older and less educated Jack.

Immediately thereafter, Zach began recommending, and the board of directors approved, a series of substantial salary increases for Zach, the CEO. Jack got only small raises. Zach upgraded his company car to a Mercedes sedan, while Jack continued with a two-year-old Chevrolet. Zach frequently forgot to give Jack notice of board and other meetings. At the meetings Jack did attend, Zach frequently shouted Jack down, or told him he was "out of order" and to "keep his mouth shut." When Jack protested to other board members, he was moved to a small office at the end of the hallway, adjacent to the door leading to the garbage dumpsters.

232. It has been three-and-one-half years since the father died. Nothing Jack has tried seems to work. He has become completely isolated from Silver Screens, his brother Zach, and other managers and board members. He wants to take action. What might it be?

(A) File suit for dissolution of the corporation on grounds that Jack has been "oppressed," in that the action of the majority shareholder and the corporation have been "highly prejudicial" to Jack.

(B) Same as Answer (A) but allege that the actions of Zach and the board have been "unduly harsh and burdensome."

(C) File a suit in the name of the corporation, alleging that the increased salary and perks Zach has received result from a breach of fiduciary duty and should be paid back to the corporation.

(D) Allege only that, as a substantial minority shareholder in Silver Screens, Jack has been denied his reasonable expectations, and is therefore oppressed and entitled to the involuntary dissolution remedy.

Weird Wireless, Inc., a publicly-held telecommunications company operating throughout the Western United States, has had to restate its earnings for the past two years. Many items that should have been listed as expenses were falsely recorded as "capital expenditures," to be deducted over five years rather than one year.

Since the earnings restatements, Weird Wireless shares have dropped 80 percent. You are the U.S. Attorney and you are conferring with the SEC lawyers assigned to the case. Weird Al, the company founder, and his brother, Weird Hal, reaped $200 million in stock option profits in the six months before bankruptcy. This is the second wireless company the Weird brothers have run into the ground.

233. What relief would you seek?

    (A) A constructive trust on their stock option profits in favor of the company.

    (B) Forfeiture of compensation (salary and bonuses) received for the period during which they were in breach of their fiduciary duties.

    (C) Forfeiture of incentive based compensation such as their $200 million in stock option profits.

    (D) Same as Answer (C) plus a lifetime or similar bar against the Weird brothers ever serving as officers or directors of another publicly-held company.

Martha is a television celebrity, known as a home decorating and lifestyle guru. She is a weekend house guest at the home of Peter Finch, the fabled stock picker. While going through the linen drawer in the Finch kitchen, Martha finds a list of stocks labeled "Magellan — recommended purchases." That night she needlepoints the ticker symbols of the stocks (15 in all) onto a pillow case which she takes back to NYC with her. She buys all 15 stocks, 14 of which turn out to be big winners. Her profits exceed $15 million.

234. In what capacity can Martha be prosecuted in federal court?

    (A) Insider, or temporary insider.

    (B) Tippee.

    (C) None. She may be a thief but she is a clever thief.

    (D) Misappropriator.

Cynthia's brother Mike runs the family business back in the Midwest (Detroit, to be exact). The business, Standard Detroit Gear, Inc., supplies parts to the automobile industry. It provides a comfortable, if not affluent, living to Mike and his family.

Cynthia lives on the West Coast. Each sibling (Cynthia and Mike) owns 37.12 percent of the company. Mike has a nice salary, company car, NBA basketball and NFL football season tickets, health insurance, and other perks. He refuses to have the company pay dividends. This has gone on for 12 years now. The shares in the company are the principal inheritance Cynthia received when her father died. She is willing to go to court to get comparable benefits. She and Mike speak to one another, but, recently, their relationship has become strained over this issue.

235. What cause of action might work?

    (A) A derivative suit against Mike for breach of fiduciary duty.

    (B) A direct suit for breach of fiduciary duty owed her by her brother and by the corporation to her as a shareholder in a closely-held corporation.

    (C) A securities fraud lawsuit in federal court.

(D) A suit for involuntary dissolution of the corporation on grounds of oppression ("denial of reasonable expectations").

236. What exactly is a "double derivative suit" and what is a possible objection to be made to the shareholder who seeks to file one?

ANSWER:

ANSWERS

1. **Answer (D) is the best answer.** Formation of a partnership, defined as "an association of two or more persons to carry on as co-owners a business for profit," UPA § 6, used to send lawyers and courts scurrying off in search of evidence pointing to intent. The 1997 Revised Act, § 202, adds "an association . . . whether or not the parties intend to form a partnership." So in many cases we examine all the facts and circumstances to determine whether a partnership was formed. For example, one court delineated eight factors a court must weigh in determining if a partnerships exists: (1) the right and duty to participate in management; (2) the right and duty to act as agent for the other owners; (3) unlimited exposure to liability; (4) participation in profits and in losses; (5) contribution (investment) in the firm; (6) ownership stake in the firm's property; (7) voting rights; and (8) form which compensation takes. *Serapion v. Martinez*, 119 F.3d 982 (1st Cir. 1997).

    Answer (A) is incorrect. Under the RUPA, lack of intention is no longer dispositive. The parties may have intended nothing in particular (they didn't think about it) but a partnership results. Nonetheless, if an agreement can be shown (written, oral, or oral sealed by a handshake), that evidence may be a clincher for the parties who desire to show that a partnership (at will) exists. Similarly, a partnership involves an arrangement to share profits, but an arrangement also to share losses may be a clincher for the party seeking to demonstrate the existence of a partnership.

    Answer (B) is incorrect. Even financial benefits determined by taking a percentage of profits may nonetheless be wages. Don't jump too fast to a conclusion that a partnership exists. Co-ownership, a husband-and-wife relationship, or a family farm or business do not necessarily imply a partnership.

    Answer (C) is incorrect. Partnership contributions will usually (not always) be in round amounts. The dollars and cents amounts of Dooley's and Flower's purchases tends to show that they were independent contractors purchasing their own equipment. At most they were employees required to purchase their own equipment. They probably were not partners although, again, standing alone this fact would not be dispositive.

    Note: The Uniform Partnership Act (1914) (UPA) has been superseded by the Revised Uniform Partnership Act (1997) (RUPA). The UPA, however, remains on the books in 10 or so jurisdictions. In nearly 40 jurisdictions, plus the District of Columbia, bar association committees have reviewed the RUPA and recommended that legislatures adopt it, which they have done.

2. It appears that Sam, Charlene, and Dave have formed a partnership. More precisely, they have formed a partnership at will. No writing is necessary for the formation of a partnership. All that is necessary for formation of a partnership is "an association of two or more persons to carry on as co-owners a business for profit." UPA § 6; RUPA § 202(a). It may be that Dave's status is that of a lender to the business, or both lender and partner. UPA § 7 provides that "[t]he receipt by a person of a share of profits of a business is prima

facie evidence that he [she] is a partner in the business, but no such inference shall be drawn if such profits were received in payment . . . as interest on a loan, though the amount of payment may vary with the profits of the business." RUPA § 202(3)(i) provides the same. Because the parties are in my office, the easy solution is to ask them what they intend Dave's status to be. They may not have thought about the issue, but it appears that a good solution might be to structure part of Dave's contribution as partner's equity and part as a loan to the partnership.

3.   I would draft a partnership agreement for them. I may also have to draft a promissory note from the partnership to Dave if the parties decide that all, or a portion, of Dave's contribution is to be structured as a loan. Three salient features of the agreement would be how the partners are to divide the profits, how the partners are to share the losses (if any), and what the duties and responsibilities of each partner will be (for example, who maintains the warehouse and inventory, who will have what sales territory, how much time is to be devoted to sales, who keeps the partnership books, etc.). If no one drafts a partnership agreement, the UPA, or RUPA, supplies a series of default rules. One way to view a partnership statute is as an "off the rack" contract that governs the partners' relationships unless they provide otherwise. If the parties do draft a partnership agreement, albeit one that is less than comprehensive, the UPA, or RUPA, functions as a "gap filler," supplying terms and provisions that are missing in the agreement.

4.   If they do not draft a partnership agreement they are partners at will. The consequences are that they will split the profits equally. Upon dissolution, "[e]ach partner shall be repaid his [her] contributions whether by way of capital or advances to the partnership property and share equally in the profits and surplus remaining after all liabilities . . . ." UPA § 18(a); RUPA § 401(b). So in the event of dissolution, at least if there is a surplus, Dave's disproportionate contribution will be protected.

It is the event of losses for which parties tend not to provide and which may cause difficulties in a partnership at will situation. A number of courts have held that in the event of a dissolution in a partnership consisting of partner who has contributed primarily capital (Dave) and partners who have contributed primarily services (Sam and Charlene), when there are losses neither party is entitled to a contribution from the other. The reasoning is that "where one party contributes money and the other labor, then in the event of loss each would lose his own capital — the one his money and the other his labor." *Kovacik v. Reed,* 315 P.2d 314 (Cal. 1957). A number of jurisdictions follow this rule. *See, e.g., Becker v. Killarney,* 532 N.E.2d 931 (Ill. App. Ct. 1988); *Snellbaker v. Herrmann,* 462 A.2d 713 (Pa. Super. Ct. 1983). This is not good for Dave, so the parties should probably draft around this counterintuitive rule, providing that Sam and Charlene in some fashion make monetary contributions in the event of losses.

5.   **Answer (D) is the best answer.** A joint venture is the association of two or more persons or entities in business for a limited purpose, and normally involves a less than total merging of the business interests and assets of the venturers. That has happened here, so **Answer (B) is a correct answer, though not the *best* answer.**

Another possibility (remote in this case) is tenants in common. Merely purchasing or leasing a piece of property together results neither in a partnership nor in a joint venture. The parties are co-owners (tenants in common) even if the parties to the arrangement perform other acts consistent with co-ownership of an investment, such as paying taxes or obtaining insurance. If they do more, such as remodel the premises, or subdivide the property, then they may well have become partners rather than tenants in common.

Back to joint venture, strictly speaking, a joint venture is not a form of business organization itself. It must assume a form. For example, if two large forest products companies jointly build, say, a paper mill costing hundreds of millions of dollars, they may form a corporation, with joint control of the board of directors, or, today, a limited liability company (LLC). The corporation or LLC would hold title to and operate the paper mill.

If, however, the co-venturers (Liam and Clare) take no affirmative steps to form a business organization such as a corporation or an LLC, their joint venture will be a partnership at will ("an association of two or more persons to carry on as co-owners a business for profit," UPA § 6(1); RUPA § 202(a)). Thus, **Answer (A) is a correct answer, but not the best answer. The best answer is Answer (D) (both Answers (A) and (B)).**

The scope of each co-venturers' authority to bind the enterprise will be limited by the scope of the venture. In *Matanuska Valley Bank v. Arnold*, 223 F.2d 778 (9th Cir. 1955), Arnold supplied money and borrowed from the bank, and Davis acted as contractor in building a house. Unbeknownst to Arnold, Davis went to the bank, borrowing more money, ostensibly to build another house, but using the money for personal purposes. When the bank sought to hold Ms. Arnold liable, the court refused to hold Ms. Arnold responsible, even though under general partnership law "[e]very partner is the agent of the partnership for the purpose of its business, and the act of every partner . . . for apparently carrying on in the usual way the business of the partnership of which he is a member binds the partnership." UPA § 9(1). RUPA § 301(1) is similar: "Every partner is the agent of the partnership for the purpose of its business."

Davis, as a joint venturer, did not have the general implied authority of a partner in an ordinary trading or commercial partnership. His authority was limited to the scope of the venture, that is, building one house. **Answer (C) is incorrect**, as Liam and Clare have taken none of the formal steps, such as filing with a state official, to form a limited liability company.

6. Sam and Charlene can just give Dave notice that they are dissolving the partnership. Dissolution "is the change in the relation of the partners caused by any partner ceasing to be associated in the carrying on . . . of the business." UPA § 29. In the absence of an agreement to the contrary, dissolution is caused "by the express will of any partner." UPA § 31; RUPA § 801(1). So they should check the terms of the partnership agreement, if any. If the partnership agreement is silent, or there is no partnership agreement, Sam and Charlene may dissolve it by simple notice to Dave, to be followed by a "winding up" of the partnership affairs.

7. Sam and Charlene may or may not have legal rights against Dave for his absences, failure to supervise, and the resulting losses. One theory may be that in his failure to supervise storage of the inventory Dave has breached the fiduciary *duty of care* he owes to his partners, Sam and Charlene. A number of courts hold, however, that a partner truly is his or her "brother's keeper," in finding that partners do not owe a fiduciary duty of care (as compared to a *duty of loyalty*) one to another. A leading case is *Ferguson v. Williams*, 670 S.W.2d 327, 331 (Tex. App. 1984) ("[W]e hold as a matter of law that negligence in the management of the affairs of a general partnership or joint venture does not create any right of action against that partner by other members of the partnership."). Cases following this rule include *Duffy v. Piazza Construction, Inc.*, 815 P.2d 267 (Wash. Ct. App. 1991), and *Johnson v. Weber*, 803 P.2d 939 (Ariz. Ct. App. 1990). RUPA § 404(c) (1993) expressly adopts this position: "A partner's duty of care to the partnership and the other partners . . . is limited to refraining from or engaging in grossly negligent or reckless conduct, intentional misconduct, or a knowing violation of law." *See also* Larry Ribstein, *A Mid-Term Assessment of the Project to Revise the Uniform Partnership Act*, 46 Bus. Law. 111, 140 (1990). Sam and Charlene may be out of luck — under one view of partnership law, they should have been stopping in at the Central City facility periodically in order to assure themselves that Dave was managing things properly.

    However, under the UPA, contrary authority exists that general partners do owe each other a limited duty of care. *See, e.g., Roper v. Thomas*, 298 S.E.2d 424 (N.C. Ct. App. 1982); *Wyler v. Feuer*, 149 Cal. Rptr. 626 (Ct. App. 1978); *Boxer v. Husky Oil Co.*, 1983 Del. Ch. LEXIS 436 (June 28, 1983); *Shinn v. Thrust IV, Inc.*, 786 P.2d 285 (Wash. Ct. App. 1990).

8. **Answer (B) is the best answer.** This question deals with the other principal prong of fiduciary duty, the duty of loyalty, and is based upon one of the most famous and oft-cited duty of loyalty cases, *Meinhard v. Salmon*, 164 N.E. 545 (N.Y. 1928) (Cardozo, J.).

    Answer (A) is incorrect. The duty of loyalty, which deals with self-dealing and other forms of venial behavior, requires that a partner or other fiduciary, such as a corporate officer or director, must in every instance act in the best interests of the partnership or corporation, rather than in their own best interests, or those of family, friends, or affiliates (principally other businesses in which they have an interest). When those interests conflict with the interests of the partnership ("conflict of interest"), the partner must serve the partnership's best interests or, at a minimum, make full disclosure and leave decisions on the matter to a decision maker who has no interest in the matter ("disinterested" partners or "disinterested" directors). A difference in partnership is that duties run not only to the entity, as with a corporation, but to every other partner.

Answer (D) is incorrect because a judge would be unlikely to find a narrow scope for the venture, thereby exonerating Jennifer. Jennifer breached her duty of loyalty by "usurpation" or "diversion" (the words are used interchangeably) of a partnership opportunity. An issue of fact may exist as to what exactly was the scope of the original partnership. In such cases, however, the tendency of most judges (as factfinders) would be to err on the side of being over inclusive. Partnership is a consensual and often somewhat intimate relationship. Judges state that partners owe each other a duty "of the utmost good faith and loyalty." Judge Cardozo stated the duty as one of "the finest loyalty" which requires not merely "honesty alone but the punctilio of an honor the most sensitive."

When a chancellor finds a fiduciary to have violated her duty of loyalty, the remedies are extreme. Note that, unlike the duty of care, which requires that the partnership or corporation have been damaged, under the duty of loyalty either damage to the entity or illicit gain to the fiduciary is sufficient. This is because loyalty in the fiduciary, and not mere prevention of harm to the entity, is the aim for which the law strives.

Answer (C) is incorrect. A feckless fiduciary may be denied compensation, or be ordered to disgorge compensation, for the period of time for which she was found to have been in violation of her duty. The plaintiff partner or partnership may ask for the classical equitable remedy of an accounting in which the wrongdoer must reconstruct for the court, or for a receiver or master appointed by the court, all of what occurred during the violation period (receipts, expenses, taxes paid, etc.). Last of all, the court may place a constructive trust on the wrongdoer's illicit gain and the fruits thereof. A constructive trust is akin to a cowboy's lasso. With it, the court ropes and pulls back to the original partnership all of the subsequent venture, "lock, stock, and barrel." Most courts will not place a trust or lien only upon the portion of the gain attributable to the opportunity, as opposed to the breaching fiduciary's skills (as suggested in Answer (C)).

Postscript: RUPA § 404(b) attempts to limit the application of rigorous common law duty of loyalty to three subduties:

(1)   To refrain from acting for an adverse party;

(2)   "[T]o account to the partnership . . . for any property, profit, or benefit derived by the partner in the conduct and winding up of the partnership business or derived from a use . . . of the partnership property, including the appropriation of a partnership opportunity"; and

(3)   "[T]o refrain from competing with the partnership."

California adopted RUPA but rephrased section 404 to state that "the duty of loyalty includes these duties." In *Enea v. Superior Court*, 132 Cal. App. 4th 1559 (2005), a case in which a partner leased partnership property to himself at less than fair price, the court found that as modified in California, RUPA § 404 contained a "comprehensive but not exhaustive list" of the duties a partner owes to the partnership.

9.   **Answer (D) is the best answer.** "Every partner is an agent of the partnership for the purpose of its business, and the act of every partner . . . for apparently carrying on in the usual way the business of the partnership of which he is a member binds the partnership." UPA § 9(1); RUPA § 301. Ordering luxury automobiles cannot, however, be said to be carrying on in the usual way the business of a law partnership. A rank-and-file partner would not have the power to bind Wycoff and Van Duzer.

With offices and titles, such as managing partner in a partnership context, or president, CEO, executive vice-president, COO, treasurer, CFO, or even purchasing agent, etc., in a corporate context, may come a form of "super agency," of sorts. The source of that authority is "inherent authority" (incidental authority, inferred authority, ostensible authority), which may be defined as the authority possessed by similar agents, with similar titles, and in similar types of businesses. Look to the left, look to the right, see what similar agents in similar corporations actually do. Treasurers sign checks. Purchasing agents purchase automobiles.

Purchasing agents, or here, managing partners of medium-sized law firms, do not order luxury automobiles, and in great numbers, to boot. Even if the transaction proposed were arguably in the realm of the managing partner's or other official's inherent authority, before the fact, in a transaction of any size, no reasonable business lawyer would rely on inherent authority. Inherent authority is more suited to smaller or routine transactions or, after the fact, for argument in arbitration or court proceedings that the other party to a contract is bound. Thus, **Answer (A) is not a good answer.**

Another maxim of agency, though, is that "the best evidence of an agent's authority may be her usual occupation." If an agent does not have inherent authority by virtue of the title or office she holds, she may have very similar authority through having done the same or similar transactions in the past. This source of authority is called "implied actual authority." Again, though, as with inherent authority, implied actual authority is more suited to smaller or routine transactions or, after the fact, for argument in arbitration or court proceedings. Thus, **Answer (B) is not a good answer.**

It is often said that, with implied actual authority, one looks to the acts of the agent. With apparent authority, which is somewhat similar, one looks to the acts of the principal. If the principal has created in third parties a reasonable apprehension that the agent has the authority to enter into the transaction, the principal will be bound because the agent is clothed with apparent authority. The principal could do so by provision to the agent of office, stationery, title, and so on, or by permitting the agent to engage in similar acts in the past and not rescinding them or otherwise objecting. In many cases in which implied actual or inherent authority is present, apparent authority also is present. But, yet again, no transactional lawyer is going to advise a client to enter into a major transaction based upon apparent authority of a managing partner. Thus, **Answer (C) is not a correct answer.**

What a lawyer will advise a client to obtain is "express actual" authority that the agent for the counterparty has the authority to bind the entity (the partnership, the corporation, the LLC) for which he is acting. A provision in the partnership agreement (or articles or bylaws in the corporate setting) may contain a broad grant of authority to the agent. More probably, the lawyer will request a resolution from a partnership or board meeting authorizing the partner or corporate official to carry out the transaction.

Here, you should request evidence that a majority of partners at Wycoff & Van Duzer approved not only the purchase of the automobiles, but the price and other terms of the transaction as well. The terms, the concepts behind them, and their use — express actual authority, implied actual authority, inherent authority, and apparent authority — are not confined to partnership law, but run through all the law of business organizations and the law of agency as well. You should fix in your mind each type of authority agents may possess and a working definition of it.

10.   **Answer (A) is the best answer.** A Ponzi scheme is a prevalent species of fraud. The scheme's promoter promises and pays high rates of return by using funds contributed later (as principal) to pay interest on funds contributed earlier, which have been spent for personal expenses or otherwise squandered. Eventually the scheme collapses when the promoter is unable to attract new investors. The form of fraud takes its name from Carlo Ponzi, an Italian immigrant in Boston who promised and paid high rates of interest to other immigrants early in the 20th century.

In a famous case with the same facts, *Rouse v. Pollard*, 21 A.2d 801 (N.J. 1941), the New Jersey Supreme Court upheld allowing the testimony prominent law firm members gave that lawyers did not invest client funds. The plaintiff failed in her attempt to recoup her losses from the wrongdoer's law firm and partners. Since that time, however, the cases have gone the opposite way.

UPA § 14 now provides that: "The partnership is bound to make good the loss (a) [w]here one partner acting within the scope of his apparent authority receives money or property of a third person and misapplies it." Several cases have held that it is the reasonable expectation of the public as to a particular calling (law, accounting, etc.) that determines what the business of a partnership is and what is "carrying on in the usual way the business of the partnership." *See, e.g., Roach v. Mead*, 722 P.2d 1229 (Or. 1986) (lawyer misapplied client funds — partnership liable); *Croisant v. Watrud*, 432 P.2d 799 (Or. 1967) (accountant wrongfully released funds to client's former husband — partnership liable).

RUPA § 305 makes it somewhat clearer: "If, in the course of the partnership's business or while acting with authority of the partnership, a partner receives or causes the partnership to receive money or property of a person not a partner, and the money is misapplied by a partner, the partnership is liable for the loss."

Answer (B) is incorrect. There simply is no evidence that Norma was "contributorily negligent."

Answers (C) and (D) are incorrect. The judge should bar the testimony of the bar association president and other leading members of the bar as irrelevant.

11.   **Answer (D) is the best answer.** Joseph must be prepared to dissolve the partnership

because there is no effective way to restrict Larry's authority and have that restriction bind third parties. As with the absence of a duty of care among partners, this outcome, too, lends support for the proposition that in a small partnership a partner truly is her brother's (sister's) keeper. This Question is based on *Covalt v. High*, 675 P.2d 999 (N.M. Ct. App. 1983), and *National Biscuit Co. v. Stroud*, 106 S.E.2d 692 (N.C. 1959).

Answers (A) and (B) are incorrect. To restrict a partner's authority requires a vote by a majority of the partners. UPA § 18(h) ("Any difference arising as to ordinary matters connected with the partnership business may be decided by a majority of the partners."); RUPA § 401(j) ("A difference arising as to a matter in the ordinary course of business of partnership may be decided by a majority of the partners."). In a two-person partnership, a majority is 50 percent plus one. If Larry refuses to cooperate, there is no way in which Joseph can vote to restrict Larry's authority. Were Joseph able to do so, he could then inform creditors of valid partnership action restricting the authority of one of the partners under UPA § 9(1) or RUPA § 304 ("Statement of Denial").

Answer (C) is incorrect. Joseph cannot associate a new partner. That action requires unanimous consent by the partners. UPA § 18(g) ("No person can become a member of a partnership without the consent of all the partners."); RUPA § 401(i) ("A person may become a partner only with the consent of all the partners."). Thus, Larry could, by withholding his consent, block any attempt to end run him by expanding the partnership.

12. This is similar to the previous problem but involves claims between two partners rather than trying to restrict a partner's authority to deal with third parties. Summers loses. UPA § 18(e) bestows equal rights in management and conduct of the partnership. The partnership must act for the hire to be enforceable against it. The partnership acts by a majority. A majority of two (50% plus 1) is two. Summers had only one vote (his own).

13. **Answer (B) is the best answer.** Because Ken and Barbie live in California, they do not have to share the losses in the same proportions as they share the profits. *Kovacik v. Reed*, 315 P.2d 314 (Cal. 1957), holds contrary to the UPA/RUPA rule stated below, when one partner is a pure capital contributor and other is a pure talent/labor contributor. "The rationale of this rule . . . is that where one party contributes money and the other contributes service, then in the event of a loss each would lose his own capital — the one his money and the other his labor."

The ordinary rule, at least when all partners are contributing capital (property and/or cash), is "[e]ach partner . . . must contribute towards the losses whether of capital or otherwise, sustained by the partnership according to his share in the profits." UPA § 18(a); *accord* RUPA § 401(b). Thus, Answer (A) would be correct in some states, but because Ken and Barbie reside in California, in Question 13, **Answer (A) is incorrect.**

Answers (C) and (D) are incorrect because, absent agreement, a partner is not entitled to remuneration for services to the partnership.

Several jurisdictions have case law expressly following the rule in *Kovacik v. Reed*. The ramification for the business lawyer is: (1) always discuss with clients how they intend to share losses as well as how they intend to share profits; and (2) memorialize their agreement in the partnership agreement. Unless the parties expressly provide otherwise, at least in the capital versus talent/labor partnership, the somewhat counterintuitive rule of *Kovacik v. Reed* might be applied.

14. Simply apply RUPA § 807 ("Settlement of Accounts Among Partners") or UPA § 40 ("Rules for Distribution"). UPA § 40(b) provides that the partnership's liabilities shall be paid as follows: (1) those owing to creditors, (2) those owing to the partners other than for capital and profits (*e.g.*, advances), (3) those owing to partners in respect of capital, and (4) those owing to partners in respect of profits. So, paying the $30,000 to creditors leaves $770,000 of $800,000 in proceeds; paying the loan or advance to Robert of $20,000 leaves $750,000; returning capital contributions to each partner ($140,000 to Roberta and $10,000 to Robert) leaves $600,000; and, thus, the profits of the partnership venture are $600,000.

How the profits are to be split depends upon the partnership agreement, if there is one, which there may well not be in an informal partnership at will such as this one. Absent agreement, UPA § 18(a) sets out the "default rule" (again, the entire partnership act has very little mandatory content and may be thought of as a series of default rules — the contract that the parties get in default of providing otherwise). The subsection provides:

"Each partner shall be repaid his contributions, whether by way of capital or advances to the partnership property and share equally in the profits and surplus remaining after all the liabilities, including those to the partners, are satisfied." RUPA § 401(b) is similar.

Thus, Robert and Roberta each take $300,000 of the partnership's $600,000 profit. This may be satisfactory to them. Robert put in a lot of labor and the relationship is one of mother and son. He is not entitled to wages. *See* UPA § 18(f) ("No partner is entitled to remuneration for acting in the partnership business, except that a surviving partner is entitled to reasonable compensation for his services in winding up the partnership affairs."); RUPA § 401(h) (same). The equal share of the profits, despite a small capital contribution, may be a "substitute" for wages.

It might be otherwise if the house had been purchased and re-sold relatively quickly. In that case, Roberta might view the rules as resulting in an inequitable wealth transfer to her son. The default provision of UPA § 18(a), or of RUPA § 401(b), thus may be a "penalty default" in any case in which partners' capital contributions are uneven, and significantly so, especially in the case of a dissolution following shortly thereafter. *Ex ante* the "penalty default" then requires any partnership in which contributions are uneven to draft around the rule, providing in their partnership agreement how profits (and losses) will be divided.

15. **Answer (B) is the best answer.** This is an improvement over the UPA which the RUPA introduced. RUPA § 601 lists 10 events of "dissociation" (withdrawal, an event in the agreement, expulsion, expulsion by unanimous vote of the partners, bankruptcy, death, appointment of a guardian or conservator, etc.). RUPA § 801 provides that only some events of dissociation require the partnership to wind up and dissolve. The ordinary consequence, however, is that the firm will continue. The conceptual background for the change is the RUPA recognition of a partnership as an entity in its own right, rather than merely an aggregate of the partners as under the UPA.

Answer (A) is not the best answer. It pertains only where the UPA still is in effect.

Answer (C) is incorrect. Dissociation is wrongful only if the partnership agreement is violated by their dissociation.

Answer (D) is incorrect. Many partnership agreements, particularly for larger or more sophisticated entities, contract around the default rules but this one does not.

16. **Answer (B) is the best answer.** The question asks you to apply partnership rules. UPA § 38(1) provides that "[w]hen dissolution is caused in any way, except in contravention of the partnership agreement, each partner . . . may have the partnership property applied to discharge its liabilities, and the surplus applied to pay in cash the net amount owing to the respective partners." *See also* RUPA § 402 ("A partner has no right to receive, and may not be required to accept, a distribution in kind."). So, if Mike wishes to go to Bora Bora and be a beach bum, he doesn't want a tavern. He wants cash. He could force the sale of the partnership's assets. Thus, **Answers (A), (C), and (D) are not the best answers.**

The statutory rule is really another "penalty" default rule. It forces Pat and Mike to bargain. Pat may decide to keep both taverns, borrowing from the bank to cash Mike out, perhaps in a lump sum, or perhaps in installments. The "fire sale" nature of the UPA § 38 rule gives Pat (and Mike) a strong incentive to reach an agreement.

Some courts have ignored the provision when the equities (and common sense) have been in favor of doing so. In *Nicholes v. Hunt*, 541 P.2d 820 (Or. 1975), one partner contributed an existing business. Just one year later the partners decided to dissolve the partnership. The other partner wanted to force an auction pursuant to UPA § 38. The court declined to do so, ordering an in-kind distribution that left the original proprietor with his original business. *See Nicholes*, 541 P.2d at 828 ("Plaintiff argues that he is entitled to purchase the 50 percent share . . . [but] defendant conceived and designed the machinery and the method of operation, which was successfully operated for a number of years before formation of the partnership at will."). Under this rule, Answers (A) and (D), where each receive a tavern and the other assets are divided equally or sold and the proceeds divided equally, could be correct.

This question and outcome (Answer (B)) are based on *Dreifuerst v. Dreifuerst*, 280 N.W.2d 335 (Wis. Ct. App. 1979) (family partnership which owned two feed mills).

17. **Answer (A) is the best answer.** Partnerships are consensual in nature. A partner's withdrawal, and the ensuing dissolution of the partnership, is wrongful only if it is in contravention of the partnership agreement. The RUPA makes this clear while the UPA does not. RUPA § 602(b) defines "wrongful" as dissolution that is "in breach of an express provision of the partnership agreement." This Question is the "smash and grab" frequently encountered in law and other professions. The stronger partner withdraws in an opportunistic manner, setting up in business alone or with someone else. Short of withdrawal, she uses her relative strength and the threat of withdrawal to extract concessions from her partners. *See generally* Robert Hillman, *Law Firms and Their Partners: The Law and Ethics of Grabbing and Leaving*, 67 Tex. L. Rev. 1 (1988).

     The weaker partner, Ken here, may try to establish that the partners' agreement was for a "definite term or particular undertaking." UPA § 31(1)(a); RUPA § 602(b)(2). There are cases finding that partners who intended to continue the partnership for a term were required to allow the partnership to earn sufficient funds to accomplish the objective understood by all the partners. A common objective may be to pay off startup expenses. Barbie's withdrawal prior to that time would be wrongful. The trouble is that Ken has no evidence that the partners joined together for a "definite term or particular undertaking." Thus, **Answer (B) is not the best answer.**

     Courts may insert fiduciary law into the partners' agreement as an implied term. The withdrawing partner will be liable if she took partnership property, used the partnership's proprietary information, and so on. Using the threat of withdrawal to extract concessions may be wrongful. *See, e.g., Page v. Page*, 359 P.2d 41 (Cal. 1961) (Traynor, J.). Barbie did not do so here. She made a "clean break." Thus, **Answer (C) is not the best answer.**

     Answer (D) is not the best answer because it is incomplete. While it is true that Ken has no claim because Barbie did not take anything that belonged to Ken, if there had been a partnership agreement with a provision protecting Ken from the dissolution, Ken would have a claim against Barbie. Partnership law does not have as an objective making all partners equal in all things. There is no perfectly level playing field. The answer to Ken is that he should have had a partnership agreement that contained a provision that would have given him some protection against a smash and grab.

18. **Answer (C) is the best answer.** The competition would be between Answers (A) and (C). A partnership is dissolved "[b]y the expulsion of any partner from the business bona fide in accordance with such power conferred by the agreement between the partners." UPA § 31(1)(d); RUPA § 601(3). In the Kingston Boats partnership, upon dissolution, the ordinary rule is that "each partner, as against his co-partners . . . may have the partnership property applied to discharge its debts, and the surplus applied to pay in cash the net amount owing to the respective partners." UPA § 38(1); RUPA § 807(a) & (b). This might make **Answer (A)**

correct.

The UPA continues, however, to provide that, "if dissolution is caused by expulsion of a partner, bona fide under the partnership agreement, and if the expelled partner is discharged from all partnership liabilities . . . he shall receive in cash only the net amount due him from the partnership." UPA § 38(1). These are the facts here.

RUPA takes a different approach. RUPA § 801 does not list expulsion of a partner as "an event of dissolution." Therefore, upon expulsion of a partner, RUPA § 701 ("Purchase of a Disassociated Partner's Interest") rather than RUPA § 807 ("Settlement of Accounts Among Partners") governs. Therefore, Answer (C) is correct under either the UPA or the RUPA, making it the best answer.

Answer (B) is incorrect. Shane would not likely succeed in a suit for wrongful dissolution against Dave and Nick, because they acted in accordance with the power given to them in the partnership agreement — the right to expel a partner.

Answer (D) is incorrect. Dave and Nick do not have to move locations and change the name of the enterprise. All they have to do is to pay Shane the value of his interest, possibly obtaining a bank loan for that purpose if they have insufficient funds on hand. "The partners who have not caused dissolution wrongfully, if they desire to continue the business in the same name, either by themselves or jointly with others, may do so, during the agreed term for the partnership and for that purpose may possess the partnership property, provided they secure the payment by bond approved by the court, or pay to any partner who has caused the dissolution wrongfully, the value of his interest in the partnership." UPA § 38(2)(b).

This Question is based on *Monteleone v. Monteleone*, 497 N.E.2d 1221 (Ill. App. Ct. 1986).

19.   **Answer (A) is the best answer.** Many partnership agreements provide that the partners may by majority, or super majority, vote to expel a partner, with or without cause. Such clauses are known as "guillotine" clauses. They are common in law firm as well as other partnership agreements. Several celebrated cases involve law firms' expulsion of partners because of political activities or failure to produce enough business. One case upheld the expulsion of a partner *after* he had successfully fought alcoholism. *See Lawlis v. Kightlinger & Gray*, 562 N.E.2d 435 (Ind. Ct. App. 1990).

There is no requirement for cause in many partnership agreements. A simple vote to expel is sufficient. Thus, **Answer (B) is incorrect.**

The tension that arises is that partners also are fiduciaries one to another. But, absent self-dealing or bad faith, courts have sided with the consensual nature of a partnership. Partners have no obligation to remain partners. Partners are bound together by shared values and expectations as to effort, collegiality, and professionalism. If a partner does not measure up to these mutual expectations, the partners should be able to exclude her from the partnership without liability for wrongful dissolution or breach of fiduciary duty. Thus, **Answer (C) is incorrect.**

What about the rules of professional responsibility? In the case upon which the question is based, the dissenting opinion cited a New York case holding that a dismissed law firm associate had a breach of contract claim after he had been dismissed for reporting another associate's misconduct. The court held an implied term of his employment contract was an obligation to comply with professional responsibility rules. A law firm associate is, however, an employee. If she has no contract, she is an employee at will. The New York court would read into the at will relationship the professional responsibility rules. A partner is not an employee. The partner-to-partner relationship has at its core trust and confidence in one's fellow partners. The New York case is not necessarily persuasive authority in a case involving expulsion of a partner rather than dismissal of an employee.

In anything but an extreme case of wrongdoing, bad faith, or the like, courts uphold expulsion of a partner if the expulsion has been pursuant to the express terms of the partnership agreement. Thus, **Answer (D) is incorrect.**

This Question is based on *Bohatch v. Butler & Binion*, 977 S.W.2d 543 (Tex. 1998).

20.   The best answer is: "Render unto Caesar what is Caesar's, render unto God what is God's." In other words, up until the date of departure, she should perform in good faith and in accordance with the letter of the partnership agreement:

(1) If the agreement requires advance notice of her withdrawal, she should give such notice. Otherwise her withdrawal will be wrongful. Once she gives notice, she may be treated as a pariah, but some discomfort is better than a suit for wrongful withdrawal.

(2) If cases are ripe for settlement, she should settle them. She should not postpone settlement to a date when her own partnership will enjoy the entire fee. She should make reasonable efforts to avoid continuances in her cases and conduct discovery at her normal pace.

(3) She should not use firm resources (copy machine, telephone, and so on) to develop her new partnership.

(4) She should work during normal working hours. Meet with the architect, the office machine sales person, and so on, on Saturdays, or after normal working hours.

(5) She may take her clients, and their files, with her, but first she must obtain their consent. The choice of representation is the client's and not the law firm's or the lawyer's. In seeking such consent, she should avoid misrepresentation or puffery. The notice must be "brief, dignified, and not disparaging of the lawyer's former firm." The notice should be sent only to persons with whom the lawyer has an active attorney-client relationship and not to other of the firm's clients.

(6) The law firm may also send to the clients solicitation letters and authorization forms.

(7) If asked, be truthful. Thus, if the firm asks which clients Megan intends to take with her (so the firm may conduct a dueling solicitation) she must provide the information. UPA § 20 provides that a partner has an obligation "to render on demand true and full information of all things affecting the partnership and the partner." *See also* RUPA § 403(c).

(8) The firm associates are employees. She should not offer them employment with the new firm before she has left the old firm. The day after she leaves, she may offer them positions with the new firm.

See generally Meehan v. Shaughnessy, 535 N.E.2d 1255 (Mass. 1989).

21. There are several provisions you might include, but the key here is not to overreach and impose unreasonable or draconian penalties on partners who wish to withdraw. Some of the provisions might include:

(1) *Covenant Not to Compete (at least for non-lawyer partnerships).* The Rules of Professional Responsibility prohibit covenants not to compete by active lawyers on the grounds that they deprive clients of their choice of representation. The only valid covenants are those which prohibit a lawyer who truly is retiring from the profession from competing with the partnership.

In other forms of service partnerships, covenants not to compete are common. Briefly, the covenant must protect only the actual, and not inchoate or potential, competitive interests of the partnership. Thus, a surgical partnership could not purport to govern the practice of dermatology on grounds that it might someday pursue that activity.

The covenant must be reasonable in geographic scope (actual not potential scope), in terms of scope of the prohibited activity, and in duration. Courts tend to disfavor covenants on grounds that they deprive persons of the means of earning their livelihood.

In the surgical partnership, a reasonable covenant might regulate only the practice of surgery in the town in which the partnership currently operates (and not nearby towns in which it might expand, or the entire Western half of the state, etc.), and only for one or two years.

(2) *Notice Provisions.* The partnership agreement might require the withdrawing partner to give, say, three months' notice to the management committee, or to the managing partner.

(3) *A Fair Charge for Work in Progress.* The attorney must be allowed to take files with her if the client desires to continue the representation. The old firm, however, will have investments in those files — unreimbursed costs, associates' time, indirect overhead charges. Partnership agreements commonly provide that the departing professional must pay some amount ("a fair charge" is one phrase used). The irony is that the payment is to the old partnership that has been dissolved by the partner's withdrawal. Thus, to the extent of their interest in the "old" partnership (say, 5%), the withdrawing partner is paying a portion of the fair charge to herself.

(4) *Right to Accrued Partnership Profits and Capital Contribution.* The partnership agreement may not unreasonably withhold or forfeit the partner's capital account. The UPA, RUPA, and tax law require that each partner have a capital account, which would consist of their capital contributions, plus accrued profits and less losses. *See* RUPA § 401(a). Courts have held that there must be a causal connection between any

deduction from the withdrawing partner's capital account and any alleged breach of duty by the withdrawing partner. If there has been no breach of any duty imposed by law or by the partnership agreement, the withdrawing partner is entitled to the return of their capital account.

22. **Answer (C) is the best answer.** Answer (D) may be an equally good or better answer, but one better understood after you have learned a bit about limited liability companies.

Answer (A) is not the best answer. A general partnership is not a good idea. The partners would be personally liable on both contract and tort claims against the partnership, which for these purposes is nothing more than an aggregate of the partners. Student tenants who fall off balconies could and would sue the partners personally. General partnership would be well suited only for a small time investment such as a duplex or small commercial property. Partnership does have the advantage of "flow through" tax treatment. A partnership files a tax return, but only an information return. The partnership profits, or losses, flow through to the partners, who report them on their individual tax returns. Improved real estate produces losses that are paper losses only, such as depreciation, which the partners want to flow through, sheltering income from other sources, such as their professional practices. All tax shelter investments that are left, such as oil and gas investments or real estate, should be organized so as to obtain flow through of depreciation, depletion, and other items which are expenses for tax purposes, but not actual out-of-pocket expenses.

Answer (B) is not the best answer. A corporation would provide the limited liability but not the flow through tax treatment essential here. The shareholders' liability would be limited to their investment, provided they set the corporation up correctly and avoid veil piercing. Corporations are "stand alone" fictional beings in their own right, rather than aggregates of human beings. As such, corporations file their own tax returns and pay taxes on their income. For a run-of-the-mill corporation, there is no "flow through" tax treatment. So here the corporation would have paper losses that would accumulate in the corporation, doing no one any good.

Answer (C), a hybrid entity that is a creature of legislative enactment known as the limited partnership, **is the best answer.** As with a corporation, the participants file a document (the "Certificate") with a state official (Secretary of State usually) that brings the legal entity into being. It does not arise solely from the interaction of the partners, as with a general partnership. The enabling law, and default contract, is the Revised Uniform Limited Partnership Act ("RULPA") (1976), which has been adopted in nearly all U.S. jurisdictions. RULPA superseded an earlier enactment, the Uniform Limited Partnership Act ("ULPA") (1916). RULPA was amended substantially in 1985. Not all jurisdictions have adopted the amendments.

ULPA required cumbersome filings of the certificate, the limited partnership agreement, and a roster of limited partners, which had to be continuously updated as partners sold or gifted their "units of participation" to others. RULPA streamlines this process. In most states with the later enactment, only the certificate need be filed. *See* RULPA § 201 (certificate need only contain name, name and address of registered agent, name and address of each general partner, and the latest date upon which the limited partnership is to dissolve, if any).

A limited partnership must have one or more general partners, who remain personally liable. The limited partners (sometimes called "sleeping partners") may not undertake active management of the partnership's business and affairs. If they do, they may lose their limited liability. *See infra* Question 23. With limited partnership, the partners obtain "flow through" tax treatment. Losses and tax credits flow through, to be reported on their personal tax returns. The limited partnership peaked in the 1970s and 80s when it was the principal vehicle for tax shelters. Oil and gas, coal mining, real estate, orchard, vineyard, cattle, airplane, equipment leasing, over-the-road trucking, and other ventures were formed using limited partnerships in which units of participation would be sold, for the most part to higher income individuals. Elimination of the investment tax credit and certain accelerated depreciation methods, and other reforms of the federal tax laws, have eliminated the feasibility of many of those tax shelters. The Internal Revenue Service also began a vigorous enforcement program to root out "abusive" tax shelters.

There are few shelters left, and no "deep shelters." Improved real estate investments, oil and gas investments, and a few other odds and ends are the only tax shelters left. And, today, those shelters that do exist would be equally likely to be organized as limited liability companies as they would limited partnerships. Nonetheless, it may be helpful to learn a bit more about limited partnerships before turning to the subject of limited liability companies (LLCs).

23.   **Answer (D) is the best answer.** Limited partners are supposed to have limited control over and participation in the business. Under the traditional standard they faced a possible loss of their limited liability if they exercised control. ULPA § 7 provides: "A limited partner shall not become liable as a general partner unless, in addition to the exercise of his rights and powers as a limited partner, he takes part in control of the business." Consequently, **Answer (A) is not the best answer.**

In *Holzman v. De Escamilla*, 195 P.2d 833 (Cal. Ct. App. 1948), two limited partners in a farming limited partnership regularly conferred with the general partner over which crops he should plant, on occasion reversing his decisions. They also had control over the partnership funds, as the banking resolution provided that checks could be signed by any two of the three partners. A suit by the trustee in bankruptcy to hold liable the limited partners for partnership debts succeeded and was affirmed. Arguably, by merely signing the checks, Jim Brady does not have control over the funds. Thus the facts in Question 21 are different from *Holzman* in which the general partner's signature is required in every case. Yet, it would be foolish to bet upon such a distinction being upheld by a court. Thus, **Answers (B) and (C) are not the best answers.**

The RULPA changes this radically. First, it introduces a number of safe harbors, activities in which limited partners now may be engaged. Second, it introduces a further requirement of reliance. A limited partner who oversteps the boundary "is liable only to persons who transact business with the limited partnership reasonably believing, based upon the limited partner's conduct, that the limited partner is a general partner." RULPA § 303(a). The safe harbors include certain business activities and exercise of what are known as a limited partner's "democracy rights." The former includes "being a contractor for or an agent or employee of the limited partnership or of a general partner." RULPA § 303(b)(1). Thus, ironically, under the RULPA, while Jill and June probably should not oversee the renovations by an interior decorator, they themselves could contract with the partnership to be the interior decorators. *See, e.g., Gast v. Petsinger*, 323 A.2d 371 (Pa. Super. Ct. 1974) (two of several limited partners wore "second hats" as paid consultants to the partnership, resulting in no loss of limited liability). Other business activity permitted includes "consulting with and advising the general partner," acting as surety for or guaranteeing partnership obligations, or winding up the partnership's business and affairs. Democratic rights include attendance at partners' meetings, bringing derivative actions in the name of the partnership, proposing and voting on dissolution, sale or pledge of substantially all the partnership's assets, incurrence of indebtedness, a change in the nature of the partnership's business, admission or removal of a general partner, and admission or removal of a limited partner.

24. **Answer (C) is the best answer.** In *Delaney v. Fidelity Lease, Ltd.*, 526 S.W.2d 543 (Tex. 1975), the Texas Supreme Court held that, by acting as directors and officers of an incorporated general partner, the limited partners had lost their limited liability. Under UPA § 7, they had taken "part in control of the business." Nearly simultaneously, the Washington Supreme Court came to the opposite conclusion. In *Frigidaire Sales Corp. v. Union Properties*, 562 P.2d 244 (Wash. 1977), the court held that service as directors and officers of an incorporated general partner was not impermissible activity. They also noted that creditors could utilize piercing the corporate veil doctrines to hold liable the limited partners if they set up or operated the corporation in an abusive manner. *Frigidaire* was similar to the Brady Bunch case. Frigidaire had supplied, on credit, the home appliances for the apartment complex that the limited partnership owned and the incorporated general partner managed. Most jurisdictions, however, have no authority one way or another on use of a corporation as a general partner. So, **choosing between Answers (A) and (B) would be guesswork, making Answer (C) the best answer.**

RULPA makes clear the ability of limited partners to act as officers and directors of an incorporated general partner, without loss of limited liability. RULPA § 303(b)(1) provides that "[a] limited partner does not participate in the control of the business within the meaning of subsection (a) solely by . . . being an officer, director, or shareholder of a general partner that is a corporation." Thus, **Answer (D) would be a correct answer but not the best answer.** It could be years before Wigmore adopts the RULPA.

Many (most) of the tax shelters that were widely sold in the 1970s and 1980s were structured as limited partnerships with a corporation serving as a general partner. The difference was that the corporation had an existence independent of the limited partners.

Often the corporate general partner was a subsidiary of a brokerage or real estate firm formed to act as general partner and/or provide management services. Today, the chances are better than even that such a real estate venture as that the Brady Bunch is involved in would utilize a limited liability company ("LLC") rather than a limited partnership. In fact, the LLC has completely eclipsed the limited partnership as the form of entity for many different kinds of ventures.

25. One difficulty is that limited partnership interests are extremely illiquid. There are firms that stand willing to purchase some limited partnership interests, but at a deep discount from probable market value. Usually, there is no market in which to sell your interest to another investor. Illiquidity makes partners' dissolution rights doubly important. RULPA § 603 provides that a limited partner may withdraw on six months' notice to the general

partner, absent a contrary agreement. Under RULPA § 604, the withdrawing partner must be paid any distributions to which she is entitled and, if not otherwise provided in the agreement, the fair value of her interest in the partnership. Those are the default rules. Usually (but not always — so it is worth checking each of Evelyn's agreements), the limited partnership agreement "provides otherwise." The agreement may provide for sale of the real estate after a holding of so many years, *e.g.*, 10 years, followed by a distribution. There may also be provision for dissolution by a vote of a majority, or a super majority, of the units of participation. If the partnership is a smaller, local "deal," perhaps Evelyn can procure the requisite vote. Overall, however, I am afraid that, after examining the agreements, I will have to tell her that it is a patchwork. She will obtain liquidity only over time.

26.   **Answer (B) is the best answer.** An area of remaining vitality for the limited partnership form of entity is the "family limited partnership." It is a device used to minimize estate taxes upon death and, short of death, gift taxes. It works something like this:

Myron conveys the winery to a limited partnership, with Myron acting as general partner. Myron gifts to his children units of participation as limited partners. Because of the illiquidity of limited partnership interests, and the limited rights to participate in control of the business, the units will have a value that is heavily discounted from their probable market value (which itself is very uncertain). Myron does have to pay gift tax on the value that exceeds $5 million, the current one-time overall exclusion, but hopefully it will not even approach that amount. The limited partnership agreement will restrict transferability of the children's interests. It also will eliminate the limited partners' withdrawal rights. As he ages, Myron will use yearly gift tax exclusions (currently $13,000 per child per year) to decrease his stake and increase that of his children. When Myron dies, his estate will have very little interest in the winery, thus avoiding (not evading) payment of significant estate taxes.

Answer (A) is incorrect. A general partnership would not work. The partners would have full right to participate in the business. They might be in Myron's hair all the time. Moreover, their control rights would increase the value of what they hold, thereby increasing gift tax payments.

Answer (C) is incorrect. For similar reasons, a corporation may not work, although with non-voting stock some of the same aims might be achieved.

Since 2001, estate taxes had been scheduled to be phased out by 2010 unless Congress acted. With little time to spare, late in 2010 Congress passed the Tax Relief, Unemployment Insurance and Jobs Creation Act (Dec. 17, 2010). The Act reinstates the federal estate tax but with a lower maximum rate (35% versus 45%) and with a larger per person exemption ($5 million).

Answer (D) is not the best answer. A limited liability company could be adapted to suit Myron's purposes (manager-managed, etc.). Currently, however, most estate planners utilize the limited partnership form.

Beyond those brief details, the "ins" and "outs" of family limited partnerships are beyond the scope of a work such as this. Family limited partnerships are mentioned here because they seem to be the last area of robust vitality for the limited partnership as a form of entity.

A new revised uniform limited partnership act has been drafted by the National Conference of Commissioners on Uniform State Laws, assisted by Professor Daniel Kleinberger, of the William Mitchell College of Law, as reporter. Few states, though, have had a chance to adopt the most recent changes.

27.   **Answer (C) is the best answer.** The "new kid on the block" is the limited liability company (LLC). It has all but crowded the limited partnership out of the field. It has also given the Sub S corporation a run for its money. An LLC may be viewed as an "incorporated partnership," but it is really much more than that. A member-managed LLC would give the Brady Bunch all three attributes they desire: limited liability, flow through tax treatment, and the ability to participate in management and control with little or no risk of general liability. No one would have to put his neck on the line, serving as general partner of the limited partnership.

Answer (A) is not the best answer. As has been seen, a corporation would not suit the Brady Bunch's needs. It has no flow through tax treatment. Losses such as depreciation would be "bottled up" in the corporation, therefore doing little good for anyone.

Answer (B) is not the best answer. There is a type of corporation that does have "flow through" tax treatment. It is a tax treatment authorized by subchapter S of the corporate chapter of the Internal Revenue Code, for electing small business corporations. The corporation may have only one class of stock, may not have any foreign nationals as shareholders, must have 75 or fewer holders of shares, and must by unanimous vote elect "Sub S" treatment by the fifteenth day of the third month of the year in which the election is to be made. *See* I.R.C. § 1362(b)(1). Sub S is often elected by incorporated businesses, such as startup retail businesses, that need limited liability but expect losses in their first several years of existence. It is sometimes also elected by profitable businesses who need to retain little in the way of profits, and who distribute all, or nearly all, of their earnings. The latter type of business is relatively rare. Sub S is generally not suitable for real estate and tax shelter type investments because the flow through of deductions is capped at the amount of the shareholder's investment ("basis"). Tax shelters often produce deductions in excess of that amount.

Answer (D) is not the best answer. A family limited partnership is still a limited partnership, with the same drawbacks.

Wyoming was the first state to grant women the right to vote. In 1977, it also became the first state to adopt a limited liability company act. Only in 1988 did a second state, Florida, adopt such a statute. Then, in 1988, the Internal Revenue Service issued a ruling upholding a Wyoming LLC as a partnership ("flow through") for tax purposes. Eight years later, every U.S. jurisdiction had adopted a limited liability company act. Because the competition among states to adopt an act unfolded quickly, there is substantial variation among statutes. Some states' bar committees drew more heavily on partnership law. Other states' bar committees drew heavily from corporate law. The resulting mishmash of laws, as well as the extreme open-endedness of the LLC device, makes getting "a handle" sometimes difficult. There is a Uniform Limited Liability Company Act (ULLCA) to which reference will be made from time to time, but it was not promulgated until 1995, at which time most jurisdictions had already adopted their own "home grown" statutes. Only a few states have therefore adopted the ULLCA.

Early LLC statutes attempted to be "bulletproof," guaranteeing partnership-type tax treatment for entities using the statute, which takes a bit of explaining. The IRS had rules to determine whether a business firm would be treated as a partnership or corporation for tax purposes. These were the so-called "*Kintner* rules," after *United States v. Kintner*, 216 F.2d 418 (9th Cir. 1954). A firm would receive corporate tax treatment only if it had three of the four essential attributes of a corporation (continuity of life, centralized management, limited liability, and free transferability of interests). If the firm had two or less, its choice of partnership flow through tax treatment would be undisturbed. Thus, early LLC statutes automatically denied entities formed under it two of the three attributes of corporateness, aside from limited liability. Thus, all LLCs in a given jurisdiction might have to have member-management and limited life (no perpetual existence) features. In 1997 the IRS gave up. It abandoned the *Kintner* rules, adopting a "check the box" regime. Non-corporate business entities will be treated as partnerships for tax purposes unless they elect corporate tax treatment by checking a box. The check the box regime has increased the usefulness of the LLC entity for many different types of business ventures.

Note: Choice of entity is a complex question that is best approached with the attitude that there often is no right answer. Put another way, choice of entity is an art rather than a science. Two equally capable business lawyers often will make different choices for the same type of enterprise. For you as a student, the goal is to obtain a comfort level and an ability to discuss some of the pros and cons. You should not have as a goal "perfect knowledge."

28.   **Answer (B) is the best answer.** The project seems made for a manager-managed LLC: flow through tax treatment for the startup years' losses, limited liability, and centralized management, but with some input by the first round of investors, should that be desirable.

LLCs, like limited partnerships, are formed by filing a certificate, or equivalent document, with a state official, usually the secretary of state. From the parties' standpoint, the significant document is the "operating agreement," a lengthy document that describes various participants' interests (usually in percentage terms), who will manage (members, a managing member, a committee), restrictions on transferability, events of dissolution (seven years, completion of the project, etc.). There are a number of sources with sample operating agreements from upon which the draftsperson may draw. *See, e.g.,* LARRY RIBSTEIN, UNINCORPORATED BUSINESS ENTITIES 409 (2d ed. 2000) ("Membership Agreement of the Chameleon Company").

LLC statutes also provide for rollover of existing entities (*e.g.,* partnerships, limited partnerships, etc.) into the LLC form. The precise procedure is to form the LLC with a subsequent merger of the pre-existing entity into the new LLC. *See, e.g.,* ULLCA §§ 901–906. The effect of conversion on creditors of a conversion is an issue. ULLCA § 903 provides that the converted entity is the same entity as the predecessor, "for all purposes." However, courts could construe rental and other payments under long-term contracts as new LLC debts (no personal liability of the members) rather than "old" partnership debts, upon which partners would have had unlimited liability.

Answer (A) is not the best answer. The Sub S alternative may work, but the corporation could have no more than 72 shareholders, plus Clare, Erika, and Rachel. All shareholders must consent initially. Thereafter, a majority must continue to consent (a Sub S election may be revoked if more than one-half of the shares consent to the revocation). I.R.C. § 1362(d)(1)(B). It could work, but would be unwieldy.

Answer (C) is not the best answer. A limited partnership requires a general partner, who remains liable. All three of these women have substantial assets they will not wish to expose to the risks of the venture. The project may be big enough to justify the expense of using an incorporated general partner. Another drawback may be that the limited partners would still have to have limited participation. A selling point may be that the early investors would have a say in course and clubhouse design. A limited partnership form of entity would be restrictive, at the least.

Answer (D) is not the best answer either. A (subchapter C) corporation would bottle up the losses for several or more years until the corporation generated more profits against which it could use those losses.

29. **Answer (B) is the best answer.** Corporate law includes a judge-made doctrine known as "piercing the corporate veil," or the doctrine of "corporate disregard," which is vast and sprawling. The doctrine provides an add-on cause of action or claim to a breach of contract or tort claim against a corporation (almost always a corporation with only a few shareholders, rather than a General Motors or a Microsoft). Plaintiffs add on a veil-piercing claim in an attempt to reach the pockets of the corporation's shareholder, which may be a parent corporation or wealthy individual shareholders. Plaintiffs claim that the corporate form, with its attendant limited liability, has somehow been abused.

There are several bases on which courts may pierce the veil: (i) thin capitalization (alone in some jurisdictions, but only in combination with other factors in other jurisdictions), (ii) intermixture of affairs of owner and the corporation, and (iii) when the court finds that a corporation has been used solely to evade a contract or statute or to work a fraud.

Answer (A) is not correct. Courts have carried over some of the piercing the corporate veil doctrine to the LLC area. Under the corporate law doctrine, intermixture of affairs is often proven in part by evidence that the participants in the corporation failed to observe formalities corporate law requires, such as shareholders' and directors' meetings, adequate books and records, including minutes of meetings, separation of owners' and corporate assets, etc. Lack of formality alone seldom wins a case for plaintiffs but, when combined with evidence of other abuses of the corporate form, may be the "tipping point."

Answer (C) is not the best answer. In the LLC area, lack of formality in operation should not carry so much weight. At least one LLC statute, California's, specifically provides that failure to observe certain formalities may not be a ground for "veil piercing" in an LLC. Cal. Corp. Code § 1701(a); *accord Hollowell v. Orleans Regional Hospital*, 1998 U.S. Dist. LEXIS 8184 (E.D. La. May 29, 1998) ("[T]he analyses between corporate veil piercing and limited liability company veil piercing may not completely overlap."), *aff'd*, 217 F.3d 379 (5th Cir. 2000); *see also New Horizons Supply Coop. v. Haack*, 590 N.W.2d 282 (Wis. Ct. App. 1999) (error to pierce LLC veil merely because LLC is treated as a partnership for tax purposes).

You always should also examine a potential veil piercing case to determine if an owner was a participant in the alleged wrongdoing, or the wrongdoer himself. If Joe negligently hired a drunk or incompetent driver, or drove the truck himself, Joe's liability would be direct. At least as to him, veil piercing would be unnecessary. *See, e.g., Pepsi-Cola Bottling Co. of*

Salisbury, Md. v. Handy, 2000 Del. Ch. LEXIS 52 (Mar. 15, 2000) (misrepresentations made by owner in purchase of land on behalf of an LLC). On this subject generally, see LARRY RIBSTEIN, UNINCORPORATED BUSINESS ENTITIES 345–348 (2d ed. 2000).

This case would not be an especially good one for veil piercing. Plaintiffs are not always entitled to a solvent or wholly solvent defendant. LLC and corporation statutes permit formation of entities for the purpose of limiting shareholder liability. What plaintiffs, and citizens at large, are entitled to is that the LLC entity form not be abused to evade foreseen, or foreseeable, obligations. Thus, **Answer (D) is incorrect.**

30.   Courts apply an "internal affairs" choice of law rule. Relationships between members and between members and manager-members and similar internal affairs are governed by the state in which the LLC filed its certificate. That state's law will provide the default rules for financial, management, fiduciary duty, and other internal governance matters, even though the LLC operates and/or is headquartered in a different state. For experienced LLC practitioners, choice of state law may be an important planning consideration, especially given some of the wide variations among state LLC statutes. The "internal affairs" choice of law rule has its genesis in corporate law. Thus, for example, an Oregon company, incorporated in Delaware, but with its headquarters and its only plant in Oregon, will nonetheless have its internal affairs and disputes about them adjudicated under Delaware (and not Oregon) law, even if the dispute is litigated in an Oregon court. Here, then, the matter *sub judice* will be determined in accordance with Nebraska law. It is an internal affair of a Nebraska LLC.

LLC statutes provide default rules. One universal LLC default rule is that, unless the operating agreement otherwise provides, an LLC is member-managed. In that case, Warren and Jim have no one else to blame for their failure to oversee Joe. If the operating agreement provided for a manager-managed LLC, and that manager was Joe, perhaps Warren and Jim may recover from Joe for breaches of fiduciary duty, but an operating agreement may well limit liability for breaches of fiduciary duty, especially the duty of care. It may limit Joe's liability to damages for reckless acts, self-dealing, or knowing violations of law. Or, it may exculpate the manager from liability altogether.

Are such provisions valid? It depends upon the extent to which an LLC statute is completely a set of default rules or, in contrast, contains some mandatory provisions. Delaware's statute gives maximum effect to operating agreements. The LLC statute is completely a set of default rules. *See* 18 DEL. CODE § 1101(b). By contrast, the ULLCA § 103 provides that certain types of provisions, including certain waivers of fiduciary duty, are unenforceable. Thus, the ULLCA has mandatory content. Which is appropriate? The former probably is in small partnership-type settings in which the operating agreement is the product of a consensual course of dealing among the members. The latter is probably the better view in larger LLCs that may be used as vehicles for passive investment, or partially passive investment schemes, such as the golf course LLC with 100 members discussed in Question 24. This is a theme that runs throughout the law of business organizations. How much mandatory content, if any, should there be in statutes? Is there an irreducible minimum or core (usually centered around fiduciary duties) in corporate law, partnership law, or the law of LLCs? Or, should statutes and cases be viewed only as default rules that the parties are free to vary by means of contract? It is a much-asked question that we cannot answer here.

31.   **Answer (B) is the best answer.** Some LLC statutes expressly authorize what the English

call a "company limited by guarantee." Under English and Commonwealth companies acts, a corporation may be "limited by shares" (the usual case) or "limited by guarantee." The latter is unknown to United States corporation law, which always provides that when issued shares are deemed "fully paid and non-assessable," but, as aforesaid, the concept has been introduced by LLC statutes. *See, e.g.,* ULLCA § 303(c). Thus, members may partly fund an LLC, standing by to cover additional debts, but only to the extent provided for in the certificate and operating agreement. It seems perfect here. The Cubs players should set up an LLC, funded in part by cash contributions and limited by guarantee in part. They can then return to concentrating on baseball. As the Cubs continue to win, and production and sales ramp up, the LLC can draw on the line of credit, backed by the limited guarantee. When the players receive their large checks for winning the National League and World Series championships, they can use the proceeds to make good on their limited guarantees, thus paying off the LLC debt.

Answer (A) is not the best answer. The LLC statute provides that each member has a capital account, as in a partnership. In that account are the members' capital contribution, less any losses, plus undistributed profits, etc. Throughout the life of the entity, members' capital accounts are periodically updated. It is very common to draft around such a default scheme. One method is to assign percentages, which seems very appropriate here. Sammy Sosa (a home run hitting king) would receive a much larger share, say 20 percent, than a seldom used relief pitcher, who might receive 2 percent or 3 percent.

Answer (C) is not the best answer for the reasons stated above. With Answer (B), the players would not have to borrow against their homes, as suggested in Answer (C).

Answer (D) is definitely a red herring. LLCs do not issue stock certificates, as corporations do, although in the highly permissible LLC world, nothing absolutely prohibits it.

One other note on finances: Like corporate law, LLC statutes provide for member liability for unlawful or illicit "distributions" (payouts to members whether in the form of a dividend or otherwise) made after an LLC has become insolvent. If the Cubs don't continue to win, and the LLC becomes unable to pay its debts as they come due, the LLC may not pay out any sums to the player-members.

32. **Answer (B) is the best answer** (although **Answers (C) and (D) may work as well**).

Answer (A) is not the best answer. The default rule is Answer (A). Most LLC statutes provide that, in the absence of a contrary agreement, the members manage the LLC. Members have partner-like authority to bind the LLC. Such an arrangement may result in chaos here. Besides, the players want to play baseball. The LLC is a mere sideline.

Some form of centralized management is in order. In an LLC usually that is done by electing to be a manager-managed LLC, although election of corporate type officers is also done in some instances. Many LLC statutes provide that a manager-management election must be noted in the articles or certificate filed with the Secretary of State, or similar official, to put third parties on notice who has authority to bind the entity. So it is important to examine the applicable statute.

Can the manager bind the LLC in extraordinary transactions (large contracts, sale of substantially all of the assets, guarantee of the debts of another, pledge or mortgage of substantial assets, etc.)? Some statutes provide that the manager has plenary power to bind the LLC unless the certificate or operating agreement limits the authority. *See, e.g.*, 6 DEL. CODE ANN. § 18-402 (any restriction on authority to be stated in the operating agreement). Under other LLC statutes, even in manager-managed LLCs, a vote of the members is necessary for extraordinary transactions.

Should the members re-elect managers from time-to-time? Or is it sufficient to provide a process for removal (majority vote of the members, super majority vote)? Most smaller LLCs in which informal dealing is the norm opt for the latter. The statutes are split on voting. Half provide for "one member, one vote," unless the LLC agreement specifically provides otherwise. Other statutes have as a default rule voting according to financial contribution. Some operating agreements provide for proxy voting, in which an absent member may constitute another member his agent for purpose of voting at a meeting of the members (a proxy is nothing more than a specialized form of agency relationship). The members may want to provide for super majority (2/3rds or 3/4ths) voting for certain extraordinary transactions of certain kinds, or unanimous voting for any change that would result in the LLC being treated as a non-partnership, or an increase in member's contribution obligations. The variations are many. Fortunately, sample operating agreements provide a starting point for the drafter, often pointing out various options that may be elected.

33. This question implicates one of the two principal fiduciary duties, the duty of care. Again, we find that the LLC statutes are split. One group of statutes provides as a default rule that the managers have only a duty to refrain from reckless conduct. *See, e.g.*, ULLCA § 409(c). This dovetails with the standard of the Revised Uniform Partnership Act § 404(c), discussed in the answer to Question 7. The other group borrows the corporate law common denominator standard applicable to directors and officers: "the care an ordinarily prudent person in a like position would exercise under similar circumstances." MBCA § 8.30(a)(2). If we follow up the corporate law analogy, we would see that the interaction of the business judgment rule and the standard of conduct would make a proactive manager liable only for decisions in which he failed to exercise any care in the making of his decision. On the other hand, for the manager who fails to make any decision or judgment at all ("asleep at the switch"), the corporate law standard remains mere negligence. The RUPA and ULLCA standard would seemingly give some protection to a manager in either instance. Here Art made a decision or judgment. He seems free of disabling conflicts of interest, or any conflicts of interest. If he exercised at least some care in forming his hunch, he may not be liable. He made a calculated guess. On the other hand, if he did nothing whatsoever to inform himself, making an "off the wall" decision (an uncalculated guess), he could be liable.

34. The second question implicates the other principal fiduciary prong, the duty of loyalty, which deals with venal conduct and self-dealing. One subset of LLC statutes adopts UPA § 21: "Every partner must account to the partnership for any benefit, and hold as trustee for it any profits derived by him without the consent of the other partners from any transaction connected with the formation, conduct, or liquidation of the partnership or from any use by him of its property." Under this rather strict rule, Art would forfeit any profits he made unless he first obtained the consent of his fellow LLC members. Other LLC statutes contain a safe harbor for member or manager transactions that are approved by a majority of the disinterested members, based upon full disclosure. Under either regime, Art should not simply go ahead. He must first make disclosure of his intentions, of his potential interest in the transaction, and of the LLC's interest, and then seek a vote of the LLC's members.

35. **Answer (B) is the best answer.** Given its partnership antecedents, the default rules in most LLC statutes track the partnership rules, that is, the member may transfer financial rights (rights to distributions and a liquidating share upon dissolution of the LLC), but not rights to participate in governance or management. A transferee may become a member only if he follows the procedures in the operating agreement for doing so or, if no such procedures are set forth, if all the members consent. *See* ULLCA § 503(a).

Answer (A) is not the best answer. The law has come to permit reasonable restrictions on alienation but not absolute prohibitions.

An LLC member is not a co-owner of the LLC's property. ULLCA § 501(a). Instead, his principal rights are his rights to distributions and his governance rights. For example, an LLC member has no right to demand the company truck for her personal use. An LLC member's transferee has the rights described above, but those are carefully circumscribed by the ULLCA default rules. Uncle George, for example, may not "require access to information concerning the company's transactions, or inspect or copy any of the company's records." ULLCA § 503(d).

There is a downside to becoming a member, or to moving from the status of transferee to the status of member. The new member is liable for any obligation of his transferor to make further contributions. He is also liable to make good any prior distributions to the extent they were unlawful (made the LLC insolvent). ULLCA § 503(b). In this hypothetical, it may well suit Uncle's George's interests best by not becoming a member and remaining only a transferee after nephew Hal goes off to San Diego.

Answer (C) is not the best answer. Many LLCs will have operating agreement provisions that restrict transfer in different ways (as in Answer (C)). For example, an agreement could permit transfer, but only after the transferring member has given a right of first refusal to fellow members.

Answer (D) is not the best answer because it would entail unnecessary work and expense.

36. **Answer (A) is the best answer,** but everything must be prefaced with the statement, as in partnership law, "unless the agreement provides otherwise," which it commonly will if sophisticated parties have negotiated and drafted the LLC operating agreement. Assuming a clean slate, however, the LLC statute will provide the rule, or default rule, if there is an agreement, but it is a less than comprehensive one. LLC statutes commonly list events of member dissociation, including death, bankruptcy, disability, and so on. *See, e.g.,* ULLCA § 801. Most lists include voluntary withdrawal, making **Answer (C) an incorrect answer.**

The consequence of voluntary withdrawal is payment to Sammy of the value of his LLC interest, at least according to first generation LLC statutes, which patterned themselves after partnership law. Second generation statutes have retained the right to disassociate, but have restricted or eliminated the right of the disassociating member to be paid the value of his interest immediately. A principal reason was that such a default right was ill suited for the family LLC, designed to pass interests in a family business to younger family members. Thus, absent contract, Sammy may withdraw. His right to receive the value of interest immediately depends upon the statute in the particular jurisdiction.

What about the other Cubs? Can they sue Sammy? This appears to be a "smash and grab," in which the stronger partner (or member) attempts to withdraw, taking the best business with him. In the partnership context, in which withdrawal causes dissolution of the partnership, one reason for drafting a partnership agreement is to modify that withdrawal right. The agreement may provide that withdrawal may occur only after proper notice, payment of a fair charge for work already done on business to be taken by the withdrawing partner, and so on. Then, any withdrawal in violation of those terms of the agreement is a "wrongful" dissolution, as discussed in the answer to Question 15. The partner may withdraw, but she will be liable in damages. LLC statutes do not make the partnership distinction between "wrongful" and "non-wrongful" dissolution. So, absent contract, Sammy may withdraw, even based upon mere whim, making **Answer (B) an incorrect answer.**

Question 36, then, illustrates the necessity for thought about the default rules and, the necessity of perhaps drafting around them. It also illustrates the necessity of thinking about the "dark side" — withdrawal, smash and grabs, making some withdrawals wrongful, and the consequences if the business is not successful.

Here, something along the lines of Answer (D) might have been a good idea. A little foresight might have led to the prediction that a "star" player, whose season really takes off, might no longer be willing to share his star power with other LLC members and may attempt a smash and grab. Drafting to make wrongful or otherwise to limit dissociation before the conclusion of the baseball season would have made sense. **Answer (D) is not the best answer** because the provision that Sammy not be allowed to withdraw until the entire baseball season is over was not specifically stated.

37. LLC statutes provide that the LLC is dissolved on member dissociation unless the non-dissociating members vote to continue. So, the Cubs remaining in the LLC should have a meeting to see what the remaining members' wishes are. Because some of them are stars in their own right, and the Cubs are having a successful season, they may well vote to continue the LLC enterprise for the remainder of the season. This rule, of course, may be changed by contractual provision. The LLC itself may be stated to be for accomplishment of a stated objective, a term of years, and so on, upon the happening of which the LLC dissolves. What happens if, at a meeting in the clubhouse to ponder Sammy Sosa's withdrawal, the remaining LLC members vote to "pack it in"? In that case, LLC statutes contain rules for distribution upon dissolution, akin to the partnership statutes. Out of the net proceeds of winding up, members first receive any distributions due them, then repayment of loans and advances, then their capital contributions, and finally a share of what remains in the proportions to their LLC interest. *See* ULLCA § 806. This is the approach of the Uniform Partnership Act, except the UPA does not give express priority to declared distributions.

38.   **Answer (D) is the best answer.** Under the Model Rules of Professional Conduct, and predecessor ethics provisions, attorneys must remain professionally and financially responsible for the work they do and for work they supervise. Therefore, lawyers have never been able to practice, and still are not able to practice, using a form of organization that accords them across-the-board limited liability. A law firm, then, may not practice by means of a corporation or a limited liability company.

Answers (A) and (B) never have been and are not now possible answers (larger law firms may, and often do, offer ancillary services, such as real estate closing or information technology, through a corporation or limited liability company, but this is because the ancillary activities do not constitute the practice of law).

Answer (C) is incorrect. Return to the partnership form would be going backwards. The firm would even lose the limited liability it now has with respect to its rental real estate.

The choice many law and other professional firms are making is to reorganize in a new form, the limited liability partnership. The LLP statutes eliminate across-the-board liability for professional activity (malpractice) as in the Professional Service Corporation acts, but retain personal liability for the partner providing the services or for employee professionals supervised by that partner. Thus, in the hypothetical posed, the firm of BLT would be liable, as would be partners 99 and 100, but partners 1–98 would escape personal liability. Oddly enough, it was the accounting and not the legal profession that pushed for the first LLP statute, which Texas adopted in 1991. Delaware soon followed with an LLP statute that is widely utilized.

One issue is whether the attorneys who sit on a firm committee that, for example, reviews opinion letters issued by lawyers under the firm's name are supervisors of the attorney, say, an associate, who actually drafted the letter. Somewhat similar (but probably weaker) contentions might be made about lawyers who sit on the firm's management committee. If the firm has a single managing partner, is she every other lawyer's supervisor as well? Some attorneys in larger firms insist on additional compensation or other accommodation before they will serve on the first sort of committee.

BLT would re-organize by filing a certificate with a state official such as the secretary of state. They would then draft a partnership agreement for the conduct of their LLP. In most respects, aside from providing for the curtailment of across-the-board professional liability, the LLP statute provides a set of default rules. The LLP form is rapidly becoming the predominant organization form for medium-sized and larger law, accounting, and other professional service firms.

39.   **Answer (B) is the best answer.** Roy and Gail should form a corporation. Once it has been incorporated and adequately capitalized (see the discussion of veil piercing below), the corporation will afford Roy and Gail limited liability, which does not mean "no liability." It means that Roy and Gail's liability will be limited to the monies and property they convey to the corporation.

   Answers (A) and (D) are not the best answers. The enterprise has become large enough that even absent risk of tort liability (although there could be cases of food poisoning), they probably wish to have limited liability. Limited liability will serve to limit Roy and Gail's personal exposure for breach of contract suits, say, if the enterprise defaults on one of the leases or fails to pay some suppliers. Ergo, any form of partnership will not do.

   Answer (C) is not the best answer. Roy and Gail should form their corporation in the state in which they do business. Incorporating in Delaware would entail added expense and is generally inappropriate for start-up corporations.

   A run of the mill corporation (a subchapter "C" corporation) accounts to the Internal Revenue Service for its profits and losses and pays its own taxes, if any. Here, however, the business plan indicates that, as with most retail businesses, the enterprise will have losses for several years. Roy and Gail could use those losses as deductions against the income they receive from dental practices and cooking shows. They want a conduit-type tax treatment in which profits or losses flow through to individual owners.

   In the first 90 days of their corporation's existence, Roy and Gail, or their accountant, should file an election to be treated as an "S" corporation. All shareholders must consent, no foreign national may hold shares, there can be only one class of stock, and the number of shareholders must be less than 75. As an electing "small business," the corporation files an information return. Roy and Gail take their pro rata share of the corporation's losses on their personal returns. When and if the corporation appears to be having a profitable year, they can consider revoking their "subchapter S election."

   Participants in a business generally elect subchapter S status in one of two situations. The first is when the corporation, as here, expects to have losses in its startup years. The second is when the corporation has profits, needs to retain few of those profits for expansion or modernization, and therefore will distribute all, or most all, its profits. Clients should be advised to avoid a Sub S election when the corporation will retain significant amounts of profit. It is bad enough to pay taxes on funds one receives. It is worse to pay taxes on funds one does not receive, which would be the case when the Sub S corporation is profitable, but retains a significant portion of the earnings.

   Today, many lawyers might achieve Roy and Gail's goals — limited liability with flow through tax treatment — by forming a limited liability company, or LLC, in lieu of a Sub S corporation.

Note: Section 302 of the Jobs Growth Tax Relief Reconciliation Act (2003) ameliorates the problem somewhat by providing that dividends payable to individual shareholders will be taxed at a reduced capital gains rate of 15 percent, rather than at ordinary income rates of 31, 34, or 36 percent. The original Bush administration proposal had been altogether to eliminate double taxation. Dividends would not have been taxable at all upon receipt by shareholders if the corporation had paid tax on the sums distributed. President Obama advocates raising the tax rate to 20 percent.

40.   **Answer (C) is the best answer.** Beginning in the 1960s, most states adopted professional service corporation acts. Generally, anyone required to be licensed (physician, lawyer, accountant, cosmetologist, dentist, veterinarian, etc.) incorporates under that act rather than under the general business corporation law. All shareholders and directors must be members in good standing of the same profession (except architects and structural engineers). Two disparate professions (surgeon and undertaker) cannot combine. The active business of the corporation must be limited to the carrying on of the profession. Passive business investments (*e.g.*, owing real estate or stocks and bonds) are permitted. The incorporated professional or professionals must place a special appellation ("PS" or "PC" are common) after the corporate name.

The acts dealt with the malpractice liability issue in one of two ways. Some acts provided that with regard to rendition of the professional service there would be no limited liability. Other acts remained silent on the theory that if professionals abused the privilege of incorporation, say, by practicing without malpractice insurance, courts would pierce the corporate veil to hold the professionals personally liable as the owners of the enterprise.

Answer (A) is incorrect. Partners are liable for the acts of every other partner for carrying on in the usual way the business of the partnership. Bar Associations used to require complete financial responsibility for each and every lawyer in a group practice. *See, e.g.*, AMERICAN BAR ASS'N, MODEL RULES OF PROFESSIONAL CONDUCT R. 5.1 (2002). Lawyers did that by practicing law together in a partnership. Today, while lawyers may have to be financially responsible for one another, they may accomplish that in ways other than remaining in a general partnership and being personally liable.

Answers (B) and (D) are not the best answers for the reasons stated above.

41.   **Answer (A) is the best answer.** The Model Business Corporation Act (MBCA), promulgated by the America Bar Association in 1950, and revised extensively in 1969 and again in 1984, is a middle of the road scheme that about 40 states have adopted, often with modifications. In addition to extensive revisions and restatements in 1969 and 1984, the ABA committee also regularly fine-tunes the statute through proposed amendments published in the Business Lawyer. The MBCA is suitable for 999 out of 1000 situations.

Answers (B) and (C) are not the best answers. Because of restrictive corporate law schemes in their states, lawyers in California used to incorporate many businesses in Nevada, which aims to be the Delaware of the West. New York law made corporate directors liable for certain wage claims. New York lawyers often incorporated clients in New Jersey. All, or most all, of those "run away" incorporations have ceased. Mature companies may re-incorporate in Delaware or Nevada, but startups seldom do.

One reason to incorporate elsewhere is that Buddy has several or more shareholders, plans many acquisitions, and is situated in one of the six or so states that still require 2/3rds, rather than majority, vote for mergers, amendment of articles, and so on. That will be the rare case. Another reason to incorporate elsewhere is that Buddy wants the right to brag to his friends and at his club ("Yeah, it's a Delaware corporation that we formed."). Bragging rights will cost money. Buddy will have to pay someone to act as his corporation's registered agent in Delaware (businesses such as Corporation Trust (CT) will do so). He will also have to pay a fee and file with the Secretary of State in Nirvana as a foreign corporation licensed to do business in that state. Bragging rights are usually not worth that much, even though the sums involved are not large (a few hundred dollars per year).

Answer (D) is not the best answer. Going offshore is an arcane subject beyond the scope of this work (although the beach time might be nice). Suffice it to say, the best advice is to stay at home in Nirvana and with the MBCA.

42. **Answer (B) is the best answer.** But few jurisdictions will have adopted the plan of domestication scheme, so Buddy and his lawyer will have to use the merger technique to change the domicile of his corporation.

Answer (A) is the second best answer. As noted, the old method of changing a corporation's domicile was through formation of a shell corporation in the new state of incorporation, a merger of the operating company into the shell, and then, if necessary, a name change for the name of the shell to the original corporate name. New MBCA §§ 9.21–9.22 (2008) outline a new procedure whereby the board of directors formulates "a plan of domestication," the shareholders vote on it, and the corporation files the "articles of domestication" with the secretary of state, "following generally the rules in Chapter 11 for adoption and approval of a plan of merger or a share exchange." The sections are quite lengthy. Follow-on sections include MBCA § 9.23 (Surrender of Charter upon Domestication); MBCA § 9.24 (Effect of Domestication); and MBCA § 9.25 (Abandonment of a Domestication).

Action on a Plan of Nonprofit Conversion. New MBCA § 9.31 now also contains authority for and specifies the procedures for such an evolution.

Action on a Plan of Entity Conversion. New subchapter E of Chapter 9 (MBCA §§ 9.50–9.57) governs other entity conversions. In the main, the chapter involves the conversion of a corporation into another creature of statute (LLC, Limited Partnership). To roll over a corporation into a non-creature of statute (*e.g.*, general partnership) would not require a conversion. A simple dissolution of the corporation would lead to a general partnership, at least in the case if more than one shareholder exists.

Again, directors formulate a Plan of Conversion (MBCA § 9.51), obtain shareholder approval (MBCA § 9.52, Action on a Plan of Entity Conversion), file Articles of Conversion (MBCA § 9.53), and work a Surrender of Charter Upon Conversion (MBCA § 9.54). Other provisions include Effects of Entity Conversion (MBCA § 9.55) and Abandonment of Entity Conversion (MBCA § 9.56).

Answers (C) and (D) are incorrect. In fact, they are nonsensical.

43. You have to draft articles of incorporation (the "charter" in Delaware, also sometimes known as the certificate of incorporation). Most modern statutes provide for "plain vanilla" articles that could fit on a postcard. For example, MBCA § 2.02(a) requires only that articles state the name (which cannot be the same as or deceptively similar to any other corporation

incorporated in the state or any foreign corporation licensed to do business in the state); the number of shares authorized; the name and street address of the registered agent (*i.e.*, may not be a post office box); and the name and address of each incorporator.

Duration is assumed to be perpetual. Purpose need not be stated. It is presumed to be "any lawful purpose." No minimum capital need be paid in and stated to have been paid in (older statutes required $500 or $1,000). No other information is required.

No lawyer worth her salt would file such articles, however, at least for a new client to whom she must prove her mettle and earn her fee. By way of example, and not limitation, MBCA § 2.02(b) sets out five optional provisions that could be in the articles. Typically, lawyers may put in a provision opting out of or limiting directors' duty of care liability; provisions for indemnification of directors (see the discussion of protecting directors below); a provision naming the first or initial board of directors; elimination of preemptive rights in further share issuances or creation of preemptive rights (the right to subscribe to further issuances for cash in proportion to one's preexisting proportionate interest, discussed below); authority to issue preferred shares and a description of the relative rights and preferences of the preferred class; restrictions on the transfer of shares (although restrictions usually are set out in a separate "buy-sell" agreement); and so on. Instead of a postcard, typical law firm articles of incorporation may run to four, five, or six typewritten pages. To save the client a trip back to the lawyer's office, the lawyer or paralegal signs the articles as incorporator. The lawyer, or paralegal, then files the document with a check for the filing fee plus the first year's corporate franchise tax. The cost runs anywhere from $150 to $250, depending upon the jurisdiction. Usually, for a small extra fee, to expedite matters the law firm can make a "counter filing" at the state capital and have the articles accepted for filing and the certificate of incorporation (if there is one) issued then and there. Thereafter, the corporation pays an annual $100 to $150 annual franchise tax for the privilege of a continued corporate franchise, along with a brief annual report form listing the officers' and directors' names and addresses. It really is pretty simple.

44.   **Answer (D) is the best answer.** Seldom will anyone draft bylaws from scratch. Bylaws deal with the frequency and preliminaries for shareholders' and directors' meetings, description of the officers' duties, what their titles will be (president or CEO, treasurer or CFO, secretary, etc.), and other internal arrangements for conduct of the corporation's business. Generally, bar association committees, or legal stationers, provide stock bylaws that may be adapted by filling in the blanks ("the annual meeting of shareholders will be held on the (third) (Tuesday) of (March)"). Many law firms have their own model bylaws. If bylaws from those sources are not forthcoming, a set of sample bylaws may well be included with the minute book you order over the telephone.

Once the minute book arrives and the bylaws are typed up, the lawyer calls the client or clients in for an organizational meeting. They elect the initial board of directors (if the articles have not already named the first board). The board then: (1) selects the depository institution (bank) for the corporation's funds and approve a corporate banking resolution; (2) approves the form of stock certificate and seal; (3) appoints the officers and set their salaries, if any; (4) approves the lease, or assignment of pre-existing lease, for the corporation's premises; (5) reviews subscriptions for shares of stock and approve or reject them; (6) values any property or non-cash consideration proposed to be used as consideration for shares; (7) approves the form of any promissory notes the corporation is to issue for loans to it, by shareholders or others; and (8) generally approves or affirmatively repudiates any contracts purportedly made on the corporation's behalf prior to the commencement of its existence (see the discussion of promoter's liability below).

The organizational meeting and the minutes thereof usually complete the work that the lawyer does for her initial incorporation fee.

Answers (A), (B), and (C) are not the best answers because they are incomplete.

45. **Answer (C) is the best answer.** *Ultra vires*, Latin for "beyond the purposes or powers," is said to be a "dying doctrine." That is not completely true. Corporations generally have all the powers natural persons have. The applicable statute will list many of those powers. *See, e.g.,* MBCA § 3.02 (listing 15 general powers). The statute will also contain a broad grant of implied power. *See, e.g., id.* (a corporation "has the same powers as an individual to do all things necessary or convenient to carry out its business and affairs").

Purpose clauses in articles of incorporation used to be lengthy statements of all the "objects" the corporation could pursue. Laws then began to authorize corporations to incorporate for "any lawful business," or "for any lawful purpose save the business of banking or insurance" (which typically are regulated industries governed by separate statutory schemes). Under these "general incorporation acts," state officials often still required that articles state what that lawful purpose was (*e.g.,* "to produce, market, and sell records, audio tapes, compact discs, sheet music, and any and all other forms of musical publication or broadcast"). Legislatures then stated that a corporation's purpose "may be, and may be stated to be, any lawful purpose." Most lawyers now utilize a general purpose clause. In fact, under the MBCA, if no purpose is stated, the purpose is assumed to be "any lawful purpose." *See* MBCA § 3.01 ("[E]very corporation 'has the purpose of engaging in any lawful business unless a more limited purpose is set forth in the articles of incorporation.' ").

When the parties who have formed a corporation have disagreements, or suspicions about each other's understanding of what are, and what are not, proper purposes for the corporation, a restrictive purpose clause might be a good idea. The clause will box in the participant who has a roving eye. She will have to come back to her fellow participants, seeking amendment or revision of the article of incorporation to pursue any new venture or extreme variant on the original purpose.

Answers (A), (B), and (D) are not the best answers because they are not the simplest way to accomplish what the clients are seeking.

46. **Answer (B) is the best answer.** Wiley's acts constitute a plain old frolic and detour by a corporate agent. Distinguish, then, *ultra vires* acts from "frolic and detours" by corporate actors and also from illegal acts. A related question is, if an act were to be illegal, isn't it always also *ultra vires*? The answer is "it ain't necessarily so." If the act is *malum in se* (a so-called "Ten Commandments" crime such as murder or theft, or a crime involving moral turpitude), then the act is both illegal and *ultra vires*. If, however, the act attributed to the corporation is merely *malum prohibitum* (illegal because the state prohibits it under the police power), the act, while illegal, is not necessarily *ultra vires*. Wiley's conduct falls in the latter category. So even if Wiley's act may be said to be a corporate act and therefore illegal, it still would not be *ultra vires*.

Answer (A) is not the best answer. *Ultra vires* is unlikely. The articles' purpose clause may read "to operate an airline between Seattle and California cities," but it is doubtful that the clause would be so narrowly drawn. More likely is a purpose clause permitting pursuit of "any lawful purpose," or one authorizing conduct of an airline business generally.

Answer (C) is not the best answer. The detour also probably is not an illegal act because no corporate high managerial agent authorized it. Alternatively, no corporate culture exists which encourages the commission of such acts. Those are two tests used by courts to find corporations criminally liable for acts of their agents.

Answer (D) is not the best answer. The facts do not indicate that any contract is involved.

47.   **Answer (A) is the best answer.** United States courts have always been reluctant to permit corporations to escape contractual performance on *ultra vires* grounds. Early on they refused to transplant the English "strict" *ultra vires* doctrine, that an *ultra vires* act was *void ab initio*. Instead, U.S. courts held *ultra vires* acts voidable, instead of void. Moreover, U.S. courts would void only executory contracts. Part performance on the other side would render the contract non-voidable on *ultra vires* grounds. Because of the strong common law interest in the stability of land titles, courts would also not apply *ultra vires* to many contracts involving real property.

MBCA § 3.04(a) codifies much of the judicial hostility to *ultra vires*, stating a general rule that "the validity of a corporate action may not be challenged on the ground that the corporation lacks or lacked power to act." MBCA § 3.02(b), however, states three exceptions. First, the attorney general of a state may bring a proceeding to dissolve a corporation under MBCA § 14.30, raising *ultra vires* acts as a ground. Second, *ultra vires* may be raised inter se, "directly or derivatively . . . against an incumbent or former director or officer . . . of the corporation." Third, "[a] corporation's power to act may be challenged . . . in a proceeding by a shareholder against the corporation to enjoin the act." The court must find that it is "equitable" to do so, but a well-disguised collusive law suit could slide by that opaque requirement. For that reason, the statutes of several non-MBCA jurisdictions, such as California and Nevada, simply provide that *ultra vires* may never be raised in a suit by or against any third party. In those jurisdictions, *ultra vires* remains viable only in a suit against the officers and directors who took the corporation down a primrose path.

This Question is based on the English case of *Ashbury Railway Carriage & Iron Co. v. Richie*, 33 Law T. Rep. N. S. 450 (1875); *see also 711 Kings Highway Corp. v. F.I.M.'s Marine Repair Service, Inc.*, 273 N.Y.S.2d 299 (Sup. Ct. 1966) (statute similar to Model Act could be used only as a defense: landlord plaintiff could not use statute "as a sword" in declaratory judgment action to have lease declared *ultra vires* and hence invalid).

Answers (B) and (D) are incorrect. There is evidence neither of any mistake of fact nor of fraudulent misrepresentation.

Answer (C) is incorrect. The Ashbury CEO does not need an attorney (you) to tell him that the price of steel *might* decline.

48.   Five reasons that the *ultra vires* doctrine has less viability today are: (1) judicial hostility to use of *ultra vires* to evade obligations; (2) broad statutory grants of implied powers; (3) widespread use of broad ("any lawful purpose") purpose clauses in articles of incorporation; (4) ease of amendment of articles; and (5) statutes such as MBCA § 3.04. Two areas of vitality remain. One is guarantee of the debts of another. A parent corporation may guarantee the debt of its subsidiary to a third party, say, the bank (a "downstream"

guarantee). [A subsidiary is a corporation that, through shareholding, is controlled by another corporation (called the "parent"). The parent corporation may own a controlling interest in the subsidiary, or it may own all of the stock ("wholly owned subsidiary").] A subsidiary might guarantee the debts of the parent (an "upstream" guarantee). Or a subsidiary might guarantee the debts of another subsidiary (a "cross stream" guarantee). A minority shareholder in the subsidiary might challenge the use of the subsidiary's resources in such a manner. She would do so on *ultra vires* grounds. Unless the guarantee is found to have been "directly beneficial" to the corporation giving it, a court will find it *ultra vires*. The second area is local government law. Units of local government (municipalities, school districts, fire districts, etc.) are organized as "municipal corporations." Municipal corporations have only the powers delegated to them by the state, and the delegation is strictly construed. *Ultra vires* lives on in the area of municipal law as a means of challenging actions that may exceed the boundaries of the delegation to the particular governmental unit. One area of former vitality for *ultra vires* no longer remains: charitable gifts, which most statutes now expressly authorize, and which courts have come to judge by application of the standard of reasonableness, rather than a binary standard of *ultra vires* or not. *See, e.g., Theodora Holding Corp. v. Henderson*, 257 A.2d 398 (Del. Ch. 1969) (gifts to pet charity controlled by corporate officer); *A.P. Smith Mfg. Co. v. Barlow*, 98 A.2d 581 (N.J. 1953) (upholding $1,500 corporate gift to Princeton University).

49.   **Answer (D) is the best answer.** No precise legal definition exists of who is, or is not, a promoter. Roughly speaking, the promoter is the one who gets the light bulb over her head, venturing out to round up resources for the budding enterprise. When a promoter or other person acts on behalf of another, in this case a corporation, or a corporation to be formed, they must indicate their representative capacity. Gyro could have done so by signing "Altoona Dunkin Donuts, By Gyro Gearloose," or by signing with a title such as "Promoter" or "President." So, even if the corporation existed, both it and Gyro would be liable because he failed to indicate his representative capacity.

But the corporation did not exist. Even if Gyro had indicated his representative capacity, an agent warrants the existence of his or her principal. Gyro would be liable for having breached that warranty. Altoona Dunkin Donuts, Inc. did not exist at the time he signed the lease agreement. The proper way for a promoter to sign, then, is to indicate both the non-existence of the principal and the promoter's representative capacity. For example: "Altoona Dunkin Donuts, Inc., a corporation to be formed, by: Gyro Gearloose, promoter."

Answers (A), (B), and (C) are not the best answers for the reasons stated above.

50.   **Answer (C) is the best answer.** The rules are very tricky. A novation is a three-party transaction in which one obligor is substituted for another on a contract. Gyro cannot provide for a present novation as the third party, the corporation, does not exist. He may, however, provide for a future novation, when the corporation does come into existence.

Answer (B) is not the best answer. It is not enough to provide in the contract that the other party will look to the corporation when it comes into existence. To be safe, the contract must also plainly state that at that point the promoter will "drop out," that is, no longer be liable. Otherwise both corporation and promoter will continue to be liable. *See, e.g., Goodman v. Darden, Doman & Stafford Assocs.*, 670 P.2d 648 (Wash. 1983) (agreement to look to the corporation does not necessarily include agreement to release the promoter); *RKO-Stanley Warner Theatres, Inc. v. Graziano*, 355 A.2d 830 (Pa. 1976) (similar).

Answer (A) is not the best answer. Taking a mere offer often is not satisfactory because, under contract law, an offer may be revoked at any time prior to acceptance. Gyro could lose the prime retail space in the week or 10 days it takes to get the corporation formed.

Answer (D) is not the best answer. Gyro could also enter into binding contracts and then look to the corporation for indemnity when it is formed. But, if there are other participants (shareholders) in Gyro's enterprise they could "stiff" him on one or all of the contracts by refusing to assume them or to indemnify Gyro. And, if the corporation never is formed, most courts hold the promoter liable. *See, e.g., Stanley J. How & Assocs., Inc. v. Boss*, 222 F. Supp. 936 (S.D. Iowa 1963) (promoter held personally liable to architect when hotel corporation, which was to be the "obligor," was never formed). For that reason, if they reach a promoter in time, many experienced lawyers advise bypassing these traditional rules in one of two ways. One is to do nothing until the corporation is formed. Prepare and file plain vanilla articles by means of a counter filing at state capital. By having a clerk or paralegal drive to the Secretary of State's office, and paying a small extra fee, the corporation can be formed in 24 or 48 hours and Gyro can act. Alternatively, some law firms maintain already formed generic "shelf corporations" just for such a scenario. The second way is to advise Gyro to take an assumable option on the rental space, for the donut machine, and so on. When the corporation comes into being, Gyro assigns the option contracts to it and no longer is on the hook. The difficulty is that an option may seem strange or suspicious to relatively unsophisticated parties. The putative landlord, for example, might say "Well, do you want the space or not?"

Because these rules are tricky — how to sign and how to provide for a future novation, etc. — over the years testing on them has been a favorite of law professors and bar examiners.

51. **Answer (A) is the best answer.** A concept known as acquiescence will result in liability if all the corporation does is abjure the contracts it does not want. Acquiescence results from knowledge, actual or constructive, of the contracts plus the passage of time. So, "time is not on their side," and they must accept or reject and notify the counterparty on those contracts they find inappropriate. *See McArthur v. Times Printing Co.*, 51 N.W. 216 (Minn. 1892) (corporation held liable to advertising solicitor hired by promoter when no one in corporation took steps affirmatively to repudiate the contract).

Answers (B) and (D) are incorrect for the reasons stated above.

Answer (C) is not the best answer. Purchasing a newspaper advertisement is one possible, but not necessary, way to achieve such a notification. A letter to each counterparty would be cheaper and would suffice. The advice to remember is that the newly formed corporation, by its flesh and blood actors, must be proactive as to the promoter's contracts it does not desire to perform.

52.   **Answer (D) is the best answer** for the reasons stated below.

Answer (A) is incorrect. De jure corporate existence is good against the world. The corporation has recognized existence as a juridical person. But, de jure status cannot exist here because Lash the lawyer never made a filing with the incorporating authority.

Answers (B) and (C) are incorrect. The fallback defense is de facto status, good against every potential claimant except the state. The defense has three elements: (1) existence of a statutory scheme permitting incorporation for the purposes stated; (2) good faith attempt to incorporate under that scheme; (3) purported use of corporate powers or activity as a corporation. *See, e.g., Cantor v. Sunshine Greenery, Inc.*, 398 A.2d 571 (N.J. Super. Ct. App. Div. 1979) (applying de facto doctrine); *see also Robertson v. Levy*, 197 A.2d 443 (D.C. 1964) (setting out de facto doctrine, but refusing to apply it). Seemingly, the de facto corporation defense would be good here as well, but in *Timberline Equip. Co. v. Davenport*, 514 P.2d 1109 (Or. 1973), the Oregon court held that the 1969 MBCA provision, which provides that "all persons who purport to act as a corporation without authority so to do shall be jointly and severally liable," abolished the de facto corporation doctrine. For policy support, the court noted the ease of incorporation under modern statutes and procedures. Under the Model Act scheme, an entity is either a corporation de jure or nothing. There is no in-between. Nonetheless, the Oregon and other courts might let Smokey and Brenda off on grounds that, unlike Soupy, they did not assume or "purport" to act as or on behalf of a corporation. Soupy would be liable.

The 1984 revision of the Model Act softened considerably this harsh result. MBCA § 2.04 provides that "[a]ll persons purporting to act as or on behalf of a corporation, *knowing there was no incorporation* under this Act, are jointly and severally liable for all liabilities created while so acting" (emphasis added). Under that standard, not only Smokey and Brenda, but also Soupy, would escape liability. Thus, **Answer (D) is the best answer.**

A related doctrine is "corporation by estoppel." If a contract creditor dealt with the entity as though it were a corporation, sending invoices in the corporate name to the corporate address, etc., and the owners of the business have changed position or otherwise relied in good faith upon their belief that a corporation exists, the creditor may be estopped to deny the corporation's existence. *See, e.g., Cranson v. International Business Machines Corp.*, 200 A.2d 33 (Md. 1964). The Official Comment to MBCA § 2.04 makes clear that estoppel is possible under the statute if, and only if, the owners had no knowledge of the defective corporate existence.

53.   This Question is at the opposite end of the spectrum from Question 49. Rather than defective birth, this Question involves corporate death. Many statutes provide that, after certain failures to file the brief annual report forms most states require, or to pay franchise taxes, say, on the third failure to file (which would be 24 months after the first missed filing date), the corporation is dissolved by operation of law. The Model Act provides that, after 60 days

failure to pay the tax or file the report, "the secretary of state may commence a proceeding to administratively dissolve a corporation." *See, e.g.*, MBCA § 14.20. Most statute also provide for a reinstatement procedure. Upon payment of back taxes, interest, and penalties, plus filing the required report form, Chunk can reinstate Mystic's corporate existence. There may, however, be an outside time limit, *e.g.*, three years after the date of dissolution. *See, e.g.*, MBCA § 14.22(a) (two years). Again, most statutes also provide that any reinstatement relates back to the date of dissolution. *See, e.g.*, MBCA § 14.22(c). A few do not and a question exists, upon which little authority exists, as to whether a reinstated corporation in such a jurisdiction may have a gap in its corporate existence. Quite a bit of variation exists among jurisdictions, so the best answer is always to check the relevant statute, but Chunk and Mystic Pizza can probably rely on your conclusion that the above represents a very typical pattern. Mystic Pizza, Inc. may be brought back to life.

54. **Answer (C) is the best answer.** Piercing the veil is a favorite theory of litigators. It is an "add on" claim filed most often when the defendant is a small corporation, on top of or after the plaintiff has alleged contract or tort claims against the corporation. The claim represents an attempt to reach the pockets of the owners, the shareholders of the corporation, and not the officer or directors. Usually, when courts pierce the veil, they pierce it as to all the owners. One ramification of that is that in a small corporation, as owner, you must keep a watch on things. You are your sister's keeper. Another is that because of the inequity involved when any number of innocent shareholders are involved, courts seldom, if ever, allow the veil to fall if more than a handful of shareholders stand behind the veil. No court would pierce the corporate veil at, say, General Motors.

Answer (D) is incorrect. Law students sometimes forget that an agent of a corporation is always liable for his own torts. If Melba served the drinks to a customer, knowing he was inebriated, she is a tortfeasor, liable directly for her tort. In that case, neither the plaintiff nor the judge needs to pierce the veil to reach Melba's (presumably) deep pocket.

Answers (A) and (B) are incorrect. Doctrinally, the area of corporate disregard is filled with statements of legal conclusions and, in Justice Cardozo's words, "enveloped in the mists of metaphor." *Berkey v. Third Ave. Ry.*, 155 N.E. 58, 61 (N.Y. Ct. App. 1926). Courts talk of inadequate or thin capitalization, but they seldom analyze what capital is for purposes of the doctrine. In finance, the capital would be what is permanently contributed to corporation, that is, the equity of $10,000. For veil piercing purposes, capital is defined more broadly. Basically, it is what the shareholders are "on the hook for" on behalf of the corporation, here, $50,000. Melba and Marvin became ultimately responsible for that amount when they guaranteed CEI's bank loan. Capital also includes liability insurance coverage, here, $100,000 — for a total of $150,000.

Most courts would find the capital here adequate. *The law allows persons to incorporate precisely to limit their liability.* If the promoters and owners do not abuse that privilege, courts will not pierce the veil. The doctrine does not look to the adequacy of capital with the benefit of hindsight and does not exist to achieve the objective of making tort and contract claimants whole in every case. It exists to prevent or police extreme abuses of the corporate form. Courts in some states, such as California, pierce the veil frequently, doing so based upon inadequacy of capital alone. *See Minton v. Cavaney*, 364 P.2d 473 (Cal. 1961). California courts use the "trifling or illusory" test which came from a corporate law treatise authored by Professor Ballantine, who taught at the University of California at Berkeley. *See* HENRY BALLANTINE, BALLANTINE ON CORPORATIONS 303 (rev. ed. 1946). Courts in other states note the ability to incorporate to limit liability and the modern day abrogation of even the most modest $500 or $1,000 minimum capital requirements which once were widespread. Those courts require, in addition to inadequacy of capital, the presence of one or both of the other two principal bases for veil piercing: intermixture of the affairs of the owner and of the corporation, or use of the corporation solely, or primarily, to evade a contract, work a fraud, or evade a statute. *See also Consumer's Co-op. of Walworth County v. Olsen*, 419 N.W.2d 211 (Wis. 1988).

When the owners utilize a corporation solely or primarily to evade (an existing) contract, or statute, or other obligation imposed by law, the court may disregard the corporation. In one case, *McLoughlin v. L. Bloom Sons Co.*, 24 Cal. Rptr. 311 (Ct. App. 1962), the owner of three shoe stores in San Jose operated them through a corporation which had signed a collective bargaining agreement with a labor union. When the corporation opened a fourth store in a new suburban mall, it utilized another corporation so as to evade unionization. The appellate court disregarded the existence of the newer corporation. There are many of these cases. *See, e.g., Culinary Workers and Bartenders Union Local No. 596 Health & Welfare Trust v. Gateway Cafe, Inc.*, 630 P.2d 1348 (Wash. 1981) (brazen purchasers of cafe used new corporation, Bypass, Inc. to attempt to evade collective bargaining agreement and unfunded union pension liabilities); *Roccograndi v. Unemployment Comp. Bd. of Review*, 178 A.2d 786 (Pa. Super. Ct. 1962) (self-employed persons incorporated wrecking business, and then took turns being "laid off" to draw unemployment compensation). *Cf. Stark v. Flemming*, 283 F.2d 410 (9th Cir. 1960) (self-employed person formed corporation and conveyed farm to corporation so as to be able to draw social security benefits as an employee; court held it was for Congress, not common law doctrines of corporate disregard, to police the practice).

This Question is based on *Baatz v. Arrow Bar*, 452 N.W.2d 138 (S.D. 1990).

55.   **Answer (B) is the best answer.** This is the second "structural situation" in which veil piercing arises. Rather than seeking to hold flesh-and-blood owners personally liable, as in Question 51 above, the plaintiff seeks to pierce the veil between a subsidiary and its parent corporation. Hypothetically, finding insufficient assets in the parent, a plaintiff could seek to pierce a second veil to reach the pockets of the owners of the parent, be they human actors or another, "grandparent" corporation.

The Question here though specifies that BEI has more than enough assets. Over the years, courts and commentators have observed that courts ought to allow more veil piercing in this situation, as the plaintiff seeks not to hold human beings, but merely another corporation, liable. In an extensive empirical study of 2,200 judicial opinions, though, Professor Robert Thompson concluded that courts do the opposite of what they say. Courts allow plaintiffs to pierce the veil less frequently in the corporate group (*e.g.*, subsidiary-parent) context. *See* Robert Thompson, *Piercing the Corporate Veil: An Empirical Study*, 76 CORNELL L. REV. 1036 (1991). This may be explained in part by the surmise that corporate groups probably have more sophisticated corporate attorneys who insure that subsidiaries are adequately capitalized and that the parent corporation does not intermix (meddle) too much in the subsidiary's affairs.

Here, though, it seems that BEI's attorney, however sophisticated, allowed conduct that would provide a good basis for veil piercing. Courts have held that mere identity of joint officers and directors in the subsidiary may be relevant evidence, but alone is not enough to justify veil piercing. Beyond identity of corporate officials, plaintiff Kenyon can prove grossly thin capitalization of the subsidiary and extensive intermeddling. The conversion (theft of customers), the abdication by AgriEast officers and directors in favor of BEI employees, and the takeover by the parent of the subsidiary's day-to-day affairs all might convince a court to hold BEI liable on veil piercing grounds. In such a case, the separate corporate identity of the subsidiary should be disregarded.

In fact, many lawyers and courts might urge or adopt a so-called "alter ego" or "instrumentality" theory. The idea is that separate existence is so lacking and intermixture of affairs is so complete that the subsidiary has become "the mere instrumentality," or "alter ego," or "agent" of the parent. The parent dominates completely the subsidiary's business and affairs. Whether "instrumentality," "alter ego," or "agency" merely constitute language used for emphasis, or independent legal theories, is uncertain. The issue, though, seems academic. Courts apply those words, or theories, based upon the same forms of conduct that forms the basis for veil piercing — *e.g.*, inadequate capitalization or intermixture (or domination) of the subsidiary's affairs.

Answers (A), (C), and (D) are not the best answers. As to Answers (A) and (C), alleging personal liability or a conspiracy to defraud may be overkill, motivate BEI corporate officers and directors to fight to the death, and eliminate any chance for settlement of the dispute. As to Answer (D), the attorney general has bigger fish to fry, would regard this as a routine veil piercing better left to litigation between the parties, and would quickly decline any invitation to become involved.

56. **Answer (C) is the best answer.** But, it is a close question. A court could well choose Answer (C) or apply an emerging doctrine known as "enterprise liability." If each tanker is put into a separate entity, adequately insured for most risks of normal operation, and other capital is contributed, separate "corporateness" may be upheld.

The lesson to be learned is that riskier segments of a business might be segregated from asset-rich or less-risky segments of the same business, if the strategy is not abused. As long as the separation is clear and maintained, capital adequate to "the business to be done or the risks of loss" is provided, and the subsidiary has a measure of functional independence, a business may pursue a segmentation strategy. It is common, for example, to put truck and other corporate vehicles into a "transportation subsidiary," which then contracts to provide services to the parent and to other subsidiaries. Those dealings must, then, be above board, clearly demarcated, and adequately capitalized (including liability insurance), but the practice clearly is legitimate. The segmentation strategy may be abused, however, when, for example, scores of subsidiaries are used rather than a handful of subsidiaries, each with little or no capitalization or function independence. *See, e.g., OTR Associates v. IBC Services, Inc.*, 801 A.2d 407 (N.J. Super. Ct. App. Div. 2002) (hundreds of subsidiaries formed and controlled from corporate headquarters for individual leases by Blimpie franchisees).

Enterprise liability has been applied when large multinationals attempt to hide behind subsidiaries' separate existence after torts have been committed by a far flung subsidiary (often a third- or fourth-tier subsidiary) operating in a distant corner of the globe. Amoco (Standard Oil of New Jersey) was held liable for the wreck of and oil spilled by the supertanker *Amoco Cadiz* off France in 1978, despite two layers of subsidiaries between the vessel's putative owner, Amoco Tankers, Inc. and the parent company. *See In re Oil Spill by Amoco Cadiz off Coast of France on Mar. 16, 1978*, 954 F.2d 1279 (7th Cir. 1992). By contrast, Westin was held not liable for a drowning at a hotel operated by its Mexican subsidiary. *See Gardemal v. Westin Hotel Co.*, 186 F.3d 588 (5th Cir. 1999). Plaintiffs have urged application of the concept to Texaco for its subsidiary's environmental degradations in Ecuador; to Royal Dutch Shell for human rights abuses by its Nigerian subsidiary; and to Union Oil of California (Unocal) for human rights violations in construction of a natural gas pipeline in Myanmar (Burma).

Enterprise liability may lie when there exists common control of various corporations and those corporations have contributed to a collective enterprise or endeavor. Facts such as common employees, use of the same parent company logo, use of a central treasury or bank account, undercapitalization, and the like support a finding of enterprise liability. From a policy standpoint, commentators have called enterprise liability in the multinational context "honest bookkeeping": that is, if the profits from an activity flow back to the headquarter's country, so, too, should the responsibility (liability) for activities undertaken by subsidiaries operating in distant regions.

Answers (A), (B), and (D) are not the best answers for the reasons stated above.

57.   **Answer (D) is the best answer.**

This Question mimics the taxi company cases, such as *Walkovszky v. Carlton*, 223 N.E.2d 6 (N.Y. 1966). New York taxi owners formed a series of "sibling" corporations. Each corporation had two taxi cabs, each of which was subject to a significant lien. Each corporation obtained the minimum liability insurance permitted under the financial responsibility law. The only significant assets of each corporation are the taxi medallions, permitting the cabs to operate in the City. A City ordinance prohibited creditors from attaching the taxi medallions. In *Mangan v. Terminal Transportation System, Inc.*, 284 N.Y.S. 183 (Sup. Ct. 1935), *aff'd per curiam*, 286 N.Y.S. 666 (App. Div. 1936), 20 or so cabs all bore the same logo on the doors (Seon Cab), operated out of the same garage, and had the same dispatcher. A tort claimant was able to convince the court to pierce the veils among the 10 or so corporations ("sideways piercing," if you will), holding the corporations to be one enterprise. This type of piercing, holding brother-sister corporations to be one entity, is the third main structural situation in which courts pierce the corporate veil. Plaintiff Walkovszky attempted to reach the assets of the flesh-and-blood owner, Carlton. Apparently, Carlton had been careful to segregate his personal affairs from those of his taxicab companies.

The case came down to inadequate capitalization. The New York Court of Appeals examined the two applicable statutes, the first of which (the business corporation act) allowed one to incorporate precisely to limit one's personal liability, and the second of which (the financial responsibility law) required $10,000 insurance coverage and no more. The court refused to hold that Walkovszky could reach Carlton's personal assets. A strong dissent pointed out that the majority's decision permitted use of the financial responsibility law to defeat the law's goal, which was as much as possible to make whole victims of auto accidents. The court remanded the case, giving Walkovszky a strong hint that he might have more luck trying to reach the assets of the brother-sister cab companies. Instead, Walkovszky filed an amended complaint alleging more acts by Carlton, still attempting to reach the pocket of the flesh-and-blood owner. The case settled soon thereafter.

In this case, Millie Mild should follow the *Mangan* court's advice, seeking to hold the 12 corporations as one enterprise. In addition she may also attempt to reach Walker's assets, but as the Question is written there is no evidence of intermixture of his personal affairs with those of the corporations.

Courts and commentators may also refer to this sideways piercing as "enterprise liability." The various brother-sister, or sibling, corporations (corporations under the control of the same owner) are operated as, or in reality are, one enterprise.

Answers (A), (B), and (C) are not the best answers for the reasons stated above.

58.   **Answer (B) is the best answer.** A tort claimant has no opportunity to investigate the affairs of the corporation whose truck or taxicab collides with her. She cannot say "don't hit me" because your insurance is insufficient and your capitalization otherwise is thin.

Answer (D) is not the best answer. Because of the strong common law interest in the stability of land titles, courts have been extremely reluctant to apply the doctrine in real property cases.

Answers (A) and (C) are not the best answers. A contract claimant does have that opportunity. That is especially true of significant creditors such as banks, who do assure themselves that the owner of an incorporated enterprise has set it up properly and continues to operate it in that fashion. Bank can ascertain whether the affairs of the owner and the corporation are sufficiently segregated, and the capital adequate "given the business to be done and the risks of loss." If banks have any doubt, they usually obtain personal guarantees of the loan by the owners of an incorporated business. Trade creditors, those who supply smaller amounts of goods and services on open account indebtedness, are another significant class of contract creditors. They often do not have the practical ability that a bank or landlord would have to investigate a corporation with which they do business. Nonetheless, numerous courts have stated that they are more willing to pierce the corporate veil in cases of tort rather than contract. In contract, the claimant had an opportunity (if only in theory) to investigate the corporation first while the tort claimant does not. In his extensive empirical study of veil piercing cases, Professor Robert Thompson found that courts do the opposite of what they say they do. *See* Robert Thompson, *Piercing the Corporate Veil: An Empirical Study*, 76 CORNELL L. REV. 1036 (1991). They pierce the veil more often in contract than in tort cases (41.98 versus 30.7%). The important point to remember, however, is the accepted wisdom and the reasoning behind it. In theory, all things being equal, a tort claimant should have a (slightly?) better chance of reaching the assets of shareholders who have abused the corporate form.

59.   Piercing the corporate veil has a procedural aspect. Intermixture of affairs by the parent corporation with those of its subsidiary may subject the parent to jurisdiction in a remote forum where the subsidiary operates. Although less likely, the reverse may be true. A subsidiary may be made to answer in the jurisdiction in which its parent corporation is headquartered or has operations. *See, e.g., Empire Steel Corp. of Texas v. Superior Court*, 366 P.2d 502 (Cal. 1961) (service on subsidiary's corporate officer in California held good against Texas parent corporation of which he was also an officer); *see also Taca Int'l Airlines, Inc. v. Rolls-Royce, Ltd.*, 201 A.2d 97 (N.J. Sup. Ct. Law Div. 1964) (service on New Jersey subsidiary held good as against Canadian parent and English grandparent corporations). Taking the allegations of the complaint as true, and assuming plaintiff Kenyon's attorneys have made some semblance of the proper argument, you should advise the judge not to dismiss for lack of territorial jurisdiction. Plaintiff Kenyon should be able to proceed in California against the out-of-state parent corporation based upon its intermeddling in the affairs of its California subsidiary.

A note of caution to the judge: she should remind the parties that, just because she has held that *in personam* jurisdiction may be asserted against BEI, her holding does not necessarily mean that plaintiff Kenyon will be able to pierce the corporate veil "on the merits," that is, after he has established his claim.

60. **Answer (A) is the best answer.** You have found a written contract of guarantee, made by someone with undoubted authority to enter into such a contract on behalf of the parent corporation, BEI. The liability of BEI would be direct. Plaintiff would no longer have to place primary reliance on his piercing the corporate veil theory.

In Question 55, the Dram Shop Act claim case against a tavern, the teaching was always to look for direct involvement of the owners of the corporation who would be personally liable for their own torts (*i.e.*, breach of the duty of care). In contracts, the rule is different. Generally speaking, corporate officers are not liable for acts constituting breach of corporate contracts. Like human actors, corporations are permitted to engage in "economic breach." If a corporation is willing to run the risk of paying damages and wishes to engage in economic breach, it must do so through human actors. Those human actors should not be held liable for acting on behalf of the corporation.

This case, however, is different. It is not a case of breach. Instead, it is a case of a human actor contracting on behalf of the corporation (which is the only way fictional beings such as corporations can act, through actual human beings). In cases of contract, always look for direct liability first — a holding out, a contract of guarantee, and so on — that may be a platform for holding the shareholder or shareholders, whether a parent corporation or a human owner liable, in addition to any veil piercing theory you may wish to pursue.

Answers (B), (C), and (D) are not the best answers for the reasons stated above.

61. **Answer (D) is the best answer.** Equitable subordination is a doctrine closely related to corporate veil piercing. It is also known as the "Deep Rock doctrine," after a leading case in which the U.S. Supreme Court recognized and approved the doctrine, *Taylor v. Standard Gas & Electric Co.*, 306 U.S. 307 (1939); *see also Pepper v. Litton*, 308 U.S. 295 (1939) (equitable subordination of wage claims by sole shareholder to claims of outside creditors upheld). Here, Grosse Bank should be attempting to "deep rock" Hans and Franz.

If Hans and Franz are able to stand "elbow to elbow" with others in the line of creditors at the bankruptcy court, absent transaction costs, each creditor will receive three-fifths of the face amount of the debts ($500,000 in debt against $300,000 in assets). Grosse Bank would receive $120,000. By contrast, if the court pushes Hans and Franz to the end of the line, treating them as a separate "subordinated" creditor class, each creditor will receive six-sevenths of the face amount of the debts ($350,000 in debt against $300,000 in assets). Grosse Bank would receive $171,600. Hans and Franz would receive zero. In effect, by subordination, the court treats Hans's and Franz's "loans" as in reality being equity, pushed down the right hand side of the balance sheet from "liabilities" to "shareholders' equity" or "capital stock." Hans and Franz receive nothing unless and until creditors have received complete (100 cents on the dollar) payment, a very unlikely prospect in any bankruptcy.

The grounds for equitable subordination are much the same as veil piercing: grossly thin capitalization and/or intermixture of the owners' affairs with those of the corporation. Thin capitalization perhaps looms a bit larger here than in run-of-the-mill veil piercing cases. In the principal case upon which the hypothetical is based, *Costello v. Fazio*, 256 F.2d 903 (9th Cir. 1958), the court found that the owners' prior experience as a partnership demonstrated what capital was necessary for the business. Here that would be $210,000. There, and probably here, the debts owing to the shareholders would be subordinated.

One additional aspect should be noted. Being subordinated, or "deep rocked," is not as catastrophic as is veil piercing. In equitable subordination, Hans and Franz lose $150,000. While very unpleasant, it is not as severe as the loss of personal assets (house, SUV, ski condo, and so on) that would occur if the court had ordered that the veil be pierced.

Answers (A), (B), and (C) are not the best answers for the reasons stated above.

62. The best answer is "No." In veil piercing and equitable subordination cases, for the most part, courts have based results on a "snapshot" of the corporation's capitalization at the time of formation and a period thereafter. If the capital is found to have been sufficient for the original business plan, courts have further held there is no additional duty to "top up" or increase the capital as the business grows or its risk profile changes. *See, e.g., Arnold v. Phillips*, 117 F.2d 497 (5th Cir. 1941). By contrast, banks and other significant creditors know that the capital of a corporation is a "pad" or "cushion" for the creditors. It is their safety margin in case of a liquidation or bankruptcy. As a business grows, banks and other creditors will urge or insist that the owners widen the "capital base" before they lend further funds, or lend funds in the first place. But, banks' and other creditors' predilections are a business, rather than a legal, matter. Courts impose no requirement to widen the "capital base" as a business grows, either under veil piercing or related doctrines such as equitable subordination.

63.   **Answer (D) is the best answer.** But, **Answer (C) would also be perfectly acceptable.** Once a corporation has been formed, it generally is then "capitalized." Think of the newly formed corporation as an empty shell, or box. Capitalization is the process of putting money and other assets into the box. Assets may include an existing business that had operated as a proprietorship or partnership, or equipment, as here, or inventory, raw material, land, or land and a building. Then from the corporation, or out of the box, come various pieces of paper representing different types of interests in the corporation. Here, the pieces of paper will be stock certificates for all three participants and promissory notes for all three as well.

       Answers (A) and (B) are not the best answers. In simple, small incorporations such as the one described, attorneys avoid getting too fancy. Attorneys cause the corporation to "issue" common stock in equal proportions to all shareholders, whether there are two, three, four, or five. Issuing common and preferred stock would be too complicated for this fact scenario. The same is true as to Answer (B), for at least one of the same reasons. The partners' expectation is probably that each will receive equal treatment, but, of course, that may be subject to negotiation.

       Common stock is usually voting stock, the most important attribute of which is the right to elect directors. It is described as the "residual interest" in the corporation because, in a liquidation, after all the liabilities have been paid, the common stockholders receive whatever remains (the residue). If the company has not been successful, the common stockholders will receive nothing. If the company has succeeded, say, been wildly successful, the common stockholders own everything after the fixed amount claims "above it" have been paid.

       MBCA § 6.01(b) sets forth the only legal requirements:

       The articles of incorporation must authorize (1) one or more classes of shares that together have unlimited voting rights, and (2) one or more classes of shares (which may be the same class or classes as those with voting rights) that together are entitled to receive the net assets of the corporation upon dissolution.

       By custom, one class, usually called common stock, has both attributes: voting and the right to receive the residual interest. "Above it" is a reference to where physically on a balance sheet the owner's equity, here represented by common stock, is placed. Owner's equity ("capital stock" or "common stock" plus retained earnings) is on the lower right side, at the bottom, below all the liabilities. Owner's equity is usually separated from liabilities by a horizontal line, as follows:

Dukes' Racing, Inc.
Initial Balance Sheet

Cash	$30,000	Capital Stock:	
Race Car	$15,000	Jesse 100 shares	$15,000
		Beau 100 shares	$15,000
		Luke 100 shares	$15,000
Total	$45,000	Total	$45,000

In a simple incorporation, the most common variant on an all common stock capital structure is a structure with stock and a promissory note (loan) for each participant (Answer (D)). The reasons are that interest on a debt is an expense to the corporation, and therefore deductible, while money paid out as dividends on shares is taxed as profits to the corporation and as income to the shareholders (double taxation — but reduced by the 2003 Tax Reform Act to 15 percent at the individual shareholder level). Also, in case of bad times and liquidation, if the use of debt has not been abused (see the Answer to Question 58), as creditors, shareholders may stand a chance of receiving something back from the liquidating corporation.

With such a capitalization, the balance sheet might look like this:

Dukes' Racing, Inc.
Initial Balance Sheet

Cash	$30,000	Capital Stock:	
Race Car	$15,000	Jesse 100 shares	$10,000
		Beau 100 shares	$10,000
		Luke 100 shares	$10,000
		Promissory Notes:	
		Jesse	$5,000
		Beau	$5,000
		Luke	$5,000
Total	$45,000	Total	$45,000

With their corporation duly formed, capitalized, and the books "set up," Beau, Luke, and Jesse are ready to go off to the races.

64.   **Answer (B) is the best answer.** Authorized shares "means the shares of all classes a domestic or foreign corporation is authorized to issue" by the articles of incorporation. MBCA § 1.40(2). Once shares are authorized, the directors have power to issue them, subject of course to their fiduciary duties. If, however, the directors bump up against the number of shares authorized, they must go back to the shareholders, seeking amendment of the articles of incorporation. The authorized share limitation on the power to issue is a loose, but important, check on the directors' power. Exceeding the number of authorized shares by issuing shares above the number contained in the articles is an "over issue." Older statutes had stiff penalties for directors in the case of over issuances. By and large, those penalties are gone now, but a shareholder should be able to enjoin an over issue. **Answer (A) is incorrect** because the corporation does have 200 unissued shares, which the directors may

reissue.

"Shares that are issued are outstanding shares until they are reacquired, redeemed, converted, or cancelled." MBCA § 6.03(a). The term "issued shares" refers to all of the shares the corporation has ever issued, whether they are in shareholders' hands or have been re-acquired by the corporation. The term "outstanding shares" refers to shares that have been issued and remaining "out there" in shareholders' hands. In olden times, when the corporation re-acquired shares, they became "treasury shares." The directors could re-issue them. Or, alternatively, in a second formal act, the directors could vote to "retire" the shares, in which case the power to reissue would be lost and the number of authorized shares reduced accordingly. The Model Act abolishes the treasury share concept (although people still use the terminology all the time). Therefore, **Answers (C) and (D) are incorrect.** MBCA § 6.31(a) provides that "[a] corporation may acquire its own shares, and shares so acquired constitute authorized but unissued shares." That is, they revert to their earlier, or earliest, status rather than remaining "in the treasury" — unless, as MBCA § 6.31(b) tells us, "the articles of incorporation prohibit the reissue of acquired shares," in which case, "the number of authorized shares is reduced by the number of shares acquired."

Here, under either the old scheme or the MBCA, the directors had 200 shares at their disposal: 100 authorized, but unissued, shares and 100 treasury shares under the old scheme, and 200 authorized, but unissued, shares under newer versions of the MBCA. Beau could not get the injunction based upon a pure technical argument. He may, however, succeed with an argument that Luke and Roscoe have violated fiduciary duties.

65.   **Answer (D) is the best answer.** Historically, there were corporate law rules that governed what could come into the corporation in kind and amount in return for stock. The MBCA eliminated them in the early 1980s and many states have followed. Although once correct, **Answer (A) is incorrect** under current versions of the MBCA. There remain several holdouts and, in foreign jurisdictions, various sets of "legal capital" rules are alive and well. It is therefore helpful to review them, if only for background purposes.

At the incorporation stage, legal capital rules dealt with the following subjects:

(1) What consideration is, or is not, eligible consideration for the issuance of stock?

(2) If eligible, does the consideration measure up in amount or does it fall short, making the contributor the recipient of "watered, bonus, or discount shares"?

(3) What is the yardstick lawyers and courts use to see if the consideration measures up in money or money's worth?

(4) Who values non-cash consideration to be received for shares?

(5) Under what standard would a court review such a valuation?

AND the answers are (or were):

(1) Statutes, including the MBCA, did not state what consideration was eligible. Rather they excluded certain forms of consideration, most frequently promissory notes and future services. Exclusion resulted from a day when corporate law, as opposed to bankruptcy and fraudulent transfer law today, had as a central purpose protection of creditors. Creditors could realize nothing from future services (involuntary servitude is banned) and very little from promissory notes given for shares. Today's MBCA eliminates all such restrictions. Modern U.S. corporate law concerns itself very little with creditor protection. *See* MBCA

§ 6.21(b) ("any tangible or intangible property or benefit to the corporation, including cash, promissory notes, services to be performed, contracts for services to be performed," etc.). MBCA § 6.21(e) suggests escrowing shares to be issued for future services, but that is merely advice as to what good practice might be.

(2) If the consideration did not measure up to aggregate "par value" of the shares received, the creditors could come knocking on the shareholder's door to recover the "water." Because this cause of action arose only upon the corporation's insolvency, which could be 10 or 15 years later, it was especially pernicious. In the hypothetical, if par were $150 ($150 × 100 shares = $15,000), Uncle Jesse could be in for a rude $10,000 surprise in the event of insolvency, given that the racecar is worth only $5,000. Bonus shares were extra shares the corporation gave to a shareholder who paid par value in cash for his initial share allotment. Discount shares arose when the shareholder paid cash, but the amount of cash was less than the aggregate par value of the shares received. Legally, the treatment of bonus and discount shares was the same as with watered shares.

(3) Par value was an arbitrary number in the sense that it was the number the attorney pulled out of thin air and put in the articles of incorporation. But, it was not arbitrary in the sense that very real consequences could follow if par were set high and a shareholder paid less than par in money or money's worth (look what might happen to Uncle Jesse here). At one time (late 19th century) par value had significance in the marketplace. Credible enterprises set their par at $50, $100, or higher per share.

In the 20th century, statutory draftspersons decided that creditors of a corporation should not look at its capital "as the source of its credit and standing in the community." Rather creditors should look at items such as credit reports (how fast do they pay their bills). So statutes were amended to provide that corporations could issue "no par stock." Few lawyers used that alternative. The convention that arose was to use par, but to set it very low (Answer (D)). The marketplace had come to regard par value as having little or no meaning. Here a lawyer might set par at $1.00 per share. Even poor Beau and Luke could come up with $100 ($1.00 × 100 shares = $100). Jesse's race car has a defensible worth well above $100. High tech and other enterprises commonly used par values of 1/1000 or 1/10,000 of a cent.

The excess paid over par value ($4,900 by Uncle Jesse) would be credited to an account called "capital surplus" by the statute. Accountants called it "paid-in-capital" or "excess paid over par or stated value." Maddeningly, lawyers and accountants sometimes have different names for the same thing.

The early 1980s MBCA amendments eliminated par value. Everything paid in with respect to shares is credited to one account ("Capital Stock"). If no par value is used, there is no longer any yardstick to use in saying there has been a shortfall. The result is that if the corporation, by its board of directors, agrees to accept X consideration for Y number of shares, the shareholder may not later be said to have received "watered, bonus or discount shares." *See also* MBCA § 6.22(a) ("A purchaser from a corporation of its own shares is not liable to the corporation or its creditors with respect to the shares except to pay the consideration for which the shares were authorized to be issued."). Thus, **Answer (B) would be incorrect** under the modern schemes. Instead, the causes of action that might arise would be by a shareholder against the directors for violating their fiduciary duties in valuing (falsely) the consideration to be received. Or a shareholder who subsequently purchased shares might sue the corporation for common law or statutory securities fraud. They would base their action on the basis of the left hand side of the balance sheet, saying the assets were overvalued and the overvaluation on the balance sheet constitutes a misrepresentation. Here, for example, if the balance sheet listed Uncle Jesse's racing car at $10,000 or $15,000, *that* would be a material misrepresentation.

(4) Statutes charge the board of directors with valuing consideration to be received for shares. *See* MBCA § 6.21(c) ("Before the corporation issues shares, the board of directors must determine that the consideration received or to be received . . . is adequate.").

(5) Without statutory language, the directors' valuation would be reviewed by a court under a deferential business judgment rule standard, discussed below. Statutes provide for a more deferential standard yet, such as "in the absence of fraud" or "in the absence of actual fraud," "the determination of the board of directors is conclusive." *See, e.g.*, MBCA § 6.21(c). In other words, even if the directors were grossly negligent in valuing consideration, a court would accept their conclusion. Only intentional misconduct would trigger further judicial inquiry. Thus, **Answer (C) is not the best answer.**

66.　It would look something like this:

Dukes' Racing, Inc.
Initial Balance Sheet

Cash	$0	Capital Stock:	
Contract Services	$15,000	Jesse 100 shares	$5,000
Promissory Note	$15,000	Beau 100 shares	$15,000
Race Car	$5,000	Luke 100 shares	$15,000
Total	$35,000	Total	$45,000

Note that there is no longer any "bright line" objection to shareholders paying different amounts for shares when they are purchasing at about the same time. Par value, when it existed, and was customarily set at more than a nominal number, served that function: it set a floor above which everyone paid. With low par, and now elimination of par altogether, par value no longer exists to perform that function. Instead, it is a consensual matter. If the parties all agree, Uncle Jesse may contribute consideration worth $5,000 and other shareholders contribute consideration arguably worth $15,000, for the same thing, to wit, 100 shares. If the parties do not consent, or their consent is procured by misrepresentations, it is now, strictly speaking, not a corporate law matter. It is matter for a fraud or securities fraud claim.

67.　**Answer (D) is the best answer.** In a modest incorporation in which the parties know one another, as in the Beau, Luke, and Uncle Jesse Questions above, lawyers dispense with subscription agreements. The parties attend the organizational meeting. At that point, they hand over their checks and receive their share certificates. That is not the case here.

Answers (A) (B), and (C) are not the best answers. When more than a handful of people are involved, or when it is important to bind an investor to an enterprise that has not yet been incorporated, attorneys draft and utilize formal subscription agreements. At common law, there were two theories of subscription agreements. One was that they were mere offers which could be revoked at any time before the corporation came into existence. The later, and more enlightened view, was that subscription agreements were also agreements among the subscribers "inter se." A subscriber could revoke an agreement only with the consent of her fellow subscribers. Today most jurisdictions have statutes on the subject. MBCA § 6.21 has five subsections dealing with the subject of subscriptions. MBCA § 6.21(a) reflects a modified "inter se" approach: "A subscription for shares entered into before incorporation is irrevocable for six months unless the subscription provides a longer period or all the subscribers agree to revocation." Once the corporation comes into being, MBCA § 6.21(e) makes clear that the subscription then becomes "a contract between the subscriber and the corporation." Acting through its board of directors, the corporation then could release the subscriber from her obligation.

Clare, Rachel, and Erika cannot merely "fork over" share certificates (Answer (B)) because the corporation has not yet been formed. They can garner signatures on subscription agreements, or garner signatures and accept checks. If they do the latter, good practice would be to deposit the checks in an escrow account, pending both incorporation and raising the $2.5 million they deem necessary to begin the enterprise. Good practice is not, however, required by law.

68.   **Answer (C) is the best answer.** Venture capitalists often take convertible preferred stock in companies in which they have made an investment. A preferred stock is "preferred" because the issuing company's articles of incorporation so provide. The stock may be preferred as to dividends (*e.g.*, 7 percent preferred, meaning 7 percent of stated value which often is $100), or preferred upon liquidation (in which case the articles set out a "liquidation preference," say, $110). Often preferred shares are preferred in both ways but, again, the articles of incorporation have to spell out the preferred's "designations, preferences, limitations and relative rights." *See* MBCA § 6.01(c) & (d).

Preferred as to dividends or distributions means that the preferred must receive its dividend before any dividend may be paid on the common. But, what happens if there are no dividends on the common for several quarters or even years? The dividend on the preferred may then forever be lost under some states' court decisions unless the articles provide that it is a "cumulative preferred." *See, e.g., Guttmann v. Illinois Central R.R.*, 189 F.2d 927 (2d Cir. 1951) (Frank, J.). On the other hand, in a startup, significant preferred stock "dividend arrearages" may drag the company down if the preferred is a cumulative preferred. So a hybrid is often used — "cumulative if earned." If the company has profits, it may chose not to distribute them but, if that is the case, a dividend arrearage begins to mount. Preferred may be "participating," in which case, after so much has been paid out on the common stock, the preferred is entitled to a second dividend, if you will. Or the preferred may be expressly made non-participating.

Some "preferred stock contracts," as the courts call the subsection of the articles spelling out the preferred's "preferences, limitations and relative rights," provide for default voting rights. The preferred does not vote (but only because the articles so provide) but, upon default of paying dividends for eight successive quarters, the articles grant the preferred the right to elect three (five? a majority?) of the directors.

Here, the preferred stock contract would provide for convertibility, that is, the preferred may be converted into common stock at a specified ratio. The ratio is set so as to make the conversion option viable only if the common stock rises significantly in price.

Preferred stock contracts are much like the childhood game of "Mr. Potato Head." Lawyers put various combinations of features into the articles depending upon what the investment bankers say will sell, the parties themselves negotiate, or in accordance with whatever the current fad is. So there could be a "7 percent cumulative (if earned) non-participating convertible preferred" with default voting rights. These features are some of the customary ones attorneys and financial officers have used, but the only limitation is their imagination. A preferred could be called "blue moon" preferred and its principal right might be to throw water balloons at the CEO if certain specified earnings targets are not met.

Answer (A) is not the best answer. Kleiner Perkins might have the greatest safety for its investment by making a loan. If, however, the company is to grow, Webvan will have to borrow from others, probably from banks. The banks will want a satisfactory "equity cushion." It will object to the venture capitalist being on the same footing as the bank. If, however, the bank borrowing is somewhat away in the future, Kleiner could take a convertible debt security. When and if bank borrowing becomes imminent, Kleiner could convert and "widen Webvan's equity base," facilitating bank borrowing.

Answer (B) is not the best answer. Usually, bank borrowing will not be far down the road so the venture capitalist takes an equity position at the start. That equity position could be all common stock. The problem is that with a $30 million infusion, Kleiner would receive so much common stock that the founders of the company would lose control of the board of directors.

Answer (D) is incorrect. Firms taking orders for groceries over the Internet have been successful.

The convention that has arisen is to use convertible preferred stock (Answer (C)). The venture capitalist stands some chance of a small recovery in the event of liquidation. In the event of great success, the venture capitalist converts the preferred into common and sells some into the market, thereby reaping its profits. Your advice for the lawyers: they have to prepare and have Webvan's current shareholders adopt a "preferred stock contract" for insertion in Webvan's articles of incorporation. What that contract contains will be the outcome of negotiations between the venture capitalist and the company in which it invests.

Some successful smaller and mid-size companies issue preferred shares to the older generation, say, members of the original founding families, to give them fixed income. Public utilities such as electric and natural gas companies traditionally (pre-Enron and pre-deregulation) issued series of preferred stock (batches labeled "series A," "series B," "series C," etc.). Utilities had steady, ample cash flows with which to pay the dividend. In turn, the steady dividends made the preferred shares attractive investments for trusts, retirement plans, and older, conservative investors. Preferred share issuances were a principal means by which utilities raised significant amounts of capital.

69. **Answer (A) is the best answer.** The capital structure of a corporation (or other form of entity) allocates the three essential ingredients of an enterprise: risk, reward, and control. For example, a senior debt security would be paid first in the event of a liquidation. It has the least risk. As a consequence, debt securities commonly have a fixed return (although there are debt securities with variable rates of payment called "income bonds") and no voting or other control rights. At the opposite end of the spectrum, common stock would be paid last in the event of a liquidation and would receive nothing if the business had not been successful. It, therefore, has the most risk of all. Because it has the most risk, common stock has the most *potential* return. If the business is wildly successful, the common stock has the residual interest: to it belongs everything left over after the fixed claims above it have been

paid. Also, because it has the most risk, the common stock would have the most, or exclusive, control, manifested in its right to elect the board of directors. In between would be preferred stock such as that discussed in the previous Question. Preferred is senior to the common, represents less risk, and therefore has less control and a fixed return (but see the discussion of participating preferred stock in the Answer to Question 65). But the preferred is junior to and riskier than the debt above it. It may therefore have a stated dividend rate higher than the debt, but only contingent or default voting rights, or no voting rights whatsoever.

The old family lawyer, though, could have used the capital structure to install a power sharing arrangement between the Golden Delicious and the Granny Smith families, not as a financial, but as a political or governance, matter. He could have split the common stock into two classes, GD stock and GS stock. Each class would be identical except that the GD stock could elect two directors and the GS stock could elect two directors. The board size could be permanently capped at four, or at five, with the fifth director chosen by the four elected directors. *See, e.g., Lehrman v. Cohen*, 222 A.2d 800 (Del. 1966) (upholding fifth director tie-breaking device). Such a power sharing arrangement would foil any "divide and conquer" strategy Gomer and the Golden Delicious family contemplated using to split up the Granny Smith family shareholders. MBCA § 7.25 outlines the mechanics of voting such shares. Now, however, Gomer and his sister may not be amenable to an amendment of the articles to split the common stock into two classes. On the other hand, there would be no harm in asking.

Answer (B) makes little sense. Why create a situation that may force the sale of interests the parties may wish to keep?

Answer (C) is also unsatisfactory. It amounts only to "closing the barn door after the horse is gone."

Answer (D) (do nothing) is not the best answer for the reasons stated above.

70.   **Answer (C) is the best answer.** In a hostile takeover bid, or tender offer (the two terms are used interchangeably), a bidder anticipates that the "target company" board of directors will not be receptive to a merger proposal. The bidder thus makes an offer directly to the target company shareholders. If the bidder obtains enough shares, the bidder elects its own people to the target board. Those new directors then propose a merger with the bidder or a subsidiary of the bidder. Hostile takeover bids are discussed in depth below.

In the mid 1980s, at the height of the U.S. takeover boom, one defense that arose was issuance of super voting stock to an inner circle of "safe" shareholders. The corporate euphemism for such a defensive use of a company's capital structure was "dual class capitalization." Dual class capitalization might be a suitable defensive measure here. By contrast, **Answers (A), (B), and (D) are not the best answers** as they would be overkill, suitable as takeover defenses only if an identifiable threat existed (if at all).

Some companies have always had dual class capitalization. For example, through a dual class capitalization, the extended Ford family continues to hold over 40 percent of the voting power of Ford Motor Co. Some hi-tech companies have gone public with dual class capitalizations already in place, reserving to the founders extraordinary voting power.

When, in the 1980s, larger public companies tried to re-arrange their capital structures in midstream, however, they encountered an obstacle. The New York Stock Exchange (NYSE) had a "one share, one vote" rule for companies that list shares on the NYSE. Fearing the loss of listings to the National Association of Securities Dealers Automatic Quotation System

(NASDAQ), which had no such rule, the NYSE prepared to capitulate to the listed companies that wished to issue super voting stock. The Securities and Exchange Commission then intervened, passing its own "one share, one vote rule." Then the Business Roundtable, an organization consisting of the CEOs of 150 of the largest U.S. corporations, took the SEC to court. In *Business Roundtable v. SEC*, 905 F.2d 406 (D.C. Cir. 1990), the court held that the SEC had exceeded any statutory mandate it may have, which by and large is limited to requiring disclosure. Corporate governance, including the voting of shares, is a matter of state and not federal law. There was then no legal obstacle to issuing super voting stock, at least as a matter of federal law.

The mechanics of issuing super voting stock vary. In the Question, for example, Fabulous could seek to amend its articles to provide that shares held for over 10 years by the same person or persons would have five times the normal voting power in the election of directors, thus vastly magnifying the inner circle's voting power. *See Williams v. Geier*, 671 A.2d 1368 (Del. 1996) (shares held at record date would have 10 votes per share, but upon any disposition would revert to one vote per share until such time as shares had been held for 36 consecutive months, at which time shares revert to 10 votes per share).

Fabulous might not need to amend its articles. Many companies have authority in their articles for "blank check" classes of stock. MBCA § 6.02(a) authorizes the practice: "If the articles of incorporation so provide, the board of directors may determine, in whole or in part, the preferences, limitations, and relative rights . . . of any class of shares before the issuance of any shares of that class." The board of directors is able to "fill in the blanks" on the blank check. The need for "blank check" authority arose in the turbulent markets of the mid 1970s, when interest rates gyrated as high as 21 percent. It was felt that when "market windows" opened temporarily, boards of directors had to be able to get new share issuances quickly to market. They would not be able to do so if they first had to convene a shareholders' meeting to amend the articles of incorporation. By the time they had done so, and returned to the market, the directors would have found that the "market window" had disappeared. Use of blank check authority to issue "super voting stock" (and also in "poison pill" takeover defenses, discussed *infra*) seems a corruption of the original purpose, but it has become an accepted practice in publicly-held corporations.

Note: The two new subjects this Question introduces, dual class capitalization (a.k.a. "super voting stock") and blank check share authority, are advanced subjects for an introductory business organizations course. They are useful subjects to know about, but will seldom come into play when the client is a small or mid-size corporation.

71. Yes. A distribution is payment made "in respect of" shareholdings. It may be in the form of a cash dividend, but could be in the form of a dividend in kind (two new tires for each shareholder), or a pro rata repurchase of stock by the corporation. MBCA § 1.40(6) defines "distribution" as follows:

A direct or indirect transfer of money or other property (except its own shares) or incurrence of indebtedness by a corporation to or for the benefit of its shareholders in respect of any of its shares. A distribution may be in the form of a declaration or payment of a dividend; a purchase, redemption, or other acquisition of shares . . . or otherwise.

A payment might be made to, say, shareholder Luke, but with respect to labor performed for the corporation. Or a payment could be made to, say, Beau, but with respect to a loan he made to the corporation. Those payments to shareholders would not be dividends because the corporation did not pay them "in respect of any of its shares." Rather they were wages paid to an employee and principal or interest paid to a lender.

Corporate law regulates distributions. A director who authorizes an "illegal" distribution is "personally liable to the corporation for the amount of the distribution that exceeds what could have distributed without violating section 6.40(a)." MBCA § 8.33(a). The liability is not strict. "[T]he party asserting liability [must establish] that when taking the action the director did not comply with [the statutory duty of care]." So, before making a distribution, a corporation should obtain the opinion of attorney (formal or informal) that the distribution is legal. The yardstick MBCA § 6.40 uses for testing the legality of distributions is "double insolvency" testing. After giving effect to the distribution, the corporation must still "be able to pay its debts as they become due in the usual course of the business," that is, solvent in terms of what is known as the "equity" sense. Also, after giving effect to the distribution, the corporation's total assets must also exceed its total liabilities, that is, the corporation must be solvent in what is known as the "bankruptcy" sense.

To apply the test, we have to take a look at the corporation's balance sheet as it might look after the events described above:

Dukes' Racing, Inc.
Balance Sheet Dec. 31, 2002

Cash	$30,000	Capital Stock:	
Contract Services	$15,000	Jesse 100 shares	$5,000
Promissory Note	$15,000	Beau 100 shares	$15,000
Race Car #1	$5,000	Luke 100 shares	$15,000
Race Car #2	$5,000		
Spare Parts	$10,000	Retained Earnings	$70,000
Motor Home	$25,000		
Total	$105,000	Total	$105,000

Testing for bankruptcy solvency is easy, as the corporation has no liabilities. Giving effect to the distribution, assets — liabilities = $70,000. The corporation would be solvent in the bankruptcy, or balance sheet, sense. Testing for equity solvency (or insolvency) is more problematic. Paying a $30,000 dividend will deprive the corporation of all its cash. Thus, it will not be able to pay its debts as they become due (if, in fact, it has any debts). The wise advice may be to pay out only $24,000–$27,000, leaving $3,000–$6,000 cash in the corporation for working capital.

72.   **Answer (D) is the best answer.** A long-term repurchase is a distribution. It must therefore be tested for legality. Thus, **Answer (C) is incorrect.** The dominant legal question is whether the transaction is subject to "up front" testing (the entire $4.5 million amount), or "installment by installment" testing (each $75,000 quarterly payment), or both. From Buddy Boy's point of view, his worry was the "insolvency cutoff" that might occur four or five years down the road if Bobby and Bart mismanaged the company. For instance, while on the golf course enjoying his retirement, Buddy Boy could learn that the corporation's lawyer had instructed the company not to send a check because the $75,000 payment would make the corporation "unable to pay its debts as they come due in the normal course of business." MBCA § 6.40. Thus, **Answer (A) is not a satisfactory answer.** As the corporate lawyer, you

must use your best efforts to avoid any such "cutoff."

About 1980, amendments to the MBCA's financial provisions answered the oft-vexing question, opting for "up front" testing. MBCA § 6.40(e) provides in pertinent part:

[T]he effect of a distribution under subsection (c) [the double insolvency test] is measured . . . in the case of a distribution by purchase, redemption, or other acquisition of the corporation's shares, as of the earlier of (i) the date money or other property is transferred or debt incurred by the corporation or (ii) the date the shareholder ceases to be a shareholder with respect to the acquired shares.

Suffice it to say, that language clearly opts for up front testing. If, as of the closing date, the tests are met, Buddy Boy will exchange his share certificate for a promissory note and a check. He will not thereafter have to worry about a legal "cutoff" ending the flow of quarterly installments to him.

Answer (B) is nonsensical and therefore incorrect. Because everyone involved in the corporation agrees to this negotiated transaction, there is no possible breach of fiduciary duty.

73. It depends. Most corporations, or other business entities for that matter, carry assets on their balance sheet at cost. They may "mark to market" assets they hold for purposes of sale, such as inventory. A securities firm, for example, might revalue the inventory of securities it holds for sale on a daily basis. But most assets (equipment, land and building, and so on) are not held for sale. Instead, a business holds them for their usefulness in producing income. Conservative accounting thus dictates that those assets remain on the books at their historical cost until such time as they actually are sold. Businesses have on their books assets they have held for a long period of time that have appreciated significantly in value (say, commercial real estate in Seattle, Denver, Chicago, or New York City that was acquired many years ago). Especially in periods of inflation, hard assets such as equipment or airplanes may have value much higher than their historical cost. Intangibles, such as patents, licenses, software may have values much higher than their carrying value on the books.

Another difficult question is whether, for purposes of consummating a transaction such as the long-term installment repurchase of Buddy Boy's shares, a corporation could "write up" assets on its books to meet the applicable test. Accountants said "no." Court decisions were mixed. Around 1980, the MBCA took on this question, answering "yes."

The board of directors may base a determination that a distribution is not prohibited under subsection (c) [double insolvency test] either on the basis of accounting practices and principles that are reasonable in the circumstances or *on a fair valuation or other method that is reasonable in the circumstances.*

MBCA § 6.40(d) (emphasis added). The comments to the section make clear that, in revaluing assets, directors are subject to their fiduciary duties. Also, if they undertake a revaluation, directors should not do so on a selective basis. If they write up some assets, they should also write down the value of other assets, if economic reality so dictates.

Let's assume a balance sheet for Buddy Boy Broadcasting to see how all of this might work:

Buddy Boy Broadcasting, Inc.
Balance Sheet Dec. 31, 2003

Cash	$400,000	Accounts Payable	$300,000
Receivables	$100,000	Bank Debt	$400,000
Equipment	$300,000		
Transmitter Site	$500,000		
FCC Licenses	$100,000	Capital Stock	$100,000
Land/Building	$300,000	Retained Earnings	$900,000
Total	$1,700,000	Total	$1,700,000

Equity solvency seems not to be a problem. After giving effect to payment of the initial $75,000 installment, the corporation has sufficient, if not abundant, cash of $325,000. Balance sheet solvency is more challenging. Under the MBCA, the corporation must have a balance sheet "surplus" equal to, or greater than, $4.5 million. The corporation has, however, only $1 million in balance sheet "surplus." After giving effect to the distribution, liabilities would exceed assets by $3.5 million. The corporation would be insolvent in the "bankruptcy sense."

Assume, though, that the corporation has held the transmitter site and the building for 25 years. Rather than guessing, the board of directors (or the attorney) hires an appraiser. Conservatively, she values the transmitter site at $1.5 million and the land and the building at $2.3 million. A $3 million write-up in the assets in that manner would increase balance sheet surplus to $4 million — close, but not quite there yet. The principle intangibles here, the radio station licenses, are on the books at cost ($100,000). Say the directors (or the attorney) brings in an expert on valuation of broadcast properties. Conservatively, she values the stations at $1 million each, for a further write up of $2.9 million. Now the corporation has $6.9 million in balance sheet surplus, far more than it needs to "back" the distribution. An attorney might then render a letter of opinion that the long-term installment repurchase of Buddy Boy's shares meets the requirements of the MBCA. And, evidencing solvency in the bankruptcy sense, the balance sheet might now look something like the following:

Buddy Boy Broadcasting, Inc.
Balance Sheet Dec. 31, 2003

Cash	$400,000	Accounts Payable	$300,000
Receivables	$100,000	Bank Debt	$400,000
Equipment	$300,000		
Transmitter Site	$1,500,000	Capital Stock	$100,000
FCC Licenses	$3,000,000	Retained Earnings	$900,000
Land/Building	$2,300,000	Revaluation Surplus	$5,900,000
Total	$7,600,000	Total	$7,600,000

74. **Answer (C) is the best answer.** The preemptive right is the shareholder's right to preserve her proportionate ownership and control interest in the corporation by having a right of refusal on any new shares the corporation proposes to issue for cash (but not in merger or for property). Right of first refusal means that the shareholder must match the terms which the third party is willing to pay. She is not entitled to purchase at par or at a price more favorable than the prospective purchaser. *See, e.g., Stokes v. Continental Trust Co.,* 78 N.E.

1090 (N.Y. 1906).

Older statutory schemes, including the 1969 MBCA, made the existence of preemptive rights presumptive. They existed unless articles of incorporation "opted out" of them. The 1985 MBCA reversed that, providing that preemptive rights presumptively do not exist. Articles of incorporation must contain an "opt in." *See* MBCA § 6.30(a) ("The shareholders of a corporation do not have a preemptive right to acquire the corporation's unissued shares except to the extent the articles of incorporation so provide."). Some jurisdictions did not follow the newest MBCA in this regard, feeling that the preemptive right was important for owners of the numerous small corporations that predominated in their state. Among other things, preemptive rights provide some "bright line" protection against dilutive share issuances sometimes seen in corporate freeze outs and squeeze outs. As an example of the latter, suppose Han, Luke, and Chewbacca each own 100 shares in a successful corporation. Hans has a falling out with Luke and Chewbacca. They propose that the corporation offer 300 shares to Darth Vader, a relative of Luke's. Han has a right of first refusal as to 100 of those shares.

Getting back to Quad's questions, early case law held that the preemptive right was not only important, it was a vested property right. Only a unanimous shareholder vote could eliminate preemptive rights once they had been installed in a corporation. That has become history. The last vested right decisions, dating from the 1950s and 1960s, have effectively been overruled. *See, e.g., Seattle Trust & Savings Bank v. McCarthy*, 617 P.2d 1023 (Wash. 1980) (preemptive right would no longer be considered vested right which could be removed only by unanimous shareholder vote). Thus, **Answer (A) is no longer correct.**

MacroSoft's lawyer evidently "opted in" to preemptive rights when he drafted the original articles of incorporation. The current MBCA sets out several exceptions to preemptive rights for corporations which do "opt in," such as shares issued to directors, officers, or employees as compensation; shares issued to satisfy conversion or option rights; shares issued within six months of incorporation; and "shares sold otherwise than for money." MBCA § 6.33(b)(3). Thus, **Answer (D) is incorrect.** Even without a statute, at common law the last two exceptions clearly existed, although at common law initial share issuances were shielded from preemptive rights if they were issued as part of the "original plan of financing."

Most closely-held and small corporations find it desirable or even imperative, to have preemptive rights in place. Corporations that are fast growing and may be approaching a public offering, or some other form of broad-based equity financing, find it imperative to eliminate preemptive rights.

Answer (B) is incorrect; federal law has nothing to say about preemptive rights. They are a matter governed by state corporation law.

75.   **Answer (D) is the best answer.** The securities lawyer's take on securities issuances is that they must be registered, or have an exemption from registration, both on the federal level and in each and every state where they will be offered. Thus, **Answer (A) is absolutely wrong. Answers (B) and (C) are both correct, but Answer (D) is the best answer.** The National Markets Improvements Act of 1996 takes away the state's power to require a registration if the corporation registers its shares with the SEC, but that level of understanding may be too complex for these questions on basic business organizations. The better mantra to carry around in your head is the unqualified first sentence of this

paragraph.

The median cost of registration with the SEC, which necessitates high payments for sophisticated accounting and lawyering services and for printing and prospectus delivery, was $980,000 in 2001. Quad and his company may be able to afford that here. For most small companies, though, the cost of an IPO is too high for the traffic to bear. The name of the game for them, and their lawyer, is finding and then complying with a suitable exemption from registration, on the federal and on the state levels.

In the case of small corporations issuing shares to a small number of persons, the thought of securities law compliance may not even cross anyone's mind. Usually there will be one or more exemptions: federal intrastate or private placement exemption, and state isolated transaction, incorporators' or limited offering exemptions. In 1981, the SEC adopted a series of exemptions and exemption safe harbors called Regulation D which under Rules 504, 505, and 506 makes federal compliance easier. If the corporation is not entitled to an exemption, its liability is strict. The only defense to a failure to register is an exemption.

Securities regulation is the subject of a separate law school course offering. It is beyond the scope of courses in basic business organizations. You should also remember this admonition: for the unschooled, or even for the schooled who lack any on-the-job training from a more experienced securities lawyer, securities law compliance work is akin to playing with gasoline. Securities lawyers have been held civilly liable for millions of dollars when they have made mistakes. Many have also been criminally convicted. Violation of the securities laws is a felony which carries a maximum sentence of 20 years and fines up to $5 million for "willful" violations. It is an extremely dangerous world out there.

76.   **Answer (D) is the best answer.** Traditionally shareholders act at meetings. There are two types of meetings: annual and special. The annual meeting, at which shareholders elect directors, has an open agenda. Special meetings have closed agendas: only the items specifically included in the notice to shareholders may be considered. For valid action to take place there must be a "quorum" present. A quorum is a majority of the shares entitled to vote on a matter, plus one. *See* MBCA § 7.25(a). For example, if there were four equal shareholders, three would have to be present to make a quorum. Here it would be eleven.

Statutes may change these common law rules. MBCA § 7.05 requires notice for both types of meetings ("A corporation shall notify shareholders of the date, time and place of each annual and special shareholders' meeting no fewer than 10 nor more than 60 days before the meeting date."). Under common law shareholders were presumed to know when the annual meeting would take place; no notice was required. MBCA § 7.02(e) carries over the closed agenda rule for special meetings: "Only business within the purposes described in the meeting notice . . . may be conducted at a special meeting." Action taken at a meeting held without notice or which exceeds the scope of the stated purpose is voidable. A shareholder who attends the meeting waives objection to the lack of notice or defective notice unless she makes "a special appearance" for the purpose of objecting. Newer MBCA versions allow a shareholder to participate on a limited basis, objecting only to matters not in the notice before they are presented. MBCA § 7.06(b).

Either the board of directors or "the person or persons authorized to do so" in the bylaws (often the board chairperson) or 10 percent of the shares may call a special meeting, MBCA § 7.02(a), although many corporations attempt to eliminate the latter power as a takeover "shark repellent." Traditionally, once it has been determined that a quorum is present, valid action is taken if a majority of those shares present votes in favor. Ten or more years ago the MBCA changed to plurality voting. Valid action is taken if the number of votes favoring a resolution exceeds those opposing it. MBCA § 7.25(c). The stated reason was that, with majority voting, abstentions are really "no" votes. Assume that at a meeting 90 of 100 shares are present. On a resolution, 44 vote "yes," 40 vote "no," and 6 "abstain." Under majority voting the measure fails: it needed 46 votes to pass. Under plurality voting the measure passes. Many states retain majority voting.

For mergers, sale of substantially all the corporation's assets, dissolution, and other "fundamental changes," the rules were different. Statutes required a majority of all the shares entitled to vote on the matter, not merely a majority of those present. And a few states' statutes still follow the original Model Act, which required a 2/3rds vote of all the shares entitled to vote on the matter. Today's MBCA § 11.03(e) states that a plan of merger "must be approved by a majority of all the votes entitled to be cast on the plan."

Answers (B), (C), and (D) will not do, as HHH wants final approval within 30 days. AA's board chair should call a special meeting, notifying all 20 shareholders and hoping that not only a quorum may be obtained, but that a majority of all, and not just a quorum, will vote for this merger.

77. Probably not. Under modern corporate law schemes, shareholders have *a right* to be "present" by person or by proxy. It is not a matter merely of grace. Also, a quorum exists if a majority is present either "in person or by proxy." *See* MBCA § 7.22 ("A shareholder may vote his shares in person or by proxy.") A proxy is nothing more than a specialized agency relationship. As such it is revocable by an express revocation, a later dated proxy given to another, or by attendance at the meeting. In any case, the proxy expires at the end of 11 months unless "a longer period is expressly provided in the appointment." MBCA § 7.22(c). Barbara gave to Tony a valid proxy, or "form of appointment" as the MBCA refers to the actual piece of paper. On the other hand, Betsy cast an absentee ballot. Absentee ballots are not used frequently in business corporations, although they are used quite often in membership not-for-profit entities such as alumni associations, golf clubs, etc. Betsy's vote would not be valid unless the AA bylaws provide for absentee voting. As stated, however, absentee voting is relatively rare in business corporations and it would be a long shot as to whether AA's bylaws authorize the practice.

78. **Answer (C) is the best answer. Once upon a time Answers (A) and (B) would have been good answers, but no longer.** For example, in a series of cases, the New York Court of Appeals struck down greater than majority voting requirements even after the New York Legislature had amended the Business Corporation Act expressly to authorize them. *See, e.g., Benintendi v. Kenton Hotel, Inc.*, 60 N.E.2d 829 (N.Y. 1945) (bylaw provision requiring unanimity struck down as invalid against public policy because they made it difficult to the corporation to conduct its business and created an undue risk of deadlock).

Nowadays, many statutes contain authority similar to that contained in MBCA § 7.27(a): "The articles of incorporation may provide for a greater quorum or voting requirement for shareholders (or voting groups of shareholders) than is provided by this Act." The wisdom of high, or higher, quorum or voting requirements is another matter. A high requirement may very well result in tyranny by a minority of shares, as courts have observed. Nonetheless, Jonah and the Whalers aside, many small and closely-held corporations want very consensual governance arrangements, akin to partnerships in which all partners make major decisions. Shareholders may want to reach consensus, or near consensus, on every important matter. The participants in many enterprises sense that majority rule can have bruising effects if the same individuals wind up on the losing side of votes most of the time.

If as an attorney you negotiate for a power sharing arrangement implemented through greater than majority quorum or voting, you have to think about amendments. Some courts have held that a mere majority may amend articles to remove the negative control arrangement. MBCA § 7.27(b) is clear on this: "An amendment . . . that adds, changes, or deletes a greater quorum or voting requirement must meet the same quorum requirement and be adopted by the same vote . . . required to take action under the quorum and voting requirements then in effect or proposed to be adopted, whichever is greater." No matter what jurisdiction's laws you are operating under, it is recommended that you always give thought to the issue of later amendments.

Answer (D) is not the best answer, for the reasons stated above.

79. **Answer (A) is the best answer.** But, first a bit about Answer (B). Rank-and-file shareholders do not owe fiduciary duties to the corporation. They have no positive duty to attend meetings or to do anything else. From 1975 onward, however, judicial precedents in a number of states (*see, e.g., Donahue v. Rodd Electrotype Co. of New England*, 328 N.E.2d 505 (Mass. 1975), and the discussion of the "*Donahue* principle" in the answer to Questions 160 and 161) hold that participants in a closely-held corporation owe fiduciary duties one to another, akin to partners in a partnership. Here, however, with 20 shareholders, it is doubtful whether AA is a closely-held corporation (one in which share transfer is restricted to keep the ownership circle "close"). The much-criticized *Gearing v. Kelly*, 227 N.Y.S.2d 897 (App. Div. 1962), intimated that, by staying away to prevent a quorum ever from assembling, a closely-held corporation shareholder might have breached her fiduciary duties. It is doubtful whether a court would follow that precedent. A minority shareholder may have no other tactical choice in certain situations than to stay away from a meeting to prevent a quorum from assembling. Thus, **Answer (B) is incorrect.**

Answer (C) is incorrect. If Betsy attends, she runs afoul of the basic rule of thumb at the shareholders' level: "Once a quorum, always a quorum." At the director's level, a quorum must be present for each and every vote, thus "quorum breaking" tactics may work. At the shareholder level, MBCA § 7.25(b) codifies the basic rule: "Once a share is represented for any purpose at a meeting, it is deemed present for quorum purposes for the remainder of the meeting and for any adjournment of that meeting."

Answer (D) is also incorrect. "Special appearances" work for protesting lack of notice or defects in the notice for a meeting. A specially appearing shareholder would be present for quorum purposes. The danger is that the specially appearing shareholder may participate in the meeting after all, thus creating the necessary quorum or waiving the defect in the notice. The best advice for Betsy is to "stay away" or, indeed, "go back to the beach."

80. **Answer (D) is the best answer.** Corporations used to freeze share transfer at a point in time well in advance of the meeting. Transfers could take place, but the corporation would not recognize them on its books (Answer (C)). Today, most boards set a record date a few weeks in advance of the shareholders' meeting. Thereafter, share transfers may occur, and the corporation will duly register them on its books, but not for voting purposes (Answer (B)). *See* MBCA § 7.07: "If the bylaws do not fix or provide for fixing a record date [say, a standard 15 days before any and all meetings], the board of directors of the corporation may fix a future date as the record date." The only restriction is that the board may not set the record date "more than 70 days before the meeting or action requiring a determination of shareholders." MBCA § 7.07(b). Older Model Act versions, and some statutes today, provide that, in the event of the failure of the directors to set a record date, the record date is the date upon which the directors called the meeting (Answer (A)).

Here, Casey is probably too late. He acquired after any possible record date. He may, however, telephone his seller, asking her for a proxy to vote the shares. However, she is not required to give Casey the proxy. She may say "no" and she does not have to explain her decision. It would have been better had Casey obtained the proxy from his seller before or at the time he acquired the shares. He could have made issuance of a proxy a condition precedent to paying for the shares. Thus, **Answers (A), (B), and (C) are not the best answers.**

These are important issues because the same or similar rules are used to decide who receives a dividend that has been declared, or a stock split, and so on. *See, e.g.*, MBCA §§ 6.23(c) & 6.40(b) (providing that, if directors do not fix a record date for respect to share dividends and distributions, respectively, the record date is the date the directors authorized the share dividend or distribution). Blackstone's metaphor for a corporation was a river. In a river, the waters constantly change as new water flows in and "old" water flows out, but it is nonetheless the same river. So, too, with a corporation, especially publicly-held ones. The identity of shareholders changes as new shareholders move in and "old" shareholders flow out, but it is still the same corporation. These rules regarding record dates, and so on, enable one to determine just who comprises the corporation at any given time, for purposes either of voting at its meeting or for receiving benefits from it.

81. **Answer (A) is the best answer,** but the best answer could well be Answer (D) if the Gores have failed to give notice of their intent to cumulate. There have been cases in which the majority forgot to cumulate its votes, allowing a substantial minority, through cumulative voting, to control the board of directors, and hence the corporation, for a year. *See, e.g., Stancil v. Bruce Stancil Refrigeration, Inc.*, 344 S.E.2d 789 (N.C. Ct. App. 1986). To eliminate such surprises, MBCA § 7.28(d) states that shareholders who have the right to cumulate may not do so unless either "the meeting notice or proxy statement accompanying the notice states conspicuously that cumulative voting is authorized" or the shareholder who wishes to cumulate gives notice to the corporation of her intention to do at least 48 hours in advance of the meeting. For purposes of this question, however, we will assume that the Gores have given the required notice.

What is "cumulative voting?" Cumulative voting is an outgrowth of the late 19th century Populist movement. At one time, 14 or so states had a requirement of cumulative voting for business corporations in their state constitutions or corporate laws. Today, only a handful of states mandate cumulative voting, the most important of which is California. In 1990, however, even California eliminated mandatory cumulative voting in publicly-held corporations, in part because California became concerned about losing hi-tech incorporations to Delaware. Cumulative voting permits a shareholder to take the number of shares she has the right to vote (say, 200), multiplied by the number of directors to be elected at the meeting (say, 5), to compute the number of votes she has (here, 1000), which she may then vote for one ("cumulate"), or less than all, of the candidates standing for election.

To be contrasted with cumulative voting is "straight" voting, in which the majority (or, under today's MBCA, a plurality) at the meeting elects all of the directors. *See* MBCA § 7.28(a) ("Unless otherwise provided in the articles of incorporation, directors elected by a plurality of the votes cast by the shares entitled to vote in the election at a meeting at which a quorum is present."). The difference between majority and plurality voting is explored in Question 73.

Almost all publicly-held companies have eliminated cumulative voting. Few state laws mandate it anymore. However, most state laws do provide that corporations may "opt in" to cumulative voting by a provision in their articles of incorporation. *See* MBCA § 7.28(b). Many corporations, and their lawyers, do so to facilitate power sharing arrangements in small and medium size corporations. Question 75 is an example of a situation in which cumulative voting might be utilized. While cumulative voting does not permit a share minority to "call the shots," it does give the minority (such as the Jonah boys) a "window" on the board's activities.

In order to ensure the election of a particular candidate, a block must control at least $\frac{S \times N}{(D+1)}$ + shares,

where S = total number of shares voting, D = total number of directors to be elected, and N = the number of directors the block wants to elect.

So, if the Gores want to elect one of the five directors, and assuming all 1,000 shares are present, the Gores would need $\frac{1,000 \times 1}{(5+1)}$ + 1 shares = 168 shares.

The Gores have 270 shares. They can safely elect one director.

The formula is generally used in two ways. First, assuming a given number of shares in a faction, the formula yields how many directors that faction can elect. Second, assuming electing a given number of directors is the goal, the formula yields how many shares the faction must have, and, therefore, may need to recruit.

Testing for two directors, the Gores would need $\frac{1,000 \times 2}{(5+1)}$ + 1 shares = 334 shares.

The Gores have 270 shares. They cannot elect two directors, unless Aunt Mary and her 200 shares do not show up to vote. In that case, the Gores would need only $\frac{800 \times 2}{(5+1)}$ + 1 shares = 268 shares.

The Gores have 270 shares. They should put themselves up for election and cumulate their votes carefully if Aunt Mary does not show (in person or by proxy) at the shareholders' meeting.

Answers (B), (C), and (D) are incorrect for the reasons stated above.

The formula does not have to be remembered. It can be brought out and dusted off in strategy sessions prior to a meeting. Instead, two salient points that should be remembered are: first, that the majority, too, has to get out the vote and cumulate properly in close cases; and, second, many shares may be locked up in attics or otherwise not voted, which may give a substantial minority an opportunity to gain an additional seat on the board of directors.

82. **Answer (B) is the best answer.** Staggering the board lessens, or eliminates altogether, the effect of cumulative voting. Therefore, **Answers (A), (C), and (D) are not the best answers.**

In a 1950s battle for control of Montgomery Ward, the incumbents staggered the board to prevent an insurgent from obtaining a toehold on the board through cumulative voting. The then effective Illinois Constitution mandated cumulative voting. In *Wolfson v. Avery*, 126 N.E.2d 701 (Ill. 1955), the Illinois Supreme Court held that classifying or staggering a board could not co-exist with the mandate for cumulative voting and was thus unconstitutional. A subsequent court case interpreting the nearly identical provision of the Arizona Constitution held that staggered boards could co-exist with mandatory cumulative voting as long as the board classification scheme did not eliminate representation for any shareholder minority, however large. In the opinion of the Arizona Supreme Court, what the state constitution required was some representation for minority shareholdings, not necessarily proportionate representation. *See Bohannan v. Corporation Commission*, 313 P.2d 379 (Ariz. 1957).

Today, statutes reconcile the conflict between cumulative voting and board classification. Many statutes, including older versions of the MBCA, provided that only a board of nine or more directors could be "staggered," and that such a board may be staggered, or classified, into no more than three classes. The result is that, under those statutes, board classification schemes may eliminate the representation of small shareholder minorities on the board, but not of a substantial minority of, say, 30 percent or more. The newest MBCA versions eliminate the requirement that a board be of some size before classification may occur. MBCA § 8.06 now simply provides that "[t]he articles of incorporation may provide for staggering the terms of directors by dividing the total number of directors into two or three groups, with each group containing one-half or one-third of the total, as near as may be."

The few states with strong policies in favor of cumulative voting, such as California, still prohibit board classification schemes, at least in non-public companies. Larger corporations disfavor cumulative voting. They note that directors owe fiduciary duties to the corporation, and not to any particular group within it, such as the shareholders who elected those directors. Companies thus oppose cumulative voting on grounds that it may promote factionalism on the board. Many, or even most, larger corporations also now classify their board of directors. Managements promote classification on grounds that it assures continuity and stability of the corporation's business strategies and policies. Board classification also serves as a defense against hostile takeover bids. Corporations stagger their board into three (and under a few states' laws, four) classes. They also resurrect a requirement that, before expiration of their term, directors may be removed only for "cause." And they eliminate the ability of a shareholder to call a special meeting for purposes of removing directors. A takeover player who has accumulated a majority of shares still may then not be able to control the board for 13 to 24 months, depending on when in the annual meeting cycle the player acquired the shares. If she acquired them immediately after an annual meeting, it may take 23–24 months to control 2/3rds of the board seats. Having borrowed heavily to purchase the shares in the first place, many takeover players are unwilling to "cool their heels," paying high interest, for such a period before they can obtain control of the target company's board of directors. Recent empirical research has demonstrated that this package of simple "shark repellent" provisions, centered around board classification, is a far more effective deterrent to hostile takeover bids than was previously thought.

83. The younger Watsons should seek a court order that a meeting be held. According to *Hoschett v. TSI International Software, Ltd.*, 683 A.2d 43 (Del. Ch. 1996), one of the few mandatory features of the Delaware corporation law is the requirement that a corporation hold an annual shareholders' meetings. Even if a single shareholder controls the votes needed to elect all of the directors, the remaining shareholders have a right to a meeting in which they may address their concerns or voice their grievances. If a shareholder requests that the meeting be held, the board of directors must convene the meeting. Statutes also reinforce this mandatory feature of corporate law. MBCA § 7.03 provides that a shareholder may go into the state court of general jurisdiction (*e.g.*, superior court, or circuit court, or court of common pleas). That court "may summarily order a meeting to be held . . . on application of any shareholder . . . entitled to participate in an annual meeting if an annual meeting was not held within the earlier of 6 months after the end of the corporation's fiscal year or 15 months after its last annual meeting." The court may also issue ancillary orders fixing the record date, the time and place of the meeting, and so forth.

84. **Answer (B) is the best answer.** MBCA § 7.04 authorizes the use of the unanimous written

consent procedure.

Answers (A) (C), and (D) are incorrect. There is no limitation on use to special rather than annual meetings or to emergencies. The attorney has the shareholders sign the consent taking certain actions. Those consents then are inserted into the corporation's minute book in lieu of minutes of a meeting.

What, then, is the difference between absentee voting, which generally is not utilized in U.S. corporations (see Question 77), and consents? Were absentee voting permitted, a meeting would be held, the votes would be counted (votes in person, votes by absentee ballot, and votes by proxy), and a majority (or plurality) would carry the day. With unanimous consents, no meeting is held but, as aforesaid, the action must be approved unanimously.

A few states, most noticeably Delaware, permit valid shareholder action by less than unanimous shareholder consents. *See* DEL. GEN. CORP. L. § 228(a). Such a procedure may present a danger in certain corporations. A majority may take action without the knowledge of the minority. With unanimous consents, the minority may refuse to sign a consent, necessitating a meeting at which the minority may at least apprize itself of action being taken.

Several publicly-held corporations incorporated in Delaware have sought to place restrictions on the use of consents. A concern exists that a takeover player may use consents to "hijack" a corporation, suddenly appearing at the corporation's offices with signed consents from 50.1 percent, or more, of the shares, removing and then replacing the incumbent directors. Other critics have pointed out that the use of consents is inappropriate for removal of directors, as they allow no opportunity for the removed director to defend herself or otherwise receive due process. Nonetheless, the Delaware courts have restricted corporations' ability to narrow the use of consents. Delaware judges have insisted that any restriction be in an amendment to the certificate of incorporation (articles of incorporation under the MBCA), which, of course, necessitates shareholder approval. *See Datapoint Corp. v. Plaza Securities Co.*, 496 A.2d 1031 (Del. 1985).

Hearing some of the criticism perhaps, California permits less-than-unanimous shareholder consents, but it does not allow their use in matters pertaining to the election of directors. CAL. CORPS. CODE § 603(d). *Accord* NEV. REV. STAT. § 78.320.

85. **Answer (D) is the best answer.** In *Schnell v. Chris-Craft Industries, Inc.*, 285 A.2d 437 (Del. 1971), the Delaware Supreme Court, reversing a contrary ruling by the Court of Chancery, instructed the chancellor to enjoin an annual meeting in a fact situation identical to this Question. Even though both actions were technically permissible under the bylaws (Answer (C)), the court refused to countenance "wrongful subversion of corporate democracy" or "impermissible manipulation of the election machinery." So far the Delaware courts have limited application of the doctrine to election of directors. While boards of director remain free, for example, to adopt radical defenses to takeover bids, directors are not free to take far less radical actions, if they pertain to election of directors.

A later Delaware case, *Blasius Industries, Inc. v. Atlas Corp.*, 564 A.2d 651 (Del. Ch. 1988), emphasized "the central importance of the franchise to the scheme of corporate governance." *Blasius* requires that directors or managers present a "compelling justification" for any manipulations and holds that the business judgment rule does not apply to shield such actions from judicial scrutiny. Courts have drawn a distinction, then, between actions taken with respect to a corporation's assets, which would be reviewed under a deferential business judgment rule standard, discussed below, and actions that tamper with the mechanics of the relationship between the shareholders and the directors. The latter will not be upheld, absent a compelling justification.

Under *Schnell* and *Blasius*, courts have enjoined advancement of meeting dates, downsizing of the board to disenfranchise certain shareholder, adjournments of a meeting when it appeared to management that it was losing a crucial vote, and eleventh hour board classification schemes. The doctrine is an important one, but its exact contours remain uncertain.

Answers (A), (B), and (C) are not the best answers for the reasons stated above.

86.   **Answer (B) is the best answer.** A proxy, of course, is nothing more than a specialized form of agency relationship. The essence of an agency relationship is the agent's loyalty and obedience to the principal. If the principal has any reason to doubt the agent's loyalty, or for no reason at all, the principal should be able to terminate the relationship. He may terminate the relationship at any time, subject of course to paying contract damages, if a contract exists.

Answer (A) is not the best answer. An essential feature of the normal principal-agent relationship then is revocability, which would apply to an ordinary proxy (Answer (A)) and make it unsatisfactory for Jennifer. In practical terms, what it boils down to is that, while the agent may be able to get damages, she cannot get her job back, at least if the principal resists.

But certain agency relationships are irrevocable. Their irrevocability will withstand a court challenge if the agency is found to be "coupled with an interest." Roughly speaking, an agency is coupled with an interest if the relationship exists to protect some independent interest of the agent as well as the interests of the principal. Independent interest of the agent means some interest beyond those agents generally have, such as being paid or otherwise benefiting from their service. Identifying which agency relationships are "coupled with an interest" is a bit like identifying pornography under Justice Potter Stewart's definition: "I know it when I see it."

All that discussion is not mere prelude. Proxies are specialized agencies. For a proxy to be irrevocable, or, more accurately, for its irrevocability to withstand court challenge, the proxy must be coupled with an interest. The same rules apply. An example: Harry Hughes owns an airline. He needs to purchase new airplanes to modernize the fleet. Harry, however, is showing signs of instability. Bank will make the loan if, and only if, Harry gives bank a proxy, styled "irrevocable," to vote some or all of his shares for the life of the loan, or until the balance has been paid down to a certain amount. The proxy would be "coupled with an interest" because it is given to protect an interest independent of a normal agent's interests, *i.e.*, to Bank as lender, as well as for the benefit of the proxy giver, Harry, who get a big loan for his airline.

MBCA § 7.22(d) sets out some examples of proxies coupled with an interest without being brave enough to attempt an overarching definition:

An appointment of a proxy is revocable unless the appointment form or the electronic transmission states that it is irrevocable and the appointment is coupled with an interest. Appointments coupled with an interest include:

• a pledgee;

- a person who purchased or agreed to purchase the shares;

- a creditor of the corporation who extended it credit under terms requiring the appointment;

- an employee of the corporation whose employment contract requires the appointment; or

- a party to a voting agreement created under section 7.31 [next Question].

Indiana and Jennifer's problem needed less in the way of analysis perhaps. Court decisions in a number of states hold that a proxy given by one shareholder to his fellow shareholder for their mutual benefit, as here, always is coupled with an interest and will he upheld irrevocable if the proxy (form of appointment) so provides (Answer (B)). *See, e.g., Haft v. Haft*, 671 A.2d 413 (Del. Ch. 1995) (irrevocable proxy to chief executive officer upheld because he was also a shareholder).

Answers (C) and (D) are not the best answers because they would be overkill here. They are discussed in the following Answer.

87. **Answer (D) is the best answer.** Both Answers (B) and (D) describe shareholder voting agreements, more commonly known as "pooling agreements."

Answer (A) would hold the Smiths together, but would not be a preferred alternative. The siblings probably would want an opportunity, at least, to comment on corporate affairs and to have their input be more than advisory. Besides, their eldest sibling might be the bossy or controlling type.

Answer (B) is not the best answer. Answer (B) was the form the agreement took in the celebrated Delaware case of *Ringling Brothers — Barnum & Bailey Combined Shows, Inc. v. Ringling*, 53 A.2d 441 (Del. 1947). The shareholder who tried to invalidate a pooling agreement she had earlier signed, but then refused to follow, argued that it was a "mere agreement to agree," and thus an illusory contract. The court disagreed, observing that a stated consequence, empowerment of the family attorney to vote the shares, followed a failure to agree. The pooling agreement was thus not illusory. The court refused, however, specifically to enforce the agreement, which provided that, in the event of breach, the recalcitrant party constituted the attorney her proxy for the voting of the shares. The court did so simply because the agreement did not adequately spell out the mechanics for enforcement. Nonetheless, because of that bit of history, statutes that deal with the subject commonly remind judges that shareholder voting agreements are specifically enforceable. *See, e.g.*, MBCA § 7.31(b) ("A voting agreement created under this section is specifically enforceable.").

Answer (C) is incorrect. There is no evidence of a need, let alone a desire, to sell.

The potential harm that the agreement of the type in Answer (D) brings to mind was an abuse of the Robber Baron era: "secret pools." Assume nine signatory shareholders. A majority of five would control the pool. Say that three of that five made a secret side agreement to vote as a majority of the three (two) agreed. The arrangement would be a "pool with a pool" which would permit two of nine, by their secret conspiracy, to control the entire group's decision making. Nonetheless, shareholder pooling agreements of both kinds are frequently entered into and statutes expressly validate them. *See, e.g.*, MBCA § 7.31(a): "Two or more shareholders may provide for the manner in which they vote their shares by signing an agreement for that purpose."

88. **Answer (C) is the best answer,** in part because it gives the author of this book an

opportunity to introduce readers to the subject of "voting trusts." A legitimate use of voting trusts is to introduce a period of stability to corporate affairs, here until the eight siblings grow up and gain some maturity. Another example is in Chapter 11 bankruptcy reorganizations. The plan of reorganization could require that voting securities be placed in a voting trust to ensure a period of political stability after the corporation emerges from the reorganization in bankruptcy. In a voting trust, shareholders literally hand over their share certificates to the trustee, who then may hand them back a piece of paper called a "certificate of beneficial interest." The certificate gives back to the shareholder all the rights of shareholding save the right to vote on all, or specified, matters. The hallmark of a voting trust is the complete separation of voting from other aspects of ownership. The shareholder gives up the right to have any binding say.

What happens if the voting trustee runs amuck? A voting trustee is a trustee. In that case, shareholders could invoke equity's historic jurisdiction over trusts and trustees, seeking an order setting the trustee straight or appointing a successor trustee.

As with secret stock pools, voting trusts begat abuses and were denounced as "vehicles for corporate kidnapping." A robber baron could pay apathetic shareholders to put their shares in a secret trust. The robber baron would then sit in the back of the meeting, inextricably controlling statutes that require voting trusts be of record at the corporation's principal place of business and that they be limited in duration, usually 10 years (15 in Delaware). An "illegal" voting trust is simply one that fails to comply with those statutory requirements. MBCA § 7.30 sets out these requirements.

Answer (A) is not the best answer because it may or may not work. The eldest may be bossy and controlling and have just as much "attitude" as the others.

Answer (B) is incorrect. There is no evidence of a need, let alone a desire, to sell.

Answer (D) does not portend much of an improvement. It still requires more to agree than disagree on any given point (a plurality).

89.   No. All of these devices are subject to a "proper purpose doctrine," if they are used to work a fraud or an illegality or to oppress minority shareholders (oppression is discussed in connection with close corporations). This somewhat nebulous, but important, judicial control limits use of these devices in schemes to evade the law or to "kidnap" corporations.

90.   **Answer (D) is the best answer.** A seeming conundrum of traditional U.S. corporate law is that, even though the shareholders own the company, they have very limited powers and even more limited powers of initiative. That is, by statute, shareholders' votes are necessary for mergers, sale of substantially all the corporation's assets, amendment of the articles of incorporation, or dissolution of the corporation, but only based upon a recommendation made to them by the board of directors. Shareholders' powers of initiative are limited to rights to elect and to remove directors. Thus, for example, if shareholders want a merger to take place, they cannot, strictly speaking, accomplish it directly. They must accomplish it indirectly. At their own expense, the shareholders must put up a slate of directors whom they believe will recommend the merger, solicit proxies, and then put their own nominees in office. Between annual meetings, they may first have to remove the incumbent board.

Answers (A), (B), and (C) are not the best answers. A central feature of every corporate law is a provision that states: "The business and affairs of the corporation shall be managed by a board of directors." In a not-so-bygone era, under this traditional model, then, the correct answer to this Question would have been (A) or possibly (B), but not today. *Auer v. Dressel*, 118 N.E.2d 590 (N.Y. 1954), modified the traditional approach. Auer held that discussion and adoption of a resolution that, even if adopted would be advisory only, is not a wholly "futile" gesture and is a proper subject for action by shareholders at a meeting. Such resolutions are not futile because, if passed, they serve to put the directors on notice that the shareholders are less than pleased and may take more strident action, such as removal and election of a new slate of directors, should conditions not improve. Nonetheless, the shareholder must propound advisory, rather than mandatory, resolutions, so the best answer is (D), rather than (C). A mandatory resolution might well be found to be "not a proper matter for consideration by shareholders under state law."

The Securities and Exchange Commission requires and regulates the solicitation of proxies to vote shares in publicly-held companies. Public companies must submit to the SEC, and send to their shareholders, an annual report, a notice of the shareholder's meeting, a proxy ("form of appointment" under the MBCA) running favor of management, and a proxy statement. The latter is a disclosure document, but one limited in scope. It contains the text of resolutions to be voted upon and disclosure that will enable a shareholder to cast an informed vote. If the shareholders were insistent about the hypothetical merger discussed above, and management was uncooperative, the shareholders would have to undertake the same process. That is to say, the shareholders would have to prepare and file their own proxy statement and form of proxy, which they would then mail to the shareholder.

When there are dueling solicitations by management and one or more shareholder groups, the process has become a "proxy contest" or "proxy fight" to control the board of directors. In a corporation of any size, a proxy fight is an expensive proposition. Insurgent shareholders have to hire a fancy (and probably expensive) lawyer, pay printing and postage costs, and incur other direct costs. Indirect costs include the risk of being sued by the company and its incumbent managers for any slip of the pen in the disclosure and advocacy the shareholders undertake.

91. You would look at the principal financial statements (balance sheets for several past years, income statements (also known as the profit & loss, or P & L statements), and the statements of cash flow). How do you obtain copies of those statements? Well, the shareholder may well have them in her files. MBCA § 16.20 provides that within 120 days following the close of the fiscal year, corporations shall send to the shareholders a copy of a balance sheet, an income statement, and "a statement of changes in shareholders' equity unless the information appears elsewhere in the financial statements." These statements "may be consolidated or combined statements of the corporation and one or more of its subsidiaries." The statements need neither be complied in accordance with generally accepted accounting principles (GAAP) nor audited by an independent accountant. If the corporation has prepared statements in accordance with GAAP for any purpose (*e.g.*, the bank), however, then the annual financial statements sent to shareholders must also be prepared on that basis.

Most small corporations, and many larger ones, do not retain an independent accountant to audit their financial statements. It is simply too expensive, although the bank may make them do it. Instead, in accordance with the statute, "the statements must be [and are] accompanied by a statement of the president or the person responsible for the corporation's accounting records." Specifically, the report must state "a reasonable belief whether the statements were prepared on the basis of [GAAP]" and, if not, the basis upon which they were prepared. Then the report must describe "any respects in which the statements were not prepared on a basis of accounting consistent with statements prepared for the previous year."

Many small corporations do not comply with some or all of these statutory requirements. In 2009, the drafters of the statute attempted to make this easier by providing that corporations may be able to deliver the documents electronically (by attachment to an email). "A public corporation may fulfill its responsibility by delivering the specified financial statements, or making them otherwise available, in any manner permitted under the applicable rules of the United States Securities and Exchange Commission." For annual documents, the SEC has implemented a "notice equals access" program, whereby corporations may send shareholders a brief notice only, stating where full sized documents may be obtained if shareholders want them. To comply with their MBCA § 16.20 duties at state law, public corporations may do the same (notice rather than actual physical delivery).

92.   The late 2010 MBCA amendments make clear that any class or series of shareholders may participate in a meeting by means of remote communications. The notice of meeting (MBCA § 7.05) must "describe the means of remote communication to be used." The basic authority for remote participation in the first place is authorized by MBCA § 7.09 (Remote Participation in Annual and Special Meetings).

Before such remote participation, the corporation must insure that it "has implemented reasonable measures:"

(1)   to verify that each person participating remotely is a shareholder, and

(2)   to provide such shareholders a reasonable opportunity to participate in the meeting and to vote on matters submitted to the shareholders, including an opportunity to communicate, and read or hear the proceedings of the meetings, substantially concurrent with such proceedings.

So, to set it up for Bert, you have to go over to the folks at Hoe to insure that they craft the notice correctly to suit Bert's situation, have a verification procedure (e.g., a password or code number), and insure that the means to be used will enable Bert to hear and to be heard.

93.   **Answer (D) is the best answer.** Obviously, this Question is typical of many law school examination questions in which a professor desires to have students set up, and then knock down, a number of "straw men," or alternatives, before settling upon and discussing "the answer."

One alternative not listed is to wage a takeover fight. Through purchases in the market, and then by a takeover bid, perhaps the "gang of five" can seek control of the company. Then they can put in a board of directors that will do their bidding. Never judge a book by its cover. These five seemingly middle-class "yuppies" could be very wealthy, so the option should be discussed briefly. A takeover, though, would cost tens of millions or hundreds of millions. Assume they reject that alternative.

Answer (A) is not the best answer. The next alternative is to wage a proxy fight, asking fellow shareholders not for their shares but for their votes. While not of the magnitude of a takeover bid or other purchase of control, this, too, is an expensive alternative, running into the tens of thousands, and possibly hundreds of thousands, of dollars. Assume that they reject this alternative as well.

Answer (B) is not the best answer. Lawsuits are some lawyers' stock-in-trade, but not here. The directors of a corporation manage its business and affairs, not the shareholders. Absent conflicts of interest, good faith decisions made by boards of directors (here on the method chosen to harvest timber) are shielded from judicial scrutiny by the "business judgment rule." Any lawsuit filed would run into the brick wall of a defense motion for summary judgment. The lawyers, and not the "gang of five," should strongly urge that this alternative not be pursued.

Answer (C) is not the best answer. Answer (C) is where many activists' natural instincts might lead them: wage a public and shareholder advocacy campaign. The "gang of five" should not go there. SEC rules define broadly what a solicitation is, including the seeking of any consent or authorization, the withholding of a consent of authorization from another, or any effort that could be construed as any of the foregoing. The 1992 amendments to the SEC's proxy rules do allow shareholders to communicate with one another how they intend to vote their shares. This "liberalization" permits a certain amount of networking among institutional and other shareholders, but nothing approaching advocacy. A public relations campaign will result in an inadvertent proxy solicitation. Unless the "gang of five" has filed formal solicitation materials with the SEC, AFP management and their lawyers can go to federal court, obtain a preliminary injunction against the illegal solicitation, and tie the insurgents in knots. The campaign to end clear cutting will be over before it really started.

The preferred answer is Answer (D). Since 1942, the SEC has had a rule, Rule 14a-8, which permits a shareholder to submit to her fellow shareholders a resolution and supporting statement, which together may not exceed 500 words. The proposal appears in management's (the company's) proxy statement, at corporate expense. Each year shareholders around the country successfully submit nearly one thousand such proposals. By and large, shareholder proposals break down into two broad categories, social responsibility issues (including environmental, as here) and "good governance" proposals. Successful submission of a proposal requires a not inconsiderable amount of expertise, including threading through a byzantine maze of grounds for the exclusion of proposals found in Rule 14a-8.

94. **Answer (C) is the best answer.** A shareholder may now only submit one proposal per company per year. If the proposal has been submitted previously and garnered less than 3 percent of the vote, the company may exclude it. Unless a proposal is merely a request that the company provide information, the rule now requires that a proposal be framed in advisory language: shareholders have no power to initiate amendments to articles or bylaws, mergers and other fundamental changes.

Thus, for example, in *Medical Committee for Human Rights v. SEC*, 432 F.2d 659 (D.C. Cir. 1970), a shareholder proposal recommending that the board of directors of Dow Chemical amend its certificate of incorporation to prohibit the sale of napalm if it would be used against human beings was includable. A prior year's proposal by the same shareholder group that Dow not sell napalm unless purchasers gave a certificate that they would not use the product against human beings was held to be excludable, on grounds that it related to "ordinary business operations."

A shareholder proposal may be excluded if:

1. it is improper under state law (not advisory or precatory);

2. it would cause the corporation to violate state, federal, or foreign law;

3.   it would result in violation of proxy rules (contains false or misleading statements);

4.   it appears to be for purposes of airing a personal grievance;

5.   it is economically irrelevant (discussed below);

6.   the corporation lacks the power or authority to implement it (*e.g.*, recommend that the board take steps to eliminate the progressive income tax);

7.   it relates to the corporation's ordinary business operations (management function exclusion);

8.   it relates to an election to the board (proper means to oppose an election is a competing proxy solicitation, not a shareholder proposal);[1]

9.   it conflicts with corporation's own proposal (*e.g.*, no "cross motions" or "dueling" proposals);

10.   the corporation has substantially complied with the shareholder's request;

11.   it is duplicative of another proposal to be submitted to the shareholders;

12.   it previously failed to meet the applicable resubmission thresholds (3%, 6%, and 10%); or

13.   it relates to the specific amount of dividends.

Answers (A) and (D) are not the best answers. The traditional means whereby a company sought to exclude a proposal was to request from the SEC a "no-action" letter (Answer (D)). The company would set forth its reasons why the proposal was excludable under one or more of the exclusions. The SEC would respond, either stating that if the company excludes the proposal "we (the SEC staff) will take no action," or that "in our opinion you must include it and here is why." If the SEC gave a no-action letter, and the shareholder strongly disagreed, then she might go to court (Answer (A)), but at this point it would be premature. *But see New York City Employees' Retirement System v. SEC*, 45 F.3d 7 (2d Cir. 1995), holding that the notice, comment, and hearing provisions of Administrative Procedure Act would not apply to the SEC's determination that proposals regarding Cracker Barrel, Inc.'s anti-gay employment policy were excludable under the "ordinary business" exclusion. This was a silent reversal of SEC past practice, so NYCERS challenged it in court (and failed). Still later, in 1998, the SEC reversed itself again, reverting to its prior interpretation that employment matters which raise important social and policy issues are proper matters for shareholder resolutions. In the end, the Cracker Barrel no-action letter thus became a dead letter.

The finer points of SEC Rule 14a-8 proposals are garnered from the SEC no-action letters rather than court decisions. In the 1998 revisions of the rule, though, the SEC indicated that it wished to reduce staff involvement, so no-action letter "production" has been reduced in recent years.

The economic irrelevance exception is less than 5 percent of the either the company's total assets, earnings or sales and is not "otherwise significantly related to the issuer's business." Although Audubon may not meet the bright line thresholds, he can argue that a food importing company has a stake in the ethical and moral dimensions and other conditions under which products are produced at their sources. In the actual case on which this

---

[1] In mid-2003, the SEC announced that it would study whether, and perhaps propose that, under certain circumstances, shareholders in publicly-held corporations should be permitted to nominate persons for directorships utilizing the corporation's solicitation materials. Such a step would be a radical departure from past SEC practice. *See, e.g., Rauchman v. Mobil Corp.*, 739 F.2d 205 (6th Cir. 1984) (Mobil properly excluded facially neutral election proposal that in effect was effort to exclude Saudi Arabian director from re-election). It also would elicit strenuous opposition from corporate America.

Question is based, *Lovenheim v. Iroquois Brands, Ltd.*, 618 F. Supp. 554 (D.D.C. 1985), the shareholder made a form of that argument, succeeding in obtaining an injunction from a federal court forcing Iroquois Brands to include the pâté de foie gras proposal.

Answer (B) is not the best answer. The SEC exempts from compliance with its solicitation filing and other requirements solicitation of 10 or fewer fellow shareholders, but the course proposed in Answer (B) would be fraught with danger. For example, the company might go to court, alleging materially false or misleading statements in the "exempt" solicitation. The court proceeding would be a great distraction even if it did not tie the shareholder activist in knots. Better to await the outcome of the traditional no-action letter process. Corporations waste money and effort attempting to exclude shareholder proposals. Somehow it becomes a test of wills for senior managers, not unlike arguing with a recalcitrant child. A better course for corporations sometimes is to include the proposal, as many of them receive insignificant support from other shareholders.

95. **Answer (B) is the best answer**, albeit an imperfect one. Most state corporate statutes, including South Dakota's, permit informal action but it must be unanimous. By affirmatively withholding their consent, though, Kristen and Hans force the "coffee klatch three" to hold a meeting. Kristin and Hans may still lose at that meeting (3-2) but maybe they can persuade one or the other of the majority to switch sides. At a minimum, Kristen and Hans will be able to express their views and to obtain a window on what is going on.

Answer (A) may be correct in some jurisdictions. Delaware, California, and a few other states permit decisions of shareholders to be by a majority vote, if reached informally. The danger with such a regime is that, without meetings, the minority not only loses but does not even know about what actions are proposed or have been approved. Nonetheless, in 2008, the ABA Committee on Corporate Laws approved an amendment to MBCA § 7.24 validating informal action by majorities. To ameliorate somewhat the lack of minority knowledge problems, MBCA § 7.04(f) provides that "if action is taken by less than the unanimous written consent of the shareholders, the corporation must give the non-consenting shareholders written notice of the action [within 10 days in most cases]." So non-consenting shareholders have at least a rearview mirror telling them, albeit briefly in most cases, what has occurred.

The other safeguard is that articles of incorporation have to provide that "action taken at a shareholders' meeting may be taken without a meeting, and without notice, if consents setting forth the action so taken are signed by the holders of shares having not less than the minimum number of votes that would be required to take the action at a meeting." MBCA § 7.04(b).

Answer (C) is incorrect. It may come to litigation, but filing suit is usually not the first answer to most legal problems.

Answer (D) is incorrect. Secretaries of state perform ministerial and administrative functions only. They never receive or file complaints. Attorneys general, on the other hand, have jurisdictions over corporations and may sue them if the corporate form is being abused. They seldom, if ever, exercise the powers which, in theory, attorneys general have over entities incorporated in their state.

96. **Answer (D) is the best answer.** You should be able to distinguish between majority and plurality voting. Since the last edition of this book, corporate governance committees have

added new wrinkles, complicating the picture. A principal wrinkle is the Pfizer, or "plurality plus" provision many companies (Pfizer was one of the first) have adopted by amending their bylaws. A wrinkle upon the wrinkle would be a bylaw that a director for whom the withhold authority vote exceeds the yes vote is not elected (no resignation required). A further wrinkle would be to authorize "no" votes in the election of directors, a step very few, if any, public corporations have taken.

As of 2007, over 100 major corporations have adopted some sort of "Pfizer policy." *See* J. Veret, *Pandora's Box, Or a Proxy with Moxie? Majority Voting, Corporate Ballot Access, and the Legend of Martin Lipton Re-Examined*, 62 Bus. Law. 1007, 1045–47 (2007).

After issuing several discussion papers on the subject, the Committee on Corporate Laws decided "not to modify the current plurality voting default rule," 61 Bus. Law. 409 (2005), which also prevails in Delaware. Del. Gen. Corp. L. § 216(3). The lynchpin of the ABA committee's effort is a new provision (MBCA § 10.22) allowing (*i.e.*, enabling but not mandating) public corporations to adopt a bylaw providing for a voting regime different from straight plurality voting. The provision enables a corporation to adopt a canned Pfizer-like variation to plurality voting.

The corporation may not do the Pfizer opt-out if (1) articles "prohibit the adoption of a bylaw pursuant to this section"; (2) articles have opted for some other variation from plurality voting, as MBCA 7.28(b) permits; or (3) the corporation has "cumulative voting." MBCA § 10.22(a). If none of those conditions are present, and the corporation opts out, the new scheme is as follows:

(1)   Shareholders must be able to vote for or against candidates for the board;

(2)   "[T]o be elected, a nominee must have received a plurality of votes entitled to vote in the election of directors at a meeting at which a quorum is present;"

(3)   But if the no votes exceed the yes votes, the elected director has a very short term, which "shall terminate on the date that is the earlier of (i) 90 days after the date on which the voting results are determined . . . or (ii) the date on which an individual is selected by the board of directors to fill the office held by such director."

Other details include the proviso that "the board of directors may select any qualified individual to fill the office of a director who received more votes against than for election." MBCA § 10.22(a)(3). Such a bylaw if adopted by the shareholders may only be amended or repealed by the shareholders, unless the bylaw otherwise provides. If adopted by the directors, either shareholders or directors may modify it. MBCA § 10.22(c).

To accommodate the new provision, and its possible use by a corporation, a number of MBCA provisions must be adapted to allow for that possibility:

•   MBCA § 8.05 (Terms of Directors): directors' terms may be bought up shorter than the next election of directors by shareholders if a § 10.22 bylaw is in effect.

•   MBCA § 8.07 (Resignation of Directors) has a new sentence added thereto: "A resignation that is conditioned upon failure to receive a specified vote for election as a director may provide that it is irrevocable."

•   MBCA § 10.20 (Amendment by the BOD or Shareholders): a board may amend or repeal bylaws except if "the articles . . . section 10.21, or, if applicable, section 10.22 reserve that power exclusively to the shareholders in whole or in part."

It gets complicated very quickly. The points to remember are three. (1) A number of modifications around majority or plurality are possible; (2) One such variation, the Pfizer scheme, is currently popular; and (3) The MBCA contains a version of the Pfizer scheme which corporations may easily adopt.

NOTE: ELECTRONIC TRANSMISSIONS AND INFORMATION TECHNOLOGY

Traditional corporate statutes contemplated presence in person at meeting or presence by proxy. The latter contemplated delivery by shareholders of signed and dated written documents (proxy cards) to the corporation, its agent, or an independent contractor the corporation has hired (*e.g.*, National Financial Services). These modes have not kept pace with the evolution of information technology. MBCA § 7.04(h) attempts to remedy part of the problem:

> An electronic transmission may be used to consent to an action if the electronic transmission contains or is accompanied by information from which the corporation can determine the date on which the electronic transmission was signed and that the electronic transmission was authorized by the shareholders, the shareholder's agent, or the shareholder's attorney-in-fact.

An electronic transmission "means any process of communication not directly involving the physical transfer of paper [fax, email] that is suitable for the retention, retrieval and reproduction of information by the recipient." MBCA § 1.40(7A). Will a texted or tweeted proxy or consent meet this definition?

No. To the MBCA the drafters have added provisions to conform with the Uniform Electronic Transmissions Act (UETA) and the Electronic Signatures in Global and National Commerce Act (E-Sign) (2009).

The first step was to add three new definitions and to change three other existing definitions. Added to MBCA § 1.40 were the following:

> (6A) "Document" means (i) any tangible medium on which information is inscribed, and includes any writing or written instrument, or (ii) an electronic record.

> (7A) "Electronic" means relating to a technology having electrical, digital, magnetic, wireless, optical, electromagnetic, or similar capabilities.

> (7B) "Electronic record" means information that is stored in an electronic or other medium and is retrievable in paper form through an automatic process used in conventional commercial practice . . . .

The changes are to "electronic transmission or electronically transmitted" (7C), "sign or signature" (22A), and "writing or written" (28).

Electronic transmission means any form or process of communication not directly involving the physical transfer of paper. Added to the definition are other tangible media capable of the retention, retrieval or reproduction of information by the recipient "and is retrievable in paper form by the recipient." What this means is that there may be paper involved but only on the receiving end when the recipient, for example, prints out a copy of an email.

On the other hand, the comment states that "[t]he terms electronic record and electronic transmission are not intended to include voice mail, text messaging, and communications using similar systems which do not automatically provide for the retrieval of date in printed or typewritten from." Systems do exist which by voice recognition software can convert voice mail into writings but use of those systems would not be the requisite transmission because such systems are not processes "used in conventional commercial practice."

Sign or signature means "with the present intent to authenticate or adopt a document," including "to execute or adopt a tangible symbol to a document" or "to attach to or logically associate with an electronic sound, symbol, or process, and includes an electronic signature in an electronic transmission." So if I type "Regards, Douglas Branson" at the end of an email, I have signed that email.

Writing or written means "any information in the form of a document," which includes electronic record (definition of document). So, for example, unanimous written consents required under MBCA § 7.24 could be electronic transmissions. An upshot would be that an attorney could do consents by sending and receiving emails from each shareholder or director.

Notices may now also be sent electronically. Extensive amendments to MBCA § 1.41 (Notices and Other Communications) make this possible:

> Notice or other communications may be delivered by electronic transmission if consented to by the recipient or if authorized by subsection (k) [articles of incorporation or bylaws may authorize or require delivery of notices].

However, the recipient may revoke consent (express or implied) to electronic delivery. Moreover, "such consent is deemed revoked if the corporation is unable to deliver two consecutive electronic transmissions given by the corporation in accordance with such consent." So, for example, if two successive emails to a shareholder bounce back, the corporation has to resort to delivery of a hard copy by U.S. mail or by courier.

Answer (D) is the best answer because Answers (A), (B), and (C) are all correct.

97.   **Answer (C) is the best answer.** These questions will undoubtedly be litigated but state law has long permitted bylaw restrictions on the nomination process, such as elucidation of qualifications for some or all the would-be nominees. Leaving nothing to chance, however, the MBCA drafters added a new subsection (c) to MBCA § 2.06 ("Bylaws"), which provides:

> The bylaws may contain . . . (1) A requirement that if the corporation solicits proxies or consents with respect to the election of directors, the corporation may include in its proxy statement and any form of proxy or consent, to the extent that and subject to such procedures or conditions as are provided by the bylaws, one or more individuals nominated by a shareholder in addition to individuals nominated by the board of directors.

The Official Comment then outlines ways in which a corporation could use such bylaws partly to nullify any right shareholders may appear to have under Dodd-Frank and the new SEC Shareholder Access Rules: "Examples of the procedures that may be included in such a bylaw include provisions that relate to the ownership of shares (including requirements as to the duration of ownership); informational requirements; restrictions on the number of directors to be nominated, or the use of the provisions by shareholders seeking to acquire control; provisions requiring the nominating shareholder to indemnify the corporation."

Besides the thinly disguised instructions on how to build a Trojan Horse (ways to partially to gut the shareholder access rule by adoption of a bylaw), the other rationale for such a statutory provision is to remove any inference which might otherwise exist that such a bylaw unduly interferes with the statutory mandate that the corporation's business and affairs be managed by, or under the supervision of, a board of directors (and not the shareholders). MBCA § 8.01.

Newly enacted DEL. GEN. CORP. L. § 112 is similar, enabling corporations to adopt bylaws both facilitating or restricting shareholder proxy access.

Answer (A) is incorrect. As noted, courts have always permitted reasonable restrictions.

Answer (B) does not go far enough. Corporations have not only the common law power described but also the power created by the new statute.

Answer (D) is probably incorrect. As noted, the U.S. Chamber of Commerce has filed suit to have the SEC Rule declared unconstitutional. The Chamber may have made an unconstitutional taking argument but I doubt it.

98. **Answer (A) is the best answer.** Activist shareholders (public employee pension funds, hedge funds) have requested various corporations to adopt bylaws providing reimbursement of some or all expenses a shareholder may have expended in propounding nominations for a company's board. New MBCA § 2.06(c)(2) is a response, enabling MBCA corporations to adopt such a bylaw if they wish to do so. MBCA § 2.06:

> (c) The bylaws may contain . . .
>
> . . . .
>
> (2) A requirement that the corporation reimburse the expenses incurred by a shareholder in soliciting proxies or consents in connection with an election of directors, to the extent and subject to such procedures or conditions as are provided in the bylaw.

Again, the comment makes clear that the bylaw can hedge the right to reimbursement in various ways, including "limitations on reimbursement based upon the amount spent by the corporation or the proportion of votes cast for the nominee."

Answer (B) is a good answer, though not the best. The necessity of specific statutory nabbing authority for a shareholder access and for a reimbursement bylaw, because otherwise such bylaws might infringe upon the board's prerogative to manage, is amplified by the MBCA Official Comment:

> Section 2.06(c) clarifies that proxy access and expense reimbursement provisions do not infringe upon the scope of authority granted to the board of directors of a corporation under section 8.01(b). *See CA, Inc. v. AFSCME Employees Pension Plan*, 953 A.2d 227, 235–37 (Del. 2008) (holding that a reimbursement bylaw regulates "procedural" rather than "substantive" matters, and is therefore a proper matter for shareholder action). Section 2.06(c) underscores the model of corporate governance embodied in the Act and reflected in section 8.01, but recognizes that different corporations may wish to grant shareholders varying rights in the selection of directors.

Answer (C) is incorrect. New DEL. GEN. CORP. L. § 113 (2009) is substantially similar to MBCA § 2.06(c)(2).

Answer (D) is incorrect. It may be unwise to put competitors on your board of directors but directors may compete with the corporation on whose board they sit and no statutory provision stands in the way of their candidacy.

99.   **Answer (A) is the best answer.** This is a famous "quorum by ambush" case, of which there are several reported instances in judicial opinions. For example, in a Victorian-era English case, the directors ambushed the Vicar (who was also a director) on the railway platform at London's Paddington Station. A principal point is that, as with shareholders, there exist prerequisites to valid action by directors. The subsidiary point is that in many instances one or the other requirement may be: (a) changed by statute; (b) waived; or (c) satisfied in an unconventional way.

Directors may meet in regular or special meetings. The board may permit directors to be present by conference telephone hookup or other "means of communication by which all directors participating may simultaneously hear each other during the meeting." Such presence is deemed physical presence. MBCA § 8.20. Meetings require notice, quorum, and vote. Statutes commonly provide that regular meetings may be held without notice. *See, e.g.,* MBCA § 8.22(a). The MBCA requires two days' notice of the date, time, and place of special meetings of the board, but dispenses with the common law requirement that the notice state the purpose of the meeting. MBCA § 8.22(b).

A quorum is a majority of a fixed-size board. If the corporation has a "variable range"-size board, a quorum is a majority of the number of directors in office immediately prior to the meeting. Under the MBCA, articles or bylaws may lower the quorum requirement, but in no case to lower than one-third. MBCA § 8.24(a) & (b). Given the presence of a quorum, valid action is by a majority of those present, or a greater percentage if articles or bylaws so provide. Absentee voting or proxy voting by directors is generally not allowed.

Given these prerequisites, how, then, could Watts and Nichols have removed Switzer?

Answers (B) and (D) are incorrect. There was no notice but, by arguing the second day, Switzer waived any lack of or defect in the notice. *See* MBCA § 8.23(b) (attendance at or participation waives defects unless director "appears specially" to protest and does not thereafter vote or assent to action taken). A quorum was present ("one, two, three" of five) and a majority of a quorum voted to remove the CEO. End of case.

Answer (C) is incorrect. On the previous day, only two directors consented to meet and there was no quorum.

Often, because of busy schedules, boards conduct much of their business by special meetings. They may receive only very informal notice that may not conform to statutory requirements. In such a case, a first order of business is to have all directors sign a written "waiver of notice," which is then inserted in the corporate minute book. MBCA § 8.23(a) legitimates the practice, whether the waiver takes place "before or after the date and time stated in the notice."

100.   The best answer is "No." Directors are not agents. They have no power to bind a corporation. They can bind the corporation acting only as a collegial body. If Holland wears

"another hat," as marketing director or vice president of this or that, or if the full board has appointed him their delegate, in that capacity he may be an agent whose acts bind the principal (the corporation). Many lay persons mistakenly believe that directors have power to bind the corporation, as agents or, indeed, as "super agents" of some sort. Reality is otherwise. The offer sheet from Maury Holland would not bind Nike.

101.   The best answer is "Yes." Recall that at the shareholder level the rule of thumb is "once a quorum, always a quorum" (see the answer to Question 79). MBCA § 7.25(b) codifies this rule. On the director level, the rule is the opposite. There must be a quorum before each and every vote. MBCA § 8.24(c). If there is not, any action taken has no validity. Quorum breaking will work. Hypothetically, a director who abused the right or exercised it in opportunistic fashion might be sued for breach of fiduciary duty. Here, though, it is the exact way in which the "system" is supposed to operate. Fred may absent himself from the meeting in progress, break the quorum, and then return on another day when his allies are present and he is better able to advocate his point of view.

102.   **Answer (B) is the best answer.** The trend in publicly-held U.S. companies is toward smaller board size. Average board size is 11, down from 13 a decade or so ago. Many high-tech and dotcoms have boards of seven or nine members.

Answers (C) and (D) are not the best answers because they call for a board that is unwieldy and much too large.

Answer (A) is not the best answer. Board focus also has changed from actively advising on business decisions to some advising, some policy making and, most centrally, monitoring of the corporation's senior executive officers. The modern board's "highest calling" is to monitor, evaluate the performance of, and, if necessary, replace the senior executives, most particularly the Chief Executive Officer. To fulfill the latter role, the board must be comprised of a majority of independent directors. Indeed, the trend is toward a super majority. Independence means directors who are free from all economic, family, and perhaps even social ties with the corporation or its senior executive officers. Thus, a count of independent directors not only excludes "insiders" (or executive directors, as some call them), but certain "outsiders" (called non-executive directors), as well. Rapidly disappearing from the board scene are investment bankers, lawyers, commercial bankers, and other professionals who, alone or through their firms, provide a substantial amount of services to the corporation. Those persons may still serve, but they may not count as "independent" in any assessment of a board's overall independence. The trend is thus to have no more two or perhaps three inside or otherwise non-independent directors. A typical pattern would be the CEO, perhaps the CFO and the CEO of a major subsidiary as the insiders on the board.

An influential blueprint has been the AMERICAN LAW INSTITUTE, PRINCIPLES OF CORPORATE GOVERNANCE AND STRUCTURE (1994) [hereinafter ALI PRINCIPLES]. The ALI Corporate Governance Project lasted from 1979 to 1994 and was controversial at its inception. It is one of the few ALI projects that does not have "Restatement" on the cover. What was controversial then has become accepted wisdom today. The ALI prescription was that "large publicly-held" companies (2000 or more shareholders) should have a majority of independent directors. Other publicly-held companies should have at least three independent directors. Almost all publicly-held companies would exceed those requirements by a significant margin today.

In a bygone era, large boards were the norm. For example, General Motors Co. long had a board of 24 directors. With such a large board, outside directors would experience difficulty "networking" and the insiders, though less than a majority, could control the agenda and decision making. A device that was used, pursuant to express statutory authority, was the executive committee. The executive committee possessed the full board's authority between meetings. Insiders would dominate the executive committee, have few board meetings (two or three per year), and run most decision making through the committee.

Today, boards of public companies meet every other month or at least quarterly. While they have not disappeared, executive committees are on the wane. Despite Enron, WorldCom, Tyco, and other scandals of recent years, corporate governance in the United States as well as elsewhere around the globe has improved dramatically from a time were boards were dominated by the CEO's cronies, most of whom were "mushroom directors" (kept in the dark with manure piled upon them). The "good governance" movement dates from at least the early 1980s and has become a worldwide phenomenon.

103. **Answer (D) is the best answer.** One way in which to view the modern public corporation's committee setup is as a structure whose main purpose is to assist the board in its more focused mission of monitoring the senior executives. The committees designed to do that are three: (1) the audit committee; (2) the nomination committee (called the governance committee at some companies); and (3) the compensation committee. Larger corporations may have many other board committees as well: capital committee, executive committee, social responsibility committee, finance, long range planning, and so on. Statutory authority for board committees is found in corporation codes. *See, e.g.,* MBCA § 8.25(a) ("Unless this Act, the articles of incorporation, or the bylaws provide otherwise, a board of directors may create one or more committees and appoint one or more members of the board of directors to serve on any such committee.").

The audit committee may be the most important. The committee focus is on the integrity of the information that goes to the full board and upon which corporate and senior executive performance will be judged. Traditionally, audit committees were comprised of two or three directors who had financial "literacy." The committee would meet with the company's independent public auditors to discuss the annual audit, adequacy of internal accounting controls and personnel, and any problem areas of which committee members were aware. After the audit, the committee would again meet with the auditors for an "exit interview." The committee might also meet one other time per year.

The newest "kid on the block" is the risk management committee, whose job it is to identify, quantify, and when necessary oversee steps to ameliorate the amount of risk or particular risks the corporation's various businesses may face. Large public corporations' boards of directors have an average of six committees.

Answers (A) and (B) are incorrect. In the 1980s, the NYSE instituted an audit committee requirement of its listed companies (Answer (B)). SOXA now requires all companies that file periodic financial reports with the SEC (approximately 16,200) to have an audit committee comprised exclusively of independent directors. Neither insiders nor lawyers, bankers, or other consultants may serve. At least one member must be a "financial expert," which the SEC has by regulation defined. By law, and federal law at that, it is now the audit committee that appoints, oversees, and determines the compensation of the company's outside auditors. By law, the audit committee has power to hire lawyers, financial advisers, and other consultants as it sees fit. SOXA also makes the audit committee the receptacle for whistleblower complaints concerning auditing and accounting matters, which the audit committee must now investigate.

Two observations. First, Congress may be putting more weight on the audit committee device than it can bear. Audit committee service may become so burdensome that many directors will not wish to serve. Second, state law traditionally governs internal corporate affairs, including corporate governance. Under the securities laws, the federal mandate was for the SEC to regulate disclosure to investors and shareholders. SOXA runs roughshod over that traditional division and does significant violence to federalism.

Answer (C) is incorrect. The nomination committee, also comprised of independent directors, serves to take the board nomination function out of the hands of the CEO, where it traditionally has resided. A purpose is to promote continued diversity and independence on the board so that the board can fulfill its function of evaluating and, if necessary, removing senior executives. In the past, there have been many instances where underperforming or misguided CEOs used their power to re-make the board into a more compliant and less critical group, thus prolonging their tenure. CEOs have appointed movie and television stars and politicians, creating "celebrity boards of directors." Although the NYSE requires companies to have a nomination committee, no legal requirement exists. The same is true for the compensation committee, the third committee many corporations have.

Compensation committees have not worked well. CEO compensation in the U.S. has become obscene, at least at large companies. In 1990, German CEOs made 21 times the average worker, Japanese CEOs 16 times, and U.S. CEOs 150 times. By 2002, CEOs of large U.S. corporations were making 531 times the average worker's pay. The reasons for this astronomical climb are many, but one is that service on the compensation committee is looked down upon. The newest, or least capable, directors are appointed to the committee. Alternatively, CEOs insure that fellow CEOs, who have a vested interest in ever-escalating CEO pay, serve on that committee. There are legal reasons as well. The ubiquity of the business judgment rule, which shields properly scripted board and board committee decisions from later judicial scrutiny, has been extended to compensation decisions, especially by the Delaware courts. They have abandoned earlier legal tests that compensation had to bear a reasonable relationship to the services rendered. These issues are discussed again in the discussion of the business judgment rule, Questions 126–34.

NOTE: THE SARBANES-OXLEY ACT OF 2002

The Sarbanes-Oxley Act of 2002 (SOXA) is an extensive federal incursion into matters traditionally relegated to state law, including state corporate law. It is a deep and multi-pronged incursion that has been touched upon from time to time in this book. *See, e.g.,* Questions cited *infra.* The bankruptcy of Enron Corp. late in 2001 and the failure of WorldCom in early summer of 2002 galvanized Congress into enacting this "reform" legislation. The Act goes off in so many different directions that it would take another 15–20 questions to cover the salient points if the treatment of SOXA adhered to the question and multiple choice answer format. In 2010, the President and Congress followed SOXA with the Dodd-Frank legislation ("The Wall Street Reform and Consumer Protection Act of 2010") which contains several additional federal incursions into corporate governance matters traditionally regulated by state law. See the note following the answer to problem 166, *infra.*

In the interests of efficiency, then, this treatment will give you what remaining knowledge of

SOXA you may need to know in a basic business organizations class by means of an "executive summary" (captions of items not previously discussed in italics):

1. Officer and Director Bar Orders. Discussed in the answers to Questions 113 and 156.

2. Prohibitions on Loans to or Arranging Credit for Corporate Officers and Directors. Discussed in the answer to Question 154.

3. *Near Real Time Securities Exchange Act Section 16(a) Reports for Corporate Officers, Directors, and 10 Percent Holders.* These individuals must report changes in their ownership to the SEC within three days rather than at the end of the month. Companies must soon thereafter post the information on corporate websites.

4. Mandatory Use of and Expanded Duties for Audit Committees of the Board of Directors. Discussed in the answer to Question 104. The audit committee now has the power to hire and fire the outside auditor. The audit committee must establish an internal hotline and investigate internal reports of financial or accounting irregularities. As discussed in the answer to Question 128, the audit committee must have at least one member who is a "financial expert."

5. CEO and CFO Quarterly (Section 302) and Annual (Section 404) Certification of Financial Statements and Internal Controls. Discussed in the answer to Question 128.

6. CEO and CFO Forfeiture of Incentive Based and Equity Compensation. Triggered by earnings restatement based upon misconduct. One year reach back. Discussed in the answer to Question 156. In 2010, the Department of Justice sought claw backs in 70 cases, indicating a late-found discovery of the utility of this SOXA provision.

7. Mandatory Code of Ethics for Senior Financial Officers. Discussed in the answer to Question 129.

8. *Rotation of Outside Audit Partner at Least Once Every Five Years.*

9. *One Year Revolving Door Limitation on Outside Auditor Going to Work for Audited Firm.*

10. *Audit Firm Registration with and Periodic Inspection by Public Company Accounting Oversight Board.*

11. *Creation of Public Company Accounting Oversight Board.*

12. Mandatory Separation of Auditing and Consulting Services in Outside Audit Firms. Cannot provide both to the same client. Discussed in the answer to Question 108.

13. *Lawyers' Section 307 Duty of Intracorporate Whistleblowing.* Trigger is "evidence of material violation of securities law or breach of fiduciary duty or similar violation by the company or an agent thereof." Applies to all lawyers, inside or outside, who do work for the corporation. First report is to the CEO or to the Chief Legal Officer (CLO). Failing "appropriate action" further duty of lawyer is to report to audit committee, the independent directors, or the full board of directors.

14. *Umbrella Protection for Whistleblowers Within the Corporation.* Creates a new federal cause of action in favor of any whistleblower who is demoted, fired, harassed, etc.

15. *Securities Law Judgments No Longer Dischargeable in Bankruptcy.*

104. **Answer (A) is the best answer,** based upon the decision in *McQuade v. Stoneham,* 189 N.E. 234 (N.Y. 1934). Perhaps the most central provision of every traditional corporate statute is the provision to the effect that the corporation's business and affairs shall be managed by or under the direction of a board of directors. *See* MBCA § 8.01(b) ("All corporate powers shall be exercised by or under the authority of, and the business and affairs of the corporation managed by or under the direction of, its board of directors."). The business and affairs of a corporation includes the appointment of its officers and other agents. Under the traditional governance model, by their contract, shareholders could not bind, "handcuff," or "sterilize" the board of directors, on decisions as to who the officers may be or on any other matter. Some courts struck down such contracts as efforts to conduct a corporation's business "as if it were a partnership."

Answer (B) is incorrect. Wettick cannot get his treasurer's job back. He might get damages if he had a contract providing for a salary. *See* MBCA § 8.44(b) ("An officer's removal does not effect the officer's contract rights, if any, with the corporation."). On the other hand, "[t]he appointment of an officer does not itself create contract rights." *Id.* § 8.44(a). It is customary for minutes of directors' meetings to record the appointment of officers and the fixing of their compensation.

A policy reason for these views is that future directors should have a full measure, or nearly full measure, of discretion, unfettered by prior restraints. Along similar lines, future shareholders should be able to elect directors with a full measure of discretion. Prior restraints on directors disenfranchises future shareholders. It is otherwise for Stan's board seat. First of all, directors generally have no power to remove fellow directors; that power resides either in the shareholders by majority vote, MBCA § 8.08, or under newer versions of the MBCA, by a court, MBCA § 8.09. Furthermore, the first part of the contract is nothing more than a shareholders' pooling agreement (see Question 84). Modern statutes make such voting agreements "specifically enforceable." To paraphrase Justice Oliver Wendell Holmes, "Indeed, to make their power felt, shareholders often must unite." Stan can get back on the board, but he cannot get back his position as treasurer.

Answers (C) and (D) are incorrect for the reasons stated above.

105. **Answer (D) is the best answer. Answer (C) is a close second.** A scant two years after its decision in *McQuade v. Stoneham,* the New York Court of Appeals, in *Clark v. Dodge,* 199 N.E. 641 (N.Y. 1936), faced a case in which, by contract, shareholders appointed each other to corporate offices. Pointedly, however, the court noted that all the shareholders were signatories to the agreement. The court then asked, "If all the shareholders agree, and a contract poses no conceivable damage to anyone, why shouldn't a court enforce it," even though technically it runs afoul of the statutory maxim that the corporation's business and affairs shall be managed by the board of directors. The court side-stepped its former ruling, **making Answers (A) and (B) incorrect.** The agreement, at least if it is unanimous, is valid.

106. The best answer is a qualified "Yes." Courts recognize the importance of such employment agreements to participants in small and closely-held corporate enterprises. Although

authority on less than unanimous agreements is scant, the few decisions that exist focus on actual harm, or the possibility of actual harm, to the non-signatory shareholders. They no longer focus on potential, or possible but less than probable, harms. *See, e.g., Glazer v. Glazer*, 374 F.2d 390 (5th Cir. 1967) (applying Tennessee law). Here, Sally is competent, with a proven track record of performance. The possibility of harm is slight. By contrast, if the signing shareholders were utilizing the agreement to put a ne'er-do-well son-in-law in office, with a long-term contract, a very real prospect of harm to the non-signing minority shareholders does raise its head.

107. **Answer (C) is the best answer.** Boards of directors may abdicate their duty to manage through long-term (or overly broad) delegations of three kinds: (1) contracts with officers or employees; (2) contracts with outsiders; or (3) delegations to committees of their own number. With regard to the first, the traditional model is that the board appoints, and re-appoints, the officers annually. Longer term appointments tie the hands of future boards of directors and tend also to disenfranchise future shareholders. See the discussion in the answer to Question 95. Lifetime, or excessively long-term, appointments were seldom, if ever, upheld. *See, e.g., Lee v. Jenkins Brothers*, 268 F.2d 357 (2d Cir. 1959) (lifetime employment contracts have met "with substantial hostility in the courts"; they "unduly restrict the power of shareholders and future boards of directors on questions of managerial policy") (applying Connecticut law). Today, courts apply a rule of reason analysis. How broad is the delegation? What is the term? What are the shareholders' other relationships to the corporation? What is the nature of the corporation: small, family-owned, closely-held, small publicly-held? And so on. The easy fix is to draft a long-term contract (not for life), but make it terminable by the corporation, or effective only so long as, "she faithfully and completely fulfills the duties of her office," or words to that effect.

Answers (A) and (B) are not the best answers for the reasons stated above.

Answer (D) is not the best answer. There is no way to evaluate Answer (D). You should always remember, though, as counsel to the company (if, indeed, that is what you are), that you represent the corporation and not any particular person within it. To evaluate Answer (D), Sally should seek advice elsewhere.

108. **Answer (D) is the best answer.** Delegations to outsiders, such as consulting firms, today have also come to be judged by "rule of reason" analysis as well. How broad is the delegation? What is the term? What are the shareholders' other relationships to the corporation? What is the nature of the corporation: small, family-owned, closely-held, small publicly-held? And so on.

The legal objections to overly broad or lengthy delegations (Answer (C)), are the same as those recited above, namely, that such delegations handcuff or tie the hands of future boards and disenfranchise future shareholders. *See, e.g., Sherman & Ellis, Inc. v. Indiana Mutual Casualty Co.*, 41 F.2d 588 (7th Cir. 1930). Consulting by major and intermediate accounting firms (Answer (A)) has proven controversial. Merely as auditors, those firms have had a conflict of interest. Their auditing fees are paid by the very entity (a publicly-held company) that they are overseeing and whose executives could be displeased by an overly rigorous annual audit. Nonetheless, in the 1980s and 1990s, public accounting firms forged onward, sometimes using auditing as a "loss leader" so that they could sell to audit clients consulting services. SOXA now forbids provision of nine categories of consulting services (legal, human resources, bookkeeping, actuarial, valuation, broker-dealer, and several others) to audit clients, so Answer (D) is correct. Accounting firms may still provide tax consulting services to audit clients. One result is that regulators and investors will have added confidence in audits' integrity. Another is that three of the "Big Four" have begun the process of "spinning off" their consulting practices into separate firms (but little has been heard from the so-called "intermediate 18" — smaller, but still sizeable, public accounting firms). The unintended consequence has been that audit fees have begun to climb precipitously, 30 and 35 percent in SOXA's first year with prediction of similar increases to follow.

These prohibitions on provision of accounting and consulting services apply to publicly-held corporations that are required to file periodic reports with the SEC. Those are corporations with a class of equity security (*e.g.*, common stock) held by 500 or more persons and $10 million in assets. Those are called "12(g) corporations," after the relevant section in the Securities Exchange Act of 1934. Corporations also come within the SEC's system, and are subject to a number of federal laws (including SOXA) if they have a class of securities listed on a national securities exchange (so-called "12(b) corporations"). Tree Top appears to be a 12(g) corporation.

Answers (A), (B), and (C) are not the best answers for the reasons stated above.

109. **Answer (D) is the best answer.** Most states now have statutes on the subject of delegations to board committees, so resort to a rule of reason, a business judgment rule analysis (Answer (A)), may be unnecessary. MBCA § 8.25(e) provides a short list of non-delegable matters:

A committee may not, however:

(1) authorize or approve distributions, except according to a formula or method, or within limits, prescribed by the board of directors;

(2) approve or propose to shareholders action that this Act requires be approved by shareholders;

(3) fill vacancies on the board of directors or . . . on any of its committees; or

(4) adopt, amend, or repeal bylaws.

Most state statutes have slightly longer lists, with seven, eight, or nine non-delegable matters. To advise an objector, or the board, counsel must always check the applicable statute. Here, at Two Fisted, Inc., the delegation exceeds permissible limits under the statute. Don Knotts should succeed in his challenge to the executive committee delegation. He does not need to resort to the argument that the delegation was overly broad and constitutes an abdication by the full board of its responsibilities (Answer (C)).

Answer (A), (B), and (C) are not the best answers for the reasons stated above.

110. **Answer (C) is the best answer.** In *Carmody v. Toll Brothers, Inc.*, 723 A.2d 1180 (Del. Ch. 1998), the court struck down the "dead hand" poison pill (Answer (A)) on grounds that it "handcuffed" future boards of directors, robbing them of the full measure of discretion they should be able to bring to bear during their board service. Less than a year later, in *Quickturn Design Systems, Inc. v. Shapiro*, 721 A.2d 1281 (Del. 1998), the Delaware Supreme Court upheld rejection of the "no hand" poison pill (Answer (B)), noting that "[o]ne of the most basic tenets of Delaware corporate law is that the board of directors has the ultimate responsibility for managing the business and affairs of the corporation." The no

hand pill "prevents a newly elected board of directors from completely discharging its fiduciary duties to protect fully the interests of Quickturn and its stockholders" and is therefore invalid.

Answers (A), (B), and (D) are not the best answers. Under the precedents discussed above, the best that can be done is adoption of a poison pill combined with a classified board, removable only for cause (Answer (C)). Such combination of devices may enable a target company to stave off a hostile bidder attaining control for many months.

As you can see, very interesting cases were resolved by application of old and time-tested corporate law principles.

111.　**Answer (C) is the best answer.** Dean and Dorothy may move ahead, but they must call a shareholders' meeting and give Knotts a chance to defend his record.

Answers (A) and (B) are incorrect. Even if statutes were silent on the subject, which once they were, shareholders had a common law right, called the right of "a motion," to remove directors. The right required sufficient cause (which was ill defined) and a shareholder vote (Answer (A)). Modern statutes change this rule. Removal is "with or without cause" (Answer (B)). *See* MBCA § 8.08(a): "The shareholders may remove one or more directors with or without cause unless the articles of incorporation provide that directors may be removed only for cause." The Model Act now makes removal not by a majority share vote, but by a plurality ("a director may be removed only if the number of votes cast to remove him exceeds the number of votes cast not to remove him").

Removal, however, may very well involve leveling charges against the director whose removal is sought, if only as a political matter (that is, to get the votes). In that case, and perhaps other cases as well, the director ought to have the right to defend herself. The cases are not plentiful (*Campbell v. Loew's, Inc.*, 134 A.2d 852 (Del. Ch. 1957), is one), but the few that exist have held directors entitled to due process. At a minimum, a director whose removal is sought should receive notice of the charges made, if any, and an opportunity to present her case to the shareholders (Answer (C)).

In the 1980s takeover boom, many corporations opted into removal only for cause by provisions in articles of incorporation or charter. Delaware adopted a "fool proof" version. If a Delaware corporation classifies its board of directors, a requirement of removal for cause only automatically springs into being. DEL. GEN. CORP. L. § 141(k).

Answer (D) is incorrect. Directors have no power to remove fellow directors. That would disenfranchise shareholders.

112.　Yes. Cumulative voting is not as important as it was even 15–20 years ago. Even California, which had mandatory cumulative voting, and prohibited staggered boards of directors because they tend to negate the effect of cumulative voting, has relented. Publicly-held companies that are incorporated in California may "opt out" of cumulative voting and have classified boards. Nonetheless, attorneys often use cumulative voting to effect power-sharing arrangements in corporations. Most corporate attorneys encounter cumulative voting arrangements periodically. As has been seen, however, modern statutes allow removal of directors with or without cause, by majority or plurality vote. In a corporation with cumulative voting, then, the following scenario could develop. Through cumulative voting, the minority (say, 16%) elects one director to a seven person board. The board immediately calls a special shareholders' meeting to remove that director. Because removal is by majority vote, and the majority has 50 percent voting power, the minority director would be removed. A further wrinkle is necessary, then, to reconcile removal by majority vote with cumulative voting. Statutes provide that a director elected cumulatively is not removed if the number of votes cast against his removal would have been sufficient to elect him in the first place. *See, e.g.*, MBCA § 8.08(c) ("If cumulative voting is authorized, a director may not be removed if the number of votes sufficient to elect him under cumulative voting exceeds the number of votes cast to remove him."). Director Knotts, therefore, should get out the vote, especially of those who elected him in the first place, if he intends to defend against his removal.

113. **Answer (A) is the best answer.** Around 1984, the Model Act drafters added a provision for judicial removal of directors. They advanced two justifications. One was the case reported, that of a cumulatively elected "bad actor" (no pun intended) director who had the votes to defeat his removal each time it was attempted. The other is the case of a badly behaving director in a large publicly-held corporation. Convening a shareholders' meeting, soliciting proxies, and so on, to remove such a director could well cost the corporation $1 million. Going to court would be (much?) cheaper. MBCA § 8.09(a) enunciates the test for removal stated in Answer (A), but requires a further finding. The court must also find that "considering the director's course of conduct and the inadequacy of other available remedies, removal would be in the best interest of the corporation." Conceivably, a court could then find that a badly behaving director was a badly behaving "genius" director whose removal was not in the best interest of the corporation. There have been no reported cases under the section.

   Answer (B) is incorrect because the SEC, and not the company, has power to seek "director and officer bar orders." The federal Penny Stock Reform Act of 1990 gave the SEC power to go to court seeking lifetime (or shorter) bar orders. The SEC, though, had to prove that the director or officer was "substantially unfit to serve." Based upon a law review article by an eminent corporate legal scholar, Jayne W. Barnard, *When Is a Corporate Executive "Substantially Unfit to Serve"?*, 70 N.C. L. REV. 1489 (1992), federal courts adopted a six-part test of "substantial unfitness to serve." The SEC chaffed under the six-part test and courts' reluctance to issue bar orders. SOXA changes the test to mere "unfitness to serve." SOXA also allows the SEC to proceed administratively against an officer or director rather than going to court. Two Fisted could lobby the SEC to utilize its new SOXA powers, banning Don Knotts from further service as a director, but Two Fisted could not do so itself.

   The state court proceeding would be best. In the proceeding, the corporation may also seek a state court "bar order" of sorts. *See* MBCA § 8.09(c): "The court, in addition to removing the director, may bar the director from reelection for a period prescribed by the court." Later, the corporation may seek damages for breach of fiduciary duty (Answer (D)), but the first priority is removal of Knotts as director.

   Answers (C) and (D) are not the best answers for the reasons stated above.

114. **Answer (C) is the best answer.** In the case on which this Question is based, *Hurley v. Ornsteen*, 42 N.E.2d 273 (Mass. 1942), the court recognized the possibility of informal action. Nonetheless, the court failed to give effect to the informal action in the case at bar because no evidence existed that the third director had ratified compromise of the debt. There also was evidence that perhaps no third director even existed, but the court ignored it.

   Answer (B) is incorrect. One old case, *Baldwin v. Canfield*, 1 N.W. 261 (Minn. 1879), struck down informal action by a board even though it was unanimous. The court's view was that directors had to sit around a table, convened in a formal meeting, in order to take valid action. Boards, especially boards of smaller companies, often acted without such formalities. Courts began to recognize reality: informal action by directors was often the norm. They recognized informal action if it had been unanimous, making Answer (B) incorrect. Then came informal action by some directors with ratification or acquiescence (knowledge plus inaction) by others (Answer (C)).

Answers (A) and (D) are not the best answers. In the last several decades, courts have used a number of devices, including estoppel (Answer (D)), to hold corporations bound by the informal acts of a majority of the directors. Some courts also will hold corporations bound by the formal acts of some directors and the informal acts of others (ratification or acquiescence) if the "total" is equal to a majority of the directors then in office. Nonetheless, before the fact, one dealing with a corporation is best off by obtaining a board resolution, or a signed unanimous directors' consent, or evidence that the acts involved are the binding acts of a duly authorized agent of the corporation. As to the latter, Director One's forgiveness of the debt may or may not bind the corporation. If she is acting only as director, directors are not agents (see Question 91), and the corporation would not be bound. By contrast, if she wore another hat (e.g., managing director or CEO), she would be an agent and her acts may well bind the corporation (Answer (A)). As you can see, however, the whole area would be fraught with problems of proof. Did Director Two's "shrug" constitute ratification? What "hats" did Director One wear? Is a majority sufficient or does the relevant case law (if there is any), by parity of reasoning to the consent statutes (discussed in the answer to Question 106), require unanimity?

115. Doug should attempt to procure a written consent signed by all of the directors then in office. Or, because it is more properly the work of the corporation's lawyer (if Edward D. Moans has one), urge that she obtain the written consent of the board members, providing you with copies. MBCA § 8.21(a) provides in part: "[a]ction required or permitted under this Act to be taken by the board of directors may be taken without a meeting if each director signs a consent describing the action to be taken and delivers it to the corporation." MBCA § 8.21(c) provides that such action is equivalent to action taken at a meeting and may be so described in documents and the like. The practice often utilized is to send a separate (but identical) piece of paper to each director. They sign and return the "consents" to the corporate secretary or to the attorney, who staples them together, placing them in the corporate minute book in lieu of minutes of an actual meeting. If any director is opposed to the action to be taken, or to the desirability of the action, or of taking the action without discussion at meeting, she may merely withhold consent. The result is that a meeting of directors must then be held if the proponents of the action wish to continue to proceed with the matter.

116. The board should be straightforward with the shareholders but live up to the best efforts provision as well. MBCA § 8.26 (2008) is a new section added to the Model Act: "A corporation may agree to submit a matter to a vote of its shareholders even if, after approving the matter, the board of directors determines it no longer recommends the matter." The best efforts or other provision of a merger agreement, or an agreement for the sale of the corporation's assets, may require the directors to convene a meeting and hold a vote on the matter. This may be so even though pursuant to a "fiduciary out" the board has changed its mind, now swearing allegiance to another better offer or one with more

advantageous terms.

A related amendment is to MBCA § 10.03 (Amendment by Board of Directors and Shareholders). Originally, the section required that with a request for shareholders to vote the board also transmit its recommendation. A pre-existing exception was "unless the board of directors makes a determination that because of conflicts of interest or other special circumstances it should not make a recommendation." A second exception has now been inserted for the situation in which section 8.26 applies, that is, a preexisting agreement required directors to submit a matter to shareholders but the board no longer has a recommendation (because of a better offer, etc.).

117. **Answer (D) is the correct answer.** Answer (D) paraphrases in part, and quotes in part, MBCA § 8.40(a) & (c). The section is extremely flexible.

Answers (A), (B), and (C) are incorrect. Older statutes required that there be one person with the title of "president" and one person with the title of "secretary," as in Answer (A). Often, in annual reports and other documents of public corporations, one will see the head person signing "President, Chief Executive Officer, and Chairman of the Board." In part, it is an exercise in egomania by corporate CEOs. More forgiving, the triple title may also exist because the corporation is incorporated in a state with an older statute which still requires a "president." The CEO title is also taken because that is what is in vogue as the title for the head person.

The new voguish titles for corporate officers (Answer (C)), none of which is legally required (with each title's equivalent from a bygone era in parentheses), are as follows: Chief Executive Officer (CEO) (President), Chief Operating Officers (COO) (Executive Vice-President), Chief Financial Officer (CFO) (Treasurer or Comptroller or both), Chief Legal Officer (CLO) (House Counsel or Vice-President and General Counsel). The corporate secretary is generally still called the "corporate secretary," but soon someone will come up with a fancier title.

Titles for corporate officers, then, are merely a matter of custom and current fads. Generally, the bylaws will name those titles and, in very general terms, delegate certain tasks to the various officers named. The only bottom line is that there must be one person designated to do what corporate secretaries traditionally have done, but that person need not have the title of secretary. It could be something such as "Recording Bozo."

In *Gantler v. Stephens*, 965 A.2d 695, 708 (Del. 2009), the Supreme Court of Delaware filled an obvious hole in Delaware jurisprudence, finally and expressly holding that "corporate officers owe fiduciary duties that are identical to those owed by corporate directors."

118. The attorney is right. Corporate officers have very little authority by virtue of their titles alone. The sources of whatever authority they do have are articles of incorporation (very rare), statute (almost never), board resolutions (frequent general delegations or transaction-specific resolutions), and bylaws (almost always, but usually exceedingly general). Those are sources of "actual authority." Another, somewhat slippery, source of authority is "inherent authority." Inherent authority (ostensible authority) is based upon what persons with the same or similar titles in corporations of the same or similar size and purpose do. It is a common denominator sort of standard. An attorney, or a business person, would very seldom rely upon inherent authority, even of a CEO, in a transaction of any size or with any novelty to it. Better viewed, inherent authority is for smaller and routine transactions. Alternatively, attorneys rely on inherent authority only after the fact, when they use it as a backstop in trying to impress or pin upon a corporation contractual responsibility for the acts of its

officers.

Surprisingly, corporate officers, including CEOs, by law alone have very little authority. It is the board of directors which manages, or under whose supervision is managed, the business and affairs of the corporation. The "buck stops" with the board, and not the CEO, and that, ultimately, is where authority to bind the corporation is found or originates. *See, e.g., Black v. Harrison Home Co.*, 99 P. 494, 497 (Cal. 1909) ("It is an elementary principle of corporation law that the president of a corporation has no power, merely because he is president, to bind the corporation by contract. The management of the affairs of a corporation ordinarily is in the hands of its board of directors."). CEOs have power to hire and fire employees, to execute contracts entered into in the ordinary course of the corporation's business, to conduct the corporation's day-to-day business, and so on. Absent delegation by the board of directors, however, CEOs have no power to bind the corporation in "extraordinary" transactions. Older cases regarded persons with the title of "President and General Manager" as having greater inherent authority than a person with merely the title "President." Whether those cases would be persuasive today is doubtful. The modern title "Chief Executive Officer" seems as or more extensive than "President and General Manager." Attorney here should advise his contractor client to obtain a board resolution authorizing the CEO to execute the construction contract on the corporation's behalf.

119.   **Answer (D) is the best answer.** The best evidence of authority one can obtain is evidence of express actual authority. As seen in the previous Question, express actual authority might be found in the bylaws, but here the purchasing agent is not what many corporate lawyers would call a "bylaw officer." This transaction might very well be done by means of a "certified board resolution." Certified means nothing more than the corporate secretary attests (certifies) that what appears in the document is a true and correct copy of the resolution passed by the board at such and such a meeting. But, what if the board of Air Wisconsin has a crowded agenda? They might not have time to do a resolution or to give the matter full board consideration. For Glenn Grant, it might be "take it or leave it."

Answers (A), (B), and (C) are not the best answers. Much of what transactional lawyers do is to insure that the fictional being (corporation, LLC, LLP, Limited Partnership, etc.) on the other side of transactions will be bound by the acts of flesh and blood humans who purport to act on the fictional being's behalf. As you may have guessed, too, there are no certain answers. If Air Wisconsin proposes to pay cash, say, $1.6 million, the payment in cash may end the problem. Also, counsel should ask, what kind of trucks are they? If they are large over-the-road trucks, that does not fit with Air Wisconsin's business. It should put the attorney on notice that further inquiry, and further assurances, may be in order because inherent authority (Answer (A)) is a doubtful proposition. By contrast, if the order is for 100 medium size pickup trucks, that may very well fit with Air Wisconsin's business. *See, e.g., General Overseas Films, Ltd. v. Robin International, Inc.*, 542 F. Supp. 684 (S.D.N.Y. 1982) (although assistant treasurer of Anaconda Copper Co. had trappings of office, his guarantee on behalf of Anaconda of loan to company constructing Russian mission in New York defied common sense — no apparent authority), *aff'd*, 718 F.2d 1085 (2d Cir. 1983).

Much of what a transactional lawyer does in these cases, then, is a combination of common sense, judgment, and the art of the possible (obtaining a personal guarantee from the purchasing agent and one or more other officers (Answer (B) is not likely possible). The best that a lawyer can get is always express actual authority. On the other end of the spectrum, when the parties are unequal in bargaining power, it may well be a "take or leave it" proposition. The lawyer's job then may be only to apprise her client of the risks, or give an informal opinion that inherent authority appears to exist; she may be able to do little else.

Third-party letters of opinion are sometimes used (Answer (C)), but here counsel would probably not willingly give a letter of opinion. The reasons are varied, but one is, because of risk, lawyers bill high amounts for legal opinions. The lawyer may know, without asking, that Air Wisconsin would not want to pay the bill. Actually, the previous Question ($19.4 million construction in Sweet Home, Oregon) might be a better opportunity for a third-party letter of opinion (third party because the letter is for the benefit of the third party contracting with the corporate client rather than for the benefit of the corporate client itself).

120. **Answer (B) is the best answer.** It is often said that the "best evidence of an agent's authority is her usual occupation." If this agent, or the person occupying the office, has engaged in the same or very similar transactions in the past, the past dealings may be evidence of implied actual authority. It may also be grounds for arguing that "apparent authority" exists (see Question 112).

Assume, then, that the Fleet Sales manager answers the following to your question in Answer (B): "Oh yeah, they are on a two-year cycle. They order 20 or 25 trucks every other year. In fact, I think this is the fourth cycle Air Wisconsin has been through since I have been here." In this instance, an attorney may safely (well, not absolutely safely) be able to opine that implied actual authority exists, especially if satisfactory answers are also received to the questions stated in Answers (A) and (D). There is no substitute for express actual authority (certified board resolution — which is what you would be going after by asking the question in Answer (C)) if you can get it. Implied actual authority's best use is for argument after the fact if the authority to enter into the transaction is disputed.

Answers (A), (C), and (D) are not the best answers for the reasons stated above.

121. Probably "Yes." By the facts as restated, no implied actual authority exists. The Air Wisconsin purchasing agent has not previously done this type of transaction with Glenn Grant. The next item on your checklist (after express actual authority and implied actual authority) is inherent authority. It is a common denominator standard: what do CEOs do? What do corporate treasurers do? What do corporate purchasing agents do? Look to the left, look to the right: what do similar agents in similar size corporations and of a similar type do? CEOs sign contracts that are in the ordinary course of the company's business. Treasurers sign checks. Purchasing agents buy things, such as pickup trucks.

Inherent, or ostensible, authority is the authority that by tradition and custom comes with the office or position.

122. **Answer (D) is the best answer** (based upon *General Overseas Films, Ltd. v. Robin International, Inc.*, 542 F. Supp. 684 (S.D.N.Y. 1982)). The proposed answers lay out the checklist an attorney, or law student, should follow. In descending order, no evidence exists of express actual authority. Next, there is no evidence of this sort of thing in the past and, hence, no implied actual authority. Next, treasurers of corporations do not guarantee the debts of completely unrelated entities, so Answer (B) (inherent authority) is incorrect. In fact, guarantee of the debts of another is always considered an "extraordinary" transaction

that may even be *ultra vires*.

There is something "fishy" here. There is no evidence of actual authority (Answer (A)) such as a board resolution. Is there a kickback to the Air Wisconsin treasurer? Has he become a rogue agent? Is Rub-A-Dub owned by the Treasurer's brother-in-law or cousin? Something does not make sense.

Back to the checklist: the last item is apparent authority (Answer (C)). In cases of apparent authority, by its own acts, the principal (here corporation) has created in third parties a reasonable apprehension that the agent in fact has the authority to enter the transaction on the principal's behalf. In most cases of implied actual authority (what has the agent done in the past) there also exists apparent authority. If the agent did the acts in the past, and the principal knew about, and did not in some way countermand or give notice of the limits on the agent's authority, a reasonable apprehension of authority and, hence, apparent authority may exist. It is said that while implied actual authority comes from examination of the past acts of the agent, apparent authority comes from examination of the past acts of the principal.

Here apparent authority may exist even though implied actual authority does not. Air Wisconsin put this person in office, gave him personalized stationery, a telephone, an email address, a fax machine, and other emoluments of office. The principal (Air Wisconsin) set up the agent (the Treasurer) so as to enable him to do things such as guarantee debts.

But back to common sense. In cases of apparent authority, the principal creates in third parties a *reasonable* apprehension that the agent has the authority to do the transaction. Any apprehension by Citizen's Bank that the Treasurer of Air Wisconsin can guarantee the bank's loan to a Denver hot tub company, for a new factory in Phoenix, is not reasonable. And, in the case upon which this hypothetical is based, that is exactly what the court decided.

Answers (A), (B), and (C) are incorrect. Citizen's Bank should not make this loan.

Both in and after law school, remember your checklist for the authority of agents, including corporate officers (who are nothing more than agents):

(1) express actual authority;

(2) implied actual authority;

(3) inherent authority; and

(4) apparent authority.

123. **Answer (D) is the best answer.** A principal difference in the standard of care applicable to corporate directors and officers is that it is quasi-subjective. It is a common denominator standard. Look to the left, look to the right, see what directors or officers in similar corporations who do similar businesses do. *See, e.g., Litwin v. Allen*, 25 N.Y.S.2d 667, 678 (Sup. Ct. 1940) ("In the last analysis, whether or not a director has discharged his duty . . . depends upon the facts and circumstances of a particular case, the kind of corporation involved, its size and financial resources, the magnitude of the transaction, and the immediacy of the problem presented."). The standard as traditionally expressed is "that amount of care and skill that a reasonably prudent person in like position in similar circumstances would exercise." In the instant case, the testimony of directors of other companies, as long as it is not overly cumulative, would be admissible, while it may not be in run-of-the-mill torts case.

Answers (A) and (B) are incorrect. Answer (B) is the tort law standard you learned in the first year of law school. What is done in the community may be excluded, or subject to a limiting jury instruction, because the entire community may be comprised of "fools" or of persons who do foolish things. A whole profession may have been laggard in the adoption of new techniques. *See, e.g., The T. J. Hooper*, 60 F.2d 737, 740 (2d Cir. 1932) (L. Hand, J.) ("[I]n most cases reasonable prudence is in fact common prudence; but strictly it is never its measure; a whole calling may have been unduly lagged in the adoption of new and available devices."). Put another way, the reasonable person standard, which is an objective standard, depends upon the reasonable person, who is everywhere, but at the same time is nowhere in particular.

Answer (C) is incorrect. The declarants are in court where they may be cross-examined. Evidence questions are beyond the scope of this work.

In the 1980s, the Model Act drafters took a number of steps to make the standard more forgiving yet. They deleted the word "skill" from the standard as they codified it, denying that a modicum of skill ever had been part and parcel of the duty of care. A few state statutes, especially in banking and insurance, do expressly include the word "skill." In 1998, the drafters attempted to make the standard of care more subjective yet. MBCA § 8.30(b) provides: "The members of a board of directors or a committee of the board . . . shall discharge their duties with the care that a person in like position would reasonably believe appropriate under the circumstances." The tenor of the change is to attempt to say that the judges of how much care is enough care are in the first instance the directors themselves, rather than a judge or an aggrieved shareholder. To some extent, this is a collapse of the business judgment rule, which is a creature wholly of case law, into the standard of conduct (see Questions 126–34). Under the business judgment rule, how much information is enough information, or how much care is enough care, is itself a business judgment. It is too soon to determine how this change in the standard, if adopted by many states, will play out in adjudicated cases. At some point, the standard could become so subjective as to be meaningless.

But what the right hand giveth, the left hand taketh away. In 2005, the ABA Committee and the ABA amended MBCA § 8.01 ("Requirement for and Functions of Board of Directors"). Shortly after injecting more of a subjective element, the Committee spelled out, for the first time, sub duties of the duty of care, adding objective elements to the equation of what the duty of care requires in particular circumstances.

In the case of a public corporation, the board's oversight responsibilities include attention to:

(1)   business performance and plans;

(2)   major risks to which the corporation is or may be exposed;

(3)   the performance and compensation of senior officers;

(4)   policies and practices to foster the corporation's compliance with law and ethical conduct;

(5)   preparation of the company's financial statements;

(6)   the effectiveness of the corporation's internal controls;

(7)   arrangements for providing adequate and timely disclosure to directors; and

(8)   the composition of the board and its committees, taking into account the important role of independent directors.

These statements of subduties were said to be necessary to bring the MBCA into line with federal requirements mandated by the Sarbanes-Oxley Act.

124.   **Answer (D) is the best answer.** Two principles should be brought to bear here. First, although no particular care and skill may be required to be a director, if an individual director does possess certain skills and knowledge (the actuary or the lawyer here), she must bring it to bear. Second, although no particular care and skill may be required as a prerequisite to being a director (the daughter or the son), upon joining a board, a director must, within a reasonable time, gain the skill, knowledge, and familiarity with the company's affairs that will enable her to function well as a director. If she is not able to do so, she should resign. *See, e.g., Francis v. United Jersey Bank*, 432 A.2d 814 (N.J. 1981) (discussed *infra*).

Many lawyers, accountants, bankers, and other persons in business-related professions (here, an actuary) no longer wish to serve on boards for the reason that they may be held to a "higher standard" — one that includes the baseline of knowledge and skill that a judge or jury believes a professional should possess.

As to the son and the daughter, an older Supreme Judicial Court of Massachusetts opinion absolved a woman director of duty of care liability for wrongdoing by her husband, the more active participant in the venture. In absolving her, in effect the court made the sexist statement, "She was only a housewife with no business experience." *Allied Freightways, Inc. v. Cholfin*, 91 N.E.2d 765 (Mass. 1950). That would not be good law today, if ever it was. *Francis v. United Jersey Bank, supra*, is more representative. The corporation was in the reinsurance brokerage business. As such, it handled millions of dollars of premiums collected by insurance agents and brokers, to be passed through to various re-insurers. The father, who ran the business, passed away. The mother, who served on the board, did nothing to learn about the business or to obtain the business sense she may have needed. Instead, in a period of protracted mourning over her husband's death, she drank heavily, to the detriment of the business. Her sons, who were active participants, looted the corporation to the extent of $10 million. "They spawned their fraud," the New Jersey Supreme Court found, "in the back water of her neglect." Her estate was held liable for the entire loss. Thus, although few if any prerequisites may exist for becoming a corporate director, once one does achieve that status she must quickly "get up to speed," gaining the skill, knowledge, and familiarity with the business appropriate to the position.

The duty of care may also be the vehicle by which shareholders seek to vindicate extremely unwise or stupid acts by corporate directors or officers, acts intentionally rather than negligently done, but with no hint of self-dealing or other venal purpose. In *Litwin v. Allen*, 25 N.Y.S.2d 667, 678 (Sup. Ct. 1940), directors of bank purchased bonds (debt securities) of the Missouri Pacific Railway, giving the seller the right to repurchase the bonds (an option) at any time in the ensuing six months, at the sales price. It was a "heads you win, tails we lose" proposition for the bank. The transaction occurred in 1930, just at the start of the Great Depression. Needless to say, the bank suffered great losses. The court found the directors liable. *See id.* at 699 ("[T]he entire arrangement was so improvident, so risky, so unusual and unnecessary as to be contrary to fundamental conceptions of prudent banking practice."). In *Hun v. Cary*, 82 N.Y. 65 (1880), directors of a failing bank used its last resources to construct a glorious new building, which did not save the bank. The directors were then held liable. They were either stupid, or they engaged in a last ditch, high stakes gamble. Conservative commentators deny that directors ever may be held liable for extremely unwise or "stupid" acts alone. The question is one that cannot be resolved here.

Answers (A), (B), and (C) are incorrect for the reasons stated above.

125.   **Answer (A) is the best answer.** Although they may exist in reality, in law there is no such thing as a specialized, honorary, or figurehead director. If a director attempted to defend a claim on the grounds that she was only a "figurehead," or a "specialized" director, she would be "hung out to dry." Thus, **Answers (B) and (C) are incorrect.**

Answer (D) is incorrect. There is no duty to attend meetings. Instead, the duty is to keep informed. However that may be, the best evidence of keeping informed may well be attendance at all, or most all, of the board's meetings. *See, e.g., Hoye v. Meek*, 795 F.2d 893 (10th Cir. 1986) (upholding duty of care liability where director and board chairman of Oklahoma corporation lived in semi-retirement in Vermont, attended few meetings, and by default allowed his son to mismanage the corporation).

Corporations have achieved the goal of having specialized directors, which may be very useful, by having a second, unofficial board. In high tech, for example, technical wizards may receive all of the pay and perks of directors, but serve on a technical "advisory board" rather than the "statutory" board of directors. In a real estate multiple listing service, a second "advisory" board consisted of community representatives whose primary interest was the community or communities in which their offices were located, and not the corporation's business overall. But, on "real" boards of directors, as Gertrude Stein might have said, "A director is a director is a director."

126.   **Answer (B) is the best answer.** This is a 21st century version of *Bates v. Dresser*, 251 U.S. 524 (1920) (Holmes, J.). The common law duty of care was the same both for officers and directors, to wit, the degree of care and skill that similarly situated persons would use in like positions. The president, however, or any other corporate officer, had to bring that standard of care to bear in many more situations and much more to day-to-day minutiae than would the average director. Consequently, **Answer (B) is a better answer than Answer (C).** In

Bates, Holmes concluded that the president of the bank should have noticed the fanciful ways of the young cashier while the directors would have no occasion to do so. He opined that the president should have called in some passbooks and compared them to the ledger while he would not have expected the directors of the bank, absent notice of some sort, to do so.

Answer (D) is incorrect. It is the directors' duty to manage or supervise the corporation's business and affairs. They can never shift that duty, or responsibility for breach of it, onto government regulators (*e.g.*, banking or insurance regulators). By law, the "buck stops" with the board of directors.

Answer (A) is incorrect. It is just a nonsense or throw-away answer.

Once again, the Model Act drafters have attempted to tinker with (twist) the common law. MBCA § 8.42 provides: "An officer, when performing in such capacity, shall act . . . with the care that a person in a like position would reasonably exercise under similar circumstances." Recall that the standard adopted in 1998 for directors attempts to be more subjective, and therefore more forgiving: "the care that a person in a like position would reasonably believe appropriate under the circumstances." It would have been simpler to have the standard of conduct be the same for officers as well as directors, as has previously always been the case.

127. **Answer (D) is the best answer.** Courts and commentators have been resistant to entreaties that they should break the duty of care down into a list of sub-duties. However, if there are sub-duties, the two principal ones would be the duty to stay informed and the duty to make inquiry (next Question).

In *Fields v. Sax*, 462 N.E.2d 983 (Ill. App. Ct. 1984), a corporation suffered financial reversals. Plaintiff shareholders sued, *inter alia*, an aged director who conducted business from his Miami hospital room during several lengthy illnesses. Even while positing "a duty to attend and participate in regular meetings of the board of directors," the court affirmed a directed verdict for the aged director. "[I]nvalids are permitted to engage in the hope of recovery, and are not called upon by reason of their illness to retire at once from this life and confine themselves to preparation for their passage into another." The duty is to stay informed, which may in certain cases necessitate attendance at most meetings. Overall, though, no mandatory rule of attendance holds sway.

Answers (A), (B), and (C) are incorrect for the reasons stated above.

128. Maybe. If directors have notice that would trigger inquiry by a reasonable director, then they have a duty to make inquiry, or cause inquiry to be made by others (*e.g.*, the CEO, the corporate attorney, or a board committee). If they cause inquiry to be made, then, "absent knowledge that makes reliance unwarranted," they are "entitled to rely [on persons or committees] to whom the board may have delegated, formally or by course of conduct, the authority or duty to perform one or more of the board's functions." MBCA § 8.30(d). Again, "absent knowledge that makes reliance unwarranted," a director is "entitled to rely on information, opinions, reports or statements, including financial statements and other financial data, prepared or presented" by the person or persons to whom the board has made a delegation. *Id.* Thus, if the board came to suspect that the person to whom they delegated the task of investigation was doing a sloppy job, or had begun drinking heavily, or had taken a kickback from the high living cashier, the board could not rely. Absent facts giving rise to an inference of knowledge, though, the board may delegate and then rely on:

(1) one or more officers or employees of the corporation whom the director reasonably believes to be reliable and competent in the functions performed or the information, opinions, reports, or statements provided;

(2) legal counsel, public accountants, or other persons retained by the corporation as to matters involving skills or expertise the director reasonably believes are matters (i) within the particular person's professional or expert competence or (ii) as to which the particular person merits confidence; or

(3) a committee of the board of directors of which the director is not a member if the director reasonably believes the committee merits confidence.

MBCA § 8.30(e).

129. **Answer (D) is the best answer.** Large companies have long had internal "antitrust compliance programs." They now also have codes of conduct and mission statements that require compliance with law. Each employee and manager must sign. Internal personnel, or outside law firms, do "legal audits," assessing risk both of criminal or civil liability in every area in which the company does business. In any area in which significant exposure exists, lawyers and managers design and put in place monitoring and compliance programs. Active monitoring and compliance is a central item on many boards' agendas. Often the overarching description of such activity is "risk management." Some large corporations now have a "risk management committee" of the board of directors whose particular task it is to monitor legal compliance.

Answer (C) is not the best answer. For CB Foods, in this day and age, an audit and monitoring and environmental compliance programs would not be merely be wise, but a requirement dictated by the duty of care.

Answers (A) and (B) are incorrect, but at one time, Answer (B) would have made sense as well. *Graham v. Allis-Chalmers Mfg. Co.*, 188 A.2d 125 (Del. 1963), involved Allis-Chalmers's part in the great electrical equipment price fixing scandal of the 1950s in which a number of companies (Allis-Chalmers included) were liable both criminally and civilly (for treble damages). In the 1930s, Allis-Chalmers had been involved in a similar, but smaller, scandal. The Delaware courts absolved the directors. The prior scandal was not enough of a "red flag." Absent suspicion of further wrongdoing, the directors had no duty to put in place a "system of watchfulness." Thirty-three years later, in *In re Caremark International, Inc. Derivative Litigation*, 698 A.2d 959 (Del. Ch. 1996), shareholders sought to hold liable directors of a home health care company whose middle managers paid kickbacks to physicians and otherwise engaged in Medicare fraud. The company paid over $250 million in fines to regulatory agencies. The reported opinion, approving settlement of the shareholder lawsuit, gave then-Chancellor Allen (now a law professor at NYU) an opportunity to comment on the contemporary relevance of *Graham*. Chancellor Allen opined that contemporary corporate boards should have in place:

> information and reporting systems . . . that are reasonably designed to provide senior management and the board itself timely, accurate information sufficient to allow management and the board . . . to reach informed judgments concerning both the corporation's compliance with law and its business performance.

Id. at 970.

Subsequently, however, the Supreme Court of Delaware has raised the bar back up, at least part way and in non-transaction settings ("oversight" responsibilities). In *Stone ex rel. Amsouth Bancorporation v. Ritter*, 911 A.2d 362 (Del. 2006), shareholders sued directors for failure to oversee staff. Employees had failed to file reports as required by the Bank Secrecy Act. Banking regulators had fined the corporation $50 million. Plaintiff shareholders alleged that the directors had failed to comply with their "*Caremark*" duties.

Mr. Justice Holland quoted the Chancellor below with approval: "Where a claim of directorial liability for corporate loss is predicated upon ignorance of liability creating activities within the corporation . . . only a sustained or systematic failure of the board to exercise oversight — such as the utter failure to assure a reasonable information and reporting system exists — will establish the lack of good faith that is a necessary condition to liability."

If a plaintiff establishes a sustained or systematic failure, taking place over a period of time, the violation is not a violation of the duty of care but of the emerging duty of good faith and the duty of loyalty. The court spoke of "good faith" as part of the "triad of fiduciary duties that includes the duties of care and loyalty." "[F]ailure to act in good faith is not conduct that results, *ipso facto*, in the direct imposition of director liability." But "a showing of bad faith conduct [sustained or systematic oversight failures] . . . is essential to establish director oversight liability [and] the fiduciary duty violated by that conduct is the duty of loyalty."

If a failure to exercise oversight escalates to a violation of the duties of good faith and of loyalty, one doctrinal result is that exculpatory provisions in the corporate charter or articles of incorporation will no longer shield the director from money damage liability. *Stone v. Ritter*, then, gives added content to two fiduciary duty areas: *Caremark* or oversight responsibilities and the duty of good faith.

At least in the financial and accounting areas, the Sarbanes-Oxley Act of 2002 (SOXA) requires that directors and officers of publicly-held companies be proactive. Effectively, those officials must see to it that the company adopts a code of conduct that "promote honest and ethical conduct, including the ethical handling of actual and apparent conflicts between personal and professional relationships" and "promote compliance with applicable" laws and regulations. More accurately, SOXA requires companies to disclose whether or not they have such a code of ethics in place. The upshot is that all public companies will put such a code in place. SOXA also requires quarterly and annual certifications by CEOs and CFOs of public companies. They must certify, under pain of criminal penalties, that the companies' financial reports do not contain any material omission or misstatement and that they fairly present in all material respects the company's financial situation. Relevant here, the CEO and CFO must also certify, quarterly (302 certifications) and again annually (404 certifications), that they have evaluated the company's "internal controls." They must report to the corporation's audit committee any deficiencies in those controls as well as any "fraud" by those in the corporation responsible for such controls. In several unfolding corporate "meltdowns," such as the Amsouth matter, the SEC has alleged knowingly false certifications and obtained guilty pleas and convictions of corporate CEOs and CFOs, for conduct that not so long ago may have at most amounted to a duty of care or duty of loyalty violation.

130.   **Answer (C) is the best answer.** Even though the duty of care may be different from the tort law reasonable person standard, many of the other analogies to tort law do work. Thus, the plaintiff must prove that the violation of duty (failure to keep informed, failure to make

inquiry, etc.) "proximately caused" the damage to the corporation. Thus, defense counsel may be able to bring to bear many of the causation arguments she learned in her law school torts course.

Answer (D) is not the best answer. Here, there is an issue of fact. A jury could find that Answer (D) is more likely, but Answer (C) provides the raw material for an attempt at a defense. In the face of a dominating director, the transaction would have occurred no matter what Dan and Val had done. Whether they voted "yes," "no," or abstained, the acquisition, and the resulting damage to the corporation would have occurred. *See, e.g., Barnes v. Andrews*, 298 F. 614 (S.D.N.Y. 1924) (finding that a protest, even if it had been made, would not have stopped the improvident transaction and, therefore, no causation).

Answers (A) and (B) are incorrect. Dan and Valerie would be presumed to have assented if they did nothing. MBCA § 8.24(d) so provides unless "his dissent or abstention from the action taken is entered in the minutes of the meeting; or . . . he delivers written notice of his dissent or abstention to the presiding officer of the meeting before its adjournment or to the corporation immediately after adjournment of the meeting."

131. Yes. The advent of "big box" store competition is similar to what occurred in the 1930s and 1940s with "chain store" competition. You can argue that the advent of "big box" retailing in Montana is an intervening cause that supersedes any duty of care violation by Ted or his fellow directors. *See, e.g., Martin v. Hardy*, 232 N.W. 197 (Mich. 1930) (directors of an "old time dry goods store," which failed, relieved of their negligence because of a superseding cause, namely, the advent of "chain store" competition in the region). The proximate cause of the damage to Country Joe's becomes the arrival of Home Depot and Wal-Mart. In the same way, regional, national, or international economic developments, or the weather, or what have you, may be argued to be a cause that supersedes any duty of care violation by corporate officers or directors.

132. **Answer (C) is the best answer.** Again, similar to the tort law negligence rubric, the last element of a duty of care claim is proof that the corporation suffered damage. As will be seen, the duty of loyalty is different: either damage to the corporation, or certain forms of illicit gain to the corporate officer or director, will suffice. See Question 135.

Answers (A) and (B) are not the best answers. In a duty of care case, the first line of defense may well be Answer (B), the business judgment rule. The defense would be a weak one here because the business judgment rule requires that at least some care (not necessarily due care) be exercised in the making of the judgment or decision. Here that burden (and also Answer (A) — due care) would be difficult to sustain. Rosten obtained no information whatsoever. He acted on a hunch based upon his astrological chart. Losing on the business judgment defense is not fatal, however. The director can fall back at trial to argue the merits of the duty of care claim, namely, that due care was in fact exercised, or that there was a superseding cause of the damage the corporation sustained, or, as here, that the corporation suffered no legally cognizable damage.

Answer (D) is incorrect for the reasons stated above.

133. **Answer (B) is the best answer.** Majority rules, but it does not rule completely. Thus, **Answer (C) is incorrect. Answers (A) and D) are not the best answers.** The limits on ratification are three in number: (1) it must be based upon relatively full and fair disclosure (which does not occur with a blanket ratification); (2) shareholders may not go so far as to

ratify fraud, illegality or the "waste" or gifting of corporate assets; and (3) the act must amount to ratification "in its so-called 'classic' form: that is to circumstances when a fully informed shareholder vote approves director action that does not *legally* require shareholder approval." In *Gantler v. Stephens*, 965 A.2d 695, 713 (Del. 2009), the Supreme Court of Delaware held that a shareholder vote could not serve double duty: a required approval of an amendment to articles of incorporation could not also serve as ratification of directors' wrongful acts. So it is possible for shareholders to ratify directors' acts amounting to a duty of care violation, thus absolving directors of liability, although sometimes it is tricky to obtain a valid shareholder ratification.

Often plaintiffs use "waste" as a conclusory statement, a means of posturing in litigation settings (*e.g.*, "these directors were so deficient that their acts amounted to a waste of corporate assets"). Waste also, though, has analytical uses. One is as a limit on the business judgment rule. Directors' acts will not be shielded from judicial scrutiny if they amount to a waste or mere gifting of corporate assets. *See, e.g., Aronoff v. Albanese*, 446 N.Y.S.2d 368 (App. Div. 1982). Another analytical use of "waste" is to describe the outer limits of shareholders' power to ratify. The American Law Institute defines waste as an "expenditure of corporate funds or a disposition of corporate assets" in which "the consideration the corporation receives is so inadequate in value that no person of ordinary sound business judgment would deem it equal with that which the corporation has paid." ALI PRINCIPLES § 1.42. Extremely foolish acts, grossly sloppy behavior, or gifts of corporate assets may amount to waste.

Here, arguably, Sam and Dave's foolish act of expansion, with little or no rational basis to support it, amounted to waste. The shareholder ratification (unless, of course, it had been unanimous) would not have therefore been effective, or so the argument would go.

134.   **Answer (D) is the best answer.** Modern duty of care analysis focuses upon senior managers' and directors' decision-making process rather than result. Over the years, attorneys and others have evolved a number of different processes intended to improve the decision-making process.

This Question is based upon the Delaware Supreme Court's controversial decision in *Smith v. Van Gorkom*, 488 A.2d 858 (Del. 1985). In that case, the directors of Trans Union Corp. did approve the transaction after only a two-hour meeting, with no deal documents, reports, or other information. While announcing a forgiving standard ("we think the concept of gross negligence is the proper standard for determining whether a business decision reached by a board of directors was an informed one"), the court held that the directors had not even met the forgiving standard. Thus, they were not entitled to the business judgment rule. Reaching the merits as well, the court found that the directors had breached the fiduciary duty of care. On remand, the Delaware Chancery Court found that a sufficient price ("intrinsic value") would have been $65 per share. The directors, who were a prestigious group, were potentially liable for $133,577,580.

Van Gorkom is a "reverse roadmap" case. If an attorney or other advisor in a major merger or other transaction, advised doing the opposite of everything that the Trans Union directors did or did not do, the advisor would have the board well on its way to compliance with fiduciary duties. The list of devices used is extensive, but a partial list would include:

(1) Utilization of internal expertise (CFO Roman and his report).

(2) Use of outside valuation experts (the Delaware Supreme Court stated that this was not, strictly speaking, necessary, but the court meant just the opposite).

(3) Place the decision in the hands of independent directors (often under the leadership of an independent director designated the "lead director").

(4) Provide the ad hoc committee with independent advisors.

(5) Have the written documents and other reports circulated.

(6) Have one or more adjournments so that directors are able to ruminate and "sleep on it."

(7) In final documents insure that the directors have a "fiduciary out," so that they may react to superior bids without breaching any contract with the first bidder.

Answer (A) is incorrect, because it involves almost no process which would tell the directors if $55 may be a good price. **Answer (B) is better, Answer (C) is better yet, and Answer (D), which is cumulative, is the best answer.**

135. **Answer (C) is the best answer.** The fallout from *Smith v. Van Gorkom* was voluminous. The finding of liability for a well-qualified group of directors not only shocked corporate America, it also coincided with a severe contraction of liability insurance coverage in the U.S., including Director and Officer (D & O) coverage that companies of any size obtain to protect their directors and senior officers. In Delaware, in June 1986, the legislature (at the behest of the corporate bar) played a "trump card" after the Delaware Supreme Court had revealed its hand in *Van Gorkom*. The legislature added to the list of optional charter provisions. DEL. GEN. CORP. L. § 102(b)(7), permitting a corporation to add to its charter:

A provision eliminating or limiting the personal liability of a director to the corporation or its stockholders for monetary damages for breach of fiduciary duty as directors, provided that such provision shall not eliminate or limit the liability of a directors for:

(i) For any breach of the director's duty of loyalty . . . ;

(ii) for acts or omissions not in good faith or which involve intentional misconduct or a knowing violation of law;

(iii) [for unlawful distributions]; or

(iv) for any transaction from which the director derived an improper personal benefit.

Very quickly every incorporating jurisdiction in the United States amended its corporate law to permit addition of such exculpatory provisions to articles on incorporation.

An important point to note is that a shareholder still may obtain injunctive relief even though the corporation has "opted out" of duty of care liability for damages. And, in large merger and other transactions, that is the game. Plaintiffs' attorneys seek to obtain a preliminary injunction against consummation of the transaction on grounds that directors breached their duty of care in the decision-making process leading up to the transaction. They thus obtain leverage over the merger participants which may enable them to obtain a "few dollars more" per share for shareholders.

MBCA § 2.02(b)(4) contains authority for exculpatory provisions in articles, but the section words the limitations on exculpation differently than does Delaware. Under the MBCA, a corporation may not eliminate "liability for (A) the amount of a financial benefit received by a director to which he is not entitled; (B) an intentional infliction of harm to the corporation or its shareholders; (C) [unlawful distributions]; or (D) an intentional violation of criminal law."

Is exculpation always a good idea? Many attorneys now always include such a provision in their standard form articles of incorporation. If the participants to an enterprise do not know each other well, it may be wise only to limit, and not eliminate, old-fashioned duty of care liability. The latter is not the situation here, one in which the participants know each other well. A knowledgeable attorney would probably include an exculpation article in articles of incorporation.

Answer (A) is not the best answer. Corporations intending to go public generally do not include preemptive rights in articles. They will have to eliminate such right before any offering can occur.

Answer (B) is not the best answer. Par value may be used, but is no longer legally required.

Answer (D) is incorrect for the reasons stated above.

136. **Answer (C) is the best answer.** How or when the duty of care or the duty of loyalty might require a director to make disclosures to fellow directors has largely been an unexplored area, although both duties undoubtedly require disclosure in certain instances. Not leaving further exploration to chance, the ABA drafters have added a new MBCA § 8.30(c) "codifying a director's obligation to disclose material information to fellow directors of the board of directors and committees of the board." The subsection provides that:

> In discharging board or committee duties a director shall disclose, or cause to be disclosed, to the other board or committee members information not already known by them but known by the director to be material to the discharge of their decision-making or oversight function, except that disclosure is not required to the extent that the director reasonably believes that doing so would violate a duty imposed by law, a legally enforceable obligation of confidentiality, or a professional ethics rule.

Sir Arthur could also comport with the duty imposed by this section by making disclosure to the full board of directors, but he may not wish to do so because such action may embarrass members of the Finance Committee.

Answers (A) and (B) are incorrect. Remaining silent, or an *ex parte* meeting with Fields, obviously would put Sir Arthur in violation of the duty of disclosure codified in MBCA § 8.30(c).

Answer (D) is not the best answer. Many attorneys and directors believe that what occurs at board or committee meetings, or what does not occur, is confidential. These beliefs came to light in 2008 when a Hewlett-Packard director spoke with a *Wall Street Journal* reporter, disclosing to her what the H-P board had done at one of its meetings. Another, officious H-P director and the H-P Director of Security decided to be bloodhounds. They hired private detectives to track down the leak of "confidential information." The detective then engaged in a number of illegal practices, including "pretexting," pretending to be telephone company employees to obtain the suspected "bad" director's phone records. Criminal prosecutions followed for those actions.

Standing alone, the beliefs of many attorneys, directors, and the officials at H-P are incorrect. Board meetings, committee meetings, and minutes of the foregoing are not necessarily confidential. Walk into any law firm which does a business practice. While minute books of corporations the firm represents may not be scattered about, they are not kept under lock and key, as would be confidential documents. So board chairs, and CEOs, who wish matters to remain confidential should issue a verbal statement at the commencement of the meeting or, better yet, obtain non-disclosure agreements (NDAs) or confidentiality agreements from directors for certain matters or periodically.

So Sir Arthur would violate no express command by telephoning a Houston Chronicle reporter but his tenure on the board might be severely shortened by his having done so.

137. **Answer (C) is the best answer.** The uniquely American business judgment rule was a creature of 19th century judge-made law. It has not subsequently been codified by statute and remains a matter wholly of common law. Yet the business judgment rule is a prominent feature in a substantial majority of cases in which shareholders allege that some or all of the directors have violated the fiduciary duties that they owe to the corporation. It is also "the rule that is not a rule." It has no mandatory content. It is not the standard of conduct for directors and officers of corporations. The standard of conduct remains the duty of care, that is, that amount of care that a reasonably prudent person would exercise in like position in similar circumstances. *See* Douglas M. Branson, *The Rule That Isn't a Rule — The Business Judgment Rule*, 36 VAL. U. L. REV. 631 (2002). Instead, the rule serves a number of other functions. It serves first and foremost as directors' front line defense to an allegation that they have breached their duty of care. The rule serves also as a means whereby courts may conserve the judicial resource, determining the majority of cases at an early point in the litigation. Last of all, in cases in which directors have been proactive, making decisions and judgments (rather than doing nothing), the rule does become the de facto standard for conduct of the board's activities.

Answers (A) and (B) are not the best answers. Courts often state the results of the rule, or the policy behind the rule, as the rule itself. Examples would be Answers (A) and (B) in this Question. Other similar statements are that "neither the directors nor the officers of a corporation are liable for mere mistakes or errors of judgment." Or, "directors of a commercial enterprise may take chances, the same kind of chances that a man [or woman] would take in his [or her] own business." Or, "absent evidence of lack of good faith or fraud on the part of directors, courts must and properly should respect the determination of directors." All of those, and many other statements by courts, encapsulate the policy behind the rule, or the results of numerous decisions under the rule, rather than the rule itself.

What then are the elements of the business judgment rule? The following four Questions delineate and then expand upon the elements of the business judgment rule. In the instant Question, the directors made an actual judgment or decision. On the surface at least, it also appears that the directors had no personal or financial interests in which decision was made, that is, they were independent and free of disabling conflicts of interest. They also exercised some care ("canvassed the markets") in informing themselves about the decision they made. Thus, although you or I, or the judge, might have made a different decision had they first confronted the situation, a judge should probably dismiss the lawsuit. The directors are charged with making the decision. Given the facts as the directors confronted them, without the benefit of hindsight, who can say that they were wrong, either as a legal or factual matter? Consequently, **Answer (D) is incorrect.**

138. **Answer (A) is the best answer. Answer (D) is not a good answer** for reasons already discussed in the answer to Question 126. The business judgment rule is not something with

which directors are required to or must comply. If they do meet its requirements, they receive a more deferential review in court. But, if they do not, they may nonetheless defend themselves on the merits; that is, that they did in fact exercise the requisite amount of care.

Now, to the Question at hand. This Question is based upon a celebrated Illinois case, *Shlensky v. Wrigley*, 237 N.E.2d 776 (Ill. App. Ct. 1968), involving chewing gum magnate Phillip K. Wrigley's refusal to install lights at Chicago's Wrigley field despite continuing financial losses by the Chicago Cubs major league baseball team. Wrigley won the court case, but many law school casebooks include the case to suggest that perhaps the court made the wrong decision (or the plaintiff's lawyer failed to make arguments he should have made).

Answer (B) is incorrect. Answer (B) is an extreme statement of the rule. The business judgment rule's first requirement is that the directors must have made a decision or judgment. Sometimes the phrasing is that they must have made their own "independent" decision or judgment. Here and in *Shlensky*, the directors merely "rubber stamped" the controlling shareholder's decision. Alternatively, in such a case a plaintiff may argue that the directors lacked the requisite independence. That is, the directors, or a critical mass of them, were beholden to and dominated by the controlling shareholder (or CEO, and so on). This argument is best seen as a fallback argument. Courts may hesitate to make a finding that otherwise reputable businesspersons are "dominated" or otherwise not their own persons.

Answer (C) is incorrect. Absence of conflicts of interest alone is insufficient. To invoke the rule successfully, directors must demonstrate that they exercised at least a modicum of care.

Returning to the decision or judgment requirement of the modern business judgment rule, directors criticize it. They say that directors, especially those with long service together, make decisions by processes of accretion. A requirement for a formal decision forces the board to act as though it were a legislative committee or a faculty meeting. The requirement forces directors to be confrontational at times, which is not conducive to longer-term board service. The answers to these criticisms are that the decision or judgment need not be a formal one, although a formal notation in board minutes may be the best evidence to prove that an actual decision was made. Defendant directors could testify that they were in agreement and a de facto decision was reached. A second answer is that a formal "up or down" vote on important issues may beneficial on some (or many) issues that arise.

139.   Yes. The second element of the rule requires that directors who are free of disabling conflicts of interest and who are independent make the decision. The ALI Principles define independence as being free of significant financial ties to the corporation or its senior managers. ALI PRINCIPLES § 1.34(a). The practice that has arisen is to exclude the non-independent directors from participating in the decision so as to enhance the probability of business judgment rule protection for any decision that may be made. *See Ivanhoe Partners v. Newmont Mining Corp.*, 533 A.2d 585 (Del. Ch.) ("enhanced business judgment rule protection" for decisions made by independent directors alone), *aff'd*, 535 A.2d 1334 (Del. 1987). A further trend is to limit the number of non-independent directors serving on the board in the first place. Many publicly-held corporations have no more than two (say, the CEO and the COO) or three (the CEO, the COO, and the outside lawyer) non-independent directors.

In the Question at hand, the easiest determination is the independence of the golf partner.

He may be the worst choice for a director, but he would be deemed independent. Most courts have rejected the argument that long-standing social or similar ties to the senior managers of a corporation compromise a director's independence. The independence of all the remaining directors is problematic at best. The lawyer is a non-executive or outside director, but he is not independent. His law firm receives substantial fees from the Barons. There is a pronounced trend away from board service by outsiders such as lawyers, commercial bankers, investment bankers, and so on, who not so many years ago served on boards of many client corporations. The radio station owner arguably has a direct financial interest in the outcome. If he votes the "wrong way," his company may lose the contract to broadcast the Barons' games. The senior VP is an insider. His lack of independence is presumed. Courts have held that consulting fees paid to directors over and above their directors' fees may render them non-independent. In the Enron debacle, the corporation paid to nearly every one of its 16 directors consulting fees ranging from $10,000 to $100,000, or more, annually. Many corporate governance gurus have posited a per se rule: Receipt of consulting fees by directors is never proper. The courts, however, have yet to go so far.

In *Orman v. Cullman*, 794 A.2d 5 (Del. Ch. 2002), a case involving the acquisition of General Cigar, Inc, by a subsidiary of Swedish Match AB, Chancellor Chandler (a former law professor at Alabama) wrote at length on disinterestedness and independence and the difference between them. He held a director who received a $75,000 consulting payment to be disinterested because, although he would receive a benefit not offered to rank-and-file shareholders, he would not "receive a personal financial benefit *from a transaction* that is not shared equally by the stockholders." Under his contract, the director would receive the same annual fee both prior to and after the merger. He received nothing "from a transaction." Independence, according to Chancellor Chandler,

> does not involve a question of whether the challenged director derives a benefit *from the transaction* that is not generally shared with the other shareholders. Rather, it involves an inquiry into whether the director's decision resulted from that director being *controlled* by another. A director can be controlled by another if in fact he is *dominated* by that other party, whether through close personal or familial relationship or through force of will. A director can also be controlled by another if the challenged director is *beholden* to the allegedly controlling entity. A director may be considered beholden to (and thus controlled by) another when the allegedly controlling entity has the unilateral power . . . to decide whether the challenged director continues to receive a benefit, financial or otherwise.

Id. at 25. Chancellor Chandler held that, at least for purposes of summary judgment, questions of fact existed as to whether a majority of the General Cigar directors were disinterested and independent. Thus, they, and their decision, were not entitled to business judgment rule protection. *See also Aronson v. Lewis*, 473 A.2d 805 (Del. 1984) (a leading case outlining elements of the business judgment rule in Delaware, defining "interest" as "meaning that directors can neither appear on both sides of a transaction nor expect to derive any personal financial benefit from it . . . as opposed to a benefit which devolves upon the corporation or all stockholders generally").

In the Question at hand, the accounting professor on the Birmingham Barons' board also chairs the audit committee. Were the Barons to be an SEC reporting company, the corporation would be subject to the Sarbanes-Oxley Act ("SOXA"). SOXA requires public companies to have an audit committee which has at least one member who is an "accounting expert." The SEC has adopted regulations defining the criterion for being an expert. SOXA also requires that all members of the audit committee be independent. By the statute's terms, receipt of any fees, directly as here or through a firm of which the audit committee is a member, renders the particular director non-independent. Lawyers, bankers, and the like, then, may serve on the board, but may not serve on the audit committee if their firm does work for the corporation. The SOXA requirement is also likely to accelerate the trend away from board service by such persons altogether.

Wimp's nephew may or may not be independent. Many courts would hold that it is an issue of fact. If the family member has no direct financial interest in the matter under consideration, and is otherwise an experienced businessperson, a court may well find him to be independent despite his familial relationship to the controlling shareholder. What if all of the foregoing directors conceded their lack of independence and recused themselves (did not participate in the decision)? In that case, the golf partner, or possibly the golf partner and Wimp's nephew, would convene in executive session, making the decision. Would the decision made be entitled to business judgment rule protection?

The Delaware Supreme Court has held that whether the existence of pervasive conflicts of interest or lack of independence disables the board from acting is a question of fact. Thus, a majority of directors could lack independence or have conflicts, but if the board scripted its decision-making process in the proper way, a decision by the independent minority could receive business judgment rule protection. At some point, though, pervasive conflicts or lack of independence infects the board processes in a fatal way. At what point that occurs is a question of fact. The instant case, however, is very near or crosses over that imprecise line.

140. **Answer (B) is the best answer.** A principal purpose of the business judgment rule is to filter or screen out cases against corporate directors, or some of them, prior to trial. Trials are fora in which questions such as "Did defendants exercise due care or reasonable care?" are determined. If the business judgment rule required directors to demonstrate that they had exercised reasonable care (Answer (A) or Answer (C)), directors would have to do that in a trial setting. The business judgment rule would fail miserably in its role as a filter or screen that, among other things, fosters conservation of judicial resources. Instead, the business judgment rule only requires that directors demonstrate that they exercised some care, while at the same time requiring proofs on several other issues (a decision or judgment, independence and lack of conflicts, etc.). As the Delaware Supreme Court phrased the standard in *Smith v. Van Gorkom*, 488 A.2d 858, 873 (Del. 1985), "We think the concept of gross negligence [some care rather than due care] is . . . the proper standard for determining whether a business judgment reached by a board of directors was an informed one."

Many corporate law practitioners now categorically state that the standard of care for directors of corporation is gross negligence. Strictly speaking, that is not true. Statutes still articulate a standard of care such as "the care that a reasonable prudent person would exercise in like position in similar circumstances." See, for example, the MBCA's latest phrasing: "the care that a person in a like position would reasonably believe appropriate in similar circumstances." MBCA § 8.30(b). Because of the intervention of the business judgment rule, however, gross negligence becomes the de facto standard of conduct in cases in which the directors have been proactive, informing themselves to the extent they believe is appropriate, and making decisions and judgments. In cases in which directors do nothing, either in the way of informing themselves or in reaching a decision, the standard remains due care or reasonable care. It is not gross negligence. One commentator has lamented the tendency of many layers to collapse the standard of conduct completely into the business judgment rule. *See* Stuart R. Cohn, *Demise of the Director's Duty of Care: Judicial Avoidance of Standards and Sanctions Through the Business Judgment Rule*, 62 Tex. L. Rev. 591 (1983) (lamenting courts' tendency to cede the standard of conduct to the business judgment rule).

Answers (A), (C), and (D) are incorrect for the reasons stated above.

141. Yes. Even though the board members made a decision or judgment, were free of disabling conflicts of interest, and exercised some care in informing themselves, in at least one widely-accepted version of the business judgment rule, the rule does not shield from judicial scrutiny "off the wall" or highly implausible judgments or decisions. Section 4.01(c) of the American Law Institute's Corporate Governance Project, a widely-accepted attempt to codify the business judgment rule that several state supreme courts have adopted as reflective of the common law in their states, requires that "directors rationally believe that the decision made was in the corporation's best interests." In several of his opinions, Delaware Chancellor William Allen has disagreed. He opined that the business judgment rule, as it has evolved in the Delaware case law, never has contained the "rational basis" requirement. *See In re Caremark International, Inc. Derivative Litigation*, 698 A.2d 959, 967–68 (Del. Ch. 1996). Several noted commentators have agreed. *See, e.g.*, Lyman Johnson, *The Modest Business Judgment Rule*, 55 Bus. Law. 625, 632 (2000). *Cf. Parnes v. Bally Entertainment Corp.*, 722 A.2d 1243, 1246 (Del. 1999) ("The presumptive validity of a business judgment is rebutted in those rare cases where the decision under attack is so far beyond the bounds of reasonable judgment that it seems essentially inexplicable."). That difference of opinion cannot be resolved here. Suffice it to note that the ALI version requires only a rational basis, not a reasonable one. Again, if the rule required proof that actions were reasonable and not merely plausible or rational, trials or other sorts of plenary hearings would be needed. The business judgment rule would not achieve its filtering or screening role. A decision to play dawn doubleheaders, or to use the corporation's resources to put a human on Mars, seems to lack a rational basis. A board's attempt to seek business judgment rule protection for such decisions would face an uphill battle.

A fifth element, applicable in some cases, is that if an overriding contract governs, the business judgment rule does not shield decisions to deviate from it. For example, in cases in which a stock option plan's provisions govern, a decision to vary from that (to backdate options, for example) is not protected. *Weiss v. Swanson*, 948 A.2d 433 (Del. Ch. 2008). Similarly, the Supreme Court of Hawaii has held that directors' decision to deviate from the applicable Protective Covenants and from the corporation's bylaws' express commands is not protected by the business judgment rule. *Hawkins v. Waikoloa Village Ass'n*, 187 P.3d 593 (Haw. Ct. App. 2008).

142. **Answer (D) is the best answer.** The "brooding omnipresence" in the business judgment rule is the requirement that the directors made their decision in good faith. Even though the technical elements of the rule are satisfied (Answers (A) and (B)), in a given case the court may still hold the action over for trial on grounds that the board's actions were not taken in good faith. Two principal categories of cases exist in which courts have done so. One category involves board action taken in knowing violation of the law, as here. In addition to the ubiquitous fiduciary duties of care and loyalty, some posit a third affirmative duty, the duty

to act lawfully. *See, e.g.,* ARTHUR R. PINTO & DOUGLAS M. BRANSON, UNDERSTANDING CORPORATE LAW 238 (3d ed. 2009). Whether factored into the equation as an affirmative duty, or under the business judgment rule's good faith requirement, decisions directors sincerely believe are in the corporation's best interests will not be protected if the directors know, or in the exercise of slight care should know, are illegal, making Answer (C) incorrect. The other category involves cases in which directors are free from disabling conflicts of interest, but are motivated by some other base motive, such as revenge, spite, or hatred. In such cases, the court may deny business judgment rule protection to the decision even though the rule's technical requirements have been met.

Two examples of the latter might be *Yates v. Holt-Smith, Inc.,* 768 N.W.2d 213 (Wis. Ct. App. 2009), a case in which directors withheld the usual year's end dividend, a decision ordinarily protected by the business judgment rule, in order to induce another principal shareholder to sell her stock. Even though no self-dealing may have been involved, vengeful or spiteful actions were. Another is *Red River Wings, Inc. v. Hoot, Inc.,* 751 N.W.2d 206 (N.D. 2008), in which the court found that out of some illicit motive the directors engaged in an overindulgence of strategic, manipulative behavior ("Machiavellian tactics") and later advanced reasons "concocted after the fact to justify their actions."

Answers (A), (B), and (C) are incorrect for the reasons stated above.

This Question is based on *Miller v. American Telephone & Telegraph Co.,* 507 F.2d 759 (3d Cir. 1974).

143.   **Answer (D) is the best answer.** In the adoption of takeover defenses, senior managers and other board members may have a tinge or more of conflict of interest. A hostile takeover, in which a bidder seeks to acquire a majority of the voting shares, usually to be followed by replacement of the incumbent managers and board members, poses a personal threat to those in charge of the target corporation. They may lose salary, fringe benefits, and the prestige of office. Nonetheless, in most cases, courts have reviewed the adoption of takeover defenses under the duty of care and the business judgment rule rather than the duty of loyalty. One reason is that in most cases counsel for the target corporation has learned to script the process in a way that will lead to review under a business judgment rule type of standard. Those with the most at stake, the full-time managers, generally are excluded from the process at some point, or altogether. *See, e.g.,* Answer (B).

Even in the hands of the independent directors, the adoption of takeover defenses differs from other types of decisions that are reviewed under a business judgment standard. Decisions that may affect the entire board and management and result in sale of the corporation differ in quality and quantity from decisions, say, to modernize a plant or market a new product line. Takeover and takeover defense decisions are surrounded by the "omnipresent specter that a board [even of independent directors] may be acting primarily in its own interests." For those and other reasons, led by the Delaware Supreme Court, corporate jurists have evolved a specialized form of the business judgment rule with which to review adoption of takeover defenses. The "response phase" business judgment rule requires of directors the usual elements: a decision or judgment, freedom from conflicts of interest, care in informing themselves on the subject matter of the decision and a rational basis for the decision made. In addition, however, the director must have "reasonable grounds for believing that a danger to corporate policy and effectiveness exist[s] because of another person's stock ownership." Once directors have in good faith developed that belief, any "defensive measure . . . must be reasonable in relation to the threat posed." This added "proportionality requirement" is also known as the "*Unocal* standard" (Answer (A)).

In *Unocal Corp. v. Mesa Petroleum Co.*, 493 A.2d 946 (Del. 1985), Union Oil of California adopted a radical selective self tender to ward off a raid by takeover player T. Boone Pickens. The court held the board's adoption of the defense was shielded from scrutiny by the business judgment rule but, in so doing, evolved a specialized version of the rule as a yardstick with which to judge adoption of takeover defenses.

In the instant Question, Answer (D), the adoption of a radical measure in response to the possible and unconfirmed acquisition of shares by the Pike brothers, fails to meet the proportionality and other elements of the *Unocal* test. By contrast, Answer (C) is a moderate response likely to withstand attack under *Unocal*.

Answers (A), (B), and (C) are incorrect for the reasons stated above.

144. **Answer (C) is the best answer.** In *Revlon, Inc. v. MacAndrews & Forbes Holdings, Inc.*, 506 A.2d 173 (Del. 1986), the Delaware Supreme Court enunciated a second version of the business judgment rule applicable to takeover activities. In addition to the "response phase" rule with its proportionality requirement, there is an "auction phase" rule that kicks in when it has become clear that the target company will be sold. At that point, directors cease being defenders of the corporate bastion, as stated above. Their role shifts to acting as auctioneers whose duty is to obtain the best price. Thus, **Answers (A) and (B) are incorrect.**

Answer (D) is incorrect. According to the facts, the independent directors (free of disabling conflicts of interest, etc.) made the decision. Mere sympathy, or empathy, for the incumbent managers does not, without more, disable them from making a choice.

Revlon has proven to be unpopular, both with target company boards of directors and, to some degree, with the Delaware courts (who have not, however, overruled it). Instead, the Delaware courts have pointed to ways in which corporations may avoid the application of *Revlon*. One is the merger of equals, or MOE. In such a case, the target company is not being sold or broken up. After consummation of the transaction, the combined entity will still be owned by a disaggregated shareholder group. There is therefore no duty to conduct an auction. The participants in a MOE are free to "just say no" to any other bid, even if that bid clearly is superior for shareholders. The leading case is *Paramount Communications, Inc. v. Time, Inc.*, 571 A.2d 1140 (Del. 1989).

Allegedly in part to preserve the "Time culture," Time had been selective in its choice of a merger partner. Ultimately, Time went forward with Warner Communications. The agreement of merger provided for a 24-person board, with equal representation for the two constituent companies. The first CEO would come from the Warner ranks; the second from Time. Enter a spoiler. Paramount made a $175 bid for Time shares, later raised to $200. In response, Warner and Time recast the original transaction, offering some Time shareholders $70 per share instead of Time-Warner stock. The board announced its opinion that the Time-Warner merger of equals offered "greater long-term value" and that, unlike Paramount, Warner did not represent a threat to the "unique" Time culture. The Delaware Supreme Court upheld the ability of a target to say "no" to what appeared to be a clearly superior bid. As a result, today most friendly transactions are structured as MOEs rather than the purchase of one company by another, even if the latter more accurately reflects the reality of what is occurring. By so structuring the acquisition, the participants are able to avoid application of *Revlon* and its duty to conduct an auction.

There have been many subsequent twists, turns, and nuances in Delaware merger and takeover jurisprudence, but those developments are beyond the scope of a work such as this. They are more properly the subject of courses in corporate finance or mergers and acquisitions.

145.   **Answer (A) is the best answer,** although all the answers are pretty good.

The derivative suit is an invention of American equity courts circa 1870. Judges permitted shareholders to step into the corporation's shoes, bringing an action in its behalf with any recovery going to the corporate treasury. The defendant may be a party who has breached a contract with the corporation, or a tortfeasor whose acts have harmed the corporation, but who, for one reason or another, the corporation's directors have not pursued. Most often, however, the alleged wrongdoer is an officer or director of the corporation and the substantive allegation is that she has breached a fiduciary duty owed to the corporation.

Just as with flesh and blood persons, fictional beings such as corporations should be able to elect not to stand on legal rights they may have. A citizen whose neighbor's trees foul his gutters may have a clear cause of action, but may elect not to pursue it. In corporate law, the question is: How does a corporation find its voice for deciding that question (*i.e.*, not to stand on rights it may have), especially given that the wrongdoer is an associate of the group, the board of directors, that ordinarily is charged with managing the corporation's business and affairs, including its litigation? The device that arose for doing so was the special litigation committee, or SLC. In the mid 1970s, U.S. corporations were wracked with allegations of illegal foreign payments (bribes) and illegal campaign contributions to President Richard Nixon's 1972 re-election campaign. Corporate lawyers seized upon the idea of a committee of the board, with special counsel, and an internal investigation and report as a means of avoiding harsh sanctions by the SEC. It was only a matter of time before those same lawyers used the committee device in the derivative action setting as well. In 1979, within months of one another, both the U.S. Supreme Court and the New York Court of Appeals gave stamps of approval to use of the SLC device. *See Burks v. Lasker*, 441 U.S. 471 (1979); *Auerbach v. Bennett*, 393 N.E.2d 994 (N.Y. 1979).

An earlier lower court opinion succinctly articulating the theory behind use of the SLC is *Gall v. Exxon Corp.*, 418 F. Supp. 508 (S.D.N.Y. 1976) (SLC to investigate allegations that Exxon and its subsidiary, Esso Italiana, had paid $59 million in bribes and improper payments to Italian political parties). It goes something like this. Assume, as here, that credible allegations of wrongdoing are made concerning a subgroup of directors/officers and thus cannot be dismissed out of hand. Assume further that the plaintiff either makes a demand on the board to take action, or files suit alleging that demand would be futile and should be excused (demand is discussed *infra* in connection with the derivative action). In either case, the ensuing process is very similar. Using powers over board size usually contained in bylaws, the board of directors adds two or three new director positions. The board appoints to those new positions persons of standing who could have no conceivable connection with the wrongdoing alleged. Those "expansion directors" hire "special counsel," usually a law firm that has not recently done legal work for the company. Together, the SLC and counsel conduct an extensive investigation, interviewing directors, officers, employees, witnesses, and so on. Counsel performs legal research as well. The SLC then appears in court (or, in the case of demand, responds to the would-be plaintiff). It asks for relief in the nature of summary judgment. To the motion it appends a lengthy report concluding perhaps that the law has not been violated but, more frequently, that pursing the litigation would "not be in the best interests of the corporation." The report attempts to quantify those factors capable of quantification and avoids makeweight factors likely to be present in every case. Appended to the committee report may be the voluminous fruits of the investigation (sworn statements, questionnaires, and so on). Counsel might then argue to the court that: the committee has made a decision or judgment; that the SLC members were independent and free of conflicts of interest; that they exercised due care, indeed great care, in investigating and analyzing the allegations; and, as the report demonstrates, there exists a rational basis for the decision reached. The conclusion: the SLC report and conclusion are entitled to great judicial deference or, indeed, are shielded from judicial scrutiny. Why? The business judgment rule.

The scenario has met with various reactions by courts. New York accords complete business judgment rule protection once directors have offered proof of their disinterestedness and their exercise of care. Answer (B) states the theory, but we have insufficient information as to the amount of care the SLC exercised. Thus, Answer (C) is not appropriate. By contrast, in *Zapata Corp. v. Maldonado*, 430 A.2d 779 (Del. 1981), the Delaware Supreme Court distinguished other decisions applying the business judgment rule, in which courts have little expertise, from decisions to dismiss litigation, in which courts have significant experience. The Delaware "*Zapata* second step" allows the trial court, in its discretion, to examine the merits of the shareholder's allegations and the SLC report, but only in "demand excused" and not in "demand refused" cases. North Carolina courts permit the discretionary second step in all cases, demand refused or demand excused. *See Alford v. Shaw*, 358 S.E.2d 323 (N.C. 1987). Massachusetts seems to require that the trial court examine not only business judgment rule elements, but the merits as well, in each and every case. *See Houle v. Low*, 556 N.E.2d 51, 57 (Mass. 1990). *In re PSE & G Shareholder Litigation*, 718 A.2d 254, 260 (N.J. Super. Ct. Ch. Div. 1998), followed *Houle v. Lowe*. Following the American Law Institute approach, Pennsylvania's Supreme Court permits further review in duty of loyalty (self-dealing) cases, but not in duty of care cases. *See Cuker v. Mikalauskas*, 692 A.2d 1042, 1049 (Pa. 1997). No state has rejected the SLC device outright, as Answer (D) suggests. Ten or so other states' high courts have put themselves into one or another of those five camps. The important point, however, is to see how the process is scripted so that dismissal of derivative litigation becomes but one more application of the ubiquitous business judgment rule.

Answers (B), (C), and (D) are not the best answers for the reasons stated above.

146. **Answer (D) is the best answer.** While damage to the corporation is an element of duty of care violations, under the duty of loyalty either damage to the principal (the corporation) or gains procured by disloyalty will suffice. Courts have also said that lack of disclosure by the director or officer is per se disloyal. "Loyalty in the agent, and not mere prevention of harm to the principal, is the aim" for which the duty of loyalty strives. *State ex rel. Hayes Oyster Co. v. Keypoint Oyster Co.*, 391 P.2d 979, 985 (Wash. 1964). Fairness may not be a defense.

Answer (A) is incorrect. In a controversial step, the ALI Corporate Governance Project re-labeled the duty of loyalty, "the duty of fair dealing." Under the ALI scheme, if Augie had paid a verifiable fair price he would have dealt fairly with the corporation and would pay only minimal damages, or no damages at all (although the ALI scheme continues the rule that lack of disclosure may be per se unfair dealing).

Answer (B) is incorrect. With good old-fashioned duty of loyalty claims, the remedy may also be extreme. Courts throw a "lasso" around all of the venture and pull it back to the corporation to whom the wrongdoing fiduciary owed his duty. The courts make no differentiation between value that may be due to the fiduciary's status and value that has been added subsequently by his efforts. This extreme remedy is known as the constructive trust.

Overall, the duty of loyalty requires the fiduciary at all times to "serve the best interests of the corporation." Courts have not defined what precisely the phrase means. Thus, while best interests of the corporation may be largely synonymous with "best interest of the owners (shareholders)," the two are not necessarily congruent. The duty requires the fiduciary to put the corporation's interests ahead of personal interests, those of friends, family, or associates, or of entities in which the latter may have an interest. It requires a large degree of selfless conduct.

Fiduciary duty is also the legal claim made against directors or officers who engage in more brazen forms of self-dealing, including embezzlement and outright theft. Thus, although prosecutors may seek criminal sanctions against "white collar" criminals, a primary civil law claim against such wrongdoers will be a claim of breach of the duty of loyalty which seeks money damages for the corporate treasury.

Answer (C) is incorrect. Resignation after the fact would do Augie no good.

What should Augie have done? There are two possibilities. He should have disclosed fully his participation, in which case he might have been "held up" for a high price, or he should have abstained altogether. Often, the latter is best advice.

This Question is based on *State ex rel. Hayes Oyster Co. v. Keypoint Oyster Co.*, 391 P.2d 979 (Wash. 1964).

147. **Answer (D) is the best answer** (although the Question posed is more a social and political

choice than a legal one, and one over which opinions vary widely). One great debate both in the corporate social responsibility movement of the 1970s and the takeover boom of the 1980s was whether corporate law itself should delineate responsibilities to constituencies other than owners. Corporate law might then spell out all of what may or may not have been subsumed in the vague phrase "the best interests of the corporation." Professor Marleen O'Connor has written extensively, advocating equivalence of employees with shareholders. *See, e.g.,* Marleen O'Connor, *Labor's Role in the American Corporate Governance Structure,* 22 COMP. LAB. L. & POL'Y J. 97 (2000); Marleen O'Connor, *Restructuring the Corporation's Nexus of Contracts: Recognizing a Fiduciary Duty to Protect Displaced Workers,* 69 N.C. L. REV. 1189 (1991). Professors Kent Greenfield and David Millon write of the communitarian model of the corporation and the obsolescence of the old shareholder-centered model. *See, e.g.,* Kent Greenfield, *There's a Forest in Those Trees: Teaching About the Role of Corporations in Society,* 34 GA. L. REV. 1011 (2000); David Million, *Communitarians, Contractarians, and the Crisis in Corporate Law,* 50 WASH. & LEE L. REV. 1373 (1993). In part, they ground their arguments on the reality that modern large publicly-held corporations have become public or quasi public institutions and not merely forms for ownership of private property. Opponents of such views point out that a responsibility to many may be a responsibility to none. Self-serving managers would be able to play one constituency off against another, ending up accountable to no one. Profit maximization and primary responsibility to owners is the best way to ensure that the pie continues to become larger, with a resulting "trickle down" and benefits for all (employees, customers, suppliers, etc.).

Lead by "rust belt" states such as Pennsylvania, some 30 states have adopted statutes similar to the Ohio statute quoted in Answer (D) or the more extreme Indiana statute mentioned in Answer (C). *See, e.g.,* Stephen M. Bainbridge, *Interpreting Nonshareholder Constituency Statutes,* 19 PEPP. L. REV. 971 (1993). All of the statutes, save one, are permissive ("directors may consider"), rather than mandatory ("shall consider" or "must consider"). Only Connecticut has a mandatory "must consider" non-shareholder constituency statute. *See* CONN. GEN. STAT. § 33-756(d) (1997). Their intent is to overrule application of cases such as *Revlon* (see Question 133), incorporated in Answer (A). Many reform groups and corporations have adopted codes of best practices (Answer (B)), both in the United States and around the world. These codes are not law. Instead, they deal in aspirations for business and corporations rather than mandatory practices. Many of the codes also contain a stakeholder chapter or otherwise include responsibilities to other constituencies as a matter of good corporate governance. Individual corporations map out or acknowledge such responsibilities in codes of ethics and mission statements.

The only mandatory legal consideration posed by the Question would be the federal plant closing law, the so-called "WARN Act," which requires advance notice and has other requirements intended to ameliorate (but not eliminate) the dislocations caused by sudden plant closures.

Answers (A), (B), and (C) are not the best answers for the reasons stated above.

148.   **Answer (C) is the best answer.** A director may be "interested" because she, or a family member or business associate, proposes to deal with the corporation (*e.g.,* to sell a parcel of land, or a piece of software, to the corporation). Alternatively, a director may be "interested" when an entity in which the director has a substantial interest (at least 10 or 15 percent ownership) proposes to deal with the corporation. In those cases, the director should make

full disclosure to the board of directors and seek the approval of a disinterested decision maker (the disinterested directors, or the shareholders in general meeting). Otherwise, she should be prepared to defend the fairness, or the "entire fairness" of the transaction. Those are easy cases.

Here, however, Amelia has no substantial ownership interest in the entity (OCC) that proposes to deal with the corporation. All she does is sit on OCC's board of directors. These cases, in which directors also sit on the board of another corporation, but have no direct pecuniary interest in the transaction, are cases of "interlocking directorates." Traditionally, corporate law has treated an interlocking directorate (common director) as a conflict of interest the same as any other. *See, e.g., Globe Woolen Co. v. Utica Gas & Electric Co.*, 121 N.E. 378 (N.Y. 1918) (Cardozo, J.). Consequently, **Answers (A) and (B) are incorrect.**

This is true regardless of whether or not the director actually participated in or influenced negotiation of the transaction. **Answer (D), therefore, is not the best answer.**

The director who sits on both boards should insure that the proposed transaction comes to the board's attention, make full disclosure, and receive approval of the disinterested directors. Alternatively, if repeat transactions are likely, especially repeat transactions at non-standard prices and terms, the director should give serious thought to eliminating the conflict by resigning from one or the other board. The latter may be advice many directors do not wish to heed. Yet the other preventive law technique (board consideration, full disclosure, and vote of the disinterested directors) may not be palatable either. The Otter Aircraft, Ltd. board may have a crowded agenda. Considering a matter immaterial in amount ($900,000) simply because there is a common director may be a great inconvenience.

The American Law Institute allows delegation of approval to a disinterested executive by means of a "standard of the corporation" adopted by the board of directors, especially if the transactions are to be at standard or market prices. ALI PRINCIPLES §§ 1.36 ("a certificate or by-law provision, or board of directors or shareholders' resolution") & 5.09 (delegation of approval to disinterested corporate official). The American Bar Association has attempted to amend the Model Act to reverse the common law, by providing that the fact of an interlocking director alone may no longer be a conflict of interest. It does so through its definition of materiality. A director interlock that constitutes a conflict must involve a director "so linked to the transaction and of such financial significance that the interest would reasonably be expected to exert an influence on the director's judgment if he were called upon to vote." MBCA § 8.60(1)(i). Under the MBCA, Answer (A) may well be the correct answer. Without a statute on the subject, the rule is that a mere director interlock is a conflict of interest if it is proposed that the two corporations deal with each other.

149. **Answer (A) is the best answer.** In the 1980s, the American Bar Association Committee on Corporate Laws, the committee responsible for the Model Business Corporation Act ("MBCA"), added "Subchapter F, Directors' Conflicting Interest Transactions," to Chapter 8, "Directors and Officers." The subchapter attempts to achieve two ends. First is the adoption of a relatively narrow and all-encompassing definition of which transactions involve "conflicting interests," **making Answer (C) incorrect.** Second is an "unassailable safe harbor" for transactions that do involve a conflict, but are approved by as few as one or two disinterested directors, given full disclosure.

The subchapter has had a mixed record of success. A number of Model Act jurisdictions have not adopted it. Perhaps one reason is that the subchapter's definition of conflicting interest transaction is too narrow and defies common sense. Common sense would dictate that doing business with an entity controlled by a director's first cousin could involve divided loyalties (on the other hand, first cousins can be relative strangers), but common sense did not prevail, **making Answer (B) incorrect.**

Under the MBCA definition, a transaction merits special treatment if "the director knows at the time of commitment that he or a related person is a party to the transaction or has a beneficial interest in or is so closely linked to the transaction and of such financial significance to the director or related person that the interest would reasonably be expected to exert an influence on the director's judgment if he were called upon to vote on the transaction." MBCA § 8.60(1)(i). Note that the director must "know" (not "should know") and that the transaction must be significant financially, and not merely socially or familial.

For purposes of the definition, the subdefinition "related party" is narrowly drawn. It excludes first cousins: "Related person of a director" means "the spouse (or a parent or sibling thereof) of the director, or a child, grandchild, sibling, parent (or spouse of any thereof) of the director, or any individual having the same home as the director, or a trust or estate of which an individual specified in this clause is a substantial beneficiary." Bob Sole could not cause his company to do business with an entity controlled by his brother-in-law ("spouse . . . or sibling thereof") without approval of disinterested directors. Under the MBCA, he could do business with his first cousin. Therefore, **Answer (D) is incorrect** as well.

150. It depends. Courts in several states (most notably, Delaware and California) have stated that nothing in interested director statutes can sanction obvious unfairness to the corporation. *See, e.g., Fliegler v. Lawrence,* 361 A.2d 218 (Del. 1976) (compliance with the disclosure and vote statute "merely removes an 'interested director' cloud"; nothing in these statutes sanctions obvious unfairness to the corporation); *Remillard Brick Co. v. Remillard-Dandini Co.,* 241 P.2d 66 (Cal. Ct. App. 1952) ("[N]othing in this statute automatically validates [interested director] transactions simply because there has been a disclosure and approval by the majority of the stockholders."). The effect of compliance with the statute (disclosure, vote of disinterested directors, or shareholders) may be to shift the burden of proof to the shareholder who challenges the unfairness of the transaction. Compliance may have some other effect, but it is not conclusive. Otherwise, directors who might somehow be in "cahoots with" or under the influence of the interested directors could approve a highly questionable transaction. Courts would be powerless to review the transaction for fairness. It is precisely this possibility of a fairness review in some cases that subchapter F of the MBCA seeks to eliminate. If the attorney advising the corporation and the interested director scripts it correctly (full disclosure, vote, etc.), under the MBCA, a court is absolutely forbidden from reviewing transactions in which the corporation buys or sells assets from or to directors or their friends, families, or associates. So the answer to this question "depends" upon whether or not the jurisdiction in question has adopted the MBCA "conflicting interest" provisions.

In *Remillard Brick,* the same two individuals were the majority shareholders of two brick and tile manufacturing companies. They caused the companies to divest their sales function to a sales corporation of which they owned all the stock. When challenged by a minority shareholder, the sales contracts were struck down: "It is a cardinal principle of corporate law that a director cannot, at the expense of the corporation, make an unfair profit from his position. He is precluded from receiving any personal advantage without fullest disclosure to and consent of *all* those affected." *Remillard Brick Co. v. Remillard-Dandini Co.,* 241 P.2d

66, 74 (Cal. Ct. App. 1952). In effect, the court read that "cardinal principle" into the statute's first sentence which provided that "[d]irectors and officers shall exercise their powers in good faith, and with a view to the interests of the corporation." *Id.* at 74.

151.   **Answer (C) is the best answer.** This Question is based upon the Delaware Supreme Court's opinion in *Marciano v. Nakash*, 535 A.2d 400 (Del. 1987), involving the company that manufactured Guess? designer jeans and jean jackets.

Interested director statutes are not something that "must be complied with." Therefore, **Answer (A) is incorrect.** Rather they are safe harbor statutes. Compliance bestows a certain amount of extra protection ("removes any interested director cloud" were the Delaware court's words in *Fliegler, supra*) or, under the MBCA's subchapter F, makes the transaction well nigh unassailable. However, the ultimate touchstone is fairness, not compliance with the statute, on which issue the interested director(s) will have the burden of proof. Hence, **Answer (B) is incorrect.** The Lauren family should be able to demonstrate from readily-available data, perhaps buttressed by expert testimony, that the interest rate was justified by the risk. Through similar types of proof, they should be able to demonstrate the fairness of the management fee. Thus, **Answer (D) is incorrect.**

By contrast, according to the *Marciano* court, had the Laurens obtained the approval of fully informed, disinterested directors, or disinterested stockholders, the statute (DEL. GEN. CORP. L. § 144(a)) "permits invocation of the business judgment rule and limits judicial review to issues of gift or waste of corporate assets with the burden of proof upon the party attacking the transaction."

The Klein family claim is probably not a good one, as the Lauren family should be able easily to prove the fairness of the actions they took (Answer (C)).

152.   **Answer (B) is the best answer.** In days gone by, perhaps Answer (A) would have been a good answer. Without the benefit of statutes, the board of directors could not muster a quorum in the case in which a majority of the directors were interested. Today a board might still seek shareholder approval, for political purposes (it looks good) or because it may result in an even more deferential standard of review than the business judgment rule standard that would apply to director approval. For example, the ALI Corporate Governance Project suggests that shareholder approval should result in a shifting of the burden of proof (to the complaining shareholder) and a change in the standard of review as well. *See, e.g.*, ALI PRINCIPLES § 5.02(a)(2)(D). Shareholder approval would result in a highly deferential "waste" standard rather than a business judgment rule standard of review. Therefore, **Answer (A) is not the best answer.**

Today, going to the shareholders for approval is not, strictly speaking, necessary. Interested director statutes permit counting the interested directors present for quorum purposes. The Model Act Subchapter F is more flexible yet: "A majority (but no fewer than two) of all the qualified [disinterested] directors on the board of directors, or on the committee, constitutes a quorum that complies with this section." The section further provides that the presence of the interested directors does not "taint" any vote ("Directors' action that complies with this section is not affected by the presence of one or vote of a director who is not a qualified director."). MBCA § 8.62(c). *Cf. Tefft v. Schaefer*, 239 P. 837 (Wash. 1925) (typical older case holding that participation of the interested director "taints" any vote of the remaining directors, no matter how favorable).

In a pinch, the corporation could always seek court approval, whether statutory authority existed or not. Sitting as chancellor, in equity, the judge could review the transaction. It might be difficult, however, to find a judge who would do so. Therefore, **Answer (C) is not the best answer.**

In most jurisdictions, it is true that the attorney general has supervisory power over corporations generally. Few attorneys general devote significant resources to that function. Obtaining review by the attorney general's office would be next to impossible in most states. Hence, **Answer (D) is not the best answer.**

153. This is a question about who rather than how many, as in the previous question. **Answer (D) is the correct answer.** Answer (C) tells us who are termed a "qualified directors," a new term coined by the MBCA drafters in 2006. Basically, a "material relationship" to a party, proceeding or transaction knocks a director out of the "qualified group" as would a "material; interest in a proceeding or transaction. MBCA § 1.43(b) states that material relationship "means familial, financial, professional employment or other relationship that would reasonably be expected to impair the objectivity of a director's judgment." But then MBCA § 1.43(c) has some carve-outs (circumstances that might fit the definition but will not knock the director out of the box). Being named as a defendant, or a director who approved the challenged transaction, will not alone disqualify. MBCA § 1.43(c)(3). Having been nominated or elected by a director or ex-director who is not qualified, as here, will not disqualify. MBCA § 1.43(c)(1). Serving on another board of directors which contains non-qualified directors will not disqualify. MBCA § 1.43(c)(2).

Answer (A) is incorrect. Barney probably can serve but the terminology most lawyers use, "interested" or "disinterested," is no longer the MBCA's nomenclature of choice. In a two-page, Rube Goldberg-like section, and throughout various provisions of the Act, the ABA attempts to substitute the term "qualified." The definition then cuts across a number of substantive MBCA sections, including § 7.44 (dismissal of derivative action by "qualified directors"); § 8.53 (authorization of advances for defense expenses by two or more "qualified directors"); § 8.55 (authorization of indemnification — same); § 8.52 (director action with regard to interested director transaction proposals to be by "qualified directors"); and § 8.70 (the new corporate opportunity safe harbor). So Barney can serve and the terminology used, "disinterested," may become outmoded.

Answer (B) is incorrect. Barney can serve because he comes within the carve-out. Therefore he is "qualified."

Answer (C) is also incorrect. For the same reason, that is, that Barney comes with the carve-out.

154. Yes. In the 19th century, director's transactions with corporations on whose board they sat simply were void. Sometime around 1900, this harsh common law began to be ameliorated. Such transactions were voidable at the instance of a complaining shareholder or the corporation, not void altogether. In 1931, California became the first jurisdiction to pass an interested director statute, which provided that if disclosure and a vote had been obtained, fairness to the corporation was a defense or, more precisely, that then the shareholder had the burden of proving that the transaction had been unfair. Conversely, if the interested director failed to comply with procedures, she would have the burden of proving fairness.

See, e.g., the discussion of *Remillard Brick Co. v. Remillard-Dandini Co.*, 241 P.2d 66 (Cal. Ct. App. 1952), in the answer to Question 150. In various forms, interested director statutes are common today. But, whether at common law or under these "safe harbor" statutes, directors had a duty to make full and fair disclosure both of their interest and of the corporation's interests in the proposed transaction. Failure to do so would negate any safe harbor protection the director thought she had otherwise obtained by seeking director or shareholder approval. Lack of disclosure would relegate the transaction back to the voidable category. Here, despite his good intentions, Luciano failed to make complete disclosure. He must therefore be prepared to prove the fairness of the price he paid for the property. Or, he should make full disclosure and seek board approval for a second time.

155. **Answer (D) is the best answer**, except in Delaware, where the best answer for a time was Answer (A). Delaware had, in effect, abandoned all meaningful review of corporate executives' compensation. Every form of compensation was reviewed under the Delaware version of the business judgment rule. *See, e.g., Brehm v. Eisner*, 746 A.2d 244, 265–66 (Del. 2000) (business judgment rule review of board decision to pay $130 million severance to Disney president who had been in the job only for one year, who had underperformed badly, and who had sought other positions from early in his tenure; case remanded for plaintiffs to attempt to plead gift or waste of corporate assets which, in theory, could overcome the business judgment rule); *Zupnick v. Goizueta*, 698 A.2d 384 (Del. Ch. 1997) (grant of options on five million shares for Coca-Cola Co. CEO's past services reviewed under business judgment rule only). *But see In re The Walt Disney Company Derivative Litigation*, 825 A.2d 275, 289 (Del. Ch. 2003) (on remand) (post-*Enron* finding that because of their "ostrich-like" behavior, directors approving employment and later severance packages were not entitled to protection; directors had merely rubberstamped CEO's actions). But, in the last analysis, after the 37-day trial which followed, the Delaware Chancellor found the Disney directors not liable for the approval of a no-fault termination and the payment of an out-sized severance to Michael Ovitz, the departing president, even though those directors had lost the protection of the business judgment rule and had to defend on no duty of care violation grounds. *In re The Walt Disney Company Derivative Litigation*, 906 A.2d 27 (Del. 2006) (Jacobs, J.).

Here, of course, business judgment rule protection might be problematical because all three directors have disabling conflicts of interest. Most statutes permit directors to fix their compensation qua directors, excusing what otherwise might be considered to be a conflict of interest. *See, e.g.*, MBCA § 8.11: "Unless the articles of incorporation or bylaws provide otherwise, the board of directors may fix the compensation of directors." Here, of course, that is not the case. The three directors are fixing their compensation as the senior executives of the corporations.

In other cases, however, the ubiquity of the business judgment rule has contributed to runaway executive compensation in large U.S. publicly-held corporations. In those corporations, technically "independent" directors (often other CEOs) staff the compensation committee of the board of directors. The committee hires a compensation consultant who prepares a report justifying ever higher levels of compensation for the CEO and other managers. If the compensation is challenged, the directors then defend on the basis of the business judgment rule. Because the attorneys have scripted it right, business judgment rule protection is virtually certain, especially in Delaware.

There used to be an ancillary test, the reasonable relationship test (Answer (B)). It achieved great prominence when the United States Supreme Court applied it in *Rogers v. Hill*, 289 U.S. 582 (1933). The court struck down an open-ended bonus arrangement for the directors of American Tobacco Co. which gave them a percentage of all profits and was uncapped in any way. Today, once in a great while, a court will invoke the reasonable relationship test, as the Arkansas Supreme Court did in the case upon which this Question is based, *Hall v. Staha*, 800 S.W.2d 396 (Ark. 1990). A fair statement, though, is that most courts leave the matter to the business judgment rule which, in the eyes of some, amounts to a complete abdication of judicial control over corporate officials' compensation.

Not so the legislature. In the Enron hearings, it came to Congress's attention that Enron executives did not even have to go the bank to borrow funds with which to exercise their lucrative stock options. They merely went to their "Enron ATM" to obtain loans, which they repaid with Enron stock. The Sarbanes-Oxley Act of 2002 ("SOXA") therefore prohibits altogether loans to, or the arranging of credit for, corporate officers and directors of SEC reporting companies (Answer (C)). This brings the law full circle. The original Model Act (1950) prohibited such loans outright. The 1969 version permitted them, but only with a shareholder vote. The 1984 Model Act treated loans mere as another form of interested director transaction, which could be shielded from attack by disclosure and a vote of disinterested directors.

Answers (A), (B), and (C) are not the best answers for the reasons stated above.

156. **Answer (B) is the best answer.** Sadly, these abuses may be the norm among some publicly-held companies. Beginning about 2002 and extending to 2007-08, shareholders discovered options abuses such as backdating at over 300 companies, including, for example, backdating options so the late Steve Jobs could profit even more from his relationship with Apple. Recognizing that, in theory at least, the BJR could protect some such abuses, the courts quickly condemned the practices as being disloyal (in the extreme) to shareholders even if the approving directors themselves received no benefit from their acts. Typical is Delaware Chancellor William Chandler's opinion in *Ryan v. Gifford*, 918 A.2d 341 (Del. Ch. 2007) ("it is difficult to conceive of a context in which a director may simultaneously lie to his shareholders (regarding his violations of a stockholder-approved plan, no less) and yet satisfy his duty of loyalty. Backdating options qualifies as one of those rare cases [in which] a transaction may be so egregious on its face that board approval cannot meet the test of business judgment"). Chancellor Chandler concludes, "I am unable to fathom a situation where the deliberate violation of a shareholder approved stock option plan and false disclosures . . . is anything but an act of bad faith."

A note about stock options: major companies adopt a qualified stock option plan for the key executives. The exercise (or "strike") price is the same as the current market price, so the plan is for "qualified" options that will not result in income to an executive until such time as he or she exercises the option and sells the stock. Such plans are then proffered to shareholders for their approval. If a plan is qualified, then recognition of the income received (the value of the option) is deferred not only to exercise but beyond to the sale of the stock in the market. Unqualified options (strike price less than the current market, no shareholder approval) are also used but they result in income to the executive at the time of the grant.

Answer (A) is incorrect. Even with non-qualified options, Delaware courts have rejected the BJR defense and found that a shareholder may be able to plead corporate waste (to which BJR would be no defense). *See Weiss v. Swanson*, 948 A.2d 433 (Del Ch. 2008) (both spring-loading and bullet-dodging option grants).

Answers (C) and (D) are incorrect. None of these practices usually passes legal muster. Shareholder advocates have brought hundreds of derivative suits challenging these practices at various corporations. One such case, involving spring-loading of options, is *In re Tyson Foods Consolidated Shareholder Litigation*, 919 A.2d 563 (Del. Ch. 2007) (any legal effort to defend such practices faces "a severe test").

If you are asked to review a stock option plan from a corporate law standpoint, there may also be several special aspects you should examine. Several 1950s cases struck down as a waste of corporate assets stock option plans which did not contain devices to insure that the option plan resulted in receipt of the benefits for which the corporations had adopted the plans. For example, one such case struck down options that were immediately exercisable without regard to whether the executive remained employed by the corporation. *See Kerbs v. California Eastern Airways*, 90 A.2d 652 (Del. 1952); *see also Gottlieb v. Heyden Chemical Corp.*, 90 A.2d 660 (Del. 1952); *cf. Beard v. Elster*, 160 A.2d 731 (Del. 1960) (options for American Airlines executives upheld because option plan contained guarantees that the consideration would be received). In *Kerbs*, the executive could depart from the company the day he received the options, but possibly reap great benefits from them five years later. Delaware has abandoned its own precedents in the area. In a case involving Coca-Cola, the board of directors granted to the CEO lucrative options on several million Coca-Cola shares in gratitude for "past services" rather than as an incentive of any kind. In Delaware, the Chancellor held, henceforth business judgment rule review will be the only kind of review for stock option plans or any other form of compensation. No special rules apply to stock options. *Zupnick v. Goizueta*, 698 A.2d 384 (Del. Ch. 1997); *see also Lewis v. Vogelstein*, 699 A.2d 327 (Del. Ch. 1997) (grant of options on 15,000 Mattel shares to "independent" directors upheld under business judgment rule; options were immediately exercisable and contained no provision for continued service, performance, or the like). Be that as it may, courts in other jurisdictions may decide that those old "special" rules still make sense for supposedly "incentive-based" compensation. The option plan should require some period of continued employment with the corporation, perhaps including employment as a prerequisite to exercise of the options.

157. **Answer (D) is the best answer.** Earnings restatements of public and other companies are necessary from time to time. Often they have a catharsis effect. From an accounting standpoint, the restatement permits a company to get its financial foundation "level and square." Failure promptly to admit error often leads to error compounding error, quarter after quarter, year after year. Finally comes an Armageddon, a large restatement that puts the entire company at risk. In the past, the usual consequence of an earnings restatement would be shareholder lawsuits for damages (Answer (A)). In the Sarbanes-Oxley Act of 2002 ("SOXA"), Congress singled out accounting restatements of publicly-held companies as a major abuse. SOXA provides for a forfeiture of all CEO and CFO incentive-based compensation (including profits from stock option exercises) for the previous 12 months if "misconduct" triggers the restatement (Answer (B)). The Act does not make clear precisely *whose* misconduct must trigger the restatement, but the language is broad enough to hold the CEO and CFO responsible if the misconduct of a person or persons who report(s) directly to the CEO and CFO triggered the restatement. As COO, Salvatore Feragamo may escape this penalty, but Versace and Gucci will have to forfeit their bonuses as well as all profits from the sale of common stock in the 12 months preceding the restatement. In this

case, it will be a substantial and painful forfeiture.

That is not all. Under the Penny Stock Reform Act of 1990, Congress gave the SEC power to go to court to seek lifetime, or shorter, bans on certain wrongdoers ever again serving as directors or officers of publicly-held companies (Answer (C)). The SEC had to demonstrate "substantial unfitness to serve." Because Congress had not defined "substantial unfitness," federal courts came to rely on a six-part test developed by Professor Jayne Barnard. *See* Jayne W. Barnard, *When Is a Corporate Executive "Substantially Unfit to Serve"?*, 70 N.C. L. REV. 1489 (1992); Jayne W. Barnard, *The SEC's Suspension and Bar Powers in Perspective*, 76 TUL. L. REV. 1253 (2002). The SEC chaffed under this test of "substantial unfitness." The Commission saw SOXA as an opportunity to remedy what it perceived to be a defect in the law. SOXA changes the test to mere "unfitness to serve." SOXA also authorizes the SEC to undertake the process administratively.

"Stock drop lawsuits" are class actions that are filed following a 15–20 percent drop in the share price of a publicly-held company. Often, with more actively traded shares, 12, 15, or even 20 lawsuits will be filed within a few days of the announcement of an earning restatement or other corporate pratfall.

Answers (A), (B), and (C) are not the best answers for the reasons stated above.

158. **Answer (B) is the best answer.** It is not true that a corporate opportunity may not be usurped (Answer (A)). A director may (1) make full disclosure to her disinterested fellow directors; (2) seek a vote that the corporation does not wish to pursue the opportunity; (3) seek perhaps an additional resolution that the director is free to take up the opportunity, and (4) have the other directors make clear why it is fair to the corporation for the director to take up the opportunity.

Bing did not do those things. Nor would he be likely to, if his attorney gave him that advice. The reason? He would fear that the corporation would pursue the opportunity, or at least attempt to foil him. Bing knows a good deal when he sees it. Instead, a director client in Bing's position might urge counsel to reach an opinion that the opportunity is not, after all, a corporate opportunity. Thus, the particular definition of corporate opportunity one adopts may be quite important. There are several tests.

One of the earliest tests was the "interest or expectancy test" — "an interest already existing, or in which [the corporation] has an expectancy growing out of an existing right." *Lagarde v. Anniston Lime & Stone Co.*, 28 So. 199 (Ala. 1899). The corporation had to have an existing contract, or contract right in the opportunity. Here, that would be true as to the second, or middle, third, because the corporation had a formal offer in hand. But, as to the final third, the corporation had no interest or expectancy (indeed, it had been turned down). Bing was free to take it up. The interest or expectancy test is a narrow definition of corporate opportunity. Sensing that, some courts also apply a "fairness" test (Answer (C)). Is it fair to the corporation for the director to take up the opportunity? *Miller v. Miller*, 222 N.W.2d 71 (Minn. 1974), is a leading "fairness test" case. A fairness test might reach the right outcome in many cases, but it seems conclusory and not particularly helpful from an analytical point of view.

In corporate opportunity cases, the gravamen of the corporation's complaint is that the director did not deal with the corporation. By contrast, Model Act Subchapter F, which attempts to create an impregnable safe harbor for transactions disinterested directors have approved, see Question 138, purports to deal with cases in which the director has dealt with the corporation. The commentary to the subchapter therefore eschews any application of it to corporate opportunity cases.

Bing's resignation (Answer (D)) would probably avail him not, because he learned of the opportunity while he was a director.

Answers (A), (C), and (D) are not the best answers for the reasons stated above.

This Question is based on *Lagarde v. Anniston Lime & Stone Co.*, 28 So. 199 (Ala. 1899).

159. **Answer (C) is the best answer.** This is the famous Delaware case of *Guth v. Loft*, 5 A.2d 503 (Del. 1939). In the opinion, the court "layered" onto the interest and expectancy test (Answer (A)) a "line of business" test (Answer (B)). An opportunity is a corporate opportunity if (1) it is the corporation's line of business, broadly defined; (2) is in a line of business in which the corporation might reasonably be expected to engage; or (3) is in a line of business in which the director or officer knows that corporation has intentions of engaging. Note, once again, the extreme remedy when a corporate official is found to have breached his or her duty of loyalty. Besides a constructive trust on the opportunity, courts also often require disgorgement of compensation received by the corporate official during the period she is found to have been in breach of her fiduciary duty.

Answers (A) and (B) are not the best answers because the court went beyond them, pronouncing both the line of business test and what the remedy would be.

Answer (D) is incorrect. Accepting it would exalt form over substance.

160. **Answer (C) is the best answer.** Lack of wherewithal means that, in some jurisdictions, including Delaware, the opportunity is not a corporate opportunity, so Answer (C) may be the best answer. *See, e.g., Broz v. Cellular Information Systems, Inc.*, 673 A.2d 148, 155 (Del. 1996); *Schreiber v. Bryan*, 396 A.2d 512, 519 (Del. Ch. 1978). Other courts have reasoned differently. They have observed that it is the directors who are ultimately in charge of raising capital for the entity. If a beneficial opportunity comes along, and lack of wherewithal affects whether the prospect is a "corporate opportunity" or not, directors may have little or no interest in helping the corporation raise funds. Those courts hold that the financial status of the corporation goes not to the issue of corporate opportunity, but to the defense of whether or not diversion of the opportunity was "fair." Those courts hold further that lack of wherewithal is a defense for usurping directors only if the corporation was insolvent. Directors have no duty to throw good money (whether their own or that of investors) after bad. *Irving Trust Co. v. Deutsch*, 73 F.2d 121 (2d Cir. 1934), is the leading case. More recent cases include *Banks v. Bryant*, 497 So. 2d 460 (Ala. 1986), and *Nicholson v. Evans*, 642 P.2d 727 (Utah 1982).

The reason that none of the suggested answers quite fits is that Celeste learned of the opportunity "by virtue of her position," a test used by some courts and adopted by the American Law Institute in its Corporate Governance Project. *See* ALI PRINCIPLES § 5.05(b)(1)(A) ("Corporate opportunity means . . . [a]ny opportunity to engage in a business activity of which a director or senior executive becomes aware . . . [i]n connection with the performance of functions as a director or senior executive, or under circumstances that should reasonably lead the director or senior executive to believe that the person offering the opportunity expects it to be offered to the corporation."). If Celeste learned of the opportunity because, even in a very loose sense, she was an officer of Hemlock, then the opportunity is a corporate opportunity that she must disclose. On the other side of the coin, she (or you, as counsel) might argue that the conversational gambit, "Say, you're with . . ." was indeed merely an opening line and nothing more, but a judge or jury could disregard that slant on the evidence. The by virtue of the position test is one that has currency.

Answer (A) is incorrect. There is no evidence Hemlock has ever been in or considered the recycling business.

Answer (B) is incorrect. Hemlock never had an "interest or expectancy" as courts use the term. Celeste can argue as in Answer (D) but Answer (C) is more of a "show stopper" defense, at least in Delaware.

Answer (C) is incorrect. Celeste telephoned acquaintances within the industry, consulted a broker-dealer about financing, and discussed her putative business plan with an SBA representative. She used corporate resources in doing those things. Stay away from any contention that Celeste's resignation was timely.

161.   **Answer (B) is the best answer.** This Question is loosely based upon a recent Delaware Supreme Court case, *Broz v. Cellular Information Systems, Inc.*, 673 A.2d 148 (Del. 1996). In his opinion, Chief Justice Veasey pointed out that a director does not have to expand her "corporate opportunity horizon" to include the scope of a prospective merger partner's business interests (Answer (A)). He also went further. He made clear that, in Delaware at least, there exist multiple tests of what opportunities are corporate opportunities and that the tests are cumulative rather than alternative. He would ask whether the corporation has an interest or expectancy in the opportunity, whether it was in the corporation's line of business (Answer (C)), and whether the corporation had the wherewithal to develop the opportunity. Similarly, the American Law Institute Corporate Governance Project contains a section delineating a test of corporate opportunity. ALI PRINCIPLES § 5.05(b). Under the ALI test, and the case law of several jurisdictions, an opportunity may also become a corporate opportunity if the director or officer uses corporate assets, information or facilities to develop the opportunity. The ALI layers on top of that list a line of business test and a by virtue of the position test. Among others, the Supreme Courts of Oregon, Maine, and Massachusetts have expressly adopted the ALI provision. *See Klinicki v. Lundgren*, 695 P.2d 906 (Or. 1985); *Northeast Harbor Golf Club, Inc. v. Harris*, 661 A.2d 1146 (Me. 1995); *Demoulas v. Demoulas Super Markets, Inc.*, 677 N.E.2d 159 (Mass. 1997). In the modern era, then, courts may well apply a multiple of tests. Think of the various tests as outwardly expanding concentric circles.

That is as it should be. In the "old economy," opportunities tended to be capital intensive and not easy to divert. In the "new economy" of high tech and dotcoms, opportunities inure much more in information and ideas, requiring more of a multi-faceted approach to defining which opportunities are corporate opportunities.

A number of the recent cases involve golf courses. In *Northeast Harbor Golf Club, Inc. v. Harris*, 661 A.2d 1146 (Me. 1995), over a number of years, the club president acquired various parcels of land adjoining the golf course, paying $380,000. Assembled together, the several parcels had a value of $1,550,000. The Maine Supreme Court adopted the ALI "by virtue of the position" etc. test, remanded for evidence on whether Ms. Harris had indeed offered the parcels first to the club, and, if she had not done so, for submission by her of evidence on why it was fair for her to acquire the parcels. *Farber v. Servan Land Co.*, 662 F.2d 371 (5th Cir. 1981), involved a golf course in Florida, operated by a corporation with 10 shareholders. When an adjoining 160 acres of land became available, the principal officers (Savin and Serianni) disclosed it to the shareholders, but acquired the land before the shareholders took any action. Shortly thereafter, the corporation and Savin/Serianni sold the whole project for $8.5 million. Savin/Serianni allocated $5 million of the proceeds to the golf course, taking $3.5 million for their land. An appraiser later found the sum allocated to the corporation almost $1 million too high. Savin/Serianni argued ratification by the board and "no harm, no foul." As to the latter, the shareholders had benefited by any usurpation of a corporate opportunity and the subsequent generous allocation of proceeds. The court held director ratification ineffective because Savin/Serianni ratified their own wrongdoing, thus nullifying its effectiveness. Nor did the court accept the "benefit argument." "*If a corporate opportunity existed* [the court found it did] *and its stockholders would have been entitled to the profits from the sale of both parcels*," and not merely part of the proceeds from the sale of the second parcel, the shareholders were entitled to all of the profits from the sale of the second parcel as well as from the sale of the golf course.

Answers (A) and (C) are not the best answers for the reasons stated above.

Answer (D) inapposite. A director may compete with the corporation on whose board they act, especially if the director was in the business before he went on the board. That principle, however, says nothing about deciding whether new opportunities that arise are corporate opportunities.

162.   No. *See Zidell v. Zidell, Inc.*, 560 P.2d 1091 (Or. 1977). Courts have held that, absent a past practice or policy of acquiring shares, purchase of shares in a corporation is not a corporate opportunity. Because no policy or past practice existed here, Ajax was free to purchase Rosen's shares. Hector may claim breach of fiduciary duty, but the corollary is that control has its privileges. He may also claim that the corporation is closely held, he is being denied his reasonable expectations, and, therefore, he is being oppressed. Oppression is a ground for invoking the statutory remedy of "involuntary dissolution." But all of this is premature. Denial of reasonable expectations envisions a pattern of conduct. The developments in the Question are recent. It is also premature because oppression will be revisited again, *infra*, in the questions on closely-held corporations. Better to tell Hector to "grin and bear it" for a while. Mark your calendar to contact him in a year or two to see what has developed.

163.   Late in 2004, the ABA Committee on Corporate Laws added new MBCA § 8.70 to the Act. Although the section does not attempt an answer to the question of which opportunities are corporate opportunities (something the previous problems help you develop, and which the ABA Committee deems to be "fact sensitive"), the section does attempt to put in place a safe harbor. The director who presents an opportunity or possible opportunity to "qualified directors" (defined in new MBCA § 1.43), or disinterested shareholders, receiving in return "a disclaimer of the corporation's interest in the matter," may take the opportunity up without fear of subsequent attacks upon the director or the transaction ("A director's taking advantage of a business opportunity may [no longer] be the subject of equitable relief, or give rise to an award of damages or other sanctions against the director."). The official committee warns though, that "the safe harbor's benefit is available only when the corporation can entertain the opportunity in a fully objective way."

On the other hand, failure to take the proposed transaction to the board "neither creates a negative inference nor alters the burden of proof in any subsequent proceeding seeking damages or equitable relief." To obtain certainty one way or another, Guth, and you as his attorney, might take the opportunity to the board, as you would a proposed interested director transaction. Fearing, though, that the board may turn him down, Guth may not want to do this, so you should get on record (memo to the file) that you so advised him (on the pros and cons of going to the board or to the shareholders).

164. **Answer (A) is the best answer.** Directors may compete with the corporation on whose board they sit but, often, directors will have to thread a byzantine maze to do so. The rule may be stated to be that a director may not engage in "bad faith competition" with the corporation on whose board she sits. *See, e.g., Atkinson v. Marquart*, 541 P.2d 556, 558 (Ariz. 1975); *Bancroft-Whitney Co. v. Glen*, 411 P.2d 921, 935 (Cal. 1966). Bad faith competition would include acts such as disparagement (commercial defamation), "passing off" (using the name of or association with the corporation to sell products or services), and use of customer lists, trade secrets, and other items of proprietary information. Also, if the incorporating jurisdiction has adopted the popular line of business definition of a corporate opportunity, the director will have to seek board permission to compete if the director was not already in the business (Answer (B)). Here, however, Waters was in the film making business before he joined Sterling.

That said and done, larger companies often include on their board managers of smaller and family-held companies in the same industry. Those directors, whose own firms compete, at least in theory, with the larger company, represent a broad experience base upon which the board and management of the larger company may draw.

Answer (C) may also be a possibility. Before taking up "Nail Polish," Waters perhaps should have sought the Sterling board's permission. Just because the board turned down the opportunity does not mean that the director is free to take it up. Some courts would imply the board's consent. Others might require that director Waters have dotted all the "i's" and crossed all the "t's" before he would be free to take up the opportunity the Sterling board had turned down.

Answers (B), (C), and (D) are not the best answers for the reasons stated above.

165. **Answer (D) is the best answer.** For decades, the better reasoned view was that directors and officers have two, possibly three, fiduciary duties (care, loyalty, and acting lawfully). Beginning in the 1980s, the Delaware Courts began adding another duty, the duty of candor, which the courts for a time also called the duty of disclosure. *See, e.g.,* Douglas M. Branson, Corporate Governance (1993) (with supplements); *Shell Petroleum v. Smith*, 606 A.2d 112 (Del. 1992); *Citron v. E.I. Dupont de Nemours*, 584 A.2d 490 (Del. Ch. 1990). In an early decision, *In re TriStar Pictures Litig.*, 634 A.2d 319 (Del. 1993), the Delaware Supreme Court also announced a *per se* rule of nominal damages ($1 or $2 per share) for violations of the duty of candor. Because large cap corporations may have one or two million, or more, shares outstanding, a rule of *per se* damages represented a bonanza for plaintiffs' lawyers.

Answers (A) and (B) are incorrect. Because directors' disclosure may be harmful to shareholders, even though directors have violated neither the duty of care nor the duty of loyalty, a new concept, the duty of candor, was necessary. But an overall, overriding duty, combined with a *per se* damages rule produced far too many opportunities for litigation. In *Loudon v. Archer Daniels Midland Co.*, 700 A.2d 135 (Del. 1997), the court faced candor allegations that directors up for reelection were or might have become defendants in a criminal price-fixing proceeding. The court cut the duty back considerably, holding that a cause of action would lie only in cases in which directors sought a necessary shareholder vote or consent. The action would not lie for failures to disclose completely in a routine election of directors unless a final adjudication had found the candidate at fault.

Malone v. Brincat, 722 A.2d 5 (Del. 1998), necessitated an exception to the limitation. Directors of Mercury Finance, a large lender of subprime automobile loans, knowingly participated in the overstatement of Mercury's earnings. A duty of candor claim will lie, even in routine matters, when directors have intentionally been untruthful.

Answer (C) is incorrect because it is nonsensical.

A few other jurisdictions have begun to evolve duty of candor jurisprudence. One is Maryland. In *Shenker v. Laureate Education, Inc.*, 983 A.2d 408 (Md. 2009), Maryland's highest court held that a *direct* rather than derivative claim would lie for shareholders' duty of candor claim against corporate directors. Certain of the directors had been less than forthcoming in structuring a leveraged buyout by a private equity firm in which the directors also held interests. The shareholders could sue them for candor violations which resulted in shareholders receiving less than they would have if directors had exercised their *Revlon* duties (maximization of shareholder return once a decision has been made to sell or break up the corporation). The court also held that MBCA § 8.30, or the Maryland version of it, was only a starting and not an ending point for listing directors' duties. Common law duties, such as candor, exist side-by-side with any list of more defined duties such as those MBCA § 8.30 contains.

166. **Answer (D) is the best answer.** This Question fills out treatment of the Delaware duty known as the duty of good faith while the previous question fleshed out the duty of candor, also a duty but not an independent one, apparently. Duty of candor violations find their basis in a duty of loyalty or care violation, while duty of good faith violations are "free standing," so to speak, illustrating how "messy" Delaware fiduciary law has become. Two of the leading Delaware good faith cases are *In re The Walt Disney Company Derivative Litigation*, 906 A.2d 27 (Del. 2006), and *Stone ex rel. Amsouth Bancorporation v. Ritter*, 911 A.2d 362 (Del. 2006).

Only "sustained or systematic failure of a board to exercise oversight" may result in liability. But if a plaintiff is able to prove a long pattern of such non-behavior, causally related to the corporation's losses, the oversight failure ("showing of bad faith conduct") becomes a duty of loyalty and not merely a duty of care violation. Given the length of service of a supermajority of the AA directors, and the ease of supervision, knowledge of prevailing market prices for bauxite ore and knowledge (actual or imputed) of the prices being charged to Bahrain, a plaintiff might make out a case. The advice to them might be to allege violation of the duty of good faith, rising to the level that they also constitute violations of the duty of loyalty.

Answer (A) is incorrect. Run-of-the-mill allegations of duty of care violations (lack of oversight) are among the most difficult to plead and prove. They are subject to a business judgment rule defense. Moreover, the corporation may well have a Delaware 102(b)(7) exculpatory provision, or its state of incorporation's equivalent, in its articles. If that is true, under Delaware law, the suit would not even state a claim for money damages.

Answer (B) is incorrect. No duty of loyalty claim would stand. These directors have neither received any improper benefit nor acted out of revenge, spite, etc.

Answer (C) is not the best answer, but may be correct. The FCPA has received renewed attention the last few years, with over 70 corporations prosecuted criminally for such violations each year. Public corporations and their employees or contractors and subcontractors may not pay any bribe or other foreign payment which would be illegal if made in the United States. An exception is made for so-called "facilitation" or grease payments which are small in amount. Corporations must also ensure that their organizations maintain books and records adequate to determine if funds are being expended and assets used in accordance with the directives of management. The latter is an anti-bribery, anti-slush fund provision. Where violations have occurred in the past, wrongdoing employees have often procured the wherewithal to pay bribes by resorting to a convenient "slush fund."

The duty of good faith is a catchall for situations in which directors have not received any improper financial or other personal benefit. In the duty of care area, the business judgment rule is a strong defense. But extreme failures of oversight of the prolonged or callous disregard sort may lead to a duty of good faith violation. In the first *Disney* opinion, the Supreme Court of Delaware listed further examples:

> A failure to act in good faith may be shown, for instance, were the Fiduciary intentionally acts with a purpose other than advancing the best interests of the corporation, where the fiduciary acts with the intent to violate applicable law, or where the fiduciary fails to act in the face of a known duty to act, demonstrating a conscious disregard for his duties. There may be other examples of bad faith yet to be proven or alleged, but these are the most salient.

In her article, *Developments in Corporate Governance: The Duty of Good Faith and Its Impact on Director Conduct*, 13 Geo. Mason L. Rev. 1037 (2006) (footnotes omitted), Professor Janet Kerr sets forth her distillation from the cases:

> [R]ecently, the following have been considered potential violations of the duty of good faith: intentional or unintentional misconduct; reckless behavior of a given duration or magnitude; conscious disregard of known risks; and behavior that cannot rationally be explained on any grounds. According to the latest cases, directors may be liable for a good faith violation if they simply do not care about the risks inherent in the transaction at hand.

NOTE ON THE DODD-FRANK ACT OF 2010 (THE WALL STREET REFORM AND CONSUMER PROTECTION ACT OF 2010)

Until the mid 1990s, corporate governance was a matter for state law, such as the state law just reviewed outlining the fiduciary duty of corporate officers and directors. Dodd-Frank, which is over 700 pages long, attempts to do many things, but among them are further federal law incursions into the subject of corporate law and corporate governance. These follow on the heels of the Private Securities Litigation Reform Act of 1995 and the Sarbanes-Oxley Act of 2002, also the subject of notes in this Q & A volume. The near-death economic experience of 2007–2009 (especially 2008) prompted Dodd-Frank but the legislation became a Christmas tree as it made its way through Congress. Its final iteration includes several corporate governance provisions.

Remember that these enactments affect only public corporations having a class of securities registered with the SEC. There are approximately 16,000 such corporations while there are

4.5 million corporations in the United States. Here are seven highpoints of the legislation, from a corporate law point of view:

1. *Say on Pay.* The Act requires here what laws and stock exchanges in the UK or in Australia have required for some time. Dodd-Frank § 951 (codified as Securities Exchange Act § 14A) requires that corporations conduct an advisory shareholder vote on executive compensation no less than every three years. The shareholders also must be asked at least every six years how they wish to revise this (*e.g.*, to every year, every other year, etc.). The corporation must tabulate and disclose the results. Accelerated filers (between $75 million and $700 million market capitalization) and large accelerated filers (over $700 million) must disclose how their compensation policies and decisions take into account say on pay results.

2. *Requirement for a Compensation Committee.* Section 952 directs the SEC to adopt rules requiring the NASDAQ and the New York Stock Exchange, as well as other self-regulatory securities organizations, to refuse to list companies that do not have a compensation committee meeting certain requirements, particularly as to independence. The committee must have independent members and independence of action, namely, freedom to hire whatever legal or compensation experts it wishes. Commentators debate as to whether the section actually does require a compensation committee in the first place, or whether it sets requirements for such a committee if a company has one. The debate seems to be about how many angels can dance on the head of a pin. The effect of the section is that major corporations will have, in addition to an audit committee Sarbanes-Oxley required, a compensation committee (what the Australians call the remuneration committee).

3. *Compensation Disclosures.* Companies must include in their annual filings clear expositions of the relationships between executive compensation and firm financial performance. Dodd-Frank § 953. One such exposition, which may be difficult for many companies to compile, must compare the CEOs salary to the median for all the corporation's other employees, be they 100,000, 200,000, or 20,000. The corporation must then express that comparison as a ratio (CEO makes 423 times median employee's wages).

4. *More Compensation Clawbacks.* Sarbanes-Oxley § 304 (2002) provides that if a corporation has to restate its financials, and the restatement is found to be due to misconduct (by whom is undefined), the CEO and the CFO must forfeit all incentive-based compensation they have received in the preceding 12 months. Due to the frequency and size of stock option profits, the clawback often will represent a significant bite (in Enron it was estimated that the clawback would have been $200 million had Sarbanes-Oxley been in effect). Dodd-Frank § 954, adding new Securities Exchange Act § 10D, creates a second clawback track. All executive officers have to return excess compensation for the three years preceding the restatement. "Excess" means the amount by which compensation was paid over the amount that would have been paid had financials been correct.

The manner in which the result comes about is convoluted. The Act directs the SEC to adopt rules requiring issuers to disclose their clawback policies. Issuers failing to adopt a clawback policy meeting the SEC rules are subject to being delisted by the NASDAQ or NYSE.

5. *Shareholder Proxy Access.* The SEC was well down the road to requiring some form of access before Congress acted, ever since SEC Chair Arthur Leavitt began advocating shareholder access in the late 1990s. What proxy access means is that an activist shareholder may nominate and seek votes for its own board candidates, who will be listed and described in the corporation's annual proxy materials. Previously, to run its own candidate, an insurgent had to spend gargantuan sums to draft and file its own rival proxy solicitation. An insurgent will still have to undertake the latter if she seeks a change in control of the corporation, or offers up a slate of candidates consisting of more than 25 percent of the total board seats.

Not every shareholder is eligible to do this — fact, few are. Only owners of 3 percent of the company's shares (likely to be larger institutional investors, such as public employee pension or activist labor union pension plans), who have owed that or a greater amount for two years or more, will be eligible. Application to smaller public companies has been deferred. All of this is pursuant to SEC Rule 14a-11, which the SEC adopted in 2011, shortly after Dodd-Frank, which gave the SEC authority to adopt proxy access rules (the SEC thought it had the authority all along), became law. The SEC stayed the effective date of the rule while the Chamber of Commerce pursued a lawsuit against the rule's implementation. In *Business Roundtable v. SEC*, 647 F.3d 1144 (D.C. Cir. 2011), the Chamber prevailed. The Court of Appeals found that the SEC failed adequately to research the costs Rule 14a-11 might impose, in violation of the Administrative Procedure Act.

6. *Disclosure re Separation* vel non *of CEO and Board Chair Offices.* The Act takes no position on the issue; it merely directs the SEC to adopt a rule requiring companies to disclose whether or not they separate the offices. Only about 15 percent of large U.S. companies separate the offices while approximately 85 percent of companies everywhere else in the world do the opposite. One view of the board is that its highest calling is to monitor and, if necessary, remove an underperforming chief executive officer. How a board can do that is problematic when the person responsible for convening the board is the very person whose removal may be sought. U.S. companies (some, not all) have responded by creating the office of "lead director" who has power to convene the board to examine the CEO's performance. Opponents of what is sometimes called a non-executive chair requirement say that such a chair often resembles a toastmaster, devoid of deep background and knowledge about the company. Other critics say that such a requirement sets up an unhealthy competition between CEO and board chair.

7. *Sarbanes-Oxley Internal Controls Attestation Relief for Small Public Companies.* SOX § 404 requires a public corporation's top officers yearly to attest that they have not detected and are unaware of any material weaknesses in the corporation's internal accounting controls. Further, the corporation must retain an independent account to attest to the CEO and CFO's opinions on internal controls. This 404 requirement costs on average $1.56 million for smaller public companies and more for larger ones. *See generally* Douglas M. Branson, *Too Many Bells? Too Many Whistles? Corporate Governance in the Post-Enron Post-WorldCom Era*," S.C. L. Rev. (2006). Dodd-Frank § 989 permanently exempts non-accelerated filers (less than $75 million market cap) from the attestation requirement and its attendant expense.

167.   **Answer (C) is the best answer.** The sisters certainly have a federal claim. Insider trading may be defined, roughly, as trading or tipping others to trade, committed by someone in a fiduciary or similar relationship of trust and confidence, while in possession of material nonpublic information. But, federal courts are crowded these days. Many federal courts exhibit hostility to securities claims (Answer (A)). State law and state court might provide a realistic alternative. Once it was not so. Around 1900, the courts, and the law generally, were bound up in legal formalisms. When faced with claims of insider trading based upon corporate officials' duty of loyalty, courts would conclude that the director or officer owed her duty to the corporation and not anyone within it. While the conduct was of a sort they in no way approved, courts would dismiss the shareholders' suit on "no duty" grounds. *See, e.g., Goodwin v. Agassiz*, 186 N.E. 659 (Mass. 1933).

Some cases shocked the conscience. In *Strong v. Repide*, 213 U.S. 419 (1909), the Supreme Court held a director who bought up shares of a sugar plantation corporation in the Philippines (then a U.S. possession) liable of insider trading. The director knew that the corporation was about to be liquidated, at a value triple what the director was paying selling shareholders. The Court concluded that when a director was in possession of knowledge constituting "special facts," the director owed a duty directly to shareholders, either to disclose the "special facts" or to refrain from trading. "Special facts" were not precisely defined, but were thought to include episodic evolutions in the corporation's life (a merger, sale of assets, liquidation, etc.). A favorable forthcoming earnings report or new contract probably did not constitute special facts.

Some state judiciaries never bogged down in legal formalism. Early on, the Kansas Supreme Court held that a selling shareholder could sue a director who had purchased her shares for $1.25 while in possession of inside information about a forthcoming extraordinary dividend of $1.00 per share. *Hotchkiss v. Fischer*, 16 P.2d 531 (Kan. 1932) ("a director negotiating with a shareholder for the purchase of shares acts in a relation of scrupulous trust and confidence"). By and large, however, state courts had difficulty reaching insider trading using the state law duty of loyalty. Following the enactment of the Securities Exchange Act of 1934, and Rule 10b-5 in 1943, federal judges and federal court decisions dominated the area. State court judges, however, read the newspapers. In the 1980s, they read of insider trading scandal after scandal, growing out of the takeover boom. They began to evolve state law. They revived and expanded the "special facts doctrine," holding that special facts were any material facts likely to have an effect on the price of a security (Answer (B)). Directors with knowledge of special facts, so defined, owed a duty not to buy or sell from their corporation's shareholders unless, of course, they disclosed their inside information. Recent state supreme courts' decisions in Colorado and West Virginia, for example, have adopted the new, and expanded, special facts doctrine, holding trading insiders liable. *See, e.g., Bailey v. Vaughan*, 359 S.E.2d 599 (W. Va. 1987) (holding liable bank director who bought up shares while knowing that bank would be sold to larger bank); *Van Schaack Holdings, Ltd. v. Van*

Schaack, 867 P.2d 892 (Colo. 1994) (director of family farming corporation bought up shares knowing new Denver airport would be located on corporation's farm land). *See generally* Douglas M. Branson, *Choosing the Appropriate Default Rule: Insider Trading Under State Law*, 45 Ala. L. Rev. 753 (1994).

States have their own securities acts, known as "blue sky laws." Most are based on one of three versions of the Uniform Securities Act, promulgated by the National Conference of Commissioners on Uniform State Laws in 1956, 1985, and 2002, respectively, though many commercially significant states (including New York, California, Texas, Florida, and Ohio) have blue sky laws that are not based on any version of the Uniform Securities Act. Blue sky laws typically contain a statutory provision that, by and large, tracks SEC Rule 10b-5. A disgruntled shareholder or investor could sue an insider under those statutory provisions as well. They have the added advantage that the statute directs the court to award a reasonable attorney's fee to the prevailing plaintiff.

The Menke sisters could bring a combined federal and state claim in federal court. They could not do so, however, in state court. The Securities Exchange Act of 1934, pursuant to which the SEC has adopted Rule 10b-5, provides for exclusive subject matter jurisdiction in the federal courts.

State court fraud (as opposed to breach of fiduciary duty) claims (Answer (D)) did not work well for a number of reasons. Insider trading claims are claims of silence while common law fraud deals mostly with misrepresentation and half truth. Fraud required face-to-face dealings (privity) which, while present here, would not be present in transaction taking place through a broker or over a stock exchange.

Answers (A), (B), and (D) are not the best answers for the reasons stated above.

168.   **Answer (A) is the best answer.** *See SEC v. Texas Gulf Sulphur Co.*, 401 F.2d 833 (2d Cir. 1968). You should know that a respectable school of thought exists, mostly among economists, that insider trading should be permitted for reasons such as those enumerated in Answer (D). Therefore, **Answer (D) is incorrect.** Because now all developed nations of the world prohibit the practice, and insider trading has become one of *the* white collar crimes of this century, that debate has taken a backseat to debate about other issues.

Until recently, the insider trading prohibition under the federal securities laws has been a matter wholly of judge-made law. Rule 10b-5 is an opaque catch-all antifraud rule which also governs misrepresentations, half truths, and omissions in the purchase or sale of any security (not just those issued by publicly-held companies). Insider trading cases are merely a subset of a subset (cases of silence or omission) of the broad array of cases Rule 10b-5 governs. The text of the rule itself offers little, if any, guidance. You should be able to deal with answers to several questions, including:

(1)   Who is an insider?

(2)   What information is inside information?

(3)   What is the nature of the prohibition?

(4)   Upon whom is the prohibition visited?

(5)   When are insiders and tippees free to trade?

(6)   What are the penalties for trading on insider information?

Return to these questions after reviewing the answers to this and the next two Questions.

As for the present Question, the Good News employees and officers might defend on grounds that they are not insiders. Insiders, though, are those "who by virtue of a fiduciary or similar relationship of trust and confidence" come into possession of inside information. *Chiarella v. United States*, 445 U.S. 222 (1980). The test would include Cal and Jack. They might say, though, that the information is not material. They were speculating. One test well does not a major gas field make. An omitted fact is a material fact if the mythical "reasonable investor would consider it important in the making of his or her decision." It is not necessarily that they would have acted in a different manner had they had the information. Materiality also is to be judged in light of the "total mix" of information available about the issuer and the developments at issue. *TSC Industries, Inc. v. Northway, Inc.*, 426 U.S. 438 (1976). Here, that total mix might include knowledge that oil and gas companies were prospecting in the Powder River country. The total mix might make the information more, rather than less, material, as is usually the case. Would the reasonable investor consider one test well important? Only oil and gas speculators would attach importance to a find such as the Good News find. But the reasonable investor is not modeled on the little old person in tennis shoes who invests for the long-term. The reasonable investor includes "the speculators and chartists of Bay and Wall Streets," as well as the long and medium term investor. (Bay Street is where the Toronto Exchange is located; chartists are traders who plot security price movements and believe that, like tea leaves, past price movements enable one to predict the future). So, if an inner circle of investors or analysts (technology specialists, dotcom followers, precious metal bugs, and so on) would consider the information important, then it is material information. Thus, **Answer (C) is incorrect.**

The nature of the prohibition is "disclose or abstain." Disclosure may be possible in the case of smaller companies or face-to-face share trading. Usually, though, it is not possible because the trading takes place in impersonal markets, the insider lacks the requisite media access, or simply the prerogative to disclose belongs to the company and not to the insider. The effective prohibition then is to abstain from trading or from deputizing someone to trade for her. She also may not "tip" others whom she should know would be likely to act (*e.g.*, trade or tip others) based upon the information.

For how long? Ferlin traded too soon. The prohibition lasts until the information has been disclosed and effectively disseminated. According to the *Texas Gulf Sulphur* court, information is effectively disseminated when it reaches the medium likely to achieve the widest circulation. That may be the home town newspaper in certain cases, and the Dow Jones wire or the *Wall Street Journal* in others (*e.g.*, large publicly-held companies). There have been a number of cases of insiders who got greedy and "jumped the gun" (that is, traded after the information had been disclosed, but before it had been disseminated). Thus, **Answer (B) is incorrect.**

One more word on policy: advocates who favor legalization of insider trading believe that it would promote the overall goals of the securities laws, that is, efficient pricing of securities and prompt disclosure of important developments. The case of Marty Robbins illustrates the counter argument. Within a corporate organization, one can envision a delay in disclosure of important developments as, one by one, up through the hierarchy, corporate officials load up on the stock (or sell, in the case of negative news). Thus, while the Vice President for Development, the Chief Financial Officers, the Chief Operating Officers, and even the CEO, in serial fashion, buy (or sell), disclosure and accurate pricing could be delayed for several days.

169.   **Answer (D) is the best answer.** Answers (B) and (C) may apply as well. The jurisdictional means under federal securities laws (Answer (C)) is not interstate commerce, but the "use of any means or instrumentality of interstate commerce." Rare is the case in which some means of interstate commerce (mail, telephone, Internet) is not used. In Vincent's case he probably telephoned the broker to place his order. Up until that point he may not have used any means or instrumentality of interstate commerce. And, what if he placed his orders with his broker face to face? We will never know.

This is the famous case of *Chiarella v. United States*, 445 U.S. 222 (1980). The prosecutors urged that the insider trading prohibition applies not only to classical insiders (directors, officers) and temporary insiders (lawyers, accountants, business consultants, oh my!), but also to "quasi insiders." The latter were defined as the "cogs and auxiliaries" of the securities business, those who by virtue of their position or employment could be expected regularly to come into possession of material non-public information. A financial printer such as Vincent Chiarella had such access. The Supreme Court found the theory interesting, but with support neither in the statute nor the common law. Quoting a landmark SEC decision, *In re Cady, Roberts & Co.*, 40 S.E.C. 907 (1961), the *Chiarella* Court noted that insider trading requires more than mere access, it requires "a relationship giving access . . . to information intended to be available only for a corporate purpose." Those kinds of relationships, the Court noted, would be fiduciary or similar relationships of trust and confidence. Chiarella had no relationship to the persons who were selling while he was buying. He was, as to them, a "stranger" (Answer (D)). The Court reversed his conviction by a 5-4 vote. Chief Justice Burger was incensed. He filed a scathing dissent. He thought that Chiarella was no better than a common thief, who stole information despite warning signs posted by his employer. Justice Burger would have affirmed the conviction on the "misappropriation" theory of insider trading, but his colleagues on the Court who shared his views thought that the Court could not affirm on the theory because the jury had not been instructed on it. Thus were planted seeds that would come to fruition 18 years later when the Court would adopt the "misappropriation theory." But Chiarella went free. And the test of who was an insider was cut back from an "access test" to persons who have access "by virtue of a fiduciary or similar relationship."

Answers (A), (B), and (C) are not the best answers for the reasons stated above.

170.   **Answer (D) is the best answer.** The SEC's theory of the case would be Answer (A). The SEC would probably not succeed because Answer (D) is an effective defense. Therefore, **Answer (A) is incorrect.**

This question is based on *SEC v. Switzer*, 590 F. Supp. 756 (W.D. Okla. 1984), in which the SEC charged then-University of Oklahoma (and later Dallas Cowboys) head football coach Barry Switzer with insider trading. Coach Switzer won because his attorney read and applied the United States Supreme Court's opinion in *Dirks v. SEC*, 463 U.S. 646 (1983). In *Dirks*, the Court recognized tipping as an offense, but only when it is consistent with, and derivative of, an insider or temporary insider's breach of his fiduciary or similar duty of trust and confidence. In turn, the Court noted, the insider breaches his duty when:

(1) he receives a benefit or expects to receive a benefit, loosely defined, from communication of the information; and

(2) the insider knows, or in the exercise of some care, should know, that the communication of the information will likely result in trading or the tipping of others to trade.

The "benefit" may be increased influence or prestige with one with whom the insider wishes to curry favor, or reciprocity ("I'll give you a good tip, with the unspoken understanding that you will do the same for me when you have sensitive information."), or continued love and affection from a family member. Raymond Dirks, the defendant, a securities analyst, received material, non-public information about a massive fraud within Equity Funding, Inc. Because the tip came from a former executive who had been dismissed (not an insider source), and his motive was revenge (not receipt of a benefit), the SEC failed to obtain an injunction.

The Supreme Court circumscribed tippee-tipper liability carefully because one person's tip is another's diligent research. Securities analysts search far and wide for tidbits of information, which they piece together into a mosaic about a company or an industry. That process, which occurs thousands of times each day, promotes market efficiency. It is an activity we wish to encourage. An overly broad and ill-defined law of tippee-tipper trading would inhibit legitimate analyst activity and market research. The *Dirks* Court also eschewed broad equality of information as a policy goal for the law of insider trading. Some individuals (analysts, New York-based traders, etc.) often will have superior information about securities. The law of insider trading is not meant to level that playing field.

In the instant case, Local CEO reaped no benefit and violated no fiduciary duty in conversing with his spouse. He also did not knowingly communicate the information to Coach Olsen. The coach is merely a (very) fortuitous eavesdropper. Hence, **Answers (A) and (B) are incorrect.** Also, with regard to Answer (B), one can say that somewhere in a chain of ever increasingly remote tippees an argument may be made that the information no longer is non-public information. In the instant case, though, if tipping had occurred, that point of remoteness would not have been reached.

Answer (C) is also incorrect. The information is information about the market for the company shares rather than classic inside information about the company itself, its assets, and its earnings. The courts have seldom explored the differences, but it is clear that they regard market information involving a change of control (at XYZ here) as visiting upon the possessor of that information a duty to "abstain or disclose."

171. **Answer (D) is the best answer.** Horatio does not have a fiduciary or similar relationship of trust or confidence. He occupies no position at all. He was terminated months ago. Hence, **Answers (A) and (B) are incorrect.** If Horatio did occupy a position, as for example, when he still worked for the bank, any duty owed would have been to the leveraged buyout ("LBO") bidder who was buying shares, not to the shareholders of the LBO target who were selling at the same time Horatio and the Club were buying.

Answer (C) is incorrect. There was no tipping. You do not even have to apply the *Dirks* analysis to see that no factual basis exists for a tipper-tippee analysis. Horatio simply stole information, in violation of a legally cognizable duty. A former agent owes a duty to his formal principal not to misuse confidential information gained in the course of, or by virtue of, the agency. In the actual case, the court made the latter finding in order to be consistent with the *Chiarella* mandate that the person occupy a fiduciary or similar relationship of trust or confidence. Other federal courts, most notably the Fourth Circuit, in *United States* *v. Bryan*, 58 F.3d 933 (4th Cir. 1995), rejected the misappropriation theory as having no foundation in the securities statutes. Bryan was the director of the West Virginia lottery. He would purchase stocks based upon his knowledge that certain companies were to receive favorable state lottery contracts.

The U.S. Supreme Court finally gave its imprimatur to the so-called misappropriation theory in *United States v. O'Hagan*, 521 U.S. 642 (1997). O'Hagan was a partner at a major Minneapolis law firm retained by Grand Met, Ltd., a British conglomerate. Grand Met retained O'Hagan's firm because Grand Met was contemplating a bid for Pillsbury, the food products company headquartered in Minneapolis. O'Hagan had not even worked on the proposed transaction. He heard of it in the hallway. Nonetheless, he bought Pillsbury shares very heavily, making five million dollars in profit when he later sold the stock. Like Horatio in this Question, if O'Hagan owed a duty to anyone, it was to the buyer and, not the seller, of Pillsbury shares. In her opinion, though, Justice Ginsburg pointed out that Rule 10b-5 protects buyers and sellers of shares, not any particular or identifiable buyer or seller. "The misappropriation theory comports with § 10(b)'s language, which requires deception 'in connection with the purchase or sale of, any security,' not deception of an identifiable purchaser or seller." Justice Ginsburg also held that the duty that must have been violated need not have to run to the same person who bought or sold shares. The duty violated may have run off in one direction, in this case to the law firm for the prospective purchaser, and the damage or harm in another direction, in this case Pillsbury shareholders who sold contemporaneous with O'Hagan's purchases.

The misappropriation theory has been criticized heavily by legal scholars and securities lawyers, but it now seems firmly in place. So, in answer to the first question posed above, who is an insider or, more accurately, who has visited upon them the "disclose or abstain prohibition," your checklist should be as follows:

(1) Does the trader have a relationship of trust and confidence with buyers or sellers?

(2) Did the trader have a temporary position of trust?

(3) Was the defendant a tipper or a tippee who traded?

(4) Did the defendant steal the non-public information in violation of a duty of trust or confidence running to someone (not necessarily the contemporaneous traders who were harmed by the defendant's trading or tipping)?

That is the somewhat murky and confusing state of the law governing insider trading in the United States.

This Question is based on *SEC v. Cherif*, 933 F.2d 403 (7th Cir. 1991).

172. The traditional answer was "yes," based on *Northwest Transportation Co. v. Beatty*, 12 App. Cas. 589 (P.C. 1887), and its progeny. Directors' duty of loyalty requires that, at every juncture, they serve "the best interests of the corporation," rather than their own or their associates' interests. By contrast, shareholders have no fiduciary duties. Individuals own shares precisely to pursue their selfish economic interests. Traditionally, the law has not required any form of selfless behavior from shareholders. The controlling shareholder stands in a slightly different position. Applying a political analogy to the corporation, "majority rules," but does not rule absolutely. One principal function of constitutional law has been to place limits on majority rule. For example, if a majority approved a statute that would require red-haired, freckled persons to be incarcerated (albeit in a minimum security facility), courts would strike down that statute as a denial of equal protection of the laws. Similarly, corporate law, including the law of fiduciary duty, places limits on majority shareholdings, whether in the form of individual ownership, or a group acting in concert. One traditional statement of the corporate law limit on majority rule was that in pursuing its own selfish interest the majority could not "go so far as to work a fraud, or an illegality, or waste corporate assets." In Dan's case, he has fully disclosed all he knows about the proposed transaction, so there is no fraud. Illegality (violating the antitrust or environmental laws, for example) does not seem to be in the picture. And a gifting or wasting of corporate assets does not seem in the offing. Dan is willing to abide by a reputable appraiser's opinion as to the value of the three ships. Waste has been defined as a transaction in which no reasonable person would agree that the corporation received the equivalent of what it gave up. Under the traditional view of the responsibilities of a controlling shareholder, Dan may vote his 61 percent in favor of the transaction.

173. **Answer (D) is the best answer.** As long as one minority shareholder remains, directors of a corporation have to put the best interests of the corporation ahead of the wishes of the majority shareholder. Here, they have not done so. They could be held liable for the amount of the damage caused by, or the illicit gain to, Kramer and CS. In turn, the directors, though, might make a cross claim against Kramer and CE (if he has been named as a defendant in the original suit), or a third-party claim (if he has not been named in the original suit). Therefore, **Answer (A) is incorrect.**

Today the primary thrust of minority shareholder complaints has come to be a direct claim against the majority shareholder (Answer (B)). The suit either does not even name the "puppet directors," or the suit against them becomes a mere sideshow. It is important to remember, however, that the directors who do the majority shareholders' bidding, unmindful of their fiduciary duties, do remain liable for their conduct (Answer (C)). Mr. Costanza should sue both the majority shareholders and the directors (Answer (D)).

As to the substance of the claims, the "indirect overhead" and "consulting and feasibility studies" may well constitute a waste of corporate assets. Under the traditional view, a majority shareholder may not pursue his majority power so far as to waste corporate assets. In the modern era, however, two things have happened. One is that courts have come to denominate the majority or controlling shareholder's (many corporations may be controlled with a substantial, but less than numerical majority, holding) duties as "fiduciary." Two is that courts have attempted to adumbrate with more particularity the limits on use by the controlling shareholder of her power.

It is important to note that, although denominated by courts as "fiduciary," the controlling shareholder's duty is not the same as a corporate director. There remains room for the shareholder to pursue selfish interests. The limits on majority or controlling shareholder power remain described as "fraud, illegality, or waste of corporate assets." The limit has been further described in terms that the majority shareholder "may not go so far as to reap a benefit to the detriment or exclusion of the minority shareholders." Two leading cases circa 1970 are *Jones v. H.F. Ahmanson & Co.*, 460 P.2d 464 (Cal. 1969) (exclusion of minority shares from holding company that would make majority shares much more liquid and, therefore, valuable), and *Sinclair Oil Corp. v. Levien*, 280 A.2d 717 (Del. 1971) (discussed in the answer to Question 174). Both articulated such a limit on majority power. Kramer and CS are certainly doing that (reaping a benefit to the detriment and exclusion of the minority) through excessive charges to CS (overhead, consulting, etc.). The extraordinary dividends may be a different matter. CS pays the dividend to all shares, including those of the minority (unless Kramer and the CS board are stupid enough to attempt a differential distribution). With respect to the dividend, the majority may well have not reaped a benefit to the detriment or exclusion of the minority.

Answers (B) and (C) are not the best answers for the reasons stated above.

174.   **Answer (A) is the best answer.** This Question is based on the facts of *Sinclair Oil Corp. v. Levien*, 280 A.2d 717 (Del. 1971), a case involving Sinclair Oil and its Venezuelan subsidiary, Sinven. The case also included a claim that the parent had caused the subsidiary to pay excessive dividends. That aspect is dealt with in the answer to Question 158. The court held that when a parent controls a subsidiary, with the parent controlling transactions and fixing the terms of its dealings with the subsidiary, the test of "intrinsic fairness" rather than the business judgment rule applies. Therefore, **Answer (C) is incorrect.** Under the test of "intrinsic fairness," the burden shifts to the parent corporation to prove that it met the applicable legal standard.

What is that legal standard? The parent may not self-deal. "Self-dealing occurs when the parent, by virtue of its domination of the subsidiary, causes the subsidiary to act in such a way that the parent receives something from the subsidiary to the exclusion of, and detriment to, minority stockholders of the subsidiary." Manipulating the contract with the Costa Rican subsidiary by failing to take up its output and by late payments fits that definition and therefore is a breach by the controlling shareholder of its fiduciary duty (Answer (A)). Hence, **Answer (D) is incorrect.**

As an aside, the excessive dividends were not self-dealing because the minority had not been excluded. They received the dividends, too.

The business opportunities were opportunities of the parent rather than the subsidiary. There was no self-dealing. "Therefore, business judgment is the proper standard by which to evaluate [the parent's] expansion policies." Therefore, **Answer (B) is incorrect.**

In corporate groups, these cases arise with some frequency. The parent corporation allocates beneficial contracts, tax benefits, and opportunities to the subsidiaries in which has the greater ownership interests and allocates burdensome contracts, tax detriments, and so on to the subsidiaries with the greatest minority ownership. You should note, however, that the same standard applies to a controlling shareholder, whether it is another corporation (a parent) or a flesh-and-blood human being.

How well does this legal standard resolve the tension between the rights of majority ownership to pursue its selfish economic interests and the protection of minority shareholdings, in part to encourage investment? That tension runs thorough many of the cases and real world situations. In the parent-subsidiary context, many parent corporations "squeeze out" the minority owners simply because the parent does not wish to have to deal with resolving those conflicts between its own and minority shareholders' interests. With a "wholly owned" subsidiary, the parent corporation has far fewer worries.

175. **Answer (B) is the best answer.** This Question raises the classic closely-held corporation problems of illiquidity and exploitation. In a small corporation with four or five participants, absent some unique corporate asset such as a patent or software, chances are that no market exists for shares. The minority owner, thus, is extremely vulnerable. With no opportunity to exit by way of sale (no liquidity), and the standard corporate law "majority rules" model, those in control may exploit her situation. *See generally* Michael P. Dooley & J.A.C. Hetherington, *Illiquidity and Exploitation: A Proposed Statutory Solution to the Remaining Close Corporation Problem*, 63 Va. L. Rev. 1 (1977).

Why should the law bother with such situations? One reason is that, in a typical closely-held corporation, the minority owner's interest may represent a significant amount of her net worth. Her stake may also be significant in absolute as well as relative terms. The traditional legal choices open to her were, by and large, unsatisfactory. She could sue to obtain an order that dividends be paid with respect to the stock. That would help some. Courts, however, exhibit great reluctance in invading the central province of boards of directors, their control over dividends. Courts have ordered dividends in very few cases usually involving a showing of protracted (10, 12, or 15 years) "bad faith." *See, e.g., Gay v. Gay's Super Markets, Inc.*, 343 A.2d 577 (Me. 1975); *Gottfried v. Gottfried*, 73 N.Y.S.2d 692 (Sup. Ct. 1947).

Ms. O'Brien may bring a traditional derivative suit. All such a suit would do is cause those in control or their associates to repay excessive salary, perks, or payments to the corporation. Ms. O'Brien would be in same position as she had been and everyone would be angry with her. Thus, **Answer (A) is not the best answer.**

A suit to involuntarily dissolve the corporation is a possibility, but it might be overkill. Therefore, **Answer (C) is not the best answer.** Besides, that subject is dealt with in Question 176.

Today, she can invoke the so-called "*Donahue* principle." In *Donahue v. Rodd Electrotype Co. of New England*, 328 N.E.2d 505 (Mass. 1975), the court held that participants in a closely-held corporation owe duties one to another, akin to partners in a partnership. The Massachusetts judges did so based upon their recognition of the special situation ("illiquidity and exploitation") closely-held corporations often present. The remedial implication is that in a closely-held corporation a shareholder may obtain "me, too" relief. She may obtain money damages equivalent to the excessive benefits the majority has taken for itself, or a share buyback, as here.

A later Massachusetts decision, *Wilkes v. Springside Nursing Home, Inc.*, 353 N.E.2d 657 (Mass. 1976), speaks to the other side of the coin, the right the majority has to "selfish ownership" due them by virtue of owning a majority of the shares (Answer (D)). "We," the court stated, "are concerned that untempered application of the strict good faith standard enunciated in *Donahue* to cases such as the one before us will result in the imposition of limitations on legitimate action by the controlling group in a close corporation."

Over 20 states have authoritative court opinions adopting the *Donahue* principle, often citing to the Massachusetts opinion and several other Massachusetts cases which elaborate on the basic principle. It has been one of the most important developments in corporate law over the last 30 years, at least from the standpoint of Main Street, as opposed to Wall Street. Thus, **Answer (D) is not the best answer.**

176.   **Answer (D) is the best answer. The next best answer may be Answer (A).** Anyway, this is a Question about which an entire law review article could be written, and many have.

First, the other alternatives can be discussed. Again, Answer (B), the traditional remedy, would do David little good. The recovery, if any, would go to the corporate treasury. David could also leave himself wide open to further retribution. Hence, **Answer (B) is not the best answer.** Second, Answer (C) is definitely an alternative, but some of Rick's perks and salary are justified from a business standpoint. David can make no legitimate claim to completely equal treatment. Therefore, **Answer (C) is not the best answer.** Besides, the *Donahue* principle and its remedial implications were the subject of the answer to Question 160.

The most extreme form of lawsuit David could bring would be a suit for "involuntary dissolution" of the corporation (as opposed to voluntary dissolution which is an orderly winding up voted on by the shareholders). In pertinent part, MBCA § 14.30 empowers a court to dissolve a corporation, *inter alia*:

(2) in a proceeding by a shareholder if it is established that:

(i) the directors are deadlocked in the management of corporate affairs, the shareholders are unable to break the deadlock, and irreparable injury to the corporation is threatened or being suffered, or the business and affairs of the corporation can no longer be conducted to the advantage of the shareholders generally, because of the deadlock;

(ii) the directors or those in control of the corporation have acted, are acting, or will act in a manner that is illegal, oppressive or fraudulent;

(iii) the shareholders are deadlocked in voting power and have failed, for a period that includes at least two consecutive annual meeting dates, to elect successors to directors whose terms have expired; or

(iv) the corporate assets are being misapplied or wasted.

This and similar provisions in particular states' laws have a long and twisted history. Courts were extremely reluctant to grant relief, reading the grounds as jurisdictional only and the grant of relief as discretionary. Reviewing those cases, early law review commentary referred to the "Sacred Cow of Corporate Existence." For example, in the deadlock cases ((i) and (iii)), the parties (either directors or shareholders) could be threatening axe murder of one by the other and courts would still not grant relief, on grounds that business was still being carried on successfully or that the public interest was involved. Of course, the continued existence of most small businesses, or not, affects the public interest not one iota.

Courts, however, were also canny. Distinguish cessation of the legal life of an entity (involuntary dissolution of the corporation) from cessation of the economic life. The latter does not follow from the former. An economically viable business will continue in some form even if a court has ordered the corporation dissolved. Often dissolution proceedings have been counterintuitive. The stronger, and not the weaker, oppressed party, seeks dissolution, knowing that they will continue the business after dissolution owning all of it rather than merely half. Seeing through the appearances, courts have divined what is going on and refused the remedy, thereby protecting the weaker party. *See, e.g., In re Radom & Neidorff, Inc.*, 119 N.E.2d 563 (N.Y. 1954) (brother sought dissolution of successful musical publishing business which he could carry on alone, without his sister, who had plagued him with petty complaints after her husband, the other half of the successful business, had died; dissolution denied).

The two biggest breakthroughs have been courts' (1) more expansive reading of "oppressive" (in case (iii) above), and (2) willingness to consider and grant lesser included remedies, such as accounting, appointment of a provisional director or a receiver, or ordering one party to buy out the other. As to the latter, empirical research by Professors Dooley and Hetherington demonstrates that, in cases in which the remedy is seriously sought, or is granted, the resolution almost always is that one party buys out the other, either in settlement or after the remedy has been granted. *See* Michael P. Dooley & J.A.C. Hetherington, *Illiquidity and Exploitation: A Proposed Statutory Solution to the Remaining Close Corporation Problem*, 63 Va. L. Rev. 1 (1977). This reason is, again, because cessation of the legal life does not entail cessation of the economic life of the enterprise. Instead, the well pled case or the court order gives the party holding it a good lever with which to obtain a decently priced buyout of their interest. Indeed, many statutes now expressly grant courts power to order buyouts.

Now, what exactly is oppression? Older decisions draw on English cases that defined it as "highly unfair and prejudicial conduct," or "burdensome, harsh and wrongful conduct . . . a lack of probity and fair dealing" by those in control of the corporation. *See, e.g., Davis v. Sheerin*, 754 S.W.2d 375 (Tex. App. 1988); *Baker v. Commercial Body Builders, Inc.*, 507 P.2d 387 (Or. 1973). It would exclude excessive salaries, bonuses and other perks by those in control, denial of due process and participation, or meaningful participation, in governance, and so on. A further difficulty was that a plaintiff needed to prove a long and continued course of such conduct. Beginning in the early 1980s, and again, based upon the English cases, the North Carolina Supreme Court made a breakthrough. It held that in closely-held corporations (the involuntary remedy is seldom sought, and never granted, in cases other than those involving smaller, closely-held corporations) oppression was the denial to a minority or other participant of their "reasonable expectations" of the corporation: employment, health care and other fringe benefits, a company car, the same perquisites other owners receive, a meaningful role in governance if they wish to have one, and so on. The focus is more on what the plaintiff has not received, rather than on what those in control do receive, and the test does not require a plaintiff to prove up such a protracted history of misery and woe. *See Meiselman v. Meiselman*, 307 S.E.2d 551 (N.C. 1983); *see also In re Kemp & Beatley, Inc.*, 473 N.E.2d 1173 (N.Y. 1984); *Brenner v. Berkowitz*, 634 A.2d 1019 (N.J. 1993).

About 20 states have authoritative decisional law adopting the "denial of reasonable expectations" test of what constitutes oppression. A few courts have noted that the expectations must be those one would logically expect a close corporation participant to have, or those clearly communicated to those in control. A shareholder may not harbor a secret, or less obvious, expectation of ownership rights and then claim that she is oppressed based upon denial of that expectation.

This Question is based, loosely, on *Meiselman v. Meiselman*, 307 S.E.2d 551 (N.C. 1983).

David would have a good case to plead. A likely outcome might be a settlement in which Rick contracts to provide David with the perks and employment conditions to which he is entitled, or buys out, perhaps by installment payments, older brother David's interest in the company.

One last note on (iv) ("assets being misapplied or wasted"): There are not many cases, but those that exist require a repeated course of conduct over several years' time. Again, the remedy for one or two acts of misapplication or waste is a suit for breach of fiduciary or some similar duty, and a payment back to the corporation. It is not the extreme remedy of involuntary dissolution.

NOTE: SPECIAL STATUTORY RECOGNITION OF THE CLOSELY-HELD CORPORATION

Aside from the special remedial provisions many states have adopted, in the 1960s and 1970s, about 15 state legislatures adopted special closely-held corporation chapters for insertion in their business corporation acts. Most were non-integrated, stand-alone chapters, but California and a few other states adopted a package of provisions that were codified in scattered sections of their state corporation codes. A few of these chapters require a special designation (*e.g.*, "Arizona Close Corporation"). Most require that original articles, or a subsequent amendment unanimously adopted, "elect" treatment under the "Close Corporation Chapter." These chapters' provisions overrule older decisions holding invalid shareholder agreements that, for example, guaranteed employment to shareholders, divided responsibilities (sales, front office, shop, etc.) among participants, provided for minimum annual distributions, individual shareholder veto power over some or all decisions, unanimous quorum and voting, and elimination of a board of directors altogether ("The business and affairs of the corporation shall be managed by, or under the direction of, the shareholders."). Older court decisions held that some, or all, of those provisions violated the statutory mandate that "the business and affairs of the corporation shall be managed by a board of directors." Another judicial phrasing was that such provisions constituted "an attempt to operate a corporation as if it were a partnership" and, hence, were invalid.

Owners (shareholders) in closely-held corporation chafe under these sorts of rulings. They need guarantee of long-term employment. They wish to act informally, on a consensual (usually unanimous) basis. They want a flat (one-layer) management structure rather than the three-level (directors, officers, employees) structure traditional corporate norms mandated. They feel that corporate formalities (directors' meetings, notices, and so on) amount to foolish play acting or, worse, a ploy by their attorney to generate additional legal fees.

In *Galler v. Galler*, 203 N.E.2d 577 (Ill. 1964), the Illinois Supreme Court discussed and recognized the concerns of participants in closely-held corporations. It upheld a comprehensive shareholders' agreement in a closely-held, profitable wholesale drug concern. A handful of state legislatures then adopted the first wave of special close corporation statutes. For example, the Delaware enactment, DEL. GEN. CORP. L. §§ 341–356, validates agreements that sterilize or handcuff the board of directors (§ 351) and also agreements that eliminate altogether governance by a board (§ 354). The development (evolution of special close corporation chapters) was overtaken and then arrested by the increased flexibility in the general corporation laws themselves. In a seminal piece, Professor Dennis Karajala pointed out that such special chapters were no longer necessary under statutes such as the Revised Model Business Corporation Act. Such modern statutes contain more than enough flexibility to accommodate the special need of the close corporation. Dennis Karajala, *A Second Look at Special Close Corporation Legislation*, 58 TEX. L. REV. (1980); Dennis Karajala, *An Analysis of Close Corporation Legislation in the United States*, 21 ARIZ. ST. L.J. 663 (1989). No one has seriously considered such a special chapter for a good many years now, but the 15 or so that exist remain on the books. Nonetheless, the MBCA drafters later added a special section (not an entire chapter). Section 7.32 provides that shareholder agreements shall be "effective among the shareholders of the corporation even though it is inconsistent with one or more other provisions of this act." Such an agreement may vary from the statutory model in, by way of example and not of limitation, the following respects:

(1) elimination or restriction of the discretion or power of the board of directors;

(2) governance of the making of distributions provided the corporation remains solvent;

(3) establishment of who the directors or officers will be;

(4) governance of voting power, in general or as to specific matters, including provisions for weighted voting or proxy voting by directors (not usually permitted);

(5) governance of use by owners of corporate property or provision of services to the corporation by shareholders;

(6) transfers to one or more persons of a veto power or the power to resolve deadlocks among owners; or

(7) requires dissolution of the corporation upon the occurrence of specified events or contingencies.

The MBCA provision requires that such agreements be limited to 10 years' duration, but the agreement may be amended or reaffirmed by all of the persons who are shareholders at the time, unless the agreement provides otherwise. Thus if, during the period of the agreement, grandmother shareholder gives or bequeaths her shares to her grandson, the grandson's assent must be obtained before the 10th anniversary for the agreement to continue.

In *Zion v. Kurtz*, 405 N.E.2d 681 (N.Y. 1980), the parties had agreed to give the minority shareholder in a Delaware corporation an absolute veto power over the "business and activities" of the corporation, in complete disregard of the corporate law norm of majority rule. The New York court upheld the provision, applying the Delaware close corporation chapter. The only difficulty was that the parties had never formally elected to be treated as a Delaware close corporation. Not to worry, the New York court held that in the shareholders' agreement Kurtz (the defendant) had agreed to do all acts "as may reasonably be required . . . to evidence and give effect to the intent and purposes of this Agreement." The court treated the close corporation election as if it had already been made. By contrast, the Delaware Supreme Court pointedly refused to apply any special rules to a small corporation that had not formally elected treatment under the Delaware close corporation statute. *See Nixon v. Blackwell*, 626 A.2d 1366 (Del. 1993) ("It would be . . . inappropriate judicial legislation for this Court to fashion a special judicially-created rule for minority investors.").

Special treatment of closely-held corporations is important but, given the great flexibility introduced by modern statutes generally, the subject is less important than it was in the 1960s or 1970s.

177.   **Answer (C) is the correct answer.** Changes to the MBCA have modified the time-tested remedy of involuntary dissolution in two ways. First, the modified section makes clear that a court may order dissolution "in a proceeding by a shareholder *of a corporation that is not a public corporation.*" Of course, everybody knew that, but better safe than sorry. The MBCA drafters also include a definition of "public corporation" elsewhere in the Act (listed or quoted NYSE, AMEX, NASDAQ, or other system owned or operated by the NASD).

If not so quoted or listed, a company is still not subject to the involuntary dissolution provision if its shares "are held by at least 300 shareholders and the shares outstanding have a market value of at least $20 million (exclusive of the value of such shares held by the corporation's subsidiaries, senior executives, directors, and beneficial owners holding more than 10 percent of such shares). MBCA § 14.30(b), promulgated 61 BUS. LAW. 1183 (2006).

To the classic, four jurisdiction grounds (director deadlock, oppression, shareholder deadlock, waste or misappropriation of assets) for dissolution, MBCA § 14.30(a)(2)(i)–(iv), the drafters have added a fifth ground, but as a separate subsection (a)(5), as in MBCA § 14.30(a)(5): "in a proceeding by a shareholder if the corporation has abandoned its business and has failed within a reasonable time to liquidate and distribute its assets and dissolve."

The new subsection is drafting overkill. The remedy is equitable (decree to dissolve) and it would be inequitable for a court even to entertain a petition of dissolution of a corporation with more than a handful of shareholders because of the likely presence of innocent shareholders.

Abandonment of the business and ensuing failure to dissolve, or a foot-dragging dissolution, is thought to be necessary as a ground for involuntary dissolution because of "the situation [which] might result from negligence or from the desire of those in control to continue enjoying salaries or other prerequisites of office from the corporation, even though it is no longer engaged in productive operations." "In any event," the Official Comment continues, "continued delay in winding up the business and dissolving will prejudice the rights of creditors and shareholders." 60 BUS. LAW. 1627 (2005). Not to say homeowners, as here.

Answer (A) is incorrect. There is no such thing as a de facto non-corporation. In fact, MBCA § 14.05(a) provides that "[a] dissolved corporation continues its corporate existence but may not carry on any business except that appropriate to wind up and liquidate its affairs."

Answer (B) is incorrect. It may not be economical to truck the hay to a market where it may be sold.

Answer (D) is almost always incorrect. Almost always there is a solution to attempt (negotiation, agreeing to arbitrate, etc.) that should be tried before filing a lawsuit.

178.   **Answer (A) is the best answer;** or, at least that is what the Pennsylvania Supreme Court held in *Seven Springs Farm, Inc. v. Croker*, 801 A.2d 1212 (Pa. 2002). **Other courts might go with Answer (B), making it the second-best answer.**

There are two schools of judicial thought with regard to share transfer restrictions. One school is that they tend to be restraints on alienation and, therefore, should be strictly construed. Thus, each and every triggering event must be spelled out in the agreement (sale to a third party, sale to a fellow shareholder, merger, disability, cessation of employment, death, gift, and so on). Courts have held that sale means sale to a third party and does not include a sale to a fellow shareholder. Along the same lines, the Pennsylvania court held that a merger is a different thing than a sale (Answer (A)). The other school holds that share transfer restrictions are ubiquitous in business life. Every closely-held corporation will have a buy-sell agreement precisely to keep participation "close." Shareholders wish to have control over who their "partners" will be in these "incorporated partnerships." *See, e.g., Concord Auto Auction, Inc. v. Rustin*, 627 F. Supp. 1526 (D. Mass. 1986) (upholding buyout of deceased owner's shares at half, or less, of fair value, noting that "specific performance of an agreement to convey will not be refused merely because the price is inadequate"). A court which followed this school might, for example, look to federal securities law, which has held for a number of years now that a merger is a sale and does not occur by some sort of metaphysical process ("operation of the law") (Answer (B)).

No matter which school is involved, however, an agreement that appears intended more to keep shareholders "in," as opposed to one geared to control the terms under which they might get "out," may be narrowly construed or struck down as a restraint on alienation (Answer (C)). Agreements which contain overly burdensome procedures (option first to fellow shareholders, followed by option to the corporation, followed by second option for other shareholders to purchase what corporation has not taken up, etc.), exceptionally low prices that might chill any thought of sale, or lack of notice of the agreement may all contain grounds for attack on the share transfer restriction. There is no evidence of that here so **Answer (C) is not the best answer.**

Many agreements use an option rather than right of first refusal. Thus the price at which other shareholder, or the corporation, may acquire shares is determined in accordance with a formula contained in the agreement: book value, appraised value, as the parties from time to time may agree, and so on. If the formula produces a price that is significantly less than probable market or fair value, courts used to hold the agreement tantamount to a restraint on alienation. The trend, however, has been to uphold the price formula and its result, no matter how large the disparity with probable market value.

Lawyers with significant involvement in business practice evolve very complex model buy-sell agreements. The agreements may have a number of triggering events, different obligations depending upon the triggering event (*e.g.*, mandatory in the case of death or disability, voluntary in case of a proposed sale, right of first refusal if a sale, but a price formula in case of other events), and different payment terms (lump sum or installments). Agreements may run 10 to 15 pages. One common feature is for the corporation to purchase life insurance on the lives of the shareholders to fund the purchase of shares from the deceased shareholder's estate.

After articles of incorporation and bylaws, the buy-sell agreement is the most frequently encountered type of agreement in business law practice. Indeed, some attorneys incorporate share transfer restrictions in articles or bylaws rather than in a separate agreement. For that reason, MBCA § 6.27 validates such agreements ("A restriction on the transfer or registration of transfer of shares is valid and enforceable against the holder or a transferee of the holder if the restriction . . . [is] noted conspicuously on the front or back of the certificate."). The MBCA section gives a number of examples of the uses to which such agreements may be put and the features that might be incorporated in such an agreement.

Answer (D) is incorrect. There is no evidence of failures to disclose, or disclosure in a misleading way, let alone evidence of intentional misrepresentation.

179.   **Answer (D) is the correct answer.** MBCA § 7.32 legitimizes comprehensive agreements even though their provisions may contravene provisions of the Act. The section itself lists eight other sections that such an agreement could contravene. The agreement must be in articles or bylaws, limited to 10 years' duration, and a legend must be placed on the margins of the stock certificates. A 2007 amendment added a new subsection 7.32(d), providing that "an argument authorized by this section shall cease to be effective when the corporation becomes a public corporation [defined by MBCA § 1.40(18A)]." Furthermore, the new subsection gives the board of directors power to delete the agreement and references to it, without a shareholder vote. Usually, a corporation will long since have rescinded such an agreement before the stage at which a public offering may be forthcoming.

Answers (A) and (B) are incorrect. But these were the responses of courts which, until at least the 1930s and sometimes later, struck down agreements which might restrict future boards. It became necessary for courts to modify their stance when it became apparent, for example, that a contract guaranteeing long-term employment may well be necessary to obtain investments or employees for the corporation. *See, e.g., Clark v. Dodge*, 199 N.E. 641 (N.Y. 1936) (upholding contract for long-term employment when all owners of the corporation had signed it). *Cf. McQuade v. Stoneham & McGraw*, 189 N.E. 234 (N.Y. 1934) (striking down long-term contract for employment as treasurer of the corporation because it would tie the hands of future boards of directors).

Answer (C) is accurate but incomplete. A large breakthrough came with *Galler v. Galler*, 203 N.E.2d 577 (1964), *supra*, when the Supreme Court of Illinois upheld an agreement which would restrict future boards not on this or that but over a whole range of issues (minimum annual dividends, who should be directors and officers, restrictions on loans, etc.). Such agreements may still go too far, as the dead hand and no hand poison pill cases show, *see Quickturn Design Systems v. Shapiro*, 721 A.2d 1281 (Del. 1998), but much more latitude is permitted today. The principal objection to such agreements is one of cost — they are expensive to draft and to put into place.

180. **Answer (B) is the best answer.**

Answer (C) is incorrect. *New York Dock Co. v. McCollum*, 16 N.Y.S.2d 844 (Sup. Ct. 1939), held that, because directors are not agents, they are not entitled to indemnification for litigation costs and amounts paid in settlement or judgment even if they acted in a good faith belief that the actions taken were in the corporation's best interests. By contrast, at common law, agents and employees are entitled to broad indemnification, even absent contract. To provide possible indemnification for directors, legislatures have passed statutes.

Corporate law indemnification statutes, however, for the most part are permissive or enabling. They have to be implemented in a particular corporation by provisions in the articles of incorporation or bylaws. The only exception is a common statutory provision for mandatory indemnification in the case in which the director had been "wholly successful" on the merits (Answer (A)). Few court outcomes are so clear, as the facts of the Question seek to demonstrate. Later statutes make mandatory indemnification of a director who has been "wholly successful, on the merits or otherwise" (Answer (B)). Thus, a director like Sam who successfully pleads a procedural defense is entitled to indemnity for some of his legal costs. MBCA § 8.52 provides: "A corporation shall indemnify a director who was wholly successful, on the merits or otherwise, in the defense of any proceeding to which he was a party because he was a director of the corporation against reasonable expenses incurred by him in connection with the proceeding." If a director holds a position (trustee of the corporate pension plan, for instance) by virtue of being a director, she is entitled to indemnification for defense costs incurred in that role as well. Thus, **Answer (A) is incorrect.**

Many corporations do implement the authority granted by the statutes. Some attorneys place in the articles or bylaws a provision such as, "The Corporation shall indemnify its directors to the fullest extent permitted by Massachusetts law." To answer this question in the real world, we would have to examine Cheers, Ltd.'s articles and bylaws to see if they contained provision for indemnification.

The other important point to note is that, even if the corporation had provision for indemnification when Sam originally became a director, articles or bylaws may be amended, particularly after a change in control of the corporation. Many directors therefore insist on a contract granting them the rights to indemnification, or greater rights, in effect at the time they began their board service.

Answer (D) is incorrect. There is nothing in the fact pattern regarding insurance. Moreover, the existence of insurance *vel non* has nothing to do with the duty to indemnify.

This Question is based on *Merritt-Chapman & Scott Corp. v. Wolfson*, 321 A.2d 138 (Del. 1974).

181. **Answer (D) is the best answer.** Many corporations go beyond a simple "indemnification to the fullest extent provided by law" (Answer (A)). They enact comprehensive provisions

providing for indemnification decisions to be made by a committee of the board or by independent legal counsel. *See, e.g.,* MBCA § 8.55. They make mandatory advance of expenses to directors who have been sued. Directors, usually through their attorney, insist that the corporation bind itself contractually to the individual director for these protections (advance expenses, purchase insurance, indemnity rights). A director may fall out of favor, or a change of control in the corporation may occur. Those newly in control may attempt to amend or rescind a bylaw or a provision in the charter or articles of incorporation. In 2011, the MBCA drafters added a provision to grandfather in whatever rights a director might have had at the time an act or omission is alleged to have occurred: "A right to indemnification or advances . . . in effect the time of the act or omission shall not be eliminated or impaired with respect to such act or omission by an amendment of the articles or bylaws or resolution of the directors." MBCA § 8.58. The provision reverses the outcome in *Schoon v. Troy Corp.,* 948 A.2d 1157 (Del Ch. 2008), in which Vice Chancellor Lamb held that a bylaw amendment could cut off rights to advances for a former director because the director had not yet been named a defendant at the time of the cut-off amendment. New DEL. GEN. CORP. L. § 145(f) is quite similar, providing that a subsequent amendment to the bylaw or charter providing for advancement of expenses or indemnification can be impaired by amendment that occurs after the act or omission that is the subject of a suit against the director.

By the way, what is the fullest extent provided by law? Under MBCA § 8.51(a),

> a corporation may indemnify an individual who is a party to a proceeding because he is a director against liability incurred in the proceeding if:
>
> (1)(i) he conducted himself in good faith; and
>
> (ii) he reasonably believed:
>
> (A) in the case of conduct in his official capacity, that his conduct was in the best interests of the corporation; and
>
> (B) in all other cases, that his conduct was at least not opposed to the best interests of the corporation; and
>
> (iii) in the case of a criminal proceeding, he had no reasonable grounds to believe his conduct was unlawful.

What if a corporation wishes to go beyond these limits, say, indemnifying a director who had reason to believe his conduct violated a criminal law, but who has repented and reformed? The Model Act is a so-called "exclusive" statute. MBCA § 8.59 provides: "A corporation may provide indemnification or advance expenses to a director or an officer only as permitted in this subchapter." MBCA § 8.54(a)(3) allows a court to provide indemnification even though the statutory limits have been exceeded if it "determines, in view of all the relevant circumstances, that it is fair and reasonable."

Delaware and a few other states have "non-exclusive" statutes. The corporation may provide for indemnification broader than that permitted by the statutes. But the indemnification provided must be "consistent with" the types of indemnification expressly permitted and not violate public policy. Thus, for example, a Delaware corporation could not utilize the statute's non-exclusivity to provide for indemnification of directors and officers who have knowingly caused the corporation to violate environmental protection statutes.

Insurance is available (Answer (B)), but the coverage available and the premium rates vary over time and almost disappeared in the mid-1980s. Even under the Model Act, insurance may be broader than statutory rights to indemnification. Thus, in theory, insurance is not only a funding source, but also a "gap filler." In practice, the opposite is true. The coverage usually available is narrower than what the statutes permit. There are deductibles or co-insurance clauses and the coverage exclusions (securities law claims, takeover activity, environmental claims, insured (director) versus insured (company)) are numerous. Smaller companies may not be able to obtain insurance at any price.

An early authoritative work is E. Norman Veasey, Jesse Finkelstein & C. Stephen Bigler, *Delaware Supports Directors with a Three-Legged Stool of Limited Liability, Indemnification, and Insurance*, 42 BUS. LAW. 399 (1987).

The fourth leg of the stool, by and large dating from the late 1980s, exculpation provisions in articles of incorporation (Answer (C)), are discussed in Question 125, which leaves for discussion only one more major subtopic, advances for expenses.

There are fewer feelings more discomforting than those experienced upon being served with a complaint and a summons in a lawsuit. For a corporate director, the first thought may be about obtaining competent legal counsel. The second thought may be about how to pay counsel's retainer and subsequent bills. Often, the corporate attorney will file an initial appearance on behalf of directors who are sued but, at the first sign that the corporation's and the directors' interests are diverging, corporate counsel must withdraw from representation of the directors. A corporation may advance expenses to a director or an officer involved in a legal proceeding. MBCA § 8.53(a)(1) & (2) provides that the director who seeks such an advance must provide two documents. One is a "written affirmation of his good faith belief that he has met the [best interests of the corporation, etc.] standard of conduct." Two is "his written undertaking to repay any funds advanced if . . . it is ultimately determined . . . that he has not met the relevant standard of conduct."

The director neither has to provide security for his undertaking to repay nor demonstrate his credit worthiness. Either the board or a committee of two or more disinterested directors may then authorize the advance. Again, though, at the commencement of board service, many directors obtain contractual rights to advances (provided that they deliver the written affirmation and the undertaking to repay) because a bylaw or article of incorporation may be amended or deleted altogether (Answer (D)). That, then, is the four-legged plus stool of director protection: indemnification, insurance, contract, exculpation, and provision for advances of expenses.

Answers (A), (B), and (C) are not the best answers for the reasons stated above.

182. **Answer (A) is the best answer.** The Model Act does provide that as to certain documents and records a shareholder has an absolute right of access. *See* MBCA § 16.02(a) (right of access to records listed in MBCA § 16.01(e), including articles of incorporation, bylaws, minutes of shareholders' meetings or other actions, all written communications to shareholders within the past three years, financial statements, a list of directors and officers and their addresses, and the most recent annual report filed with the secretary of state). The shareholder list is not one of them — although MBCA § 7.20(b) does provide that at a shareholders' meeting the shareholders' list must be available for inspection. So, **Answer (D) is incorrect.**

The shareholders' list is among a second group of documents to which the MBCA says a shareholder *may* have access, but only after showing "good faith and proper purpose." MBCA § 16.02(c) (which purpose she must "describe with reasonable particularity"). Victoria must therefore allege, and be prepared to prove, that her purpose is a proper one (Answer (B)). Generally, though, courts have held a wide variety of purposes to be proper purposes: conduct of a feasibility study for a proxy fight or takeover bid, valuation of one's shares, investigation of possible wrongdoing or, as here, to inform fellow shareholders of the pendency of litigation. In fact, *Compaq Computer Corp. v. Horton*, 631 A.2d 1 (Del. 1993), is precisely such a case. The court articulated a long list of examples of what proper purposes might be. Hence, **Answer (B) is incorrect.**

In *State ex rel. Pillsbury v. Honeywell, Inc.*, 191 N.W.2d 406 (Minn. 1971), an heir to the Pillsbury baking fortune was an anti-Vietnam war activist and also a shareholder of Honeywell. Honeywell manufactured fuses for bombs that would be utilized in conduct of the war. The Minnesota Supreme Court denied Mr. Pillsbury access to Honeywell's books and records, holding that a purely political or social purpose was not a proper purpose. There must be an economic or business reason.

In *Conservative Caucus Research, Analysis & Education Foundation, Inc. v. Chevron Corp.*, 525 A.2d 569 (Del. Ch. 1987), the Delaware court declined to follow *Pillsbury*, but the court found an economic purpose anyway. The plaintiff sought a stockholder list to communicate with other shareholders the *economic risks* for Chevron of doing business in Angola. That the plaintiff may also have had a social or political purpose was irrelevant. Under Delaware law, "[a] proper purpose having been stated, all others are irrelevant." Courts do not weigh or blend various bits of evidence to ascertain the shareholder's dominant purpose, which they then judge as being proper or improper.

The proper purpose burden is a normal one of a preponderance (not a "greater than normal evidentiary burden"). Although only one proper purpose is necessary, courts will look beneath a plaintiff's allegation to ascertain her true motives. Courts do not accept a plaintiff's statements at face value. For example, although investigating alleged waste and mismanagement is a proper purpose, the court in *Thomas & Betts Corp. v. Leviton Mfg. Co.,*

681 A.2d 1026 (Del. 1996), looked beyond the plaintiff's statements, finding its real purpose to have been the "highly opportunistic" one to acquire leverage in a takeover attempt. The court then proceeded to allow more limited access because, as a "locked in" shareholder, the plaintiff was entitled to access to books and records, but only insofar as necessary to enable it to value its shareholding.

In Delaware, if all the shareholder seeks is the shareholder list, the burden is on the corporation to prove improper purpose. If the shareholder seeks access to any other books and records, the burden of proving proper purpose is on the shareholder. As has been seen, the MBCA has a different schematic of automatic access to some documents with a "good faith and proper purpose" requirement for any other.

Examples of improper purposes might include writing harassing letters to shareholders or obtaining the list in order to sell a product or service of some sort. "[M]ere curiosity or desire for a fishing expedition" is an improper purpose. *Security First Corp. v. U.S. Die Casting & Development Co.*, 687 A.2d 563, 568 (Del. 1997). **Answer (C) is incorrect** because no evidence supports that this is a fishing expedition.

A shareholder contemplating litigation against the corporation may, as a strategic matter, attempt access to corporate books and records before filing a lawsuit. In some instances, access at that time might be easier than through discovery procedures after a lawsuit has been filed. Of course, any shareholder would be well advised to conduct such a quest on somewhat of a stealth basis.

Postscript: The Supreme Court of Delaware has been busy in the books and records area. In *Seinfeld v. Verizon Communications, Inc.*, 909 A.2d 117 (Del. 2006), a shareholder attempted to get access to pay records for the three highest-paid corporate officers of Verizon, who were receiving over-the-top compensation. Denied access, the shareholder filed a so-called DEL. GEN. CORP. L. § 220 action to obtain access. The Supreme Court approved the corporation's denial of access, which the Court of Chancery had affirmed. It was not sufficient to show the high levels of compensation. To make out a proper purpose for access to books and records, shareholder Seinfeld had to show that those high levels arguably were due to some sort of wrongdoing: "[w]e reaffirm the well-established law of Delaware that stockholders seeking inspection under section 220 must present 'some evidence' from which a court can infer that mismanagement, waste or wrongdoing may have occurred."

In *City of Westland Police and Fire Retirement System v. Axcelis Technologies, Inc.*, 1 A.3d 281 (Del. 2010), the court applied *Seinfeld* to the specific context of election of corporate directors. Reversing the Court of Chancery, Mr. Justice Jacobs found it "difficult to understand how determining an individual's suitability to serve as a corporate director is not related to a person's interest as a stockholder" (the statutory test for access). But what the court seemed to give, it quickly took away: "[A] plaintiff who states a proper purpose must also present some evidence from which [the court] could infer that there are legitimate concerns regarding a director's suitability [*Seinfeld* applied to the election context]. [The] shareholder must establish a credible basis to infer that the director is unsuitable. [Also] the shareholder must prove that the information it seeks is necessary and essential to assessing whether a director is unsuitable to stand for reelection."

So the Delaware Supreme Court has been putting all sorts of hurdles in the path of a shareholder seeking access to books and records, a path that used to be relatively free of obstacles. At the same time, the court has been urging shareholders to use whatever access they have to obtain information before filing suit. Many would say the latter is somewhat of an empty gesture in view of the former. Nonetheless, in *King v. VeriFone*, 12 A.3d 1140 (Del. 2011), the court struck down a Court of Chancery-imposed further roadblock for a derivative action plaintiff to obtain DEL. GEN. CORP. L. § 220 access to corporate books and records. King, the plaintiff, had done it backwards. He filed the derivative action (in California) first. After the California federal court dismissed the action, without prejudice, for failure to plead sufficient facts of why demand was refused, the plaintiff came 3000 miles back across the country. He filed his § 220 action in Delaware, alleging a proper purpose, namely, to find material about whether the directors might be unqualified. "No," said Vice-Chancellor Strine. By electing to go the derivative action route first, the plaintiff lost whatever proper purpose she may previously have had. Carefully reviewing the prior precedents, the Supreme Court rejected Chancellor Strine's "election rationale." While recognizing the waste and inefficiency in doing it backwards, the court nonetheless held "that it is a proper purpose under Section 220 to inspect books and records that would aid the plaintiff in pleading demand futility in a to-be-amended complaint in a plenary derivative action, where the earlier-filed plenary complaint was dismissed on demand futility-related grounds without prejudice and with leave to amend. That holding should not be read as an endorsement by the Court of proceeding in that way."

183.   His claim might be breach of the duty of loyalty against the Manleys, who put their family interests over the best interests of the corporation. His claim against Baker and Andreen might be for breach of their duty of care, as they have done nothing and failed to attend meetings or otherwise keep informed. His claim against the fabricator would be a straight breach of contract claim. Overall, the nature of his claim is derivative. He is alleging violations of duties owed to the corporation and damage to the corporation directly. His own injury, reflected in the diminution of the value of his shares, is indirect rather than direct. In a derivative action, the shareholder steps into the shoes of the corporation, again, to vindicate its rights, and the monetary relief, if any, goes to the corporate treasury.

American courts of equity invented the derivative action in the 1870s. Because the alleged wrongdoers in corporate disputes often were the persons in charge of the corporation's business and affairs, including litigation in its behalf, or a portion of their number, it was thought necessary to invent a device whereby a shareholder could step forward to act in the corporation's stead. A derivative action may also proceed against third parties, such as the truck fabricator here, for breach of contract or tort claims the corporation may have, but that was not the original reason for creation of the derivative action device. Usually, such a claim against third parties is more of an uphill fight, as the directors' decision not to pursue litigation against some third party is the directors' decision to make, and not the shareholders', and further, absent conflicts of interest, that decision will be protected from judicial scrutiny by the business judgment rule.

184.   **Answer (C) is the best answer.** Generally speaking, derivative actions (Answer (A)) are to be avoided by disgruntled shareholders, although in straight breach of fiduciary duty cases it is difficult to avoid derivative claims. Derivative litigation is procedurally complex. Further, over the last 25 or so years, defense lawyers and law reformers have developed a number of devices, such as the special litigation committee ("SLC") of the board and the universal demand requirement, which facilitate efforts to sidetrack or altogether derail derivative

litigation. Thus, **Answer (A) is not the best answer.**

Those who represent shareholders attempt to bring claims that are direct rather than derivative (**Answer (B), which is good, but not as good as Answer (C)**). Those direct claims proceed as ordinary civil actions with the recovery, if any, going to the shareholders rather than to the corporate treasury. The first category of direct claim proceeds under the separate and distinct injury rule. If an individual shareholder, or subset of shareholders, has suffered some direct injury, he may proceed in a direct action. *See, e.g., Hanson v. Kake Tribal Corp.*, 939 P.2d 1320 (Alaska 1997) (allegation that some rank-and-file shareholders received a financial benefit while others were excluded constituted "distinct and special injury" — action was direct and not derivative). Even if all shareholders have suffered, if the injury results from a breach of the contract the shareholder has with the corporation or the denial of some right associated by law with shareholding, the whole shareholder group may proceed directly (Answer (C)). Examples include *ultra vires* acts and other breaches of the shareholder contract (found in articles and bylaws), lack of disclosure or disclosure in a misleading way, denial or diminution of voting rights (as here), dilution of shareholders' financial interests with no business purpose therefore, and similar kinds of acts. *See, e.g., Parnes v. Bally Entertainment Corp.*, 722 A.2d 1243 (Del. 1999) (allegation that corporate officials denied shareholders rights to fair process leading up to merger approval was direct rather than derivative). A third exception is the close corporation exception. Holding that the derivative action is too procedurally complex in corporations with two to four shareholders, and the risk of multiple actions is small, courts in about 20 states have accepted a close corporation exception. *See, e.g., Richards v. Bryan*, 879 P.2d 638 (Kan. Ct. App. 1994). ALI PRINCIPLES § 7.01(d) recommends that, in her discretion, a judge may permit a close corporation dispute to proceed as a direct action. *See, e.g., Barth v. Barth*, 659 N.E.2d 559, 562 (Ind. Ct. App. 1995) (adopting the ALI approach). A notable holdout is Delaware. Its courts have refused to recognize a close corporation exception. *See Bagdon v. Bridgestone/Firestone, Inc.*, 916 F.2d 379, 384 (7th Cir. 1990) (Easterbrook, J., reviewing Delaware cases).

In this Question, David Falconer may proceed directly, both as to the dividend claim and as to the wrongful sale of all, or substantially all, the assets of the corporation. A further question is whether he wishes to proceed as a representative of a class of persons who are similarly situated, or in an individual action. Therefore, **Answer (D) is incorrect.**

185.   There may well be adverse publicity. Derivative claims against public companies have come to be known as "strike suits." A strike suit is one brought with very little basis therefore, or no investigation of whether an adequate basis exists, principally to obtain attorney's fees from the corporate treasury for the plaintiff shareholder's attorney. This pejorative appellation arose in the 1920s and 1930s. Because of the great number of shareholders in most public companies, the resulting danger of multiplicity of suits, and some strike suit abuses by attorneys, legislatures listened to advocates of reform. They enacted a number of procedural hurdles for plaintiffs in derivative suits. Many, but not all, of the measures enacted in this "first wave" of reform have disappeared, but the pattern among jurisdictions is very uneven. One reform was a requirement that, upon a court order, the plaintiff be required to post security for costs. A typical court order would require the plaintiff to post a bond. A bond is nothing more than a written promise to pay, but the court would also require the plaintiff to collateralize the bond, either by putting up in cash or negotiable securities, say, 10 percent of the bond amount, or by having a commercial surety (often an insurance

company) guarantee payment of the bond if and when payment becomes due.

Security for costs means costs; it does not mean defense attorneys' fees, which are likely to be large. Over and over courts have emphasized that security for costs measures do not amount to adoption of the English rule of fee shifting in which the losing party must pay the winning party's attorneys' fees. *See, e.g., De Bow v. Lakewood Hotel & Land Ass'n*, 145 A.2d 493 (N.J. Super. Ct. App. Div. 1958). Nonetheless, in many cases, defense attorneys attempt to get security for an amount of costs that includes some or all of their fees. The amounts courts have ordered as security for costs have been quite low, as judges are hesitant to close the courthouse door to any particular class of plaintiffs. Thus, they have required bonds in amounts such as $10,000, $15,000, or $25,000. Nonetheless, when a plaintiff shareholder owning 100, 200, or 500 shares has to collateralize that bond, say, by putting up $2,500, many "strike suit" plaintiffs do not come back to the attorney's office. Many states have eliminated their security for costs statutes, but in many other states the measures are still on the books.

Can't many of these hurdles be evaded by filing suit in another state? No. While seemingly procedural, courts have held that most of these incidents of the derivative suit are part of the important distribution and balance of power among shareholders, directors, and corporate officials. Hence they are treated as substantive for choice of law purposes. The law of the state of incorporation (*e.g.*, Delaware or California) rather than that of the forum state governs many prerequisites to derivative litigation. *See Kamen v. Kemper Financial Services, Inc.*, 500 U.S. 90 (1991) (demand requirement is substantive rather than procedural); *Starrels v. First National Bank of Chicago*, 870 F.2d 1168 (7th Cir. 1989) (same); *cf. Cohen v. Beneficial Industrial Loan Corp.*, 337 U.S. 541 (1949) (law of forum, rather than incorporating state, governs security for costs because it is procedural, rather than substantive).

186. **Answer (D) is the best answer.** Part of the first wave of strike suit reforms was to put the plaintiff under a magnifying glass (sometimes high-powered, sometimes low-powered), if not under a microscope. Part of the reason is that derivative litigation is a subspecies of class litigation. Given an adequate plaintiff and adequate representation overall, the outcome will be res judicata as to all the shareholders. So, some of the examination of the plaintiff is judicially inspired. *See Cohen v. Beneficial Industrial Loan Corp.*, 337 U.S. 541, 550 (1949) ("He sues, not for himself alone, but as representative of a class comprising all who are similarly situated."). Some is also legislatively mandated (*e.g.*, contemporaneous ownership and record ownership).

In this Question, many of the litmus tests for a plaintiff are implicated:

A. Contemporaneous Ownership (Answer (A)). The plaintiff must be an owner at the time of the wrong complained of, or have had the shares devolve upon her by operation of the law (bequest, intestate succession, etc.). MBCA § 7.41(1); FED. R. CIV. P. 23.1. The obvious abuse at which the requirement aims is the purchase of a lawsuit. One who knows of wrongdoing in a corporation who then purchases the shares is not a contemporaneous owner. *See, e.g., Bangor Punta Operations, Inc. v. Bangor & Aroostook R.R.*, 417 U.S. 703 (1974) (acquirer of railroad sued its former owner for breaches of fiduciary duty; held, no contemporaneous ownership). Here Phillip only purchased his shares one month ago. He might try to argue a "continuing wrong theory." He was an owner in the tail end of the period over which the continuing wrong occurred. But, it does not look good.

B. Continuous Owner. The plaintiff must remain a shareholder continuously, through trial and the pendency of any appeals. If there is a merger into another corporation, and the plaintiff becomes a shareholder of a new successor corporation, the plaintiff loses standing. She may have a new claim, for nondisclosure of the past wrongdoing and its effect on valuation of the "old" shares in the merger, but the derivative action will disappear because of the merger.

C. Record Owner (on the Records of the Corporation) (Answer (B)). This requirement, often statutory, persists in some jurisdictions, even though today over 99 percent of publicly-held shares are in "street" (after Wall Street) or, more accurately, nominee names. Investors hold shares in street or nominee name for convenience's sake. After a sale, it is a great inconvenience to retrieve a stock certificate from the safety deposit box in order to take it downtown to the broker's office, all of which must be accomplished in three business days. It is far easier if the certificate has been left immobilized in a vault in New York, with change of ownership recorded by computer. Record ownership requirements, where they exist, have no purpose any longer, save as a trap for the unwary. When they do exist, the plaintiff's attorney must insure that the named plaintiff orders, and receives, a share certificate before suit is commenced. This may entail a delay of up to three months or so. Many broker dealer firms also charge an extra fee of $25 or $35. Ownership in nominee name, rather than record ownership, has become the overwhelming norm today. So, even if Phillip were to persuade the court based upon a continuing wrong theory that he has contemporaneous ownership, he would still be vulnerable to a motion to dismiss because he is not a record owner.

D. Clean Hands (Answer (C)). The derivative action is a creature of equity. The maxims of equity apply. Plaintiff must have clean hands. Saul may be subject to objection based upon this ground. He has had an agenda of harassment of South Shore Bank and its directors, going back some years.

E. Adequate Representation (the Shareholder). Overlapping with the clean hands requirement is the adequate representation requirement. Courts have rejected arguments based on the age or disability of the shareholder plaintiff. Aged persons, and disabled persons, should have access to the courts as well. They have also rejected arguments based upon the nationality or mother tongue of the plaintiff. A person whose native tongue is Hebrew or Polish should have access to the courts. *See, e.g., Surowitz v. Hilton Hotels Corp.*, 383 U.S. 363 (1966) (Polish immigrant who had limited grasp of English). More importantly, there is no good reason to say that an aged, Polish speaking person, for example, will not vigorously represent the interests of her fellow shareholders.

In *In re Fuqua Industries, Inc. Shareholder Litigation*, 752 A.2d 126 (Del. Ch. 1999), Chancellor Chandler faced contentions that a plaintiff who owned 8,000 shares had become ill and lost her grasp of the case. He reaffirmed prior Delaware holdings that a shareholder plaintiff's lack of proficiency in law and finance or poor health will not bar her from the courthouse so long as she has support from competent advisors or attorneys and has no disabling conflicts of interest. He also held an owner of only 25 shares to be an adequate representative because "Freberg does in fact understand the basic nature of the derivative claims brought in his name, even if barely so."

Instead of the physical, or linguistic, makeup of the plaintiff, what courts focus on is motivation, or probable motivation. Does the plaintiff have an agenda that is the same as or similar to her fellow shareholders? Or does she have a side agenda, an axe to grind, that may prevent her from representing the rank-and-file shareholders' interest? Courts have refused to let disgruntled former employees, who also happened to own shares in the company, to proceed in a derivative action when it is probable that their primary motivation is to right some wrong suffered as an employee. Here, a court might very well find that Saul wishes to pursue the action to vindicate his side agenda, as a customer and a wannabe director, rather than as a rank-and-file shareholder.

F. Adequate Representation (the Attorney) (Answer (D)). As much as plaintiff's characteristics and motivation, courts focus on plaintiff's attorney's characteristics. Does she have the seasoning, age, and experience to see the matter through? Here, of course, Avi meets none of those requirements. The matter may easily be resolved, however, by having Avi associate a more seasoned attorney for prosecution of this case.

All in all, as attorney for South Shore Bank, you would have a very good chance at stopping this derivative suit at an early point in the litigation.

Answers (A), (B), and (C) are not the best answers for the reasons stated above.

187. **Answer (B) is the best answer.** This Question is based on *Brown v. Tenney*, 532 N.E.2d 230 (Ill. 1988), in which the defendant argued as in Answer (A), but the court recognized a double derivative action (Answer (B)). In theory, a triple or quadruple derivative action is a possibility. If PYU owned a subsidiary that, in turn, owned Club One, Hans's suit would be a triple derivative action. The double (or triple) derivative action is best understood as an exception to the contemporaneous ownership rule. Thus, **Answer (A) is not the best answer.**

Answer (C) is incorrect. Although a derivative action plaintiff must have clean hands, no evidence exists that Hans has done anything that would disqualify him.

Answer (D) is correct but is not the best answer. Whether or not Hans is an adequate representative is not an issue because, for one, Hans is representing only himself. There are no other shareholders he seeks to represent.

188. **Answer (C) is the best answer.** State law seldom requires that court papers be verified. The attorney signs most pleadings, based upon "information and belief" (Answer (A)). Only in certain family matters (child custody disputes, etc.) and in derivative actions are there widespread verification requirements. In a derivative action, the plaintiff shareholder must sign, stating that, based upon a reasonable investigation, she believes the matters stated to be true (Answer (B)).

Verification would be a significant hurdle were it not for Mr. Justice Hugo Black's opinion in *Surowitz v. Hilton Hotels Corp.*, 383 U.S. 363 (1966). Ms. Surowitz was an elderly Polish lady who spoke broken English. She had a lawyer son-in-law named Irving Brilliant. Mr. Brilliant had investigated alleged wrongdoing in the Hilton Company. He prepared a complaint in his mother-in-law's name. She glanced over it, signing the attestation at the end. At her deposition, she revealed that she knew little, if anything, about the events underlying the complaint. She also testified that she had confidence in her son-in-law. The federal district court dismissed the complaint. In the Supreme Court, Justice Black stated that all verification means is that some one, not necessarily the plaintiff, has investigated the matters plead and believes them to be true (Answer (C)). He described the verification requirement as strictly an anti-strike suit provision. A strike suit is a baseless pleading filed by an unscrupulous attorney attempting to extort attorney's fees from the defendant corporation. That was not the case in Ms. Surowitz situation. He ordered her claim reinstated.

Even though state law verification requirements have been neutralized to a degree by cases such as *Surowitz*, Federal Rule of Civil Procedure 11 still applies. By filing a complaint or other court paper, the attorney vouches that he has investigated the factual matters alleged and that the legal claims are supported by law or by a good faith argument for the extension of existing law. Moreover, if any federal securities law claims are pled, the Private Securities Litigation Reform Act of 1995 may apply. That statute requires the court to conduct a mandatory Rule 11 review of all the pleadings filed in the case. If the court finds a Rule 11 violation in the original complaint, all of the defense attorney's fees are shifted on to the plaintiff. Ergo, even given a somewhat relaxed view of verification requirements, where they exist, there are a number of other constraints that operate on pleading in corporate and securities law court cases.

Answers (A), (B), and (D) are not the best answers for the reasons stated above.

189. **Answer (D) is the best answer.** Codes of civil procedure require a derivative action plaintiff to allege the facts, if any, as to whether or not a demand has been made (Answer (A)). *See, e.g.*, FED. R. CIV. P. 23.1. But the demand requirement itself is substantive, not procedural. It is a corporate law requirement, under the "internal affairs" choice of law rule governed by the law of the state of incorporation. See Question 168. Thus, **Answer (A) is not the best answer.**

Common law demand has three branches: demand refused, demand accepted, and demand excused. *See Kamen v. Kemper Financial Services, Inc.*, 500 U.S. 90 (1991) (overruling court of appeals' attempt to impose universal demand as a matter of federal common law). Two of those three branches represent possible adverse outcomes for a plaintiff. Under demand refused, plaintiff makes a demand, usually by letter. If the board of directors undertakes a reasonable investigation (often utilizing a committee, assisted by independent legal counsel), and concludes that pursuit of the claims would not be in the best interests of the corporation, the directors will notify plaintiff that demand has been refused. Plaintiff may thereafter file a complaint in court, but it may be a short court appearance. The corporation will move to dismiss, pleading the business judgment rule. If the rule requirements have been met (decision or judgment, disinterested directors, some care, and a rational basis), the court will dismiss plaintiff's case. Management of the corporation's business and affairs, including litigation in its behalf, is entrusted to the board of directors, and the board has spoken ("demand refused"). Courts in Delaware and several other jurisdictions will not review the merits of a recommendation that derivative litigation be dismissed in "demand refused" cases, even on a discretionary basis, if the board or board committee process brought the recommendation within the ambit of the business judgment rule.

Plaintiffs view demand accepted with equal trepidation. If demand is accepted, then the parties are re-aligned. The corporation, which had been a nominal defendant, becomes the plaintiff in an amended complaint. The plaintiff and her attorney drop out of the picture. If the corporation reaches a settlement with the alleged wrongdoers, traditionally there is no requirement that the corporation have the court approve the settlement or that it notify the plaintiff of the settlement terms. *See, e.g., Wolf v. Barkes*, 348 F.2d 994 (2d Cir. 1965); *cf.* ALI PRINCIPLES § 7.15(a). The corporation may voluntarily proffer the settlement to the court for approval so that the settlement will have maximum res judicata effect in blocking other shareholder suits, but it need not do so. What a plaintiff worries about is a "sweetheart settlement" between the corporation and the defendants following "demand accepted."

Traditionally, then, a plaintiff seeks to have "demand excused" (Answer (B)). There are several sub-branches to this branch (threat of irreparable harm, close corporation, and deadlock on the board regarding the demand), but the most frequent is "futility."

Alleging demand futility has become increasingly difficult over the last 15–20 years. A plaintiff must allege "particularized facts" as to why a critical mass of directors (which may well be more than a majority) is disabled from acting upon the demand. Social ties with the wrongdoers or the corporate officers, receipt of normal directors' fees, or threat of suit if demand is wrongfully dealt with do not disable. Material pecuniary ties to the corporation, to the transaction challenged, or to the wrongdoers, or familial relationships with the foregoing, do tend to disable. Receipt of significant consulting fees or legal or accounting fees will disable. Insider status (corporate officer or high level employee) will disable. Thus, **Answer (B) is not the best answer.**

The legal test for demand futility seems forgiving ("reasonable doubt as to whether the directors who approved the challenged transaction, or ['and' in the original] the directors who would have been asked to deal with the demand, were or would have been entitled to business judgment rule protection"), but is rather strict as applied. *Aronson v. Lewis*, 473 A.2d 805 (Del. 1984), enunciates the Delaware test for demand futility, but must be read in conjunction with *Grobow v. Perot*, 539 A.2d 180, 189 (Del. 1988), which corrects a typographical error in *Aronson*: Demand will be excused if plaintiff pleads particularized facts that create a reasonable doubt *either* that "the directors are disinterested and independent" *or* that "the challenged transaction was otherwise not the product of a valid exercise of business judgment." Nonetheless, from plaintiffs' viewpoint, demand excused is the preferred branch of the common law demand requirement, by far.

Here, a case may be made that the critical mass of the directors (Richie and his father) are not disinterested and that they constitute a critical mass of the board. Relying on futility, and the threat of irreparable harm as well (Answer (C)), Potsie can ignore Fonzarelli's fax, proceeding directly to court with the filing of a complaint alleging demand is excused. **Answer (C) is good, but not as good as Answer (D).**

Note: You may have made a mistake in going to Arthur's office. He may argue that your actions constituted the making of a demand on behalf of your client. Under *Spiegel v. Buntrock*, 571 A.2d 767 (Del. 1990), by making a demand, the plaintiff is deemed to have conceded the disinterestedness and independence of the board for purposes of dealing with the demand. Spiegel thus makes the fork in the road a pronounced one. Any dealings with the corporation or the board may result in loss of the demand futility court option ("spent arrow in the quiver," in the Delaware court's words). In that way, the decision discourages attempts at out-of-court dispute resolution. *Scattered Corp. v. Chicago Stock Exchange, Inc.*, 701 A.2d 70 (Del. 1997), softens the effect of *Spiegel*. There the court held that making a demand does not concede independence conclusively. "Failure of an otherwise independent appearing board or committee to act independently is a failure to carry out its fiduciary duties in good faith or to conduct a reasonable investigation. Such failure could constitute wrongful refusal."

190.   **Answer (A) is the best answer.** Answer (C) is the answer the Iowa Supreme Court reached in *Miller v. Register & Tribune Syndicate, Inc.*, 336 N.W.2d 709 (Iowa 1983). Few, if any, courts have followed that decision, in part because it could disable a corporation altogether from dealing with derivative litigation. Hence, **Answer (C) is not the best answer.**

Answers (B) and (D) are somewhat repetitive. They mimic some of the common criticism of acceptance of the Special Litigation Committee ("SLC") device.

Answer (A) is the correct answer. In 1979, within months of one another, the United States Supreme Court and the New York Court of Appeals heard cases in which boards of directors had appointed SLCs to deal with litigation filed in the corporations' behalf. *See Burks v. Lasker*, 441 U.S. 471 (1979); *Auerbach v. Bennett*, 393 N.E.2d 994 (N.Y. 1979). See also the earlier case of *Gall v. Exxon Corp.*, 418 F. Supp. 508 (S.D.N.Y. 1976), accepting in theory the power of an SLC to investigate and dismiss claims alleging payment of $59 million in bribes and illegal payments to Italian political parties.

In *Burks*, involving an investment company (mutual fund) chartered under state law, but regulated by the federal Investment Company Act of 1940, reading a trio of ancient precedents, the Supreme Court held that the SLC device was a recognized one and that no federal law or policy prevented its use. *Burks v. Lasker*, 441 U.S. 471 (1979).

In *Auerbach*, the court held that a reviewing court's authority would be limited to business judgment rule issues, although the corporation and the board of directors would have the burden of proof on those issues. Thus, if the SLC had been comprised of independent directors, had exercised care in investigating the facts and the law, and had reached a decision or judgment that the pursuit of litigation would not be in the "corporation's best interests," the business judgment rule protected that decision from any judicial scrutiny. In other words, under New York law, there then could be no review of the committee's decision on the merits. Note also that the committee's finding does not have to be that "the law has not been violated" (although it could be that). All that is necessary is a finding that the lawsuit is "not in the corporation's best interests." *Auerbach v. Bennett*, 393 N.E.2d 994 (N.Y. 1979).

The rationale is that a corporation, just as a flesh and blood person may wish to do, may elect not to stand on legal rights it may have. Just as you may elect not to sue your neighbor for loud music at his parties, and work it out amicably or otherwise, a corporation should have a mechanism for doing the same thing. That mechanism has come to be the SLC. It works something like this. Upon filing of a colorable complaint, the board will use its power over the bylaws to amend them (in cases of obviously frivolous litigation the full board may act without use of an SLC). The board will increase the board's size, adding two or three "expansion" directors. Those directors are persons who could not have had any conceivable connection with the alleged wrongdoing. They are also persons of great rectitude and perhaps prominence in the community (*e.g.*, the dean of local university's business school, an

Anglican or Methodist bishop). The board then constitutes the expansion directors as the SLC. The SLC then retains "independent counsel," who should be a lawyer, and law firm, that has done no legal work for the corporation in the past four or five years, if ever. Together, the SLC and independent counsel investigate, interviewing witnesses, perhaps under oath, sending out questionnaires to company employees, and doing a legal analysis of the claims made.

Eight months after Arthur Fonzarelli obtained his continuance, the SLC files a motion for summary judgment. To it, the SLC attaches the results of its investigation and its report, which usually concludes that pursuing the litigation would not be in the corporation's best interests. At least in New York, and several other states that have case law following the New York position, the court must dismiss the lawsuit if it finds that the committee met the prerequisites for application of the business judgment rule. Even if the court disagrees with the contents or analysis in the SLC report, if a rational basis for the recommendation exists, the court must dismiss the derivative suit.

In *Joy v. North*, 692 F.2d 880 (2d Cir. 1982), Judge Winter cautioned against SLCs using, and judges accepting, use of makeweight factors to support an SLC's recommendation. Makeweight factors, likely to be present in every case and not easily quantifiable, would include items such as drain on executive and employee time or effect on corporate morale caused by continuance of the shareholder suit.

191. The Wisconsin court may follow the lead of any of the following jurisdictions:

New York (strong business judgment rule position). In *Auerbach v. Bennett*, 393 N.E.2d 994 (N.Y. 1979), the New York Court of Appeals held that, if the prerequisites for application of the business judgment rule had been proven, a trial court may not review on the merits a special litigation committee recommendation. Several other state courts have adopted this view. *See, e.g., Lewis ex rel. Citizens Savings Bank & Trust Co. v. Boyd*, 838 S.W.2d 215 (Tenn. Ct. App. 1992); *Hirsch v. Jones Intercable, Inc.*, 984 P.2d 629 (Colo. 1999). The salient difference between an SLC case and a routine business judgment rule case is that in the former, the directors have the burden of proof, while in the latter, disinterestedness, good faith, and the like are presumed.

Delaware and Connecticut (*Zapata* second step in demand excused cases). In *Zapata Corp. v. Maldonado*, 430 A.2d 779 (Del. 1981), the Delaware Supreme Court announced that, contrary to the New York position, trial courts in Delaware could, in their discretion, look at the merits of an SLC recommendation, but only in demand excused cases. This discretionary review beyond the elements of the business judgment rule has become known as the "*Zapata* second step." In *Joy v. North*, 692 F.2d 880 (2d Cir. 1982), Judge Winter made an educated *Erie* guess that Connecticut would follow the Delaware approach.

North Carolina and Georgia (*Zapata* second step in demand excused and demand refused cases). *Alford v. Shaw*, 358 S.E.2d 323 (N.C. 1987), holds that a trial court may, in its discretion, undertake a *Zapata* second step review. *Millsap v. American Family Corp.*, 430 S.E.2d 385 (Ga. Ct. App. 1993), adopts the *Alford v. Shaw* view in principle.

Massachusetts (mandatory review). In *Houle v. Low*, 556 N.E.2d 51, 57 (Mass. 1990), the Massachusetts Supreme Judicial Court held that a trial court should review the merits of an SLC recommendation.

Pennsylvania (*Zapata* second step in duty of loyalty, but not in duty of care cases). In

Cuker v. Mikalauskas, 692 A.2d 1042 (Pa. 1997), the Pennsylvania Supreme Court adopted *in toto* the American Law Institute Corporate Governance Project provisions, which it appended to its opinion. In cases in which self-dealing and conflicts of interests are alleged, the trial court may review the merits of the SLC report. In a duty of care case, the trial court is limited to an examination of the investigation and other elements of the business judgment rule.

As a defendant, Richie will argue for the New York position, because the case involves self-dealing. Potsie would be content if the Wisconsin court adopts any of the other four positions.

192. The lynchpin of each of these suggested legislative enactments is "universal demand." The suggested enactments would eliminate the demand excused branch of the common law, or at least the futility sub branch thereof. If a shareholder plaintiff had serious doubts as to whether there existed a sufficient number of disinterested directors, she would have to make demand anyway and await the corporation's response. The reason for elimination of the futility sub-branch of demand excused is its inefficiency. After a shareholder plaintiff files her court complaint, alleging that demand was excused, the defendants almost always move to dismiss the complaint, on grounds that demand was required. There follows a mini trial, or a "trial within the trial," to make findings of fact as to whether or not demand was excused. It may delay a case's progress for eight, ten, or more months.

Assuming, then, with a universal demand requirement, demand made and demand refused, what happens next? The two proposals differ radically. Under the ALI proposal, the court could then review the diligence and independence of the board members or committee making the refusal decision. ALI PRINCIPLES § 7.09. In a close case, or one in which the court had suspicions or unresolved doubts, at least in cases of self-dealing, the court could examine the merits of the refusal decision. *Id.* § 7.10. The ALI thus makes demand universal, but downplays demand somewhat. The ABA approach makes the universal demand stage all-important. The ABA provision simply provides that, if the elements of the business judgment rule are met, there can be no judicial review of a board's or board committee's decision to refuse a shareholder demand. MBCA § 7.44(a). The ABA provision has not had as widespread adoption as it should have because it attempts to be too preclusive. Even business lawyers on state bar association committees can see the wisdom of having the "relief valve" of judicial review available in close or doubtful cases. They trust that their state court judges will not utilize it too frequently.

Now, what, if anything, has the Wisconsin Legislature done? The Wisconsin Legislature has adopted the MBCA derivative action provisions. *See* WIS. STAT. § 180.0744, based upon MBCA § 7.44. Thus, in Wisconsin, universal demand exists. Moreover, courts may not engage in the *Zapata* second step, reviewing the SLC's recommendation on the merits. For that reason, in *Einhorn v. Culea*, 612 N.W.2d 78 (Wis. 2000), Chief Justice Abrahamson emphasized the special care with which trial courts should review the independence, and perhaps the diligence, of an SLC:

> Judicial review to determine whether the members of the committee are independent and whether the committee's procedure complies with the statute is of the utmost importance, because the court is bound by the substantive decisions of a properly constituted . . . committee . . . . We conclude the legislature intended a [trial] court to examine carefully whether members of a special litigation committee are

independent.

Einhorn, 612 N.W.2d at 86–87. Later, she noted, "It is vital for a [trial] court to review whether each member of a special litigation committee is independent. The [SLC] is, after all, the 'only instance in American Jurisprudence where a defendant can free itself from a suit by merely appointing a committee to review the allegations of the complaint.' " *Id.* at 91 (quoting *Lewis v. Fuqua*, 502 A.2d 962, 967 (Del. Ch. 1985)). Chief Justice Abrahamson outlined seven factors courts should closely examine:

1. A committee member's status as a defendant. Optimally no SLC member should be a defendant, but the suit may be one in which plaintiffs named all directors on a pro forma basis.

2. A committee member's participation in or approval of the alleged wrongdoing.

3. A committee member's past or present business or economic dealings with an individual defendant.

4. A committee member's past or present personal, family or social relations with individual defendants.

5. A committee member's past or present business or economic relations with the corporation.

6. The number of members on the SLC. The more members, the less weight a court might give to one particular disabling interest of one member.

7. The roles of corporate counsel and independent counsel.

193.   Yes and no. The original theory of derivative litigation, based loosely upon an early English case, *Foss v. Harbottle*, 2 Hare 461 (1843), was that the complaining shareholder should also be required to make a demand upon the shareholders if the acts she complains of are capable of being ratified by a shareholder majority vote. *See, e.g., Wolgin v. Simon*, 722 F.2d 389 (8th Cir. 1983) (holding demand on shareholders still required under Missouri law). Conceivably, the shareholders could convene a meeting, ratifying the alleged wrongdoing. By contrast, if the complaining shareholder alleged fraud, *ultra vires* or illegal acts by directors, or a gift or wasting of corporate assets, demand on the shareholders would be excused. Shareholders are not able to ratify those acts (unless they do so unanimously). Demand on shareholders might also be excused when the alleged wrongdoers hold a majority of the shares. The leading "no demand" case is *Mayer v. Adams*, 141 A.2d 458 (Del. 1958) (also holding that because violation of fiduciary duty claims may also be viewed as claims of "constructive fraud," and fraud cannot be ratified, demand on shareholders was not required — an exception which well nigh swallows the rule in Delaware). Some statutes pointedly omit any reference to demand on shareholders. *See, e.g.,* Cal. Corp. Code § 800(b); N.Y. Bus. Corp. L. § 626; *see also Syracuse Television, Inc. v. Channel 9, Syracuse, Inc.*, 273 N.Y.S.2d 16 (Sup. Ct. 1966) (requirement was eliminated in 1963 because "it was considered too onerous" to make a demand on shareholders). The Model Act is coy, speaking only of a demand "on the corporation." MBCA § 7.42(1). The ALI is more straightforward. It provides that "[d]emand on shareholders should not be required." ALI Principles § 7.03(c). The latter is undoubtedly the correct modern view. In corporations of any size, the focus of demand and other matters relating to derivative litigation should be on the board of directors and not upon the shareholders. But Potsie should not depend upon it. He (or his lawyer) has to be

prepared to respond to a defense contention that demand on the shareholders is required. Here the response is that demand is not required when the wrongdoer (Richie) holds a majority (52%) of the shares.

194.   **Answer (B) is the best answer.** Both Answers (C) (cosmetic settlement) and (D) are, or may be, true statements, but Answer (B) contains the overriding legal principle. Thus, **Answers (C) and (D) are not the best answers.**

The true party in interest in most derivative litigation, or all shareholder litigation for that matter, at least in publicly-held corporations, is the attorney. The reason is that, even if only moderate successes are obtained, the shareholder's attorney's fees have to be paid from the corporate treasury. In large corporations, the fee may run into tens of millions, or hundreds of millions, of dollars. Thus, the shareholders' champion is the attorney. Sometimes, he is a less than faithful champion.

In the cosmetic settlement (Answer (C)), the plaintiff's attorney agrees to settle the case for very little in the way of meaningful relief, and that of the "therapeutics" variety, in return for a substantial fee. The shareholder plaintiff often exerts little influence because he is a professional plaintiff who owns 10–20 shares in several hundred companies. A gentleman named Harry Lewis, a non-practicing lawyer by training, was the paradigmatic professional plaintiff through much of the 1970s and 1980s, who would be plaintiff in 30 or 40 cases at any given time. The defense attorneys, after they have billed a substantial number of hours, for which they will be paid, then wish merely to see the case go away. They therefore agree to the cosmetic settlement.

The attorney, who produces either a common fund (Answer (A)), or a common benefit, is entitled to a fee. If the corporate "therapeutics" (amendment of a bylaw, demotion of certain personnel, amendment of the code of conduct) follow the filing of a colorable lawsuit, many courts entertain a presumption of causation based upon the sequence of events. *See, e.g., Tandycrafts, Inc. v. Initio Partners*, 562 A.2d 1162, 1165 (Del. 1989); *Allied Artists Pictures Corp. v. Baron*, 413 A.2d 876 (Del. 1980). Thus, **Answer (A) is incorrect** because it wrongly states that an attorney's fee may be ordered or approved for payment by the corporation *only* in cases in which the attorney's efforts have created a common fund of some sort that benefits all shareholders.

Traditionally, courts used a percentage of the recovery method to compute the attorney's fee. If the attorney's efforts produced, say, a real fund of $60 million to be paid out to shareholders, or to the corporate treasury, a court might well approve a fee of 20 percent or 25 percent of that amount, or $12 to $15 million. As the stakes became larger, and settlements were more on the order of $600 million rather than $60 million, the fees became, seemingly, obscene in amount. Many courts turned to an alternative computation method, the lodestar method, described in the Question. The attorneys (there usually will be several) total their billable hours and multiply that number by their normal billing rate. That product is the lodestar. They then request the judge to apply a multiplier to the lodestar to produce the fee. Judges rarely, if ever, apply a multiplier less than 1.0 (but they may reduce the hours) or more than 2.0.

The lodestar method produced yet another trial within a trial (or after a trial or settlement). In many cases, other than bargained for and agreed upon cosmetic settlements, defense attorneys began to nit-pick about every hour or expense plaintiffs billed. They fought protracted battles over the multiplier the court should utilize. The trend since the 1990s has been a return to the percentage of recovery method of fee computation. *See, e.g., In re Activision Securities Litigation*, 723 F. Supp. 1373, 1375 (N.D. Cal. 1989) ("Is this lodestar process necessary? Under a cost benefit analysis, the answer would be a resounding 'no.'"); ALI PRINCIPLES § 7.17. The percentage of the recovery method produces roughly the same amount in fees, is less likely to result in inflation of billable hours, and is far less susceptible to unseemly squabbling among attorneys. Some courts, however, still utilize the lodestar method and some, require plaintiff's attorneys to make a dual submission (lodestar and percentage of recovery).

One irony of the whole process is that, while many corporate officials rail against frivolous litigation, we have a fee computation method that encourages attorneys to bet on "long shots." If a case is a long shot, the battle will be fierce and long, and the billable hours greater. Because of novel legal issues and the difficulty of the case, the multiplier applied, or percentage of the recovery or settlement granted, will be greater. Meanwhile, the plaintiff's attorney who takes a solid case, goes about it in a workmanlike and professional way, and in short order produces a settlement acceptable and fair to all parties, is likely to receive, on a relative basis, a much smaller fee. That is but another illustration of the "law of unforeseen consequences."

195. **Answer (B) is the best answer.** Of course, this is a question about strategy, so there often will not be a right or correct answer.

Following the judicial embrace of the special litigation committee, or SLC, use of SLCs became the inevitable response to derivative claims filed by shareholders (Answer (A)). And an effective response the SLC turned out to be. In fact, the SLC device became a "show stopper" as far as derivative claims were concerned. The new game for plaintiff shareholders became statement of direct rather than derivative claims, packaging those claims as a class action on behalf of all the shares that alleged injury or denial of a right associated with shareholding (the right to full and fair disclosure here). Direct and derivative claims might be combined (Answer (C)), but the direct disclosure claims would be sidetracked for a year or more while the SLC process ran its course with respect to the derivative claims. Therefore, **Answers (A) and (C) are not the best answers.**

Answer (D) requires a bit of explanation. Many merger and acquisition cases state that "appraisal is the exclusive remedy." Those court statements are incomplete. They mean that appraisal is the exclusive remedy if the shareholder's only complaint is the sufficiency of what he is to receive in the merger (shares of another company or cash). If he voted "No," and notified the company promptly of his decision to seek appraisal, he may proceed to court. The court will appraise the value of his shares and award him damages. The court will compare the value of the new shares to the value of his old shares, or the amount of cash offered him versus the value of his old shares. The Model Act appraisal process is described in MBCA §§ 13.20–13.31. However, if the process leading to approval of the merger had been manipulated, or corrupted, as here, often by misleading disclosure, shareholders may object. Appraisal is not the exclusive remedy because value or price is not their sole objection. *See, e.g., Weinberger v. UOP, Inc.*, 457 A.2d 701, 711 (Del. 1983) ("The concept of fairness has two basic aspects: fair dealing and fair price. The former embraces questions of when the transaction was timed, how it was initiated, structured and negotiated, disclosed to the directors, and how the approvals of the directors and the stockholders were obtained."). Often, plaintiff's lawyers will seek an injunction before the merger is consummated on ground that the process or course of dealing was unfair. Of course, their real objection is value. They use an injunction to obtain an increase in the consideration offered, and accordingly, a very large attorney's fee based upon the increase in price obtained. Appraisal actions may be brought as class actions. Members of the class will have had to have voted "No." In other, non-appraisal actions, often the complaint is that, based upon non-disclosure, or misleading disclosure, and manipulation of the process, they voted "Yes."

But appraisal actions are fraught with difficulty. They are expensive because appraisers and investment bankers' services will have to be obtained. Then, too, in some older Delaware cases, the shareholders who went to the time and trouble of an appraisal action received less, not more, than they would have received in the merger to which they objected. *See Gibbons v. Schenley Industries, Inc.*, 339 A.2d 460 (Del. Ch. 1975) (plaintiffs who dissented from $53 merger received only $33.86 in appraisal proceeding). Therefore, **Answer (D) is not the best answer.**

The point of this Question is that derivative claims have come to be thought of as claims to be avoided. There was a massive shift from derivative claims and derivative actions to direct claims and to class actions. By far, the largest subset of those direct claims was claims of non-disclosure or misleading disclosure under the federal securities laws. To stem that tide, major accounting firms, the high-tech industry, and other interest groups went to Congress to obtain legislative relief in the form of the Private Securities Litigation Reform Act of 1995 (PSLRA), which is the subject of the next Question.

196.   **Answer (B) is the best answer.** All the answers contain probable strategic moves, but Answer (B) would be the first in the sequence.

Following their initial public offering ("IPO"), many high-tech companies would experience a 15–20 percent drop in the price of their shares upon the release of the slightest adverse news or quarterly results. The announcement would be followed by 10, 15 or 20 "stock drop" lawsuits, skeletal complaints often brought in the name of professional plaintiffs, such as Harry Lewis, to be followed by months of discovery. Based upon what they found in discovery, plaintiffs' lawyers would file amended complaints, sometimes (with leave of court) "fourth" and "fifth" amended complaints. Attorneys would fight for the court to name them "lead counsel." Lead counsel would parcel out the work and coordinate strategy among the attorneys who, at that point, would be participants in a consolidated action. This phenomenon was leading to high-tech corporate "crib death," in one rhetorical flourish current at the time.

The major accounting firms, who were frequently named as co-defendants in "stock drop" lawsuits, contributed millions of dollars and led an intensive lobbying effort on Capitol Hill. Representatives of various high-tech enterprises joined in the effort. The result is the Private Securities Litigation Reform Act of 1995 ("PSLRA"), which is a complicated statute with many disparate elements (as is the 2002 Sarbanes-Oxley legislation). All of the strategies suggested in the answers to this Question arise from provisions of the PSLRA. One way in which to view the PSLRA is as an "add on" code of civil procedure, which supplements the Federal Rules when a complaint alleges securities law class claims. It requires the plaintiff in a federal securities law class action to "jump through a number of additional hoops." The PSLRA is described in, *inter alia*, Douglas M. Branson, *Running the Gauntlet: A Description of the Arduous, and Now Often Fatal, Journey for Plaintiffs in*

Federal Securities Law Actions, 65 U. Cin. L. Rev. 3 (1996).

Advertisement of Suit. Simultaneously with the filing of the action, the plaintiff must place an advertisement in a periodical with national circulation, advising potentially interested parties of the pendency of the suit.

Plaintiff's Certification (Answer (B)). With the complaint, the plaintiff must file a sworn statement that she has not been a plaintiff in more than three actions in the past three years, that she is not being compensated for serving as plaintiff, and so on. This add-on procedure strives to all but eliminate the use of professional plaintiffs.

Most Appropriate Plaintiff Upset Procedure (Answer (A)). Within 90 days, other investors may appear before the court. The court is to presume that the investor with the largest financial stake is the most appropriate plaintiff. He, or she, may then upset, or oust, the plaintiff who originally brought the action. The aim was to have interested institutional investors substitute for fly-by-night, but not necessarily professional, plaintiffs such as Devore. To date, institutions have shown only little interest in so doing. There is a split among decisions as to whether a number of smaller investors may aggregate their holdings in order to contend for treatment as most appropriate plaintiff. In the question, it may be a Hobson's choice for the defense, substituting a well-financed institution (Golden Bear) for a plaintiff with nominal holdings and not much staying power. On the other hand, the defense may thereby obtain a plaintiff who acts logically and professionally in the conduct of the lawsuit.

Stay on Discovery. While a motion to dismiss is pending, the plaintiff is permitted no discovery whatsoever. As a result of this provision, defendants always file an early motion to dismiss the complaint.

Heightened Pleading Standards (Answer (C)). The first motion to dismiss to be filed will state that fraud has not been pled with the requisite particularity and in accordance with the PSLRA pleading standards. Fed. R. Civ. P. 9 has long provided that fraud must be pled with particularity (who, what, when, where, and how, as in Journalism 101), but that state of mind may be averred generally. The PSLRA now requires a plaintiff to plead with particularity why and how each and every named defendant acted with the requisite state of mind (recklessly, or knowingly or intentionally).

In the Advent Software Question, there are really two claims. One claim is failure to disclose at the IPO stage. The other is of delayed disclosure, while certain insiders sold their shares. A current question is whether pleading "motive and opportunity" suffices. Here the CFO and other employee's motive would have been to bail out before public shareholders; the opportunity was presented to them because they had access to the non-public information about the write-off. Some courts accept "motive and opportunity" as satisfying the PSLRA standard. Other courts require the pleading of additional facts, for example, here demonstrating that the delay in disclosure was not merely negligent or inadvertent.

The pleading stage is one at which many of the early PSLRA battles have been fought.

Mandatory Rule 11 Review (Answer (D)). The judge *must* conduct a review of all pleadings filed in the federal securities case, levying sanctions against the attorneys filing any court paper not based upon an adequate factual investigation or legal argument. If, in her review, the judge finds that a Rule 11 violation exists in the plaintiff's complaint, she is to shift all costs, including defense attorneys' fees, onto the plaintiff and her attorney. This fee shifting provision has caused all, or most all, of the smaller law firms who once did this practice to withdraw. Perversely, this provision, and other PSLRA elements, has had the effect of making some of the larger firms stronger, with larger market shares, rather than the intended effect of weakening them.

Eliminating Securities Fraud as a Predicate Act for Racketeer Influenced and Corrupt Organizations Act ("RICO"). RICO, which provides for treble damages and attorney's fees, requires two or more predicate acts over a 10-year period to establish a "pattern." RICO names the federal statutory violations that may constitute predicate acts. Plaintiffs often attempt to make out RICO claims against large national accounting and securities firms, who would be joined as co-defendants in many "stock drop" law suits. The PSLRA eliminates securities fraud from the list of potential predicate acts.

The PSLRA contains much more, including revision of the rules about joint and several liability, and restoration of aiding and abetting liability, but only in suits brought by the SEC. The PSLRA will be dealt with in depth in the course in securities regulation at your law school. The evolution of law in the area of shareholder litigation has involved neutralization of the derivative suit through use especially of the special litigation committee. Those developments caused a turn to federal securities law class actions. In turn, the PSLRA partially blocked the federal courthouse door to some of those claims. Where was plaintiffs' attorney to turn to next? State courts, of course, which is the subject of the next Question in the ever-unfolding saga of shareholder litigation in the United States.

Answers (A), (C), and (D) are not the best answers for the reasons given above.

197. **Answer (D) is the best answer.** Following enactment of the Private Securities Litigation Reform Act of 1995 ("PSLRA"), plaintiffs' attorneys turned to state courts. As discussed in the answer to Question 152, each state has its own securities regulation scheme. Post-PSLRA, attorneys filed state law claims against corporations and their officers in state court, got the discovery which they could not obtain in federal court because of the PSLRA, dismissed the state court suit, and filed a fattened complaint in federal court. Or, plaintiffs' attorneys might elect just to remain in state court. Federal courts are not the universally superior fora they once were. Often, the plaintiff is not able to bring federal claims in state court. Of course, the ordinary rule is otherwise. Unless specifically ruled out, under federal statutory schemes, concurrent jurisdiction, state and federal, is the norm. But the Securities Exchange Act of 1934, pursuant to which the SEC has enacted Rule 10b-5, provides for exclusive federal jurisdiction (oddly enough, under the slightly more complex Securities Act of 1933, which governs public offerings of securities, there is concurrent jurisdiction). The defense would move to dismiss any federal claim, such as a Rule 10b-5 claim, for lack of subject matter jurisdiction (Answer (C)).

The same interests that lobbied for the PSLRA (national accounting firms, high-tech companies, and so on) viewed evasion of the PSLRA through state court filings with alarm. They returned to Capitol Hill. Congress passed a relatively concise statute, the Securities Litigation Uniform Standards Act of 1998 ("SLUSA"), which provides that, in any class or group action under state securities or common law that purports to represent more than 50 holders of a "covered security," any defendant may remove the lawsuit from state court to federal court, where the PSLRA will apply (Answer B)). A group action would be one in which 50 or more shareholders appear as named plaintiffs, thus evading court supervision (including determination of attorney's fees) under the class action rules. In the same way (signing up a number of named plaintiffs), an attorney might seek to avoid PSLRA and SLUSA. Roughly speaking, a covered security is one issued by a company that files periodic reports with the SEC.

But nothing can ever be so simple as that. In the legislative process leading up to SLUSA's enactment, practitioners from Delaware argued for, and obtained, an exemption in the statute, known as the "Delaware carve out." It takes a bit of explaining. The traditional view has been that, short of fraud, affirmative disclosure obligations for companies and their directors have their source in federal law. Approximately 25 years ago, the Delaware courts began to change all of that. They posited a state fiduciary duty that, in certain instances, requires affirmative disclosure. They called it the "duty of candor." At times, the judges have retreated from that bolder label, like the artist formerly known as Prince, calling the duty formerly known as candor by another name, the duty of disclosure. Practitioners, and certain of the Delaware judges, still refer to the duty of candor. The doctrine has uncertain contours. At its core, as a matter of state corporate law, the duty of candor requires full and fair disclosure whenever the directors seek shareholder assent, as in a merger or other acquisition, or amendment of the articles or charter. The doctrine does not require full disclosure in the routine, annual election of directors. In *Loudon v. Archer-Daniels-Midland Co.*, 700 A.2d 135 (Del. 1997), the Delaware Supreme Court held that the annual proxy statement's failure to disclose criminal investigations by the Justice Department did not give rise to a cause of action for damages under the duty of candor. There is no need to engage in such "self flagellatory" disclosure short of a final adjudication of wrongdoing.

Then, in *Malone v. Brincat*, 722 A.2d 5 (Del. 1998), the doctrine took another twist. In a case involving routine disclosure, this time of quarterly and annual earnings, the directors of Mercury Finance had for a period of years covered up the utter financial ruin of the company. The Delaware Supreme Court held that the duty of candor does give rise to an action for damages whenever directors have knowingly or intentionally breached it, whether in an instance of seeking shareholder assent, or in making important, but routine, disclosures, as in *Malone*. Appellate opinions in several other states have adopted the duty of candor phrasing and doctrine, although the decisions are far from numerous.

One way in which to file and remain in state court is to file only claims that fit within SLUSA's Delaware duty of candor "carve-out." Another is to file a lawsuit in state court containing only Securities Act of 1933 claims over which state courts have concurrent jurisdiction and which are not removable under SLUSA.

Answers (A), (B), and (C) are not the best answers for the reasons given above.

198.   **Answer (A) is the best answer.** Deal structure is a complex question, involving tax law, securities law, labor law (*e.g.*, integration of seniority lists and union representation conflicts), management succession, and a host of other issues. Often, a dozen or more attorneys from a law firm will work on various aspects of a corporate combination. A basic business organizations class can give students only the most rudimentary primer on this subject.

Corporate combinations, at least friendly ones, begin with an agreement between senior managers, often memorialized in a "letter of intent," or "memorandum of understanding," which courts have ruled are more than mere agreements to agree. They are binding contracts, although perhaps loosely so. At the letter of intent stage, or shortly thereafter, a deal structure has to be settled upon. Here, it appears that a merger, even a merger of equals, would suit the parties' needs. The corporate statute of the states of incorporation of the constituent corporations will have a separate chapter devoted to "merger," or "merger and consolidation." *See, e.g.*, MBCA Ch. 11.

In merger, the boards of directors of the respective corporations formulate a plan of merger. They then must present it to the shareholders for a vote. The "Plan of Merger" or "Agreement of Merger," will specify which is to be the surviving entity, who is to receive what (in terms or shares of stock of the surviving corporation, or cash), what warranties and representations the parties make to one another, and a myriad of details. The shareholders of the two corporations then vote (2/3rds of all the shares, not merely those present at the meeting, in the old days) (now a majority in most jurisdictions). *See, e.g.*, MBCA § 11.03(e) ("majority vote of all the votes entitled to be cast on the plan by [each] voting group"). The latest MBCA change is to permit mergers to be approved by a majority of shareholders at a meeting, given a quorum. In effect, then, a merger could be approved by as few as 25 percent of the shares. After the vote, articles of merger, together with a certificate describing the meeting and the votes by which the shareholders approved, are filed in the Secretary of States' offices. When the articles of merger are "filed," say, here naming Alaska Airlines, renamed Alaska-Aloha, as the surviving corporation, the acquired corporation ceases to exist, by operation of the law. Poof! It is gone. Aloha! All the Aloha shareholders become Alaska, or Alaska-Aloha, shareholders, even though it may be months before they actually receive a share certificate. Or, with a device introduced in the late 1960s, called a "cash merger," which most state statutes now authorize, if a majority votes "Yes," and articles of merger are filed, the target corporation ceases to exist and its former shareholders (all of them, not just the majority who approved) become entitled to X dollars per share in cash.

There are several types of statutory mergers. If the surviving corporation is to be an entirely new entity, into which both of the constituent corporations are to be merged, the transaction is often called a "consolidation" rather than a merger. The Model Act drops the term consolidation, but many lawyers still use the term to distinguish such transactions from those in which one of the constituents corporations is the survivor. Many state statutes authorize use of "short form mergers." *See, e.g.*, MBCA § 11.04 (merger of 90 percent owned subsidiary). In a case in which a parent corporation owns 90 or 95 percent of the shares of a subsidiary, the parent may merge the subsidiary into another subsidiary and the 5 or 10 percent minority has no voting rights.

Another form of merger is the "small scale merger," which Delaware, Michigan, and a few other states have. *See* DEL. GEN. CORP. L. § 251(f). In that type of transaction, the statute excuses a shareholder vote in the acquiring, or surviving, corporation. Generally, the vote is excused if the outstanding voting shares of the acquiring corporation will not be increased by more than a stated percentage (15 or 20) as a result of the merger (20% in Delaware).

The other alternatives are all viable. Purchasing shares in the market before a merger (Answer (B)) is not illegal if only the corporation (Alaska here), and not its executives, do it. It is after all, self-developed inside information, upon which Alaska would be free to trade. Many corporations refrain from the practice because of the hard feeling it might cause among target company shareholders who sold, thereby foregoing the (presumably) higher merger consideration. Cash tender offers (takeover bids) (Answer (C)) conjure up vision of hostile acquisitions, but that is not always the case. The parties here could structure their friendly acquisition as either a cash or stock takeover bid (Answer (D)), but it would eventually have to be followed by a merger to consolidate the two airlines' operations. The merger would be a forgone conclusion, though, because due to the tender offer, the acquiring company would already own a substantial share block.

Answers (B), (C), and (D) are not the best answers for the reasons given above.

199.   **Answer (C) is the best answer.** In the usual statutory arrangement, the chapter that follows the chapter on merger is titled "sale of assets." *See, e.g.*, MBCA Ch. 12. The sale of assets chapter will set out a similar procedure (directors formulate a plan, shareholder vote, and so on) to that of the merger chapter. A principal difference from merger is that, in a sale of assets transaction, the target corporation does not disappear by "operation of the law." After the smoke clears, the target, or selling, corporation will still exist, holding the cash or stock received for the assets. It could re-invest those proceeds to go into an entirely new line of business. Or, as is usually the case, it could distribute the shares or cash received to its shareholders. But, even after a distribution to its shareholders, the selling corporation would still exist, if only as a corporate shell. It takes a separate, voluntary act of dissolution for the target to disappear. No operation of the law at work here.

What triggers the necessity of the formalities (a plan, shareholder vote, etc.)? Will the sale of one plant or facility do it? The statutes say "all or substantially all" of the assets. They further provide that formalities are required only when the assets are sold "other than in the regular course of business." *See, e.g.*, MBCA § 12.02. The courts use a qualitative rather than a quantitative test. Thus, sale of a key plant and the production that goes with it, even though quantitatively less than 50 percent of the assets, could be a "sale of assets," subject to the statute. *Cf.* MBCA § 12.01, official comment. ("The phrase 'substantially all' is synonymous with 'nearly all.' "). Generally, unless otherwise stated, a sale of assets means all of the assets, subject to all of the liabilities. An agreement of purchase could, however, purchase only some assets, subject only to some, or to none, of the liabilities. The possibilities are endless.

In the Question at hand, CMM wishes to avoid successor liability, if it can. Merger of the two entities (Answer (A)) may automatically result in successor liability. Thus, **Answer (A) is not the best answer.** Purchase of assets (Answer (B)), not subject to liabilities, or subject to some liabilities but not to others, may be a start on this issue (which is far beyond the ken of most business organization classes). However, **Answer (B) is not the best answer.**

Another agenda item is preservation of cash, a goal not served by Answers (A), (B), and (D) (stock tender offer), which would severely deplete cash. Thus, **Answer (D) is not the best answer.** In merger, dissenters' rights spring into being. If any number of M & N shareholders vote "No," dissent, and seek appraisal of their shares, payment to them may be a significant cash drain, even if the court does not appraise the shares at a number vastly higher than the value of their merger consideration (CMM shares). This is a wild card element in the equation that, along with the successor liability issue, tips the balance strongly against merger. Many statutes (Delaware's, for example) do not grant dissenters' rights in sale of assets transactions. Always check the statute, but, here, a stock for assets transaction may suit well CMM's needs (obviously, cash for assets would not preserve cash). You might suggest a stock for assets deal structure as the starting point for discussion on this one.

200. **Answer (C) is the best answer.** In a "reverse" transaction, the true target, or acquired corporation, is the surviving corporation for legal purposes (that is, is specified in the articles of merger as the surviving corporation). A reverse merger would result in Fisher Broadcasting being the survivor here. Its name later may be changed to Alaska-Aloha, or any other name. The objective, continuous ownership and non-forfeiture of the broadcast licenses, would be achieved. So, Answer (A) could work out to achieve your objectives, but Answer (A) would be cumbersome and not in accordance with the economic reality of what is occurring. Consequently, **Answer (A) is not the best answer.** Instead, for a variety of reasons, many acquisitions are structured as triangular transactions, which may also be reverse (Answer (C)). The acquiring company forms an acquisition subsidiary ("AA Acquisition Corp."). Alaska-Aloha then drops down into the acquisition subsidiary, AA Acquisition, cash or shares sufficient to make the acquisition (here AA shares). The merger then takes place between the acquisition subsidiary and the target (here, Fisher Broadcasting). There may be triangular sale of assets transactions as well as triangular mergers. The acquisition subsidiary acquires the assets of the target rather than merging with it. Further, here, the "triangular" merger (sketch the triangle on a piece of paper) occurs as a "reverse" transaction. Articles of merger specify that the survivor will be the target Fisher Broadcasting. When the smoke clears, Fisher Broadcasting will have continuously existed and not forfeited its FCC licenses, but also will have moved "over," so to speak, to be a wholly owned subsidiary of Alaska-Aloha.

Answer (B) is incorrect. Stock for assets would not work at all. The broadcast licenses are assets of the selling corporation. The attempt to transfer them, along with the other assets, may well result in their forfeiture back to the FCC.

Back to reverse triangular mergers: this structure may be used for a whole host of reasons other than the regulatory one explicated here. To preserve a valuable brand name, or for tradition's sake, the transaction may be reverse. For purposes of limited liability (segmentation of risks), or to preserve the separate management team, the transaction may involve use of an acquisition subsidiary and, therefore, be triangular. Thus, **Answer (D) ("It**

cannot be done.") is incorrect.

Before this book says "aloha" altogether to the subject of mergers and friendly acquisitions, let's have one more illustration of the hows and whys of triangular acquisitions.

201.   **Answer (B) is the best answer.** Triangular mergers are utilized for a variety of reasons (preserve a valuable brand, maintain a veil of liability between acquired and acquiring companies, for other management or organizational reasons, and so on). One other reason is to avoid a shareholder vote in the acquiring company. More accurately, there still must be a shareholder vote, but the number of shareholders is one, rather than 30,000. That is to say, the parent corporation votes the shares of the acquisition subsidiary, all of which the parent corporation owns. Those shares are voted by resolution of the board of directors of the parent corporation. If the parent board has 11 directors, approval of the merger requires a "Yes" vote by six individuals (a majority of 11) rather than 30,000 individuals, a low cost or no cost proposition.

In this case, then, GE forms a subsidiary, GE Acquisition Corp. Or, perhaps GE uses an existing subsidiary, perhaps even another software firm that it already owns, to make the acquisition. GE drops into that subsidiary sufficient GE shares to make the acquisition. On the GE side, the GE board of directors votes (on behalf of the sole shareholder of the subsidiary) in favor of Advent Software's merger into the GE subsidiary. On the Advent Software side of the transaction, there will still have to be a shareholders' meeting and solicitation of proxies but, on the Advent side, that process will be far less expensive.

Answer (A) is not the best answer. Re-incorporating in a jurisdiction such as Delaware, which has a small-scale merger statute, would not solve the immediate problem. Re-incorporation would also require a special shareholders' meeting, solicitation of proxies, and the $2.7 million expenditure.

Answer (C) is not the best answer. Cash for stock, or cash for assets, does not require a shareholder vote, but would require the parties to re-negotiate the deal, which they may not wish to do. They have agreed on stock for stock and merger.

Answer (D) is not the best answer. Answer (D) is a pure figment of the author's imagination, but real lawyers do come up with deal structures bearing names similar to that.

You can now telephone the GE corporate secretary to report that, indeed, there is a better way, a triangular transaction. Whether you remonstrate with her about her rudeness is a separate question, the answer to which is personal to you. On to hostile takeovers, and the jargon of Middle Ages warfare.

202.   **Answer (B) is the best answer.** A takeover bid, or tender offer, is an offer to purchase made directly to a company's shareholders, for cash or for stock, without the intervention of any intermediary, such as a stock exchange. The bid, or offer, has as its objective control, or a measure of control, in the target company. The bidder (GE here) offers to purchase target company shares tendered to a neutral depository, usually a bank (hence, tender offer). The offer may be conditional on obtaining a certain percentage (*e.g.*, at least 51%), only for a certain percent (51%), or for "any or all" shares tendered. The bidder makes the offer by a written offer to purchase, which also simultaneously with first use it files with the SEC, as exhibit "1" to SEC Schedule 14D. Therefore, **Answer (D) ("It cannot be done.") is**

incorrect.

A proxy contest, or proxy fight (Answer (A)), is the other principal means of taking over a company by hostile means. Proxy contests entail delays, for regulatory filings to be made with the SEC and for the actual solicitation process. So, too, does a stock tender offer (Answer (C)) entail delay, as the shares to be offered must be registered with the SEC (unless the transaction fits within an exemption from registration requirements). A large company such as GE may also have shares sufficient for smaller acquisitions already registered and "on the shelf," but shelf registration under SEC Rule 415 is beyond the scope of this book. Thus, **Answers (A) and (C) are not the best answers.**

The cash takeover has as its advantages "secrecy, speed, simplicity and savings." As to the last of those, purchase of shares may cost much more than solicitation of votes but, in case success is not achieved, shares may be retained for investment or sold. With solicitation of proxies, if success is not achieved, the expenditure is gone, with nothing to show for it.

A bidder usually begins by purchasing target company shares in the market. A person or group may purchase up to 4.99 percent of a public company's shares without a regulatory filing. Once the purchaser (individual or group acting in concert) exceeds 5 percent, within 10 days they must file with the SEC a brief disclosure document, Schedule 13D. Hence, once the 5 percent threshold has been reached, in phase two, bidders step up their market purchasing in the 10-day "window" which follows. The average hostile takeover bidder owns about 14 percent of the target company by the time it files with the SEC and gives the target company notice.

Phase three is the takeover bid itself. Bidders offer to pay a premium over market price sufficient at least to obtain 51 percent control. In the 1980s, for many periods over which empirical studies were made, that average, or median, premium was around 55 percent over pre-bid market price. Usually, then, target company shareholders are very receptive to (happy with?) (overjoyed with?) takeover bids.

Phase four involves use of the shares, and votes, obtained via the market purchasing and the takeover bid to install the bidder's own nominees as directors of the target company.

Phase five, which does not always necessarily follow, involves the recommendation by the new target company board of a merger into the takeover bidder or a subsidiary of the takeover bidder. This is often called the "back end" or "second stage" of a two stage takeover bid (which really involves four or five stages) while the takeover bid is the "front end" of the deal or "first stage." The merger is a "cash merger" in which the minority shares are offered cash. They are thus squeezed out of the company. No more public shareholders will be left. The reason for the "squeeze out" merger transaction is so that the bidder may fully get its hands on the assets and cash flow of the target company. There is often a strong impetus to do so because the bidder will have obtained many of the funds used to purchase the shares through bank borrowing or offerings of high yield debt securities ("junk bonds"). Access to the target's cash flow and assets enables the bidder quickly to pare down that debt and associated costs (interest).

The hostile takeover was unknown in the United States until the mid 1960s, when a number of other new things became known as well. But, that is a different story. The early 1960s takeover bids involved abuses, such as unnamed bidders (using a "blind trust"), or "Saturday Night Specials," in which target shareholders were given as few as five days to accept the offer and tender their shares, or to reject it. Inevitably, the abuses lead to federal regulation, in the form of the Williams Act (named after Senator Harrison Williams of New Jersey, its chief sponsor). The Williams Act amended sections 13 and 14 of the Securities Exchange Act of 1934. It is the subject of the next item, an executive summary of the legislation.

One more observation: it is important to note that a tender offer, or takeover bid, may be the mechanism used for a friendly transaction, in which the target company directors tender their shares and urge or recommend that the rank-and-file shareholders do so as well. Usually, however, the nomenclature, tender offer or takeover bid, conjures up visions of hotly-contested battles for corporate control.

NOTE: FEDERAL REGULATION OF TENDER OFFERS (WILLIAMS ACT)

What follows is a brief summary of the salient provisions of the 1968 federal regulation of tender offers:

Section 13d (Schedule 13D) Status Filing. Within 10 days of achieving 5 percent ownership of a public company, the acquiring person (or group) must file Schedule 13D with the SEC. The schedule calls for disclosure of only a few items, such as: identity of the acquiring party, actual ownership at the time of filing, sources of any borrowing made in order to purchase shares, and intentions regarding the company (investment, representation on the target board of directors, takeover, etc.).

The practice of "parking" shares with friends and allies, with a tacit agreement that the bidder will make good any loss on the shares, so as to avoid the 13D filing and tipping off the target, is also known as "warehousing." Many of the celebrated criminal prosecutions of the 1980s takeover boom, such as those of Ivan Boesky and junk bond king Michael Milken, were for illegal stock parking.

Section 14d (Schedule 14D) Action Filing. Regardless of any ownership, at the time of commencement of a tender offer with the objective of acquiring more than 5 percent of a class of the target company's shares, the bidder must file a Schedule 14D, which, like Schedule 13D, is a very brief filing. The bidder may, or may not, have a previous Schedule 13D on file with the SEC. The written offer to purchase, which will be circulated among target company shareholders, is appended to the Schedule 14D filed with the SEC. The 14D filing "kicks off" the formal takeover bid.

21- to 60-Day Rule. Most federal securities regulation, at least prior to the 2002 Sarbanes-Oxley legislation, requires only disclosure. Historically, federal securities law contains very few substantive commands ("Dos" and "Don'ts").

An exception is regulation of tender offers. A tender offer must be open for a minimum of 21 days, thus preventing a "Saturday Night Special" takeover bid. At the other end, if the bidder has not paid for the shares tendered and 60 days have elapsed from commencement of the offer, the bidder must allow tendering shareholders to withdraw. This prevents a bidder from tying up shares without paying for them, or while the bidder seeks funding that it should have lined up in the first place.

Pro Rata Takeup Rule. If a tender offer is for less than all of the target company shares (*e.g.*, 50%), and the offer is oversubscribed, the bidder must take up pro rata shares tendered in the first 21 days (*e.g.*, 70%). Thus, the bidder may not take up 100 percent of friends' or cronies' shares, and less of strangers' shares. In the example, the bidder must take up 5/7ths of each tendering shareholder's shares.

Increase in Consideration Rule. If during the course of a takeover, the bidder raises the amount of consideration to be paid, say, for example, in answering the competing bid of a white knight, the bidder must pay that increased amount both to previously tendering and subsequently tendering target company shareholders. This rule prevents a bidder from making a series of escalating sub-offers for 5 or 10 percent each, which would result in a lower overall average acquisition cost for the takeover bidder. In other words, the bidder may not make a series of stairstep offers, each at a slightly higher premium than the previous offer. The bidder must pay all tendering shareholders the same ("highest price rule").

Specialized Antifraud Rule. The federal catch-all antifraud rule, SEC Rule 10b-5, prohibits misrepresentations, misleading statements, and material omissions "in connection with the purchase or sale of a security." The federal courts have interpreted the language as a standing requirement. Unless the plaintiff actually purchased or sold securities, she may not go past the courthouse door. *Blue Chip Stamps v. Manor Drug Stores*, 421 U.S. 723 (1975), is the leading case, reaffirming the purchaser-seller standing rule enunciated in *Birnbaum v. Newport Steel Corp.*, 193 F.2d 461 (2d Cir. 1952).

By contrast, in a tender offer situation, the complaining shareholder may not have sold, having seen through the misrepresentations or misleading statements made by the bidder. She still may object, on grounds that the misleading statements are stampeding her fellow shareholders into tendering their shares. The takeover bid may succeed when, had the representations made been accurate, it would not have.

The Williams Act, therefore, contains a specialized antifraud rule that prohibits misrepresentations, misleading statements, and omissions "in connection with any tender offer." Two things to note about the rule: First, it is a statute enacted by Congress rather than a rule, such as Rule 10b-5, adopted by the SEC. The state of mind may therefore be lower. In some instances, a target shareholder may sue the bidder for negligent misstatement. Second, it applies to "any tender offer," not to just those for shares of SEC reporting companies (as is true of the rest of the legislation). All that is necessary to invoke the section is that the bidder have used "means or instrumentalities of interstate commerce," such as the mails, telephone lines, or the Internet.

203.   **Answer (D) is the best answer.** Early on the courts decided that, if the process is scripted correctly (independent directors approve the adoption), courts would review adoption of takeover defenses utilizing duty of care and deferential business judgment rule concepts rather than duty of loyalty analysis. Therefore, **Answer (A) is incorrect.** In *Moran v. Household International, Inc.*, 500 A.2d 1346 (Del. 1985), the Delaware Supreme Court reviewed a poison pill plan under the business judgment rule, holding that the directors who adopted the plan had been reasonably informed and had been free of disabling conflicts of interest. Their decision, or the wisdom thereof, therefore, was shielded from scrutiny by the business judgment rule itself.

Board classification schemes are takeover defenses which recent research has shown are especially effective. *See* Lucian A. Bebchuk, John C. Coates IV & Guhan Subramanian, *The Powerful Antitakeover Effect of Staggered Boards: Theory, Evidence, and Policy*, 54 STAN. L. REV. 887 (2002). A takeover bidder may have to wait as long as 23 plus months to control the board of a target company even though the bidder owns a majority of the shares. That lag time in actually implementing control may give a bidder, and its lenders, pause in the first place. Thus, clear authority exists for adoption of both defenses, **making Answer (D) the**

correct answer, and Answers (B) and (C) partially correct.

In no particular order, other defensive measures include:

Golden Parachutes. These are generous severance benefits (three to five times annual compensation) guaranteed the senior executives should they leave the target company for any reason after a change of control (discharged, early retirement, and so on). In the aggregate, parachutes alone are not enough to deter a determined bidder. Strictly speaking, then, golden parachutes are not takeover defenses, but usually they are included in any discussion of defenses.

Green Mail. Green mail is the repurchase from a bidder of its toehold or larger position at, or slightly above, current market price by the target company. Because the bidder overall will have an average cost that is lower than that, the bidder will make a substantial profit. Payment of greenmail, and receipt of it, generally is considered one of the more reprehensible forms of conduct in the takeover game.

White Squire Transaction. This is the issuance of a block of voting stock, or contingent voting stock (convertible preferred securities), to a trusted ally, but in an amount less than would enable them then to take control. The amount often is in the range of 15–20 percent of the voting power.

White Knight. A white knight is a friendly merger partner who will compete with the hostile bidder for control of the target company. A less desirable, but still preferable, partner is a "gray knight."

Leg Up Option. To entice a white knight to enter the fray, or to lock up a deal with a friendly first bidder, certain devices are used. One is a grant of an option to acquire a substantial percentage of authorized, but unissued, voting stock in the target, often in the 15–20 percent range. The target may also grant the recipient the option of very favorable payment terms (*e.g.*, 10-year promissory note).

Lockup Option. This is the same idea as the "leg up" option, but granting to the recipient a right to virtual control. This defensive device probably would not withstand scrutiny because it would be "draconian" or "preclusive," precluding acceptance by shareholders of even the most lucrative offer imaginable.

Crown Jewel Option. The target grants to an ally an option to acquire a prized division, subsidiary, or facility, often on favorable terms. The hostile bidder may obtain control, but of a company that has lost value because of the option's exercise.

Scorched Earth Defense. The crown jewel option carried to the extreme, so that the hostile bidder will find no value left in the company.

Self Tender. The target competes with the bidder in purchasing shares, thereby increasing the price the bidder will have to pay and reducing the size of the pool of shares ("the float") that the bidder may be able to purchase.

Management Buyout (MBO). Either with a hostile bid on the horizon, or as a preemptive strike, the managers borrow money, using the assets and cash flow of the target company as security for the loans. The managers, often with a buyout firm such as Kravis, Kohlberg & Roberts or Forstman Little as a partner, buy all of the publicly-held shares, taking the firm private. In effect, an MBO represents "self manufacture" of a white knight.

The lexicon, moves, and countermoves in the takeover game are colorful and seemingly endless. It is now time to turn further to development of the legal standards under which adoption of defenses will be judged.

204.   **Answer (D) is the best answer.** This Question is based upon the celebrated Delaware decision in *Unocal Corp. v. Mesa Petroleum Co.*, 493 A.2d 946 (Del. 1985). Takeover player T. Boone Pickens, who had made runs at several of the large oil companies (Cities Service, Phillips Petroleum, and Gulf Oil), announced a partial bid for Unocal shares at $54 per share. Unocal responded with a selective defensive self tender for Unocal shares at $72. Mesa Petroleum, a public company of which Pickens was CEO and which he used as his takeover vehicle, sued, challenging the discrimination against it. The Delaware Supreme Court reviewed what a "bad man" Pickens was and, under the business judgment rule, upheld the defense. The court avoided the discriminatory feature of the plan by announcing that, while Delaware forbids discrimination among shares, it does not necessarily forbid discrimination among shareholders, a distinction that, frankly, has never made sense to this author. Nonetheless, subsequently, the Delaware courts have invoked this principle from time to time. Hence, **Answer (A) is incorrect.**

As is often the case, though, the Delaware court used the occasion to refine the applicable doctrine. Because a takeover bid is an episodic development in the life of a company, and one in which directors share jurisdiction with shareholders, it is unlike a decision to modernize a plant or expand a product line, types of decisions over which directors do have exclusive jurisdiction. Accordingly, the adoption of takeover defenses must be governed by a modified (and less deferential) version of the business judgment rule, rather than the business judgment rule recited in Answer (C). Therefore, **Answer (C) is incorrect.**

In adopting takeover defenses, the directors must, after a reasonable investigation, have developed a "reasonable grounds for believing that a danger to corporate policy and effectiveness [exists] because of another person's stock ownership." Following development of such a belief, in adopting a defense the directors must come within the ambit of the business judgment rule and, in addition, the defense adopted must be "reasonable in relation to the threat posed." The business judgment rule with the added "proportionality" element is known by various names, including the *Unocal* standard and the "response phase" business judgment rule. It has become ubiquitous in Delaware takeover jurisprudence, but not without twists and turns along the way.

In the instant case, the only hard information in the directors' possession is that Vader Enterprises has acquired 12 percent. They have a strong suspicion that a hostile bid will follow. Although both are judgment calls, the self tender is less radical than is the crown jewel option. Thus, **Answer (B), stating that both defenses are overreactions and will be struck down as "disproportionate to the threat posed," is incorrect.**

205.   **Answer (C) is the best answer.** This question is based (loosely) on another of the celebrated Delaware takeover opinions during the 1980s takeover boom, *Revlon, Inc. v. MacAndrews & Forbes Holdings, Inc.*, 506 A.2d 173 (Del. 1986). The quotation in Answer (C) is from the court's opinion. Here, by their rescission of the crown jewel option, and their dealings with at least one of the bidders, the directors of Hoyne seem to have indicated that, indeed, they have ceased being defenders of the corporate bastion and that the company is "for sale." Answers (A) and (B) are inconsistent with the directors' duties flowing from the company

"being for sale." Therefore, **Answers (A) and (B) are not the best answers. Answer (D)** ("It cannot be done.") **is incorrect.**

Do they need to accept the slightly higher bid when they believe that the Aspen $21.00 bid is close enough and is better for the company overall? These are tough questions, the resolution of which makes target company directors earn their pay. Here is what Justice Moore had to say about those issues:

> *Unocal* permits consideration of other corporate constituencies. Although such considerations may be permissible, there are fundamental limitations on that prerogative. A board may have regard for various constituencies in discharging its responsibilities, provided there are rationally related benefits accruing to the stockholders. However, such concern for non-stockholders is inappropriate when an auction among active bidders is in progress, and the object no longer is to protect or maintain the corporate enterprise but to sell it to the highest bidder.

Id. at 182 (citation omitted). Thus arise *Revlon* duties, termed by some the "auction phase business judgment rule" under which directors' actions will be reviewed once the sale or breakup of the target company has become inevitable.

Since *Revlon*, the Delaware Supreme Court has limited the instances in which the duty will apply. It is almost as though, with *Revlon*, the court let the genie out of the bottle. Since that time, the court seems intent on stuffing the genie back into the bottle (or at least partly so). *See, e.g., Paramount Communications, Inc. v. Time, Inc.*, 571 A.2d 1140 (Del. 1989). It is highly likely that the board could recommend a slightly inferior offer (Aspen's bid here) without running afoul of its *Revlon* duties. The latter statement could be made with a higher confidence level, though, if the Hoyne board of directors let the bidding process run its course.

State legislatures have responded to Delaware takeover jurisprudence by, among other things, adopting so-called non-shareholder constituency statutes. Pennsylvania's was the first, but most states now have these statutes as part of their takeover (more accurately, "anti-takeover") legislation. The statutes expressly permit a board of directors, in adopting takeover defenses or in responding to a takeover bid, to consider other stakeholders' interests as well. Those stakeholders include employees, suppliers, consumers, and communities, states, and countries in which the company has a facility or operation. As discussed in the answer to Question 147, non-shareholder constituency statutes are typically permissive. Only Connecticut's statute requires directors to consider non-shareholder interests.

In subsequent cases, too, the Delaware courts have somewhat softened *Revlon* duties and, as aforesaid, limited the instances in which *Revlon* applies. It is to one of those instances to which we now turn.

206. **Answer (B) is the best answer.** This question is based upon yet another landmark Delaware case, in this instance, *Paramount Communications, Inc. v. Time, Inc.*, 571 A.2d 1140 (Del. 1989), modifying the *Revlon* rule and **making Answer (A) incorrect.** Time was permitted to say "just say no" to a clearly superior bid by Paramount in favor of its "merger of equals" ("MOEs") with Warner Communications. Time pointed to the carefully constructed makeup of the prospective Time-Warner Co., the CEO succession plan, and the necessity of permitting the Time board of directors to choose the "partnership" that would best preserve the unique "Time culture." The Delaware court pointed out that, in a true merger of equals,

the target company is not "for sale." Because breakup or sale of the company is not in the works, or even remotely likely, and after the transaction a pool of disaggregated shareholders will still own the new company, *Revlon* does not apply. A result is that M & A attorneys attempt to structure all friendly transactions as MOEs, even if it necessitates use of a large shoehorn to do so. The losers are the shareholders, who often have an inferior deal crammed down their throats as a "merger of equals," which coincidentally offers much greater job protection to the senior managers and directors of the company.

Those same attorneys include in each friendly "deal," whether it takes the form of a merger or some other legal form, stringent "deal protection" (or lockup) measures (no shop, no talk, engagement (hello) fees, termination (goodbye) fees, and so on). Viewed in one way, the purpose of deal protection is to force target company directors to disregard or to slight their fiduciary duties, such as their *Revlon* duty to try to obtain the best deal for shareholders. The common antidote to deal protection is the "fiduciary out" clause. If in the good faith opinion of the directors they must talk to or solicit other bidders, they may do so without violating the merger or other agreement. If the Hoyne directors insisted upon such a clause, it would go part way toward compliance with what fiduciary duty would require. In combination, **Answers (C) and (D) might be an alternative to Answer (B).**

M & A lawyers' response is increasingly to add qualifications to the fiduciary out clause. It may be invoked only in the case of a firm written offer from another bidder and not a mere indication of interest. The target company directors must obtain a written opinion of counsel that the firm offer and directors' fiduciary duty require them to provide the information, talk to the new bidder, and so on. Delaware courts have indicated some unease as to the extent to which M & A agreements pressure directors into situations in which they might be violating their fiduciary duties, but have, so far, not struck any blows directly against deal protection measures. There is, however, one important Delaware precedent that does provide raw material for attacking extreme forms of deal protection.

207.   **Answer (B) is the best answer.** Following its defeat in its attempt at an acquisition of Time (discussed in the answer to Question 144), Paramount undertook a strategic alliance with Viacom, the entertainment conglomerate controlled by media mogul Sumner Redstone. Applying the teachings of *Paramount v. Time*, 571 A.2d 1140 (Del. 1989), the parties (Paramount and Viacom) structured the transaction as a merger. Marvin Davis, the controlling Paramount shareholder, would be CEO of the new entity. Redstone would be the controlling shareholder. Davis and Redstone worked these details out over dinner in New York.

To "lock up" their transaction, in the merger agreement, Paramount agreed to three deal protection measures. First was a "no shop" clause which forbade Paramount officials from talking to any other bidder unless the bidder made "an unsolicited written, bona fide proposal which is not subject to any material contingencies regarding financing." Second was an agreement to pay a "termination fee" of $100 million to Viacom should the transaction not be consummated. Third was a contingent option on 19.9 percent of Paramount's shares that could be exercised by Viacom if the merger was not consummated, using a "senior subordinated note of questionable marketability" for payment. Alternatively, Viacom could insist that Paramount pay Viacom the cash difference between the option price and the market price of the 19.9 percent interest.

A second bidder did emerge. QVC Network, creator of the Home Shopping Network, made a cash bid, first at $80 per share, later at $90 per share. The offer was contingent on Paramount invalidating the contingent option given to Viacom. Thinking they were on firm ground under *Paramount v. Time*, the Paramount directors chose to stand by their deal with Viacom which, though it had been sweetened was nonetheless inferior to the QVC proposal (roughly, $85 versus $90).

In *Paramount Communications Inc. v. QVC Network Inc.*, 637 A.2d 34 (Del. 1993), Chief Justice Norman Veasey closely examined the Paramount-Viacom merger, finding it not to be a merger of equals but, in fact, a sale of control. Paramount would gain a new controlling shareholder in the form of Sumner Redstone. Because the transaction involved a sale of control, *Revlon* duties to seek the best price devolved upon the Paramount directors. Through their counsel, the Paramount directors protested: "We have signed an agreement with provisions (no shop, termination fee, share option) that binds us to the transaction with Viacom." Justice Veasey responded with a ringing endorsement of fiduciary duty:

> [Contractual] provisions, whether or not they are presumptively valid in the abstract, may not validly define or limit the directors' fiduciary duties under Delaware law or prevent the paramount directors from carrying out their fiduciary duties under Delaware law. To the extent such provisions are inconsistent with those duties, they are invalid and unenforceable.

Id. at 48. Thus, **Answers (A), (C), and (D) are incorrect.**

In the Hoyne Industries question, then, a court may closely examine the transaction to determine if it truly is a merger of equals. If it is not, the LSE directors must seek the best terms for the shareholders, regardless of what their agreement with LSE states. That is especially true if the third-party bid is clearly superior. Fiduciary duty and *Revlon* may not require the directors to forsake the sure thing for a transaction that is 50 cents or one dollar better. *Revlon* and *Paramount v. QVC* do require the directors to take seriously a clearly superior bid that is $5 better.

The deal protection measures may be held unenforceable. If they are not, then the target directors may be sued for breach of contract. For that reason, directors faced with offers to "buy the company" feel that they are in the hot seat. They may respond to that possibility by requiring the second bidder to agree to "hold harmless," or indemnify, the directors for any liabilities arising in a breach of contract suit by the first bidder.

As seen in the preceding Question, target company directors also commonly will respond by putting a "fiduciary out" clause in the agreement with the first bidder. Such an "out" states that target directors may, under certain conditions, deal with another bidder without violating the "no shop" or "no talk" provisions of the merger or other agreement. The primary condition is that the directors determine their fiduciary duties require them to deal with another party. Again, M & A lawyers attempt to add other provisions to the fiduciary out clause, making it more difficult for directors to invoke it. The provision may require a definitive offer, that is fully financed, and that is "clearly superior" to the first bid. The provision may also require the directors to obtain a written opinion of counsel explaining precisely how and why fiduciary duty requires the directors to deal with the newly arrived bidder. Sooner or later some of these stringent deal protection measures and limited fiduciary out clauses will run afoul of Justice Veasey's pronouncement that nothing in a contract can override directors' fiduciary duties. How and when that will happen is beyond the scope of this book. To learn more of the intricacies of friendly and hostile takeovers and other mergers and acquisitions, you should take the course in mergers and acquisitions, if your law school offers the subject. Many of the texts on corporate finance also contain a large volume of material on takeovers, mergers, and other acquisitions.

208. **Answer (D) is the best answer.** Federal securities laws do not preempt state regulation in the securities field, either expressly or impliedly. States may supplement federal regulation with the only preemption limitation being that states may not enact regulations that make compliance with federal and state enactments impossible.

Takeover bids disrupt local economies. Takeover bidders ("raiders") move plants to the Sunbelt or to Mexico. They lay off employees. For that reason, very early on, corporate managers hired lobbyists and headed for their respective state capitals. There they found responsive legislators who assisted in the enactment of "first generation" state takeover statutes. These statutes contained various sorts of provisions, including requirements for additional disclosure beyond what the federal Williams Act (see the answer to Question 202) requires. They provided for delays in addition to the federal 21-day rule. They often provided for hearings by the state securities commission on an offer, which entailed additional delay. And, the statutes often exerted extraterritorial jurisdiction. They applied to a takeover bid for shares of corporations incorporated in the state, with principal headquarters in the state, or with a major plant or facility within the state.

In *Edgar v. MITE Corp.*, 457 U.S. 624 (1982), the Supreme Court examined the Illinois takeover statute, finding it unconstitutional. Plaintiffs alleged that the extraterritorial feature violated the due process clause of the Fourteenth Amendment and made other arguments. The Court, however, rested on the Commerce Clause, or more particularly, the negative Commerce Clause which prohibits states from imposing significant burdens on interstate commerce, in this case commerce in the shares of publicly traded corporations. First generation state takeover statute became dead letters. But, in the milieu of the 1980s with all its financial excesses, local corporations and local economies still felt vulnerable. Next door to Illinois, in Indiana, a smaller public company, Arvin Industries, through its counsel, proposed a much more restrained version of state regulation. The regulation purported to govern only companies incorporated in Indiana. Further, it dealt only with an "internal affairs" matter traditionally relegated to the exclusive jurisdiction of the states, namely, share voting. The Indiana "control share" regulation provided that, when an acquirer of shares crosses certain thresholds, such as 20 percent, again at 33⅓ percent, and again at 50 percent, the acquired shares lack voting rights, unless a shareholders' meeting is called and the remaining shares, by majority vote, elect to restore the voting power to the acquirer's shares.

Shareholders love takeover bids, with their large premiums over market price. So, they very well might convene a meeting, restoring voting power to the takeover player. That process, however, will entail significant delay. Delay aids the takeover target, which may utilize the time to hire additional lawyers, New York investment bankers, adopt radical takeover defenses, or find a white knight or white squire (friendly merger partner or ally).

In *CTS Corp. v. Dynamics Corp. of America*, 481 U.S. 69 (1987), the Supreme Court found the Indiana control share takeover statute, limited as it was to matters traditionally regulated by laws in the state of incorporation, to be constitutional. Justice Scalia concurred in the Court's opinion, noting that "a law can be both economic folly and constitutional." State statutes such as Indiana's erect barriers to the free movement of capital and labor among the states and, for that reason, are economic folly in the eyes of many.

The CTS decision lead to a flood of state enactments styled "second generation" state takeover statutes. They are of three types:

Control Share Statutes (Answer (B)). These enactments are similar to the Indiana statute. Over 20 states have enacted control shares laws.

Non-Shareholder Constituency Statutes (Answer (A)). These statutes are discussed in the answers to Questions 147 and 205.

Business Combinations Statutes (Answer (C)). Probably the most effective of the state anti-takeover statutes, the first business combination statute, was enacted by New York following the *CTS* decision. The statutes prohibit, for a period of years following a change of control (5 years in New York), a list of enumerated transactions, ranging in number from 12 to 20 or so, depending upon the state. Prohibited transactions include sale of significant assets, merger into the bidder corporation or its subsidiary, increasing significantly the takeover target's debt load, or even raising the salaries and benefits of the senior management. The notion is to delay significantly the takeover bidder's ability to get its hands on the assets or cash flow of the target corporation to (get its arm "into the cookie jar").

Most takeover players borrow heavily to finance the purchase of target company shares. Before extending credit, however, the bank or other lender will examine closely the potential sources of repayment. By closing off the ability of the takeover player to use the assets or cash flow of the target *ex post* (after the fact), *ex ante* (before the fact) business combination statutes vastly deplete sources of potential borrowing for takeover bidders.

Answers (A), (B), and (C) are not the best answers. The best answer is Answer (D) which combines the actions stated in Answers (A), (B), and (C).

Three notes on state anti-takeover statutes:

1. Generally, patterning themselves after the Indiana statute, they limit their reach to corporations incorporated in the state.

2. Many of them allow corporations to "opt out" of the statute's protection and significant numbers of corporations do so. Pennsylvania, which has all three forms of second generation statutes, has had as high as 60 percent of the state's public companies "opting out" of one or more of the state's three takeover laws.

3. The laws have been especially effective in curbing hostile takeovers. The demise of the junk bond market (which provided funding for many takeover players) and the enactment of second-generation state anti-takeover statutes killed the hostile takeover as it was known in the 1980s. Today, the only hostile bids that have a chance of success are the so-called "super premium" hostile bids with premiums of 100 percent or more over market price. Those forms of bids force target company directors to think long and hard about what their fiduciary duties require, including disarming shark repellent defenses (poison pill plans in particular) and opting out of the protection of the applicable state anti-takeover statute.

209. **Answer (C) is the best answer.** In a partnership, a majority vote would be necessary to impose a valid restriction on a partner's authority. A majority is 50 percent plus one. In a partnership of two persons, 50 percent plus one (a majority) is two.

    Answers (A) and (B) are incorrect because any restriction unilaterally imposed by Grant has not been approved by a majority. It would be invalid as an act of the partnership.

    Answer (D) is incorrect. A suit for breach of fiduciary duty against Joseph may or may not stop or deter him. If Joseph has few assets, a suit may have little effect. In small partnerships, in case of deadlock (*e.g.*, one versus one, two versus two), the only recourse may be to dissolve the partnership, which will be dissolved by the withdrawal of any partner (Grant here).

210. The principal ramification is that you are your partner's keeper. Without the duty of care, as a partner, you must take an active role in monitoring (if not managing) the conduct of the business and monitor the activities of your partners for carrying on, in the usual way, the business of the partnership.

211. **Answer (D) is the best answer.** Underscoring their conclusions with observations about the consensual nature of partnerships, courts have upheld such clauses in the face of a number of policy objections. Partners who have been expelled by a vote of their partners because of political activities, including actions taken as a state senator, or reporting of violations of ethics rules by partners in a law partnership, or who as an alcoholic had recovered from their illness, have failed to win damages for wrongful expulsion.

    Answer (A) is incorrect because the clause referred to does not specifically provide that expulsion may be without any cause whatsoever, as guillotine clauses commonly do.

    Answer (B) is incorrect. It is the argument former partners have made but which most courts have not accepted.

    Answer (C) is incorrect because no evidence exists that the remaining partners served their own selfish interests rather than "the best interests of the partnership." Note that the First Amendment has no applicability because no governmental action is involved.

212. A. His withdrawal would be in violation of the partnership agreement in that the partnership has a stated term, viz., until all of the bank debt had been paid. Withdrawal before that time violates the partnership agreement and is therefore wrongful. Randy could recover damages from Roger for wrongful dissolution.

    B. If the partnership agreement is sophisticated it may provide that a withdrawing partner also has to pay a "fair charge" for cases taken with him and work done or expenditures made with regard to those cases. The ethics rules make the choice of attorney exclusively the clients'. So a partnership cannot legally forbid the withdrawing partner from taking clients.

It can, however, put in place a provision reasonably calculated to preserve and protect the remaining partners' economic interests. Roger may well be violating this sort of common partnership agreement provision.

C. If Roger has been untruthful, or has used partnership assets or information to develop his new practice, he may be in breach of his fiduciary duty of loyalty, which requires that, while still a partner, he serve exclusively the best interests of the partnership.

213.   **Answer (B) is the best answer.** Corporate law has a doctrine known as corporate disregard, or piercing the corporate veil. One ground for piercing is intermixture of the affairs of the owner and of the corporation. Failure to observe corporate formalities is evidence of intermixture of affairs.

    Answer (A) is incorrect because the question involves a limited liability company, which contemplates more informal dealing and less strict observance of formalities, than do corporation and corporate legal doctrines.

    Answer (C) is incorrect. There is a requirement for maintaining books and records, but violation of it does not necessarily lead to loss of limited liability on the owners' part.

    Answer (D) is incorrect. Limited liability entities (corporations, LLCs) engage in ultra hazardous (blasting, crop dusting, etc.) activities all the time. The only requirement is that they have capital (owners' contributions and liability insurance) sufficient to cover the foreseeable risk of the venture.

214.   Yes. The LLC would protect the owners from large tort or contract liabilities. It would also allow "flow through" of startup losses to the members, who could utilize the losses to shelter income from other sources. Last of all, unlike a limited partnership, LLC members could enjoy those benefits while also participating in decision making (*e.g.,* clubhouse and golf course design). They would not lose their limited liability by doing so.

215.   **Answer (A) is the best answer.** This LLP form of entity was designed with accounting and law firms in mind. Ethics rules provide that lawyers must remain financially responsible for legal work they do or supervise. The upshot of that was that lawyers continued to practice as general partners, or under professional service corporations acts which specifically provided that there would be no limited liability with regard to claims arising from rendition of the professional service. Under LLP statutes, the general idea is that the partner who does the work, or supervises or otherwise participates in it still remains liable for liabilities (*e.g.,* malpractice) arising from that work but the other partners are not liable.

    Answers (B) and (C) are incorrect because the limited liability they provide is too broad. Practicing law in a business corporation or LLC may well violate legal ethics rules because the supervising lawyers would be shielded from liability altogether.

    Answer (D) is incorrect because, as explained, the general partnership has been eclipsed by the LLP as the optimal solution.

216.   **Answer (D) is the best answer.** To avoid liability, an agent for a corporation to be formed must do all three things: indicate the non-existence of her principal; indicate her representative capacity; and provide for a novation *in futuro* when the corporation does

come into existence.

Answer (A) is incorrect. An agent warrants the existence of her principal. She can be held liable herself for breach of that warranty if the principal does not exist, but her correct action in this regard alone is not enough to escape liability.

Answer (B) is incorrect. Courts have held that if a promoter or corporate official signs XYZ Co., Gyro Gearloose, both parties will be bound. He must recite a title (President, Promoter, etc.) or use other words indicating representative capacity (*e.g.*, "by"). But, again, indication of representative capacity alone, while necessary, is insufficient to get Gyro "off the hook."

Answer (C) is incorrect. Again, it must be done but itself is insufficient.

These rules are so complicated that many attorneys advise promoters to wait until the corporation has been formed before signing contracts. Alternatively, if the promoter just cannot wait, the promoter should take an option which she then assigns to the corporation when it does come into existence.

217. It is a matter of expenses. If Joe has you form a Delaware corporation, you will have to find and pay a service company to act as the corporation's registered agent in Delaware. The corporation will also have to pay Delaware franchise taxes. The corporation will then have to come back to Montana, register as a foreign corporation licensed to do business in Montana, and pay an annual tax or fee in Montana. The corporation will also have to maintain a registered agent in Montana (although that could just be Joe himself). The costs of "running away" are not large — several hundred dollars per year at most — but it adds up. Today, under modern statutes, the advice 99.9 percent of the time is to incorporate in the jurisdiction where your principal place of business will be.

218. **Answer (C) is the best answer.** The Model Act provides that the defense of *ultra vires* (beyond the purpose or powers of the corporation) may be raised only in a proceeding brought by a shareholder, and only if the court finds that it is equitable to allow the defense.

Answer (A) is incorrect. LC has not been enriched; it has only evaded a loss.

Answer (B) is incorrect. Modern corporation statutes do contain broad grants of implied powers (*e.g.*, "to do all things necessary or convenient to carry out its business and affairs," MBCA § 3.02) but to say plumbing supply is implied by the purpose of "sales of lumber and plywood products" is too much of a stretch.

Answer (D) is incorrect. Before the *ultra vires* statutes were enacted, court decisions held that *ultra vires* could be raised only in cases of executory contracts (where neither side has performed in whole or in part). Here, however, the contract was executory.

219. **Answer (B) is the best answer.** MBCA § 2.04 provides that "[a]ll persons purporting to act as or on behalf of a corporation, knowing there was no incorporation under this Act, are jointly and severally liable." Dr. X and Dr. Y thought that the corporation did exist; they had no knowledge to the contrary.

Answer (A) is incorrect. Courts have held that the above-quoted MBCA and predecessor provisions abolish the common law de facto incorporation doctrine.

Answer (C) is incorrect. The lack of knowledge defense would be stronger and more certain than the more nebulous defense that Dr. X and Dr. Y never "purported to act."

Answer (D) is incorrect. Although corporations are now either de jure or non-existent, with no middle ground such as de facto existence, Dr. X and Dr. Y's lack of knowledge that the corporation had not been formed provides a defense.

220. **Answer (C) is the best answer.** The reason for some debt is that interest on debt is deductible (an expense) to the corporation. By contrast, payment with respect to shares is taxed once as profit for the corporation and again as dividend income to the shareholders, albeit now only at a modest 15 percent rate. Moreover, upon any forced liquidation, shareholders will be able to stand elbow-to-elbow with the unsecured creditors as to the contribution that has been structured as a loan, as long as the shareholders have not "thinly capitalized" the corporation. **Answer (A) may suffice as well.** A second alternative when all participants in the venture are making equal contributions is to have the corporation just issue common stock. This alternative has the virtue of simplicity.

Answer (B) is incorrect. There is not now, or in the foreseeable future, any need to authorize convertible participating or any other kind of preferred stock.

Answer (D) is incorrect for similar reasons. The business plan contemplates only modest expansion, if at all.

221. **Answer (B) is the best answer.** This problem requires you to apply a statutory test for the legality of distributions (a cash dividend is one type of distribution). Here, payment of the dividend would cause a cash flow squeeze (if, indeed, the funds could be borrowed to make the distribution). The corporation would be left with little or no cash and $300,000 in accounts payable.

Answer (A) is incorrect. It uses terminology ("impairment of capital") which has become obsolete since the demise of the old "legal capital rules."

Answer (C) is incorrect. Giving effect to the dividend, Pear will still be solvent in the balance sheet sense ($500,000 in assets and $300,000 in liabilities). The difficulty lies with solvency in the equity sense.

Answer (D) is incorrect, but only in a technical sense. The first piece of advice would be "do not pay the dividend," as in Answer (B). The second piece of advice will be that, after the passage of time and collection of sufficient receivables, Bill, Pauline, and Steve may cause the corporation to pay the dividend on legal basis.

222. **Answer (D) is the best answer.** To preserve inviolate shareholders' proportionate interests in the corporation several steps are necessary. A share transfer restriction would limit the ability of a shareholder to sell out to an "outsider" without giving the remaining shareholders an option (or right of first refusal) on the selling shareholder's shares. Such an agreement would not, however, govern issuances of new shares by the corporation. Thus, **answer (A) is incorrect.** Preemptive rights govern issuance of new shares, requiring that the corporation give each shareholder the right to preserve her proportionate ownership and control (voting) interest. Yet, standing alone, preemptive rights alone are not sufficient.

Answer (C) is incorrect. Under the latest versions of the MBCA, in the articles of incorporation, the corporation must "opt into" preemptive rights. Under older versions, preemptive rights existed automatically, unless the articles "opted out" of them. Under

MBCA § 6.30, however, even a corporation that "opts in" will find a number of exceptions to the statutory provisions (*e.g.*, issuances to directors, officers, or employees, shares sold for other than money). In addition to opting into preemptive rights, a cautious practitioner might negate some or all of those exceptions in the corporation's articles. Ergo, **Answer (B) is incorrect.**

223. **Answer (C) is the best answer.** SEC Rule 14a-8 allows the activist shareholders to utilize management's annual proxy solicitation to present a proposed resolution and supporting statement to Northern Pines's remaining shareholders. While not without difficulties, the rule is a low cost way to achieve some of their aims.

Answer (A) is incorrect. In all probability, the directors would assert, and the court would accept, a business judgment rule defense to the action. It is the directors, and not the shareholders, who manage the corporation's business and affairs, including the methods by which the corporation harvests its timber.

Answer (B) is incorrect. "Enlisting support" would constitute a solicitation under the SEC's rules, which define solicitation very broadly. Because no proxy statement had been filed with the SEC, it would also be an illegal solicitation, which a court would quickly enjoin.

Answer (D) is incorrect. A full fledged proxy contest would be exceedingly expensive. Better to try to use a Rule 14a-8 proposal to begin to get their views across and perhaps begin to persuade the directors.

224. First, stagger (classify) the board of directors into three classes, with each class to be elected for a three-year term (as a prerequisite, under some statutes, it may be necessary to amend the bylaws to increase the board to nine or more directors). Then, adopt a requirement that directors may be removed only for cause. Finally, limit the ability of 10 percent shareholders to call special shareholders' meetings.

225. **Answer (B) is the best answer.** The hallmark of a voting trust is a complete separation of voting from the other attributes of share ownership. Voting trusts are sometimes used to impose stability upon a corporation emerging from bankruptcy or beset by arguments among shareholders.

Answer (A) is incorrect. If the siblings fight all of the time, they are likely to fight over this alternative. In addition, at age 23, Paulette seems very young to be entrusted with all of the family's power within the corporation.

Answer (C) is incorrect. A pooling arrangement would require that the parties thereto first attempt to reach an agreement of sorts (four siblings would have to agree), which they have shown themselves incapable of doing. Moreover, rule by majority rather than consensus is likely to exacerbate resentments and hard feelings that build up over time.

Answer (D) is incorrect. Achieving unanimity would be even more difficult that a majority vote, as in Answer (C).

226. **Answer (B) is the best answer.** In the mid 1980s the Model Act added a provision for judicial removal of a director. Answer (B) tracks the language of the provision. A stated reason for the adoption was the difficulty of removing a badly acting director who had been elected by means of cumulative voting.

Answers (A) and (D) are incorrect. A director elected cumulatively will not be removed by majority vote if the number of votes cast against his removal would have been sufficient to elect him in the first place. This common provision would give Bruce Lee power to block his removal by the normal process (majority vote).

Answer (C) is incorrect. Under the MBCA you may now go to court to seek the removal of a badly acting director who had been elected by means of cumulative voting.

227. Five elements of the business judgment rule "safe harbor" for directors and senior executives are:

A. A judgment or decision, sometimes referred to as an "independent decision" (as opposed to "rubber stamping" decisions of the CEO or other senior managers).

B. Absence of disabling conflicts of interest and independence of the decision maker(s).

C. Some care exercised in informing themselves about the subject matter of the decision.

D. A rational (plausible) basis for the decision made (not necessarily a reasonable basis).

E. Overriding element of good faith (not acting out of spite or revenge, or unlawfully).

228. **Answer (C) is the best answer.** The limits of shareholder ratification are said to be "fraud, illegality, or a gift or wasting of corporate assets." Within those limits, shareholders may, subject to full and fair disclosure, vote to ratify violations by directors or officers of the duty of care or the duty of loyalty.

Answer (D) is incorrect. Such a ratification need not be by unanimous vote.

Answer (B) is incorrect. Such blanket ratifications are worthless because they are not made pursuant to full and fair disclosure, which must include all the bad news.

Answer (A) is incorrect, although it may be a close question. "Waste" is defined as an exchange in which no reasonable person could say that the corporation received the rough equivalent of what it gave up in the transaction or endeavor. Undoubtedly, someone could be found to testify that what Sam and David did was a gamble, indeed a very unwise gamble, but that some prospect existed, however small, that the corporation might receive a return at least equivalent to its investment.

229. **Answer (C) is the best answer.** Directors' protection has four elements ("the four legged stool"): indemnification, insurance, opting out of duty of care liability, and a contract guaranteeing to an individual director that the first three elements will stay in place despite a change of control, a falling out with the other directors, and so on.

Answer (A) is incorrect. Stock ownership alone provides no direct, and only a modicum of indirect, protection.

Answer (B) is incorrect. Insurance may not be renewed in some future year. It may not be obtainable at all. Even if it is obtained, and renewed, insurance alone does not afford complete protection because of deductibles, policy exclusions, and the like.

Answer (D) is incorrect. It, too, does not go far enough. Provisions implementing the authority granted by the statute, which by and large are enabling only and not mandatory, can always be amended or revoked by a subsequent board majority.

230. **Answer (C) is the best answer.** This is the Delaware *Unocal* standard, after *Unocal v. Mesa*

Petroleum, 493 A.2d 946 (Del. 1985). In addition to satisfying other elements of the business judgment rule, in adopting takeover defenses, a target corporation board of directors must conduct an investigation and satisfy themselves that a credible threat exists to the corporation's policies or way of doing business. Then any defense adopted must be reasonable (proportionate) in relation to the threat posed.

Answer (A) is incorrect. As aforesaid, courts have evolved a more demanding version of the business judgment rule applicable to adoption of takeover defenses.

Answer (B) is incorrect. It is incomplete. The director must investigate *and* insure that any defense adopted is reasonable in relation to the threat posed, as in Answer (C).

Answer (D) is incorrect. An irreversible (preclusive) defense is per se unreasonable.

231. **Answer (B) is the best answer.** The answer states the correct triage when a colorable derivative suit has been filed against corporate directors: form an SLC, staff it with "expansion directors," and hire reputable independent counsel for the committee.

Answer (A) is incorrect. It is incomplete. The SLC will need independent counsel to aid it in the conduct of its investigation and to research and apply the applicable law.

Answer (C) is incorrect. It leaves too much to chance (*i.e.*, in the normal discovery process). Also, the question of whether a derivative suit should proceed is not strictly just a matter of law. The corporation may choose not to stand on legal rights it has because doing so would not be in the corporation's best overall interests. That decision is to be made in the first instance by the directors, or the SLC, and not by a court.

Answer (D) is incorrect. A "reasonable doubt" exists as to whether the directors, had they acted on any hypothetical demand, would have been entitled to business judgment rule protection. The directors' receipt of consulting fees could lead to a finding that they are not free of conflicts of interest, or that they are not dominated by a controlling shareholder. They thus would not be entitled to business judgment rule protection for the decision they made with respect to the hypothetical demand.

232. **Answer (D) is correct.** The most drastic, and effective, close corporation remedy is a suit for involuntary dissolution of the corporation on oppression grounds. The evolving test in U.S. courts has been merely that the plaintiff minority shareholder has been denied his "reasonable expectations" (of a job, of fringe benefits, of participation in governance).

Answers (A) and (B) are incorrect. These are older tests of oppression. They may be alleged in addition to "denial of reasonable expectations" but today would not be the primary allegation.

Answer (C) is incorrect. A derivative suit would only result in a payment back to the corporation. It may well leave Jack in a worse position with brother Zach still in control and more angry than ever.

233. **Answer (D) is the best answer.** These are federal law remedies made available to/against publicly-held companies by the Sarbanes-Oxley Act of 2002. A United States attorney might well seek to invoke these remedies as part of a criminal prosecution.

Answer (A) is incorrect. This remedy would lie but in a state court proceeding for breach of fiduciary duty (or as a pendent claim in a civil suit in federal court).

Answer (B) is incorrect. This classic remedy for breach of fiduciary duty would lie as well but, again, in state court.

Answer (C) is incorrect because it is incomplete. Because Weird Al and Weird Hal have done this before, a lifetime or similar ban from serving as a director or officer of a public company would be in order.

234. **Answer (C) is the best answer.** If anything, her actions are ordinary theft which busy state court prosecutors may be loathe to pursue.

Answer (A) is incorrect. Martha is neither a classic insider (director, officer) nor a temporary insider (attorney, accountant, consultant, banker) to whom material non-public information may be entrusted, but only for corporate purposes.

Answer (B) is incorrect. Martha would only be a tippee if Peter Finch were a tipper. He would be a tipper only if he breached his fiduciary duty in providing the information to Martha. He would have breached his fiduciary duty if he received some sort of benefit, broadly defined, for providing the information to Martha. He neither provided the information nor breached any duty.

Answer (D) is incorrect. The last category of persons against whom the "disclose or abstain" rule is invoked are persons who flat out steal (misappropriate) information but they must do so in violation of a fiduciary or similar duty to someone (former employer, law firm). Martha violated no such duty when she purloined the ticker symbols from the Finch linen drawer.

235. **Answer (B) is the best answer.** Many courts have now held that, in a closely-held corporation, the participants and the corporation all owe duties one to another, akin to partners in a partnership, and not just to the corporation. This is known as the *Donahue* principle, after *Donahue v. Rodd Electrotype Co.*, 328 N.E.2d 505 (Mass. 1975). The remedial implication is that a shareholder such as Cynthia may obtain "me, too" relief. She may be able to obtain the same perks, or the monetary equivalent, as her brother Mike enjoys.

Answer (A) is incorrect. A traditional derivative suit results only in a payback to the corporate treasury. It would leave Cynthia in the same position as before the lawsuit. In addition, it may just harden Mike's resolve and rend asunder any relationship they may have had as brother and sister.

Answer (C) is incorrect. There are no grounds for such a suit. There exists neither misleading disclosure or nondisclosure nor a purchase or sale of securities.

Answer (D) is incorrect. All Cynthia wants is some return on her shares and some of the same benefits her brother enjoys. A suit for involuntary dissolution would be overkill.

236. A double derivative suit is a suit by a shareholder in a subsidiary corporation complaining of wrongdoing by officers or directors of the parent corporation. A variant is a suit by a shareholder in the parent complaining of wrongdoing in a subsidiary. The objection is that the complaining shareholder did not contemporaneously own shares at the time of the wrong complained of. Instead, she owned shares in another corporation (the subsidiary). Most courts, nonetheless, permit the action to proceed, explicitly or implicitly recognizing a double derivative action exception to the "contemporaneous ownership rule."

INDEX

INDEX